Clashing Views
on Controversial Issues
in Crime and Criminology

2nd edition

Clashing Views
on Controversial Issues
in Crime and Criminology

2nd edition

Edited, Selected,
and with Introductions by

Richard C. Monk
Valdosta State College

The Dushkin Publishing Group, Inc.

To Dan and Elsie Monk, my parents,
who first taught me the importance of
debating controversial issues

Taking Sides ® is a registered trademark of
The Dushkin Publishing Group, Inc.

Library of Congress Catalog Card Number:
90-81840

Manufactured in the United States of America

Second Edition, First Printing
ISBN: 0-87967-929-8

The Dushkin Publishing Group, Inc.
Sluice Dock, Guilford, CT 06437

PREFACE

To those who share the age-old hope that man's inhumanity to man can
be diminished.
> —*Harry Elmer Barnes and Howard Becker*

Comprehension without critical evaluation is impossible.
> —*Hegel*

This volume contains thirty-eight essays presented in a pro and con format.
A total of nineteen different clashing issues within crime and criminology
are debated. The issues are arranged in four broad topical areas that touch
upon some of the most important and interesting aspects of criminology and
criminal justice.

I have included a mix of fundamental issues and newly emerging ones.
Some of the authors unabashedly write for a popular audience primarily to
grind their own axes and/or to arouse public sentiment. Other articles are
written by some of the most profound thinkers within the social sciences and
deal with vital theoretical issues in crime and criminology (for example, the
functionality of crime). I have not shirked my obligation to provide you with
the best discussions on relevant issues available, even if the discussions are
sometimes technical and/or theoretical and require you to think deeply about
the issue at hand before making up your mind.

In order to assist you in your voyage into controversial criminological
issues, I have supplied you with an introduction to each issue and an issue
postscript, which follows the YES and NO readings. All the postscripts have
detailed suggestions for further reading should you want to pursue the
topics raised in an issue. While my primary concern was to get the authors'
ideas up front so that you could be immersed in them, fight with them,
embrace some of them, than make your own decisions, I have not been
averse to "editorializing." Now and then my own disdain (or support) for
certain ideas will be more manifest than on other occasions. Do not be
bashful about debating the authors and their ideas, or your editor as well. I
definitely could be wrong and may need your critical evaluation!

I feel strongly that the only way that irrationalities and cruelties among
men and women can be reduced is through critical evaluation of the issues at
hand. It is hoped that this volume can assist you and your generation in
keeping criminology and criminal justice vital areas of study. I feel that one
realistic way to achieve this goal is through reintroducing the necessary art of
systematic and informed debate over clashing issues in crime and
criminology.

Changes to this edition There are six completely new issues: *Are Dutch
Prisons Superior to Others?* (Issue 7), which has been included not only to

meet our goal of moving toward a comparative frame of reference but also because the controversy sensitizes us to real methodological problems in evaluating crime control policies; *Should Plea Bargaining Continue to Be an Accepted Practice?* (Issue 10); *Does Arrest Reduce Domestic Violence?* (Issue 13); *Do Boot Camps Work?* (Issue 14); *Are Drug Arrests of Pregnant Women Discriminatory?* (Issue 16); and *Should Juveniles Be Executed?* (Issue 18). And for a couple of other issues, the readings have been updated.

Supplements An Instructor's Manual with Test Questions (multiple-choice and essay) is available through the publisher for the instructor using *Taking Sides* in the classroom. And a general guidebook, which discusses methods and techniques for integrating the pro-con approach into any classroom setting, is also available.

Acknowledgments Many people always contribute to any worthwhile project. Among those more directly involved in this project whom I would like to thank are the authors of these excellent and stimulating articles. Also, my thanks to my many students over the years who have contributed to the criminological dialogue, most recently Kamil Madina, who lived the inhumanity of an American prison. Many reviewers of drafts of this edition were especially helpful. Among those are Tom Gitchoff and Joel Henderson of San Diego State University; Alex Hooke of Villa Julie College; Kurt Finsterbusch of the University of Maryland; Horst Senger of Sun Valley, California; Stefan Goodwin of Morgan State University; Don Nielsen of the State University of New York at Oneonta; Nancy and Dwight Black of Longwood, Florida; Ingegerd Harder of Danmarks Sygeplejerskehøjskole ved Aarhus Universitet; my colleagues at Valdosta State College Zug Standing Bear, Louis Levy, John Curtis, Kathleen Lowney, Kathleen Lancaster, and Jack Hasling. Their support and encouragement are gratefully acknowledged. Thanks also go to Mike Butera of the University of Nebraska at Omaha and Lin Huff-Corzine of Kansas State University for their comments and suggestions for the second edition. Finally, someone must have once said that an author or an editor is only as good as his or her publisher. Without doubt, this *Taking Sides* would not have seen the light of day without the professional assistance and ingenious prodding of Mimi Egan, program manager, of The Dushkin Publishing Group, and the work of the staff there. Naturally, I remain solely responsible for errors.

R. C. Monk
Lake Park, GA

CONTENTS IN BRIEF

CONTENTS

Classic sociologist Emile Durkheim (1858-1917) theorizes that crime exists in all societies because it reaffirms moral boundaries and at times assists needed social changes. American University philosopher Jeffrey Reiman responds that crime is functional not because it promotes social solidarity but because it provides an ideology to justify the status quo.

Marxist criminologist Richard Quinney theorizes that crime is largely socially constructed by society's elites to control the less powerful. Harvard sociologist Daniel Bell argues that fits of social control are the result more likely of middle-class moral indignation rather than policies benefiting the elite. He believes that crime is often the ingenious activity of members of emerging ethnic groups who seek a piece of the pie by providing services to others.

Florida State University criminologist C. R. Jeffery argues that physiological and chemical imbalances are frequently the precipitants of criminal behavior;

therefore, he says that research into causes and possible cures might be better placed in the hands of medical researchers. *Crime and Social Justice* editors Tony Platt and Paul Takagi, characterizing Jeffery's proposals as ridiculous and dangerous, contend that his ideas suffer from a poor understanding of biology, history, and criminology.

UCLA professor James Q. Wilson and Harvard psychologist Richard J. Herrnstein argue that the focus of crime study ought to be on persons who "hit, rape, murder, steal, and threaten." American University professor Jeffrey Reiman contends that a focus on street crimes is little more than a cover-up for more serious crimes such as pollution, medical malpractice, and dangerous working conditions that go uncorrected.

British criminologists A. Keith Bottomley and Ken Pease, while acknowledging problems with official statistics, nonetheless maintain that they are extremely useful for both analyzing crime and generating a more humane criminal justice system. Social critic Bruce Jackson disagrees, claiming that official statistics are virtually worthless for understanding the types, rates, or distributions of crime.

University of California criminal justice researcher Elliott Currie compares the U.S. rate of violent crimes with those of other industrial nations and concludes that both the reality and the threat of crime are escalating. State University of New York criminal justice administration professor Kevin N. Wright counters that the so-called crime wave is a creation of the mass media. He argues that the claim of an increasing rate of crime is a major myth of criminology.

Editor and university professor of criminology David Downes concludes from his extensive comparative research that the Dutch prison system is fairer and more humane than others, and he holds it up as an ideal for England and other industrialized nations. Editor and University of Amsterdam criminologist Herman Franke ridicules Downes's methodology of research, interpretations, and conclusions. He argues that Downes, like many others, has been fooled by Dutch propaganda into falling for the "myth" of their penal superiority.

PART 3 SOCIAL CONTROL AND THE CRIMINAL JUSTICE SYSTEM   141

University of California, Riverside, criminologist Adalberto Aguirre, Jr., and Riverside Community College professor David Baker insist that in the most crucial prison sentence possible—the imposition of the death penalty—racial discrimination remains a fact of life. Florida International University criminologist William Wilbanks raises several important issues in his defense of the U.S. criminal justice system. While acknowledging that there are racist police officers, district attorneys, and judges, he contends that, overall, criminal justice is fair.

Former Office of Juvenile Justice and Delinquency Prevention administrator Alfred S. Regnery says that children commit one-third of all crimes yet are not held accountable for their acts and calls for a return to the doctrine of deterrence because the old rehabilitation philosophy has clearly failed. Ball State University criminologists Stephen J. Brodt and J. Steven Smith reject Regnery's view of juvenile delinquency as well as the solutions he proposes, assert that claims of juveniles getting away with murder are greatly exaggerated, and argue that rehabilitation remains a workable ideal.

University of Nebraska, Omaha, professor Samuel Walker, while acknowledging that plea bargaining is an imperfect component of the criminal justice system, still feels that it is an integral part of both the courtroom work group and the manufacturing and maintenance of justice. Wisconsin circuit court judge Ralph Fine argues that criminals are hardly punished for even the most heinous crimes due to plea bargaining and, citing studies that Walker draws from, concludes that elimination of plea bargaining increases justice.

Brian Forst, on the faculty at George Washington University, says that we now have the capacity to identify repeat offenders (in his words, "real *convicted* offenders") who pose a threat to society, so we should give them longer sentences, which will keep them off the streets and significantly reduce crime. Professor of criminal justice Andrew von Hirsch argues that we do not have the ability to identify such criminals nor would it be just to give them longer sentences even if we knew for certain who they were.

Columbia Law School professor Jack Greenberg maintains that capital punishment is unfairly administered and ineffective, both as a deterrent and as a punishment. Fordham University professor Ernest van den Haag challenges those who claim that capital punishment is barbaric and unfair and insists that capital punishment does deter criminals and is just retribution for terrible crimes.

Attorney Joan Meier, after surveying several studies and reports on domestic violence, concludes that these victims must be supported by the police and courts and claims that, even if research did not show assault deterrence resulting from arrests, spouse attackers should still be dealt with punitively because their crime is so odious. University of Colorado criminologists Dunford, Huizinga, and Elliott, registering far more caution after their study of alleged domestic assault cases, cite among their surprising findings that the incidences of future assaults did not increase or decrease as a consequence of arrest. They also suggest alternative strategies besides arrest, which they imply is probably not a panacea.

National Institute of Justice scientist Doris MacKenzie and Louisiana State
University coauthors Gould, Riechers, and Shaw examine several "shock-
incarceration," or military boot camp-style, prisons and find them relatively
inexpensive, frequently helpful, and usually humane. Michigan State University criminal justice researcher Merry Morash and University of South
Dakota political scientist Lila Rucker reject both the concept and the use of
such boot camps for rehabilitation, insisting that they are inhumane and are
more likely to reinforce violence and other negative reactions by inmates.

Josh Sugarmann, formerly with the National Coalition to Ban Handguns,
identifies several problems with legalized handguns, including what he
describes as unacceptably high rates of suicides with guns, family homicides,
and accidents. Massachusetts Institute of Technology sociologist James D.
Wright argues that small handguns have many legitimate uses and that
banning them would not reduce crime.

Boston University professors Mariner, Glantz, and Annas flatly reject prosecuting drug-abusing pregnant women. They cite the difficulty of ascertaining a causal relationship between drug abuse and specific harm to neonates and argue that such prosecution only adds to the existing discrimination these women face. State's attorney Paul Logli contends that the state's role in protecting those citizens who are least able to protect themselves mandates the prosecution of drug-abusing mothers, both as a deterrent to criminal and destructive behavior and as a reason for drug-abusing mothers to discontinue their addiction.

American University School of Justice professor Arnold S. Trebach pulls no punches by insisting that the war against illegal drugs is lost and says that the only sensible path remaining is immediately to make many drugs legal. John Kaplan, from Stanford Law School, counters that legalization is not the answer and instead the lesser evil is to step up our fight against hard-core drug use and sales in order to reduce crime.

Supreme Court justice Antonin Scalia, joined by Chief Justice Rehnquist and Justice White, assails the plurality and concurring opinion in *Thompson v. Oklahoma,* which vacated the death penalty against Wayne Thompson, who at 15 brutally murdered his brother-in-law, and argues that states have the right to impose the death penalty on those under 18. Cleveland State University professor Victor L. Streib insists that executing citizens under 18 violates contemporary standards of decency and that capital punishment for juveniles makes no measurable contributions to justice because they simply do not have the reasoning abilities of adults and executing them serves neither retribution nor deterrence.

Frank Carrington, attorney and executive director of Victims Assistance
Legal Organization, and Sacramento municipal court judge George
Nicholson are convinced that the victims' movement "has arrived." After
reviewing its progress within various court systems and committees, they
conclude that the movement has been a success in spite of some remaining
hurdles. Political scientist Robert Elias contends that the victims' movement
has hurt both victims and defendants in several unexpected ways, and he
sees it as only helping certain people within the criminal justice system that
may not have any real interest in either victims or their rights.

INTRODUCTION

The Study of Crime and Criminology
Richard C. Monk

By almost any measurement of "what is important," crime continues to rank at or near the top of America's priorities and concerns. Local, state, and federal crime fighting and crime control budgets often involve the highest expenditures—typically numbering in the billions of dollars—for the police, courts, and prisons. The losses from crime in lives and in dollars are equally high. The perception of crime expressed as fear is very high among most Americans. For instance, a recent Gallup Poll reveals that some 62 percent of all women and over 25 percent of all men state that there are areas within a mile of their home in which they would be afraid to walk at night.

Many suggest that the 1988 presidential election was won by George Bush in part because he succeeded in labeling his opponent as "soft on crime." Since the 1960s, following the Omnibus Safe Streets Act, billions of federal dollars have been spent to create law enforcement training programs, to buy equipment for local police, to fund hundreds of massive research studies, and to create new state and federal crime control agencies and research centers (for example, Bureau of Justice Statistics). Unfortunately, many politicians and criminal justice administrators, most of the public, and a growing number of criminologists view these efforts as dismal failures.

Intellectually, one can also discern a definite shift in scholarly attitudes toward crime, criminals, and crime control. In the early years of this century, criminologists registered optimism about conquering crime. The assumption was that if we simply started to research crime systematically, utilizing the cognitive tools of science based upon rationality and empirical investigation free of sensationalism and biases, then significant advances would follow. John Lewis Gillin in 1926 in his popular criminology text said:

> Criminal statistics are becoming more reliable every year. . . . It is time that calm, scientific study, rather than sensational journalistic methods be devoted to the problem of crime and criminals. Only so can popular fallacies concerning what makes the criminal and how to treat him be exploded, and a sound program for the treatment and the prevention of crime be established.

A short time later, the preeminent criminologist Thorsten Sellin, as cited by F. Zimring and G. Hawkins in *Capital Punishment and the American Agenda* (1986), wrote what might be considered the basis of the modern scientific research approach to crime:

[It] is characteristic of modern man, reared in an age of scientific orientation, that he wishes to use scientific thoughtways in the approach to his problems. He does not like to be considered irrational. When he formulates public policies, he wants to think that such policies are based on scientific facts. . . .

It appears that current criminologists are imbued with a more realistic understanding of both the complexities of the twentieth century and crime and criminals. In the words of Peter Berger, in his book *The Heretical Imperative*, current academic thinking is probably more likely to be influenced by an awareness that

> . . . the institutional pluralization that marks modernity affects not only human actions but also human consciousness: Modern men and women find themselves confronted not only by multiple options of possible courses of action but also by multiple options of possible ways of thinking about the world.

This volume attempts to assist you in examining both possible options for action and possible ways of thinking about crime, criminals, and criminology. I am not particularly optimistic, however, that the problem of the twentieth century will be solved by the twenty-first century.

CRIME: DEFINITIONS AND CAUSES

Ideological Issues

Any theory or explanation of crime obviously has several dimensions built into it from the start. First, even the most "scientific" or "neutral" theory will reflect to some extent the existing ideological or political sentiments of the day. At the very least, most criminological theories can be classified as conservative, radical, or liberal, or some analytical combination of these three political perspectives.

In theory, a scientific explanation of some phenomenon, including one of crime and criminals, is supposed to be value-free, uncontaminated by emotions and political circumstances. Yet funding decisions are often based on prevailing political concerns with public demands, and consequently the formulation of theory and the pursuits of research programs for scholars are affected. For instance, the disciplinary area of criminal justice administration, which has rapidly matured since the 1960s largely as a direct result of the massive infusion of federal funds, reflects concerns quite different from those of traditional criminology. Basically, criminal justice eschews any search for *causes* of criminal behavior. Instead, it tends to serve the needs of political funding agencies, which respond to the public's demand for solutions to the crime problem, and is therefore an atheoretical, applied academic discipline. The focus is on the development of strategies for administering more effectively the courts, the police, and the prisons.

Images of Society

A second dimension of any theory of crime causation, which also sometimes overlaps with ideological issues, is the image of society and of men and women contained within the theory. If criminals are seen as evil men and women contaminating an otherwise "pure" and "perfectable" society, then the explanation of crime that follows from this thinking will probably be a conservative one. That is, crime is a consequence of the individual offender's pathology.

By contrast, if crime is seen as a reaction against the inequities of the capitalist society or system, then the system, according to a crude variant of radical or Marxist criminology, is exclusively to blame. This theory's image of men and women is that they are inherently good but the system is bad and, through oppression, drives many to commit crimes.

The liberal image of men and women is that they are potentially good but that, through a combination of factors ranging from socialization to unfortunate circumstances, they can make mistakes. Reform of certain aspects of either society or individuals, or both, is suggested by this theoretical perspective.

Theory and Treatment

A third dimension of any theory of crime is an inherent treatment modality. The conservative explanation of crime would recommend punishment. As noted, the liberal perspective would recommend "treatment" and/or "rehabilitation" as well as possible economic reforms in society. A biological theory would have as part of its implicit treatment modality either sterilization, chemical therapy, or some kind of medical remedies directed at the individual offender.

Research Programs

A fourth dimension of criminological theories is that, in addition to having, however implicit, built-in ideological biases, images of society and of men and women, and a concomitant treatment modality, they will have a specific research program. That is, each contains a particular methodological agenda. This, along with the other dimensions of a theory, is influenced by and influences the conceptualization of key theoretic concepts such as "crime" and "criminal." The exact scope of a theory is largely a result of how the element that the theory purports to explain is specifically defined. For instance, noted criminologist Edwin H. Sutherland's (1883–1950) classic definition of criminology is the study of the making of laws, the breaking of laws, and society's responses to these processes. This is a very comprehensive approach to criminology and technically includes both criminology and criminal justice. In actuality, criminologists have traditionally focused more heavily on studying the causes, rates, and distributions of crime. Criminal justice scholars have focused almost exclusively on society's responses to lawbreaking; that is, the criminal justice system. However, this historical distinction between the two has recently shown signs of collapse.

Other definitions and their concomitant theoretic frame of reference have been more narrow in scope. As a consequence, their research methodologies have also been more narrow than those working within Sutherland's tradition. For instance, a legalistic approach to criminology might emphasize simply the passage of laws. European criminologists, for example, for generations emphasized the study of laws. American criminologists, by contrast, have studied criminals, crime, and prisons far more extensively.

A LOOK AT SOME THEORIES

Some criminologists develop novel definitions of crime. James Q. Wilson, for instance (Issue 4), centers his theory of crime around predatory street crimes and ignores all other types. His work, to some extent, is reminiscent of the Italian jurist Garofalo, who in 1914 defined crimes as offenses against society's ideas of "pity" and "probity." The offense also has to be injurious to society, Garofalo wrote.

The acts of defining and explaining some phenomenon, then, automatically set the boundaries for both the discipline itself and what is to be researched in that discipline (what kinds of crimes, who commits crime). For example, both formally and informally, rape was not considered a crime in many parts of the world. Informally, in the United States, it was often not treated as a crime, or at least not as a serious crime, although laws were always on the books against it. Until the past several years, it was not considered possible for a husband to rape his wife. Indeed, in some states it was assumed that if a woman had invited a man to her home, then rape could not have occurred (only voluntary sexual intercourse). Thus, what your theory of crime consists of, how it defines crime, and what acts are included as crimes will all have a tremendous impact on your research and policy recommendations. That is why it is very important to inquire about a scholar's particular theoretic frame of reference.

Criminology in the United States grew up in the late 1800s basically as an applied study of the effects of prisons on criminals. It later received "academic respectability" through its inclusion within sociology departments at the turn of the century (for example, the University of Chicago). Almost from the very beginning, criminology as a subdiscipline of sociology emphasized a reformist, scientific orientation. It was assumed that, by scientifically understanding crime, criminals could be better controlled and helped. Thus, crime would be reduced. Most of the early theories, though, were a grab bag of different superstitions, Protestant reform sentiments, and pop biology and psychology, with some vague sociological or structural ideas thrown in. Generally, the sociological aspects of criminological theorizing were restricted to a focus upon the organization (or more typically, the perceived disorganization) of the family, the community, and the school. (See for instance, Gillin's *Criminology and Penology* [1926]).

Throughout the 1940s and 1950s, the dominant theory within American criminology, by far, was that of Sutherland and later Sutherland and Cressey. This perspective, though vast and complicated in many ways, is usually reduced to representing the symbolic interactionist sociological frame of reference. Within American sociology since the 1960s, there have been three dominant paradigms or theories explaining social behavior. These are the symbolic interactionist, the structural functional, and the conflict or radical perspectives.

As indicated, most criminological work was set within the symbolic interactionist frame of reference for several years. The emphasis was placed on how criminals were socialized into a world of crime through their interactions with criminal others. The importance of learning symbols, attitudes, and values conducive of crime commission from knowledgeable, experienced criminals was stressed. Later, the role (sometimes a fatal role) of labeling was incorporated into this perspective. The interaction between the police and alleged criminals, the courts and alleged criminals, was emphasized. However, economic factors as well as political ones were generally ignored by this perspective.

The structural functional perspective derives its thinking largely from the sociology of Emile Durkheim (see Issue 1). It has been elaborated on by a number of American sociologists. The most important bearer of Durkheim's tradition has been Robert Merton, whose elaborations upon Durkheim's work include his famous means-end scheme approach to explaining deviant behavior (first published in 1938). Later theorists writing in this tradition include Kingsley Davis and, more recently, Kai Erickson.

Structural functionalists attempt to determine what patterns of interaction or structures exist in various groups. They investigate what these patterns contribute to the maintenance of that group and of the society to which the group belongs. In the United States, for example, dating patterns and their relation to marriage are studied. Marriage patterns and their relation to the economy, to religion, and so on are traced. In addition, structural functionalists want to know about what consequences patterns of behavior have for groups, for members of groups, for society as a whole. Such consequences can be both positive and negative, intentional and unintentional.

Radical or Marxist sociologists are similar to structural functionalists in that they frequently look at the entire society and try to determine how its various component parts interrelate. However, the radical or conflict theorist (these terms are often used interchangeably) generally sees as the core definers of society's interests those who dominate the economy. By contrast, structural functionalists seem to assume core values that are shared by members of society regardless of their position vis-à-vis the economy (whether they are workers, managers, or owners).

For the structural functionalist, crime results from people having their goals or values blocked. An example would be poor teenagers who share the American goal of material success but through lack of education, discrimination, and so on are not able to achieve success through the prescribed channels. Therefore, they commit crimes as a "short cut."

The Marxist would argue, by contrast, that often the system itself through oppression pressures the criminal to commit crimes. There are many variants of radical criminology. However, earlier variants insisted that criminals were often guilty only of political acts. The radical criminologists would also emphasize the unfair treatment society's disadvantaged are subjected to by agents of the criminal justice system, such as the police on the beat harrassing the poor, the courts' unfair sentencing of them, and the prison's mistreatment of its inmates, usually poorer citizens. To the radical criminologist, the criminal justice system is little more than a handmaiden serving to protect the interests of the rich. The structural functionalists, then, obviously view crime in a very different way.

SOME FINAL THOUGHTS

It is interesting to note that the public, the police, and sometimes the courts often find scientific explanations threatening. Many police officers feel that criminologists in searching for structural causes of crime attempt to "excuse" delinquents, who the police may feel deserve a "good kick in the ass" along with jail instead of "help" and "treatment." The public and the police currently are more comfortable with explanations of crime that assume individual responsibility for criminal acts. The courts, too, may object to studies that show racial patterns in sentencing and possibly expose prejudice. To judges and other officials, the "causes" of their sentencing and processing of criminals are a result of legal factors, not racial and/or economic ones.

Thus, as you begin your voyage into academic criminology and criminal justice, you should be aware of the fact that there are many scientific explanations of crime, some of which are politically and even morally threatening to various interest groups. At the same time, though, for you and your generation to have the capacity to help solve the crime problem, you will have to be able to sort out the competing explanations with their respective images of human beings and resulting crime treatment models. To ignore rationally assessing these controversial issues is to risk perpetuating the ignorance and myths that characterize many of the current crime theories and policies—the unanticipated and unintended consequence of which is frequently to magnify the crime problem instead of solving it.

PART 1

Crime: Definitions and Causes

Exactly what is crime and who commits it and why remain core questions for the public and professionals alike. Although a definition and an explanation of crime would appear to be straightforward matters, in reality both are difficult to come by. Even assessing the harm that criminals do is problematic. Some, for instance, suggest that crime is functional and necessary in all societies. Others say that we are concerned about the wrong kinds of crime. These questions are important for criminologists and policymakers.

Is Crime Functional?

Is Crime Created by Society's Elites?

Is Criminal Behavior Biologically Determined?

Is Street Crime More Serious Than White-Collar Crime?

ISSUE 1

Is Crime Functional?

YES: Emile Durkheim, from *Rules of Sociological Method* (Free Press, 1950)

NO: Jeffrey H. Reiman, from *The Rich Get Richer and the Poor Get Prison: Ideology, Class, and Criminal Justice,* Second Edition (Macmillan, 1984)

ISSUE SUMMARY

YES: Classic sociologist Emile Durkheim (1858–1917) theorizes that crime exists in all societies because it reaffirms moral boundaries and at times assists needed social changes.

NO: American University philosopher Jeffrey Reiman responds that crime is functional not because it promotes social solidarity but because it provides an ideology to justify the status quo.

Thousands of years after Cain slew Abel, we continue to ask: What is crime? Who commits it? And why? The importance given to these questions, and their answers, varies between different categories of people, although we have little certainty that any one group's meanings and interpretations are superior to those of another.

For example, younger and older people have different perceptions of crime (older people are more likely to fear even crime though younger people are far more likely to be victims of crime). Public officials also disagree about crime. Many a politician during an election year has inflated the number of crimes committed and has attributed crimes to forces and influences that only the politician, if elected, can combat. Much of the 1988 presidential election, apparently, was decided by the "crime issue."

Criminological and criminal justice scholars, although generally slightly less shrill and self-serving than politicians in their definitions and explanations of crime, are also very likely to disagree among themselves about what crime is and its causes. They, unlike politicians, do not follow four-year cycles in their crime conceptualizations, but they do reflect trends. For example, twenty years ago most criminologists probably reflected a "liberal ideology" in their crime explanations and suggested treatments. Today some are more likely to reflect an ideologically "conservative" scholarly bias. Radical or Marxist criminologists continue to have a marginal position within the discipline.

The seminal essay, excerpted here, by Durkheim argues that deviancy, including crime, is functional and exists in all societies because it is needed to establish moral boundaries and to distinguish between those who obey and those who disobey society's rules. Although it was written almost one hundred years ago, Durkheim's original structural or sociological approach continues to be relied on by criminological and criminal justice scholars.

There are, of course, many variants of the sociological approach to crime, its definitions, and causes. However, Durkheim's approach is central for many criminologists and especially *structural functionalists*. Structural functionalists attempt to determine what patterns of interaction or structures exist in various groups. They investigate what these patterns contribute to the maintenance of a group and of the society to which the group belongs. In the United States, for example, dating patterns and their relation to marriage are studied. Marriage patterns and their relation to the economy, to religion, and so on are traced. In addition, structural functionalists want to know about the consequences of patterns of behavior for groups, for members of groups, and for society as a whole. Such consequences can be both positive and negative, intentional and unintentional.

Durkheim selects a pattern of behavior, in this case deviant acts, and attempts to determine what it contributes to the maintenance of society, what its consequences might be, including intended and unintended ones. With crime, Durkheim's genius lies in his assertion that it is functional (not necessarily good and certainly not encourageable), and his theories help establish moral boundaries. They also provide a sense of propriety and a feeling of righteousness for those who do not commit crimes as they share sentiments of moral indignation about those who do violate society's norms. Durkheim says that crime also allows for social change. It prevents a society from having too much rigidity and from becoming too slavish in its obedience to norms.

American University philosopher and criminal justice professor Jeffrey Reiman acknowledges his debt to Durkheim and to a contemporary follower of some of Durkheim's ideas, Kai Erickson. Then Reiman challenges their functional analysis of crime, asserting that crime is functional not, as Durkheim contends, because it generates social solidarity in reaction to it but instead because it provides a convenient ideology by which to justify existing inequities in wealth.

YES

Emile Durkheim

THE NORMAL AND THE PATHOLOGICAL

Crime is present not only in the majority of societies of one particular species but in all societies of all types. There is no society that is not confronted with the problem of criminality. Its form changes; the acts thus characterized are not the same everywhere; but, everywhere and always, there have been men who have behaved in such a way as to draw upon themselves penal repression. If, in proportion as societies pass from the lower to the higher types, the rate of criminality, i.e., the relation between the yearly number of crimes and the population, tended to decline, it might be believed that crime, while still normal, is tending to lose this character of normality. But we have no reason to believe that such a regression is substantiated. Many facts would seem rather to indicate a movement in the opposite direction. From the beginning of the [nineteenth] century, statistics enable us to follow the course of criminality. It has everywhere increased. In France the increase is nearly 300 percent. There is, then, no phenomenon that presents more indisputably all the symptoms of normality, since it appears closely connected with the conditions of all collective life. To make of crime a form of social morbidity would be to admit that morbidity is not something accidental, but, on the contrary, that in certain cases it grows out of the fundamental constitution of the living organism; it would result in wiping out all distinction between the physiological and the pathological. No doubt it is possible that crime itself will have abnormal forms, as, for example, when its rate is unusually high. This excess is, indeed, undoubtedly morbid in nature. What is normal, simply, is the existence of criminality, provided that it attains and does not exceed, for each social type, a certain level, which it is perhaps not impossible to fix in conformity with the preceding rules.[1]

Here we are, then, in the presence of a conclusion in appearance quite paradoxical. Let us make no mistake. To classify crime among the phenomena of normal sociology is not to say merely that it is an inevitable, although regrettable phenomenon, due to the incorrigible wickedness of men; it is to affirm that it is a factor in public health, an integral part of all healthy societies. This result is, at first glance, surprising enough to have puzzled even ourselves for a long time. Once this first surprise has been overcome, however, it is not difficult to find reasons explaining this normality and at the same time confirming it.

In the first place crime is normal because a society exempt from it is utterly impossible. Crime, we have shown elsewhere, consists of an act that offends certain very strong collective sentiments. In a society in which criminal acts are no longer committed, the sentiments they offend would have to be found without exception in all individual consciousnesses, and they must be found to exist with the same degree as sentiments contrary to them. Assuming that this condition could actually be realized, crime would not thereby disappear; it would only change its form, for the very cause which would thus dry up the sources of criminality would immediately open up new ones.

Indeed, for the collective sentiments which are protected by the penal law of a people at a specified moment of its history to take possession of the public conscience or for them to acquire a stronger hold where they have an insufficient grip, they must acquire an intensity greater than that which they had hitherto had. The community as a whole must experience them more vividly, for it can acquire from no other source the greater force necessary to control these individuals who formerly were the most refractory. For murderers to disappear, the horror of bloodshed must become greater in those social strata from which murderers are recruited; but, first it must become greater throughout the entire society. Moreover, the very absence of crime would directly contribute to produce this horror; because any sentiment seems much more respectable when it is always and uniformly respected.

One easily overlooks the consideration that these strong states of the common consciousness cannot be thus reinforced without reinforcing at the same time the more feeble states, whose violation previously gave birth to mere infraction of convention—since the weaker ones are only the prolongation, the attenuated form, of the stronger. Thus robbery and simple bad taste injure the same single altruistic sentiment, the respect for that which is another's. However, this same sentiment is less grievously offended by bad taste than by robbery; and since, in addition, the average consciousness had not sufficient intensity to react keenly to the bad taste, it is treated with greater tolerance. That is why the person guilty of bad taste is merely blamed, whereas the thief is punished. But, if this sentiment grows stronger, to the point of silencing in all consciousnesses the inclination which disposes man to steal, he will become more sensitive to the offenses which, until then, touched him but lightly. He will react against them, then, with more energy; they will be the object of greater opprobrium, which will transform certain of them from the simple moral faults that they were and give them the quality of crimes. For example, improper contracts, or contracts improperly executed, which only incur public blame or civil damages, will become offenses in law.

Imagine a society of saints, a perfect cloister of exemplary individuals. Crimes, properly so called, will there be unknown; but faults which appear venial to the layman will create there the same scandal that the ordinary offense does in ordinary consciousnesses. If, then, this society has the power to judge and punish, it will define these acts as criminal and will treat them as such. For the same reason, the perfect and upright man judges his smallest failings with a severity that the majority reserve for acts more truly in the nature of an offense. Formerly, acts of violence against persons were more frequent than they are today, because respect for individual dignity was less strong. As this has increased, these crimes have become more rare; and also, many acts violating this sentiment have been introduced into the penal law which were not included there in primitive times.[2]

In order to exhaust all the hypotheses logically possible, it will perhaps be asked why this unanimity does not extend to all collective sentiments without exception. Why should not even the most feeble sentiment gather enough energy to prevent all dissent? The moral consciousness of the society would be present in its entirety in all the individuals, with a vitality sufficient to prevent all acts offending it—the purely conventional faults as well as the crimes. But a uniformity so universal and absolute is utterly impossible; for the immediate physical milieu in which each one of us is placed, the hereditary antecedents, and the social influences vary from one individual to the next, and consequently diversify consciousnesses. It is impossible for all to be alike, if only because each one has his own organism and that these organisms occupy different areas in space. That is why, even among the lower peoples, where individual originality is very little developed, it nevertheless does exist.

Thus, since there cannot be a society in which the individuals do not differ more or less from the collective type, it is also inevitable that, among these divergences, there are some with a criminal character. What confers this character upon them is not the intrinsic quality of a given act but that definition which the collective conscience lends them. If the collective conscience is stronger, if it has enough authority practically to suppress these divergences, it will also be more sensitive, more exacting; and, reacting against the slightest deviations with the energy it otherwise displays only against more considerable infractions, it will attribute to them the same gravity as formerly to crimes. In other words, it will designate them as criminal.

Crime is, then, necessary; it is bound up with fundamental conditions of all social life, and by that very fact it is useful, because these conditions of which it is a part are themselves indispensable to the normal evolution of morality and law.

Indeed, it is no longer possible today to dispute the fact that law and morality vary from one social type to the next, nor that they change within the same type if the conditions of life are modified. But, in order that these transformations may be possible, the collective sentiments at the basis of morality must not be hostile to change, and consequently must have but moderate energy. If they were too strong, they would no longer be plastic. Every pattern is an obstacle to new patterns, to the extent that the first pattern is inflexible. The better a structure is articulated, the more it offers a healthy resistance to all modification; and this is equally true of functional, as of anatomical, organization. If there were no crimes, this condition could not have been fulfilled; for such a hypothesis presupposes that collective sentiments have arrived at a degree of intensity unexampled in history. Nothing is good indefinitely and to an unlimited extent. The authority which the moral conscience enjoys must not be excessive; otherwise no one would dare criticize it, and it would too easily congeal into an immutable form. To make progress, individual originality must be able to express itself. In order that the originality of the idealist whose dreams transcend this century may find expression, it is necessary that the originality of the criminal, who is below the level of his time, shall also be possible. One does not occur without the other.

Nor is this all. Aside from this indirect utility, it happens that crime itself plays a useful role in this evolution. Crime implies not only that the way remains open to necessary changes but that in certain cases it directly prepares these changes. Where crime exists, collective sentiments are sufficiently flexible to take on a new form, and crime sometimes helps to determine the form they will take. How many times, indeed, it is only an anticipation of future morality—a step toward what will be! According to Athenian law, Socrates was a criminal, and his condemnation was no more than just. However, his crime, namely, the independence of his thought, rendered a service not only to humanity but to his country. It served to prepare a new morality and faith which the Athenians needed, since the traditions by which they had lived until then were no longer in harmony with the current conditions of life. Nor is the case of Socrates unique; it is reproduced periodically in history. It would never have been possible to establish the freedom of thought we now enjoy if the regulations prohibiting it had not been violated before being solemnly abrogated. At that time, however, the violation was a crime, since it was an offense against sentiments still very keen in the average con-

science. And yet this crime was useful as a prelude to reforms which daily become more necessary. Liberal philosophy had as its precursors the heretics of all kinds who were justly punished by secular authorities during the entire course of the Middle Ages and until the eve of modern times.

From this point of view the fundamental facts of criminality present themselves to us in an entirely new light. Contrary to current ideas, the criminal no longer seems a totally unsociable being, a sort of parasitic element, a strange and unassimilable body, introduced into the midst of society.[3] On the contrary, he plays a definite role in social life. Crime, for its part, must no longer be conceived as an evil that cannot be too much suppressed. There is no occasion for self-congratulation when the crime rate drops noticeably below the average level, for we may be certain that this apparent progress is associated with some social disorder. Thus, the number of assault cases never falls so low as in times of want.[4] With the drop in the crime rate, and as a reaction to it, comes a revision, or the need of a revision in the theory of punishment. If, indeed, crime is a disease, its punishment is its remedy and cannot be otherwise conceived; thus, all the discussions it arouses bear on the point of determining what the punishment must be in order to fulfil this role of remedy. If crime is not pathological at all, the object of punishment cannot be to cure it, and its true function must be sought elsewhere.

NOTES

1. From the fact that crime is a phenomenon of normal sociology, it does not follow that the criminal is an individual normally constituted from the biological and psychological points of

view. The two questions are independent of each other. This independence will be better understood when we have shown, later on, the difference between psychological and sociological facts.

2. Calumny, insults, slander, fraud, etc.

3. We have ourselves committed the error of speaking thus of the criminal, because of a failure to apply our rule (*Division du travail social*, pp. 395–96).

4. Although crime is a fact of normal sociology, it does not follow that we must not abhor it. Pain itself has nothing desirable about it; the individual dislikes it as society does crime, and yet it is a function of normal physiology. Not only is it necessarily derived from the very constitution of every living organism, but it plays a useful role in life, for which reason it cannot be replaced. It would, then, be a singular distortion of our thought to present it as an apology for crime. We would not even think of protesting against such an interpretation, did we not know to what strange accusations and misunderstandings one exposes oneself when one undertakes to study moral facts objectively and to speak of them in a different language from that of the layman.

NO

Jeffrey H. Reiman

HOW CRIME PAYS

Kai T. Erikson has suggested in his book *Wayward Puritans* that societies derive benefit from the existence of crime and thus there is reason to believe that social institutions work to maintain rather than to eliminate crime. Since the Pyrrhic defeat theory* draws heavily upon this insight, it will serve to clarify my own view if we compare it with Erikson's.

Professor Erikson's theory is based on the view of crime that finds expression in one of the classic books on sociological theory, *The Division of Labor in Society*, by Emile Durkheim. Writing toward the end of the nineteenth century, Durkheim "had suggested that crime (and by extension other forms of deviation) may actually perform a needed service to society by drawing people together in a common posture of anger and indignation. The deviant individual violates rules of conduct which the rest of the community holds in high respect; and when these people come together to express their outrage over the offense and to bear witness against the offender, they develop a tighter bond of solidarity than existed earlier.[1]

The solidarity that holds a community together, in this view, is a function of the intensity with which the members of the community share a living sense of the group's cultural identity, of the boundary between acceptable and unacceptable behavior that gives the group its distinctive nature. It is necessary, then, for the existence of a community *as a community* that its members learn and constantly relearn the location of its "boundaries." And, writes Erikson, these boundaries are learned in dramatic confrontations with

> policing agents whose special business it is to guard the cultural integrity of the community. Whether these confrontations take the form of criminal trials,

*[*Earlier in Reiman's book* The Rich Get Richer and the Poor Get Prison, *from which this reading is taken, he writes: "I propose we can make more sense out of criminal justice policy by assuming that its goal is to maintain crime than by assuming that its goal is to reduce crime. . . . I call this . . . the* Pyrrhic defeat *theory. A 'Pyrrhic victory' is one in which a military victory is purchased at such a cost . . . that it amounts to a defeat. The Pyrrhic defeat theory argues that the failure of the criminal justice system yields such benefits to those in positions of power that it amounts to success."—*Ed.]

excommunication hearings, court-martial, or even case conferences, they act as boundary-maintaining devices in the sense that they demonstrate to whatever audience is concerned where the line is drawn between behavior that belongs in the special universe of the group and behavior that does not.[2]

In brief, this means not only that a community makes good use of unacceptable behavior *but that it positively needs unacceptable behavior.* Not only does unacceptable behavior cast in relief the terrain of behavior acceptable to the community but also it reinforces the intensity with which the members of the community identify that terrain as their shared territory. On this view, *deviant behavior is an ingredient in the glue that holds a community together.* "This," Erikson continues,

raises a delicate theoretical issue. If we grant that human groups often derive benefit from deviant behavior, can we then assume that they are organized in such a way as to promote this resource? Can we assume, in other words, that forces operate in the social structure to recruit offenders and to commit them to long periods of service in the deviant ranks? . . .

Looking at the matter from a long-range historical perspective, it is fair to conclude that prisons have done a conspicuously poor job of reforming the convicts placed in their custody; but the very consistency of this failure may have a peculiar logic of its own. Perhaps we find it difficult to change the worst of our penal practices because we expect the prison to harden the inmate's commitment to deviant forms of behavior and draw him more deeply into the deviant ranks.[3]

In other words, based on Durkheim's recognition that societies benefit from the existence of deviants, Erikson entertains the view that societies have institutions whose unannounced function is to recruit and maintain a reliable supply of deviants. Modified for our purposes, Erikson's view would become the hypothesis that the American criminal justice system fails to reduce crime because a visible criminal population is essential to maintaining the "boundaries" that mark the cultural identity of American society and to maintaining the solidarity between those who share that identity. In other words, in its failure, the criminal justice system succeeds in providing some of the cement necessary to hold American society together as a society.

It is not my intention to do battle with the Durkheim-Erikson thesis. Rather, my aim is to acknowledge my debt to that thesis and state the difference between it and the view that I will defend. The debt is to the insight that societies may promote behavior that they seem to desire to stamp out, that failure to eliminate deviance may be a success of some sort.

The difference, on the other hand, is this. Both Durkheim and Erikson jump from the *general* proposition that the failure to eliminate deviance promotes social solidarity to the *specific* conclusion that the form in which this failure occurs in a particular society can be explained by the contribution that that failure makes to promoting consensus on shared beliefs and thus feelings of social solidarity. This is a "jump" because it leaves out the important question of how it is that a social group forms its particular consensus around one set of shared beliefs rather than another. That is, Durkheim and Erikson implicitly assume that a consensus already exists (at least virtually) and that deviance is promoted in order to manifest and reinforce it. This leads to the view that social institutions reflect beliefs that are already in people's heads and already largely and spontaneously shared by all of them. In my view, even if it is granted that societies work to strengthen feelings of social solidarity, the set of beliefs about the world around which those feelings will crystallize are by no means already in people's heads and spontaneously shared. A consensus is made, not born, although, again, I do not mean that it is made intentionally. It is created by social institutions, not just reflected by social institutions. Thus, the failure to stamp out deviance does not simply reinforce a consensus that already exists; it is part of the process by which a very particular consensus is created. In developing the Pyrrhic defeat theory, I try to show how the failure of criminal justice works to create and reinforce a very particular set of beliefs about the world, about what is dangerous and what is not, who is a threat and who is not. And this does not merely shore up general feelings of social solidarity; it allows those feelings to be attached to a social order characterized by striking disparities of wealth, power, and privilege; and considerable injustice.

. . . THE SYSTEM MUST ACTUALLY FIGHT crime—or at least some crime—but only enough to keep it from getting out of hand and to keep the struggle against crime vividly and dramatically in the public's view—never enough to reduce or eliminate crime. I call this way of looking at criminal justice policy the *Pyrrhic defeat* theory.

It will prevent confusion . . . if the reader remembers the following two features of the Pyrrhic defeat theory of criminal justice: *First,* though I maintain that our failing criminal justice system exists in part because its failure provides benefits to those with power and wealth, I do not maintain that those with power and wealth intentionally make the system fail in order to gain those benefits. *Second,* central to my analysis of the criminal justice system is the claim that the acts that the system defines as criminal are not the only or even the most dangerous acts in our society—rather they are primarily the dangerous acts committed by poor people in our society. Thus, note that when I speak of the criminal justice system I mean more than the familiar institutions of police, courts, and prisons. I mean the entire system that runs from the decisions of lawmakers about what acts are criminal all the way to the decisions of judges and parole boards about who will be in prison to pay for these acts.

I claim no particular originality for the Pyrrhic defeat theory. It is a child of the marriage of several streams of western social theory. And although this will be discussed at greater length in what follows, it will serve clarity to indicate from the start the parents and the grandparents of this child. The idea that crime serves important functions for a society come from Emile Durkheim. The notion that public policy can best be understood as serving the interests of the rich and powerful in a society stems from Karl Marx. From Kai Erikson is derived the notion that the institutions that are designed to fight crime serve instead to contribute to its existence. And from Richard Quinney comes the concept of the "reality" of crime as *created* in the process that runs from the definition of some acts as "criminal" in the law to the treatment of some persons as "criminals" by the agents of the law. The Pyrrhic defeat theory combines these ideas into the view that the failure of criminal justice policy becomes intelligible when we see that it creates the "reality" of crime as the work of the poor and thus projects an image that serves the interests of the rich and powerful in American society.

The Pyrrhic defeat theory veers away from traditional Marxist accounts of legal institutions insofar as such accounts generally emphasize the *repressive* function of the criminal justice system, while my view emphasizes its *ideological* function. On the whole, Marxists see the criminal justice system as serving the powerful by *successfully* repressing the poor. My view is that the system serves the powerful by its *failure* to reduce crime, not by its success.

NOTES

1. Kai T. Erickson, *Wayward Puritans* (New York: John Wiley, copyright © 1966), p. 4. Reprinted by permission of John Wiley & Sons, Inc.
2. Ibid. p. 11.
3. Ibid. pp. 13–15. [Emphasis added.]

POSTSCRIPT

Is Crime Functional?

One of the first American sociologists who attempted to use the insights of Durkheim was Robert Merton in his classic article "Social Structure and Anomie," *American Sociological Review* (1938). Merton attempted to show the bearing that culturally established goals and legitimate means for achieving them or their absence has upon criminogenic behavior.

For a very different formulation of crime written by a contemporary of Durkheim that reflects the more traditional, practical, applied criminology of both England and the United States, see Gordon Rylands's *Crime: Its Causes and Remedy* (Unwin, 1889).

An early Marxist perspective on crime that, curiously, is probably closer to Durkheim's thinking than to Reiman's is William A. Bonger's *Criminality and Economic Conditions* (Little, Brown, 1916). An excellent work that sets up clearly the distinction within the social sciences between the Marxist, or conflict, perspective and the "conservative," or structural functional, perspective and their concomitant approaches to social issues, ranging from accounting for social order to crime and deviance, is *Class and Class Conflict in Industrial Societies*, by Ralph Dahrendorf (Stanford University Press, 1959).

Another delineation of the two major theoretical and ideological perspectives within sociology is the classic article by John Horton, "Order and Conflict Theories of Social Problems as Competing Ideologies." This was originally published in the *American Journal of Sociology* (May 1966). Several fairly recent books and articles discuss the Marxist (critical, conflict) approach to crime and criminal justice. These include W. B. Groves and R. J. Sampson's "Critical Theory and Criminology," *Social Problems* 33: 558–580 (October/December 1986); Jock Young's *Realist Criminology* (Gowe, 1987); and David Greenberg, editor, *Crime and Capitalism* (Mayfield, 1981).

An outstanding discussion from a feminist perspective of the creation of deviancy and crime through the passage of laws can be found in "The Criminal Law and Women," chapter 1 of *The Criminal Justice System and Women*, edited by B. R. Price and N. J. Sokoloff (Clark Boardman, 1982).

One of the most insightful articles on the conservative-liberal ideological bias within criminal justice is Walter Miller's "Ideology and Criminal Justice Policy," *Journal of Criminal Law and Criminology* 64 (1973). For an article that discusses criminological theories from a school's perspective, see "Scientific Research Programs, Theory and Schools Interregnum in Criminology and Criminal Justice," *Contemporary Criminal Justice*, by R. C. Monk (February 1988). Two new theory books include J. R. Lilly et al., *Criminological Theory: Contexts and Consequences* (Sage, 1989) and *A General Theory of Crime*, by M. R. Gottfredson and T. Hirschi (Stanford University Press, 1990).

ISSUE 2

Is Crime Created by Society's Elites?

YES: Richard Quinney, from *The Social Reality of Crime* (Little, Brown, & Co., 1970)

NO: Daniel Bell, from *The End of Ideology* (Free Press, 1960)

ISSUE SUMMARY

YES: Marxist criminologist Richard Quinney theorizes that crime is largely socially constructed by society's elites to control the less powerful.

NO: Harvard sociologist Daniel Bell argues that fits of social control are more likely to be the result of middle-class moral indignation rather than policies benefiting the elite. For Bell, crime is often the ingenious acts of members of emerging ethnic groups who seek a piece of the pie by providing services to others.

Who, or what, creates crime? Is it created by criminals who ingeniously figure out ways to commit newer and better crimes to harm us? Or could it be that crime is actually created by laws? After all, in the West we have had the tradition based on Roman jurisprudence that if there is no law to be broken, then there is no crime. Thus, it seems obvious that it must be laws that cause crime, does it not? This tradition, by the way, is quite different from that of the Soviet system. Until December 1988 in the Soviet Union, a crime could be any act defined by authorities (the political elite) as harmful to the state. Thus, crimes in the U.S.S.R. included all acts that were proscribed by criminal statutes plus any act not so covered that could be defined as a harm against the state. Mikhail Gorbachev, now president of the U.S.S.R., proposed changing this so that crimes are simply any acts prohibited by law.

In the Soviet Union, the United States, or anywhere, the problem remains: Where do laws come from? To whom do they really apply? Why are some laws enforced and others not? Why are some people almost always the target of law enforcement and others let alone?

In theory, laws originate in American society from the people (by the people and for the people). They are based on legislative or judicial decisions supposedly for benign, neutral reasons reflecting the will of the people, applied equally. What could be simpler or more obvious? As you probably already know, nothing is that simple in criminology and criminal justice.

A symbolic interactionist (discussed in this volume's introduction) would emphasize that laws basically are negotiated by various groups of people and especially by moral crusaders, who want to impress others with their tidy, sanitized versions of correct conduct. Laws for the symbolic interactionist are also frequently reflections of collective behavior, of the sentiments of the masses crystallized around a controversial issue (for example, the fear of drugs grows, and politicians call for legal changes in order to maintain support from their constituents). Laws, then, come from bargaining, compromising, and modifying standards to express both instrumental (practical necessities) and symbolic (expressive) realities.

To structural functionalists, laws are basically the embodiment of shared values and beliefs. In a democracy, the courts and/or legislative bodies are carrying out their mandated task of serving the will of the people and protecting the Constitution. The laws are neutral rules that are there for the benefit of everyone. When excessive lawbreaking occurs, this is symptomatic of deeper structural strains that are in need of remedy. Frequently, laws are effective mechanisms themselves by which to control existing societal strains and/or bring them to resolution.

A Marxist would view laws as the embodiment of the capitalist's oppression of the working classes. Laws reflect the needs and interests of society's rich, its elites, not justice or the people. To the radical Marxist, laws are a sort of giant conspiracy by which the elite maintain their own high status at the expense of the rest of society.

Historically, law has been to many a mixed blessing. At one level, it was seen as preventing all of us from being engulfed by crime, as bringing order to chaos. But it also has been viewed as capricious, as manufacturing unnecessary crimes for the interest of some third party (for example, society's elites).

"Is Crime Created by Society's Elites?" features radical sociologist Richard Quinney, who graphically shows, in both his discussion and in a series of formal propositions, that crime is constructed by society's wealthy to control those with less power. Those having power formulate and benefit from crime policy.

Reflecting almost another world, Daniel Bell, in his witty article filled with colorful historical observations, argues that crime is an American way of life. While he agrees that, as morality shifts, so do both our definitions of crime and the types of crimes we worry about, Bell sees crime as considerably more functional for the public, the elite, and criminals themselves.

YES

Richard Quinney

THE SOCIAL REALITY OF CRIME

ASSUMPTIONS

In studying any social phenomenon we must hold to some general perspective. Two of those used by sociologists, and by most social analysts for that matter, are the *static* and the *dynamic* interpretations of society. Either is equally plausible, though most sociologists take the static viewpoint. This emphasis has relegated forces and events, such as deviance and crime, which do not appear to be conducive to stability and consensus, to the pathologies of society.

My theory of crime, however, is based on the dynamic perspective. The theory is based on these assumptions: (1) process, (2) conflict, (3) power, and (4) social action.

Process. The dynamic aspect of social relations may be referred to as "social process." Though in analyzing society we use static descriptions, that is, we define the structure and function of social relations, we must be aware that social phenomena fluctuate continually.

We apply this assumption to all social phenomena that have duration and undergo change, that is, all those which interest the sociologist. A social process is a continuous series of actions, taking place in time, and leading to a special kind of result: "a system of social change taking place within a defined situation and exhibiting a particular order of change through the operation of forces present from the first within the situation." Any particular phenomenon, in turn, is viewed as contributing to the dynamics of the total process. As in the "modern systems approach," social phenomena are seen as generating out of an interrelated whole. The methodological implication of the process assumption is that any social phenomenon may be viewed as part of a complex network of events, structures, and underlying processes.

Conflict. In any society conflicts between persons, social units, or cultural elements are inevitable, the normal consequences of social life. Conflict is especially prevalent in societies with diverse value systems and normative groups. Experience teaches that we cannot expect to find consensus on all or most values and norms in such societies.

Two models of society contrast sharply: one is regarded as "conflict" and the other, "consensus." With the consensus model we describe social structure as a functionally integrated system held together in equilibrium. In the conflict model, on the other hand, we find that societies and social organizations are shaped by diversity, coercion, and change. The differences between these contending but complementary conceptions of society have been best characterized by Dahrendorf. According to his study, we assume in postulating the consensus (or integrative) model of society that: (1) society is a relatively persistent, stable structure, (2) it is well integrated, (3) every element has a function—it helps maintain the system, and (4) a functioning social structure is based on a consensus on values. For the conflict (or coercion) model of society, on the other hand, we assume that: (1) at every point society is subject to change, (2) it displays at every point dissensus and conflict, (3) every element contributes to change, and (4) it is based on the coercion of some of its members by others. In other words, society is held together by force and constraint and is characterized by ubiquitous conflicts that result in continuous change: "values are ruling rather than common, enforced rather than accepted, at any given point of time."

Although in society as a whole conflict may be general, according to the conflict model, it is still likely that we will find stability and consensus on values among subunits in the society. Groups with their own cultural elements are found in most societies, leading to social differentiation with conflict between the social units; nonetheless integration and stability may appear within specific social groups: "Although the total larger society may be diverse internally and may form only a loosely integrated system, within each subculture there may be high integration of institutions and close conformity of individuals to the patterns sanctioned by their own group.

Conflict need not necessarily disrupt society. Some sociologists have been interested in the *functions* of social conflict, "that is to say, with those consequences of social conflict which make for an increase rather than a decrease in the adaptation or adjustment of particular social relationships or groups." It seems that conflict can promote cooperation, establish group boundaries, and unite social factions. Furthermore, it may lead to new patterns that may in the long run be beneficial to the whole society or to parts of it. Any doubts about its functional possibilities have been dispelled by Dahrendorf: "I would suggest . . .that all that is creativity, innovation, and development in the life of the individual, his group, and his society is due, to no small extent, to the operation of conflicts between group and group, individual and individual, emotion and emotion within one individual. This fundamental fact alone seems to me to justify the value judgment that conflict is essentially 'good' and 'desirable.' " Conflict is not always the disruptive agent in a society; at certain times it may be meaningful to see it as a cohesive force.

Power. The conflict conception of society leads us to assume that coherence is assured in any social unit by coercion and constraint. In other words, *power* is the basic characteristic of social organization. "This means that in every social organization some positions are entrusted with a right to exercise control over other positions in order to ensure effective coercion; it means in other words, that there is a differential distribution of power and authority." Thus, conflict and power are inextricably linked in the conception of society presented here. The differential distribution of power produces conflict between competing groups, and conflict, in turn, is rooted in the competition for power. Wherever men live together conflict and a struggle for power will be found.

Power, then, is the ability of persons and groups to determine the conduct of other persons and groups. It is utilized not for its own sake, but is the vehicle for the enforcement of scarce values in society, whether values are material, moral, or otherwise. The use of power affects the distribution of values and values affect the distribution of power. The "authoritative allocation of values" is essential to any society. In any society, institutional means are used to officially establish and enforce sets of values for the entire population.

Power and the allocation of values are basic in forming *public policy*. Groups with special *interests* become so well organized that they are able to influence the policies that are to affect all persons. These interest groups exert their influence at every level and branch of government in order to have their own values and interests represented in the policy decisions. Any interest group's ability to influence public policy depends on the group's position in the political power structure. Furthermore, access to the formation of public policy is unequally distributed because of the structural arrangements of the political state. "Access

is one of the advantages unequally distributed by such arrangements; that is, in consequence of the structural peculiarities of our government some groups have better and more varied opportunities to influence key points of decision than do others." Groups that have the power to gain access to the decision-making process also inevitably control the lives of others.

A major assumption in my conception of society, therefore, is the importance of interest groups in shaping public policy. Public polity is formed so as to represent the interests and values of groups that are in positions of power. Rather than accept the pluralistic conception of the political process, which assumes that all groups make themselves heard in policy decision-making, I am relying upon a conception that assumes an unequal distribution of power in formulating and administering public policy.

Social Action. An assumption of man that is consistent with the conflict-power conception of society asserts that man's actions are purposive and meaningful, that man engages in voluntary behavior. This *humanistic* conception of man contrasts with the oversocialized conception of man. Man is, after all, capable of considering alternative actions, of breaking from the established social order. Once he gains an awareness of self, by being a member of society, he is able to choose his actions. The extent to which he does conform depends in large measure upon his own self-control. Nonconformity may also be part of the process of finding self-identity. It is thus *against* something that the self can emerge.

By conceiving of man as able to reason and choose courses of action, we may see him as changing and becoming, rather than merely being. The kind of culture that man develops shapes his ability to be creative. Through his culture he may develop the capacity to have greater freedom of action. Not only is he shaped by his physical, social, and cultural experiences, he is able to select what he is to experience and develop. The belief in realizing unutilized human potential is growing and should be incorporated in a contemporary conception of human behavior.

The *social action* frame of reference that serves as the basis of the humanistic conception of man is drawn from the work of such writers as Weber, Znaniecki, MacIver, Nadel, Parsons, and Becker. It was originally suggested by Max Weber: "Action is social in so far as, by virtue of the subjective meaning attached to it by the acting individual (or individuals), it takes account of the behavior of others and is thereby oriented in its own course." Hence, human behavior is *intentional*, has *meaning* for the actors, is *goal-oriented*, and takes place with an *awareness* of the consequences of behavior.

Because man engages in social action, a *social reality* is created. That is, man in interaction with others constructs a meaningful world of everyday life.

It is the world of cultural objects and social institutions into which we are all born, within which we have to find our bearings, and with which we have to come to terms. From the outset, we, the actors on the social scene, experience the world we live in as a world both of nature and of culture, not as a private but as an intersubjective one, that is, as a world common to all of us, either actually given or potentially accessible to everyone; and this involves intercommunication and language. [Alfred Schultz, *The Problem of Social Reality:*

Collected Papers I (The Hague: Martinus Nijhoff, 1962), p. 53.]

Social reality consists of both the social meanings and the products of the subjective world of persons. Man, accordingly, constructs activities and patterns of actions as he attaches meaning to his everyday existence. Social reality is thus both a *conceptual reality* and a *phenomenal reality*. Having constructed social reality, man finds a world of meanings and events that is real to him as a conscious social being.

THEORY: THE SOCIAL REALITY OF CRIME

The theory contains six propositions and a number of statements within the propositions. With the first proposition I define crime. The next four are the explanatory units. In the final proposition the other five are collected to form a composite describing the social reality of crime. The propositions and their integration into a theory of crime reflect the assumptions about explanation and about man and society outlined above.

PROPOSITION 1 (DEFINITION OF CRIME): *Crime is a definition of human conduct that is created by authorized agents in a politically organized society.*

This is the essential starting point in the theory—a definition of crime—which itself is based on the concept of definition. Crime is a *definition* of behavior that is conferred on some persons by others. Agents of the law (legislators, police, prosecutors, and judges), representing segments of a politically organized society, are responsible for formulating and administering criminal law. Persons and behaviors, therefore, become criminal because of the *formulation* and *application* of criminal definitions. Thus, *crime is created*.

By viewing crime as a definition, we are able to avoid the commonly used "clinical perspective," which leads one to concentrate on the quality of the act and to assume that criminal behavior is an individual pathology. Crime is not inherent in behavior, but is a judgment made by some about the actions and characteristics of others. This proposition allows us to focus on the formulation and administration of the criminal law as it touches upon the behaviors that become defined as criminal. Crime is seen as a result of a process which culminates in the defining of persons and behaviors as criminal. It follows, then, that *the greater the number of criminal definitions formulated and applied, the greater the amount of crime.*

PROPOSITION 2 (FORMULATIONS OF CRIMINAL DEFINITIONS): *Criminal definitions describe behaviors that conflict with the interests of the segments of society that have the power to shape public policy.*

Criminal definitions are formulated according to the interests of those *segments* (types of social groupings) of society which have the *power* to translate their interests into *public policy*. The interests—based on desires, values, and norms—which are ultimately incorporated into the criminal law are those which are treasured by the dominant interest groups in the society. In other words, those who have the ability to have their interests represented in public policy regulate the formulation of criminal definitions.

That criminal definitions are formulated is one of the most obvious manifestations of *conflict* in society. By formulating criminal law (including legislative statutes, administrative rulings, and judicial decisions), some segments of society protect and perpetuate their own interests. Criminal definitions exist, therefore, because some segments of society are in conflict with others. By formulating criminal definitions these segments are able to control the behavior of persons in other segments. It follows that *the greater the conflict in interests between the segments of a society, the greater the probability that the power segments will formulate criminal definitions.*

The interests of the power segments of society are reflected not only in the content of criminal definitions and the kinds of penal sanctions attached to them, but also in the *legal policies* stipulating how those who come to be denied as "criminal" are to be handled. Hence, procedural rules are created for enforcing and administering the criminal law. Policies are also established on programs for treating and punishing the criminally defined and for controlling and preventing crime. In the initial criminal definitions or the subsequent procedures, and in correctional and penal programs or policies of crime control and prevention, the segments of society that have power and interests to protect are instrumental in regulating the behavior of those who have conflicting interests and less power. Finally, law changes with modifications in the interest structure. When the interests that underlie a criminal law are no longer relevant to groups in power, the law will be reinterpreted or altered to incorporate the dominant interests. Hence, the *probability that criminal definitions will be formulated is increased by such factors as (1) changing social conditions, (2) emerging interests, (3) increasing demands that political, economic, and religious interests be protected, and (4) changing conceptions of the public interest.* The social history of law reflects changes in the interest structure of society.

PROPOSITION 3 (APPLICATION OF CRIMINAL DEFINITIONS): *Criminal definitions are applied by the segments of society that have the power to shape the enforcement and administration of criminal law.*

The powerful interests intervene in all stages in which criminal definitions are created. Since interests cannot be effectively protected by merely formulating criminal law, enforcement and administration of the law are required. The interests of the powerful, therefore, operate in *applying* criminal definitions. Consequently, crime is "political behavior and the criminal becomes in fact a member of a 'minority group' without sufficient public support to dominate the control of the police power of the state. Those whose interests conflict with the interests represented in the law must either change their behavior or possibly find it defined as "criminal."

The probability that criminal definitions will be applied varies according to the extent to which the behaviors of the powerless conflict with the interests of the power segments. Law enforcement efforts and judicial activity are likely to be increased when the interests of the powerful are threatened by the opposition's behavior. Fluctuations and variations in the application of criminal definitions reflect shifts in the relations of the various segments in the power structure of society.

Obviously, the criminal law is not applied directly by the powerful segments. They delegate enforcement and administration of the law to authorized *legal agents*, who, nevertheless, represent their interests. In fact, the security in office of legal agents depends on their ability to represent the society's dominant interests.

Because the interest groups responsible for creating criminal definitions are physically separated from the groups to which the authority to enforce and administer law is delegated, local conditions affect the manner in which criminal definitions are applied. In particular, communities vary in the law enforcement and administration of justice they expect. Application is also affected by the visibility of acts in a community and by its norms about reporting possible offenses. Especially important are the occupational organization and ideology of the legal agents. Thus, *the probability that criminal definitions will be applied is influenced by such law enforcement and administration, (2) the visibility and public reporting of offenses, and (3) the occupational organization, ideology, and actions of the legal agents to whom the authority to enforce and administer criminal law is delegated.* Such factors determine how the dominant interests of society are implemented in the application of criminal definitions.

The probability that criminal definitions will be applied in *specific situations* depends on the actions of the legal agents. In the final analysis, a criminal definition is applied according to an *evaluation* by someone charged with the authority to enforce and administer the law. In the course of "criminalization," a criminal label may be affixed to a person because of real or fancied attributes: "Indeed, a person is evaluated, either favorably or unfavorably, not because he *does* something, or even because he *is* something, but because others react to their perceptions of him as offensive or inoffensive." Evaluation by the definers is affected by the way in which the suspect handles the situation, but ultimately their evaluations and subsequent decisions determine the criminality of human acts. Hence, *the more legal agents evaluate behaviors and persons as worthy of criminal definition, the greater the probability that criminal definitions will be applied.*

PROPOSITION 4 (DEVELOPMENT OF BEHAVIOR PATTERNS IN RELATION TO CRIMINAL DEFINITIONS): *Behavior patterns are structured in segmentally organized society in relation to criminal definitions, and within this context persons engage in actions that have relative probabilities of being defined as criminal.*

Although behavior varies, all behaviors are similar in that they represent the *behavior patterns* of segments of society. Therefore, all persons—whether they create criminal definitions or are the objects of criminal definitions—act according to *normative systems* learned in relative social and cultural settings. Since it is not the quality of the behavior but the action taken against the behavior that makes it criminal, that which is defined as criminal in any society is relative to the behavior patterns of the segments of society that formulate and apply criminal definitions. Consequently, *persons in the segments of society whose behavior patterns are not represented in formulating and applying criminal definitions are more likely to act in ways that will be defined as criminal than those in the segments that formulate and apply criminal definitions.*

Once behavior patterns are established with some regularity within the respective segments of society, individuals are provided with a framework for developing *personal action patterns*. These patterns continually develop for each person as he moves from one experience to another. It is the development of these patterns that gives his behavior its own substance in relation to criminal definitions.

Man constructs his own patterns of action in participating with others. It follows, then, that *the probability that a person will develop action patterns that have a high potential of being defined as criminal depends on the relative substance of (1) structured opportunities, (2) learning experiences, (3) interpersonal associations and identifications, and (4) self-conceptions.* Throughout his experiences, each person creates a conception of himself as a social being. Thus prepared, he behaves according to the anticipated consequences of his actions.

During experiences shared by the criminal definers and the criminally defined, personal action patterns develop among the criminally defined because they are so defined. After such persons have had continued experience in being criminally defined, they learn to manipulate the application of criminal definitions.

Furthermore, those who have been defined as criminal begin to conceive of themselves as criminal; as they adjust to the definitions imposed upon them, they learn to play the role of the criminal. Because of others' reactions, therefore, persons may develop personal action patterns that increase the likelihood of their being defined as criminal in the future. That is, *increased experience with criminal definitions increases the probability of developing actions that may be subsequently defined as criminal.*

Thus, both the criminal definers and the criminally defined are involved in reciprocal action patterns. The patterns of both the definers and the defined are shaped by their common, continued, and related experiences. The fate of each is bound to that of the other.

PROPOSITION 5 (CONSTRUCTION OF CRIMINAL CONCEPTIONS): *Conceptions of crime are constructed and diffused in the segments of society by various means of communication.*

The "real world" is a social construction: man with the help of others creates the world in which he lives. Social reality is thus the world a group of people create and believe in as their own. This reality is constructed according to the kind of "knowledge" they develop, the ideas they are exposed to, the manner in which they select information to fit the world they are shaping, and the manner in which they interpret these conceptions. Man behaves in reference to the *social meanings* he attaches to his experiences.

Among the constructions that develop in a society are those which determine what man regards as crime. Wherever we find the concept of crime, there we will find conceptions about the relevance of crime, the offender's characteristics, and the relation of crime to the social order. These conceptions are constructed by communication. In fact, *the construction of criminal conceptions depends on the portrayal of crime in all personal and mass communications.* By such means, criminal conceptions are constructed and diffused in the segments of a society. The most critical conceptions are those held by the power segments of society. These are the conceptions that are certain of becoming incorporated into the social reality of crime. In general, then, *the more the power segments are concerned about crime, the greater the probability that criminal definitions will be created and that behavior patterns will develop in opposition to criminal definitions.* The formulation and application of criminal definitions and the development of behavior patterns re-lated to criminal definitions are thus joined in full circle by the construction of criminal conceptions.

PROPOSITION 6 (THE SOCIAL REALITY OF CRIME): *The social reality of crime is constructed by the formulation and application of criminal definitions, the development of behavior patterns related to criminal definitions, and the construction of criminal conceptions.*

These five propositions can be collected into a composite. The theory, accordingly, describes and explains phenomena that increase the probability of crime in society, resulting in the social reality of crime.

Since the first proposition is a definition and the sixth is a composite, the body of the theory consists of the four middle propositions. These form a model, as diagrammed in Figure 1.1, which relates the propositions into a theoretical system. Each proposition is related to the others forming a theoretical system of developmental propositions interacting with one another. The phenomena denoted in the propositions and their relationships culminate in what is regarded as the amount and character of crime in a society at any given time, that is, in the social reality of crime.

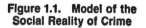

Figure 1.1. Model of the Social Reality of Crime

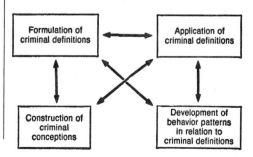

A THEORECTICAL PERSPECTIVE FOR STUDYING CRIME

The theory as I have formulated it is inspired by a change currently altering our view of the world. This change, found at all levels of society, has to do with the world that we all construct and, at the same time, pretend to separate ourselves from in assessing our experiences. Sociologists, sensing the problematic nature of existence, have begun to revise their theoretical orientation, as well as their methods and subjects of investigation.

For the study of crime, a revision in thought is directing attention to the process by which criminal definitions are formulated and applied. In the theory of the social reality of crime I have attempted to show how a theory of crime can be consistent with some revisionist assumptions about theoretical explanation and about man and society. The theory is cumulative in that the framework incorporates the diverse findings from criminology.

The synthesis has been brought about by conceiving of crime as a constructive process and by formulating a theory according to a system of propositions. The theory is integrative in that all relevant phenomena contribute to the process of creating criminal definitions, the development of the behaviors of those who are involved in criminal defining situations, and the construction of criminal conceptions. The result is the social reality of crime that is constantly being constructed in society.

NO
Daniel Bell

CRIME AS AN AMERICAN WAY OF LIFE

In the 1890's the Reverend Dr. Charles Parkhurst, shocked at the open police protection afforded New York's bordellos, demanded a state inquiry. In the Lexow investigation that followed, the young and dashing William Travers Jerome staged a set of public hearings that created sensation after sensation. He badgered "Clubber" Williams, First Inspector of the Police Department, to account for wealth and property far greater than could have been saved on his salary; it was earned, the Clubber explained laconically, through land speculation "in Japan." Heavy-set Captain Schmittberger, the "collector" for the "Tenderloin precincts"—Broadway's fabulous concentration of hotels, theaters, restaurants, gaming houses, and saloons—related in detail how protection money was distributed among the police force. Crooks, police-men, public officials, businessmen, all paraded across the stage, each adding his chapter to a sordid story of corruption and crime. The upshot of these revelations was reform—the election of William L. Strong, a stalwart busi-nessman, as mayor, and the naming of Theodore Roosevelt as police commissioner.

It did not last, of course, just as previous reform victories had not lasted. Yet the ritual drama was re-enacted. Thirty years ago the Seabury investiga-tion in New York uncovered the tin-box brigade and the thirty-three little McQuades. Jimmy Walker was ousted as Mayor and in came Fiorello LaGuardia. Tom Dewey became district attorney, broke the industrial rackets, sent Lucky Luciano to jail, and went to the governor's chair in Albany. Then reform was again swallowed up in the insatiable maw of corruption until in 1950 Kefauver* and his committee counsel Rudolph Halley threw a new beam of light into the seemingly bottomless pit.

How [to] explain this repetitious cycle? Obviously the simple moralistic distinction between "good guys" and "bad guys," so deep at the root of the

---

*[Special Congressional Committee to investigate crime in interstate commerce, which operated from 1950 to 1951 and was headed by Tennessee senator Estes Kefauver.—ED.]

From Daniel Bell, *The End of Ideology* (Free Press, 1960). Reprinted by permission of the author.

reform impulse, bears little relation to the role of organized crime in American society. What, then, does?

THE . . . LADDER
[OF SOCIAL MOBILITY]

Americans have had an extraordinary talent for compromise in politics and extremism in morality. The most shameless political deals (and "steals") have been rationalized as expedient and realistically necessary. Yet in no other country have there been such spectacular attempts to curb human appetites and brand them as illicit, and nowhere else such glaring failures. From the start America was at one and the same time a frontier community where "everything goes," and the fair country of the Blue Laws. At the turn of the century the cleavage developed between the Big City and the small-town conscience. Crime as a growing business was fed by the revenues from prostitution, liquor, and gambling that a wide-open urban society encouraged and that a middle-class Protestant ethos tried to suppress with a ferocity unmatched in any other civilized country. Catholic cultures have rarely imposed such restrictions and have rarely suffered such excesses. Even in prim and proper Anglican England, prostitution is a commonplace of Piccadilly night life, and gambling is one of the largest and most popular industries. In America the enforcement of public morals has been a continuing feature of our history.

Some truth may lie in Max Scheler's generalization that moral indignation is a peculiar fact of middle-class psychology and represents a disguised form of repressed envy. The larger truth lies perhaps in the brawling nature of American development and in the social character

of crime. Crime, in many ways, is a Coney Island mirror, caricaturing the morals and manners of a society. The jungle quality of the American business community, particularly at the turn of the century, was reflected in the mode of "business" practiced by the coarse gangster elements, most of them from new immigrant families, who were "getting ahead," just as Horatio Alger had urged. In the older, Protestant tradition the intensive acquisitiveness . . . was rationalized by a compulsive moral fervor . . . [F]or the young criminal, hunting in the asphalt jungle of the crowded city, it was not the businessman with his wily manipulation of numbers but the "man with the gun" who was the American hero. "No amount of commercial prosperity," once wrote Teddy Roosevelt, "can supply the lack of the heroic virtues." The American was "the hunter, cowboy, frontiersman, the soldier, the naval hero"—and in the crowded slums, the gangster. He was a man with a gun, acquiring by personal merit what was denied him by complex orderings of stratified society. And the duel with the law was the morality play par excellence: the gangster, with whom ride our own illicit desires, and the prosecutor, representing final judgment and the force of the law.

Yet all this was acted out in a wider context. The desires satisfied in extra-legal fashion were more than a hunger for the "forbidden fruits" of conventional morality. They also involved, in the complex and ever shifting structure of group, class, and ethnic stratification, which is the warp and woof of America's "open" society, such "normal" goals as independence through a business of one's own, and such "moral" aspirations as the desire for social advancement and social prestige. *For crime, in the language of the sociologists, has a "functional" role in the society, and the urban rackets—the illicit activity organized for continuing profit, rather than individual illegal acts—is one of the . . . ladders of social mobility in American life.* [emphasis added—ED.] Indeed, it is not too much to say that the whole question of organized crime in America cannot be understood unless one appreciates (1) the distinctive role of organized gambling as a function of a mass-consumption economy; (2) the specific role of various immigrant groups as they, one after another, became involved in marginal business and crime; and (3) the relation of crime to the changing character of the urban political machines.

GATSBY'S MODEL

As a society changes, so does, in lagging fashion, its type of crime. As American society became more "organized," as the American businessman became more "civilized" and less "buccaneering," so did the American racketeer. And just as there were important changes in the structure of business enterprise, so the "institutionalized" criminal enterprise was transformed too.

In the America of the last fifty years the main drift of society has been toward the rationalization of industry, the domestication of the crude self-made captain of industry into the respectable man of manners, and the emergence of a mass-consumption economy. The most significant transformation in the field of "institutionalized" crime in the 1940's was the increasing importance of gambling as against other kinds of illegal activity. And, as a multi-billion-dollar business, gambling underwent a transition parallel to the changes in American enterprise as a whole. This parallel was exemplified in many ways: in gambling's industrial organization (e.g., the growth of a complex technology such as the national racing-wire service and the minimization of risks by such techniques as lay-off betting); in its respectability, as was evidenced in the opening of smart and popular gambling casinos in resort towns and in "satellite" adjuncts to metropolitan areas; in its functional role in a mass-consumption economy . . . in the social acceptance of the gamblers in the important status world of sport and entertainment, i.e., "café society."

In seeking to "legitimize" itself, gambling had quite often actually become a force against older and more vicious forms of illegal activity. In 1946, for example, when a Chicago mobster, Pat Manno, went down to Dallas, Texas, to take over gambling in the area for the Accardo-Guzik combine, he reassured the sheriff as follows: "Something I'm against, that's dope peddlers, pickpockets, hired killers. That's one thing I can't stomach." . . .

Jimmy Cannon once reported that when the gambling raids started in Chicago the "combine" protested that, in upsetting existing stable relations, the police were only opening the way for ambitious young punks and hoodlums to start trouble. Nor is there today, as there was twenty or even forty years ago, prostitution of major organized scope in the United States. Aside from the fact that manners and morals have changed, prostitution *as an industry* doesn't pay as well as gambling. Besides, its existence threatened the tacit moral acceptance and quasi-respectability that gamblers and gambling have secured in the American way of life. It was, as any operator in the field might tell you, "bad for business."

The criminal world of the 1940's, its tone set by the captains of the gambling industry, is in startling contrast to the state of affairs in the decade before. If a Kefauver report had been written then, the main "names" would have been Lepke and Gurrah, Dutch Schultz, Jack "Legs" Diamond, Lucky Luciano, and, reaching back a little further, Arnold Rothstein, the czar of the underworld. These men (with the exception of Luciano, who was involved in narcotics and prostitution) were in the main "industrial racketeers." Rothstein, the model for Wolfsheim the gambler in F. Scott Fitzgerald's The Great Gatsby, had a larger function: he was, as Frank Costello became later, the financier of the underworld, the pioneer big businessman of crime who, understanding the logic of coordination, sought to *organize* crime as a source of regular income. . . .

In other types of racketeering, such as the trucking of perishable foods and waterfront loading, where the racketeers entrenched themselves as middlemen— taking up, by default, a service that neither shippers nor truckers wanted to assume—a pattern of accommodation was roughly worked out, and the rackets assumed a quasi-legal veneer. On the waterfront, old-time racketeers perform the necessary function of loading—but at an exorbitant price—and this monopoly was recognized by both the union and the shippers, and tacitly by the government.

But in the last decade and a half, industrial racketeering has not offered much in the way of opportunity. *Like American capitalism itself, crime shifted its emphasis from production to consumption.* The focus of crime became the direct exploitation of the citizen as consumer, largely through gambling. And while the protection of these huge revenues was inextricably linked to politics, the relation between gambling and "the mobs" became more complicated.

BIG-BUSINESS BOOKIES

. . . If one considers the amount of dollars bet on sports alone—an estimated six billion on baseball, a billion on football pools, another billion on basketball, six billion on horse racing—then Elmo Roper's judgment that "only the food, steel, auto, chemical, and machine-tool industries have a greater volume of business" does not seem too farfetched.

While gambling has long flourished in the United States, the influx of the big mobsters into the industry—and its expansion—started in the thirties, when repeal of Prohibition forced them to look about for new avenues of enterprise. (The change, one might say crudely, was in the "democratization" of gambling. In New York of the 1860's, 1870's, and 1880's, one found elegant establishments where the wealthy men of the city, bankers, and sportsmen gambled. The saloon was the home of the worker. The middle class of the time did not gamble. In the changing mores of America, the rise of gambling in the 1930's and 1940's meant the introduction of the middle class to gambling and casinos as a way of life.) Gambling, which had begun to flower under the nourishment of rising incomes, was the most lucrative field in sight. To a large extent the shift from bootlegging to gambling was a mere transfer of business operations. . . . Across the country, many mobsters went into bookmaking. As other rackets diminished and gambling, particularly horse-race betting, flourished in the forties, a struggle erupted over the control of racing information. . . .

GAMBLERS AND GUYS

While Americans made gambling illegal, they did not in their hearts think of it as wicked—even the churches benefitted from the bingo and lottery crazes. So they gambled—and gamblers flourished. Against this open canvas, the indignant tones of Senator Wiley and the shocked righteousness of Senator Tobey during the Kefauver investigation rang oddly. Yet it was probably this very tone of surprise that gave the activity of the Kefauver Committee its piquant quality. Here were some senators who seemingly did not know the facts of life, as most Americans did. Here . . . was the old New England Puritan conscience poking around in industrial America, in a world it had made but never seen. Here was old-fashioned moral indignation, at a time when cynicism was rampant in public life. . . .

Most intriguing of all were the opinions of James J. Carroll, the St. Louis "betting commissioner," who for years had been widely quoted on the sports pages of the country as setting odds on the Kentucky Derby winter book and the baseball pennant races. . . .

Asked why people gamble, Carroll distilled his experiences of fifty years with a remark that deserves a place in American social history: "I really don't know how to answer the question," he said, "I think gambling is a biological necessity for certain types. I think it is the quality that gives substance to their daydreams."

In a sense, the entire Kefauver materials, unintentionally, seem to document that remark. For what the committee revealed time and time again was a picture of gambling as a basic institution in American life, flourishing openly and accepted widely. In many of the small towns, the gambling joint is as open as a liquor establishment. . . .

Apart from the gamblers, there were the mobsters. But what Senator Kefauver and company failed to understand was that the mobsters, like the gamblers, and like the entire gangdom generally, were seeking to become quasi-respectable and establish a place for themselves in American life. For the mobsters, by and large, had immigrant roots, and crime, as the pattern showed, was a route of social ascent and place in American life.

THE MYTH OF THE MAFIA

The mobsters were able, where they wished, to "muscle in" on the gambling business because the established gamblers were wholly vulnerable, not being able to call on the law for protection. The senators, however, refusing to make any distinction between a gambler and a gangster, found it convenient to talk loosely of a nationwide conspiracy of "illegal" elements. . . .

Unfortunately for a good story—and the existence of the Mafia would be a whale of a story—neither the Senate Crime Committee in its testimony, nor Kefauver in his book, presented any real evidence that the Mafia exists as a functioning organization. One finds police officials asserting before the Kefauver committee their *belief* in the Mafia; the Narcotics Bureau *thinks* that a worldwide dope ring allegedly run by Luciano is part of the Mafia; but the only other "evidence" presented . . . is that certain crimes bear "the earmarks of the Mafia."

Why did the Senate Crime Committee plump so hard for its theory of a Mafia and a national crime syndicate? In part, they may have been misled by their own hearsay. . . .

The salient reason, perhaps, why the Kefauver Committee was taken in by its own myth of an omnipotent Mafia and a despotic Costello was its failure to assimilate and understand three of the more relevant sociological facts about institutionalized crime in its relation to the political life of large urban communities in America, namely: (1) the rise of the American Italian community, as part of the inevitable process of ethnic succession, to positions of importance in politics, a process that has been occurring independently but also simultaneously in most cities with large Italian constituencies—New York, Chicago, Kansas City, Los Angeles; (2) the fact that there are individual Italians who play prominent, often leading roles today in gambling and in the mobs; and (3) the fact that Italian gamblers and mobsters often possessed "status" within the Italian community itself and a "pull" in city politics. These three times are indeed related— but not so as to form a "plot."

THE JEWS . . . THE IRISH . . . THE ITALIANS

The Italian community has achieved wealth and political influence much later and in a harder way than previous immigrant groups. Early Jewish wealth, that of the German Jews of the late nineteenth century, was made largely in banking and merchandising. To that extent, the dominant group in the Jewish community was outside of, and independent of, the urban political machines. Later Jewish wealth, among the East European immigrants, was built in the garment trades, though with some involvement with the Jewish gangster, who was typically an industrial racketeer. . . . Among Jewish lawyers, a small minority . . . rose through politics and occasionally touched the fringes of crime. . . . Irish immigrant wealth in the northern urban centers, concentrated largely in construction, trucking, and the waterfront, has, to a substantial extent, been wealth accumulated in and through political alliance, e.g., favoritism in city contracts.

Control of the politics of the city thus has been crucial for the continuance of Irish political wealth. This alliance of Irish immigrant wealth and politics has been reciprocal; many noted Irish political figures lent their names as important window-dressing for business corporations . . . while Irish businessmen have lent their wealth to further the careers of Irish politicians. Irish mobsters have rarely achieved status in the Irish community, but have served as integral arms of the politicians, as strong-arm men on election day.

The Italians found the more obvious big-city paths from rags to riches preempted. In part this was due to the character of the early Italian immigrant. Most of them were unskilled and from rural stock. Jacob Riis could remark in the nineties, "the Italian comes in at the bottom and stays there." These dispossessed agricultural laborers found jobs as ditch-diggers, on the railroads as section hands, along the docks, in the service occupations, as shoemakers, barbers, garment workers, and stayed there. Many were fleeced by the "padrone" system; a few achieved wealth from truck farming, wine growing, and marketing produce, but this "marginal wealth" was not the source of coherent and stable political power. . . .

The children of the immigrants, the second and third generation, became wise in the ways of the urban slums. Excluded from the political ladder—in the early thirties there were almost no Italians on the city payroll in top jobs, nor in books of the period can one find discussion of Italian political leaders—and finding few open routes to wealth, some turned to illicit ways. In the children's court statistics of the 1930's, the largest group of delinquents were the Italian; nor were there any Italian communal or social agencies to cope with these problems. Yet it was, oddly enough, the quondam racketeer, seeking to become respectable, who provided one of the major supports for the drive to win a political voice for Italians in the power structure of the urban political machines.

This rise of the Italian political bloc was connected, at least in the major northern urban centers, with another important development which tended to make the traditional relation between the politician and the protected or tolerated illicit operator more close than it had been in the past. This is the fact that the urban political machines had to evolve new forms of fund-raising, since the big business contributions, which once went heavily into municipal politics, now—with the shift in the locus of power—go largely into national affairs. (The ensuing corruption in national politics, as recent Congressional investigations show, is no petty matter; the scruples of businessmen do not seem much superior to those of the gamblers.) . . .

Frank Costello made his money originally in bootlegging. After repeal, his big break came when Huey Long,* desperate for ready cash to fight the old-line political machines, invited Costello to install slot machines in Louisiana. Costello did, and he flourished. . . . Subsequently, Costello invested his money in New York real estate (including 79 Wall Street, which he later sold), the Copacabana night club, and a leading brand of Scotch whiskey.

Costello's political opportunity came when a money-hungry Tammany . . . turned to him for financial support. The Italian community in New York has for years nursed a grievance against the Irish and, to a lesser extent, the Jewish political groups for monopolizing political power. They complained about the lack of judicial jobs, the small number—usually one—of Italian congressmen, the lack of representation on the state tickets. But the Italians lacked the means to make their ambition a reality. Although they formed a large voting bloc, there was rarely sufficient wealth to finance political clubs. Italian immigrants, largely poor peasants from southern Italy and Sicily, lacked the mercantile experience of the Jews and the political experience gained in the seventy-five-year history of Irish immigration. . . .

During this period, other Italian political leaders were also coming to the fore. Generoso Pope, whose Colonial Sand and Stone Company began to prosper through political contacts, became an important political figure, especially when his purchase of the two largest Italian-language dailies (later merged into one), and of a radio station, gave him almost a monopoly of channels to Italian-speaking opinion of the city. Through Generoso Pope, and through Costello, the Italians became a major political force in New York.

*[Huey Long was a flamboyant Louisiana politician who was assassinated in 1935 while serving as governor.—ED.]

That the urban machines, largely Democratic, have financed their heavy campaign costs in this fashion rather than having to turn to the "moneyed interests" explains in some part why these machines were able, in part, to support the New and Fair Deals without suffering the pressures they might have been subjected to had their source of money supply been the business groups. Although he has never publicly revealed his political convictions, it is likely that Frank Costello was a fervent admirer of Franklin D. Roosevelt and his efforts to aid the common man. The basic measures of the New Deal, which most Americans today agree were necessary for the public good, would not have been possible without the support of the "corrupt" big-city machines.

THE "NEW" MONEY—AND THE OLD

There is little question that men of Italian origin appeared in most of the leading roles in the high drama of gambling and mobs, just as twenty years ago the children of East European Jews were the most prominent figures in organized crime, and before that individuals of Irish descent were similarly prominent. To some extent statistical accident and the tendency of newspapers to emphasize the few sensational figures gives a greater illusion about the domination of illicit activities by a single ethnic group than all the facts warrant. In many cities, particularly in the South and on the West Coast, the mob and gambling fraternity consisted of many other groups, and often, predominantly, of native white Protestants. Yet it is clear that in the major northern urban centers there was a distinct ethnic sequence in the modes of

obtaining illicit wealth and that, uniquely in the case of the recent Italian elements, the former bootleggers and gamblers provided considerable leverage for the growth of political influence as well. . . . And the motive in establishing Italian political prestige in New York was generous rather than scheming for personal advantage. For Costello it was largely a case of ethnic pride. As in earlier American eras, organized illegality became a stepladder of social ascent.

To the world at large, the news and pictures of Frank Sinatra, for example, mingling with former Italian mobsters could come somewhat as a shock. Yet to Sinatra, and to many Italians, these were men who had grown up in their neighborhoods and who were, in some instances, by-words in the community for their helpfulness and their charities. The early Italian gangsters were hoodlums—rough, unlettered, and young (Al Capone was only twenty-nine at the height of his power). Those who survived learned to adapt. . . . Their homes are in respectable suburbs. They sent their children to good schools and sought to avoid publicity. . . .

As happens with all "new" money in American society, the rough and ready contractors, the construction people, trucking entrepreneurs, as well as racketeers, polished up their manners and sought recognition and respectability in their own ethnic as well as in the general community. The "shanty" Irish became the "lace curtain" Irish, and then moved out for wider recognition. Sometimes acceptance came first in established "American" society, and this was a certificate for later recognition by the ethnic community, a process well illustrated by the belated acceptance in established Negro society of such figures as Sugar Ray

Robinson and Joe Louis, as well as leading popular entertainers.

Yet, after all, the foundation of many a distinguished older American fortune was laid by sharp practices and morally reprehensible methods. The pioneers of American capitalism were not graduated from Harvard's School of business Administration. The early settlers and founding fathers, as well as those who "won the West" and built up cattle, mining, and other fortunes, often did so by shady speculations and not inconsiderable amount of violence. They ignored, circumvented, or stretched the law when it stood in the way of America's destiny and their own—or were themselves the law when it served their purposes. This has not prevented them and their descendants from feeling proper moral outrage when, under the changed circumstances of the crowded urban environments, latecomers pursued equally ruthless tactics.

THE EMBOURGEOISEMENT OF CRIME

Ironically, the social development which made possible the rise to political influence sounds, too, the knell of the rough Italian gangster. For it is the growing number of Italians with professional training and legitimate business success that both prompts and permits the Italian group to wield increasing political influence; and increasingly it is the professionals and businessmen who provide models for Italian youth today, models that hardly existed twenty years ago. Ironically, the headlines and exposés of "crime" of the Italian "gangsters" came years after the fact. Many of the top "crime" figures had long ago forsworn violence, and even their income, in large part, was derived from legitimate investments. . . .

But passing, too, is a political pattern, the system of political "bosses" which in its reciprocal relation provided "protection" for, and was fed revenue from, crime. The collapse of the "boss" system was a product of the Roosevelt era. . . . Within the urban centers, the old Irish-dominated political machines in New York, Boston, Newark, and Chicago have fallen apart. The decentralization of the metropolitan centers, the growth of suburbs and satellite towns, the breakup of the old ecological patterns of slum and transient belts, the rise of functional groups, the increasing middle-class character of American life, all contribute to this decline.

With the rationalization and absorption of some illicit activities into the structure of the economy, the passing of an older generation that had established a hegemony over crime, the general rise of minority groups to social position, and the breakup of the urban boss system, the pattern of crime we have discussed is passing as well. Crime, of course, remains as long as passion and the desire for gain remain. But the kind of big, organized city crime, as we have known it for the past seventy-five years, was based on more than these universal motives. It was based on certain characteristics of the American economy, American ethnic groups, and American politics. The changes in all these areas mean that, in the form we have known it, it too will change.

POSTSCRIPT

Is Crime Created by Society's Elites?

Current theory within criminology and criminal justice probably reflects a combination of Bell and Quinney's thinking. Many criminologists agree with Bell's contention that crime is functional for various subcultures in American society. However, it would appear that as long as America remains a pluralistic society, it is more difficult to identify specific crimes with specific ethnic groups.

Most would probably agree with Quinney's assertion that crime is socially constructed: It results from the symbols we use linked with the prevailing ideologies of dominant interest groups. Yet crime is not a mirror reflection of elite needs. The relationship between elites and social control is much more complicated.

In recent criminological scholarly history, one of the most insightful articles tackling the issue of the origins and payoffs of laws is William Chamblis's "A Sociological Analysis of the Law of Vagrancy," *Social Problems* 12 (1964). For a current study that challenges the contention that crimes result from the hegemonic status of society's elites, see John Tierney's "Viewpoint: Romantic Fictions: The Re-Emergence of the Crime as Politics Debate," *Sociological Review* (February 1988). Another empirical study that challenges the thesis that crime results from elite interests is "The Process of Criminalization: The Case of Computer Crime Laws," by R. C. Holinger and L. Lanza-Kaduce, *Criminology* (February 1988). Also see *Uneasy Virtue: The Politics of Prostitution and the American Reform Tradition*, by B. M. Hobson (Basic Books, 1987).

For a stimulating discussion of the role of symbols and moral crusades in creating social problems including crime, see Joseph Gusfield's *Culture of Public Problems* (University of Chicago Press, 1981).

Works that address the issue of elites among criminals and their influences include A. A. Block and W. J. Chambliss's, *Organizing Crime* (Elsevier, 1981); James W. Coleman's, *The Criminal Elite* (St. Martin's Press, 1985); D. R. Simon and D. S. Eitzen's, *Elite Deviance* (Allyn and Bacon, 1985); and the *Social Justice* issue dealing with "Variety of State and Corporate Crime" (Summer 1989).

For recent works that deal with the Mafia and other agents of organized crime in a fashion somewhat similar to Bell's treatment, you might want to read "From Organized Crime to Organization Men: Yuppie Mobsters Opt for Briefcases Over Guns," by Eva Pomice, *U.S. News and World Report* (May 16, 1988). Also of interest is J. L. Albini's *The American Mafia* (Appleton-Century-Crofts, 1971).

A useful classic that continues to be a good representative of the "conservative" formulation of who is a criminal is Paul Tappan's "Who Is the Criminal," *American Sociological Review* (February 1947).

A more academic work that deals with the underlying assumptions of scholars working in criminal justice but is nonetheless useful in helping to classify both disciplinary and ideological issues is *Two Views of Criminology and Criminal Justice: Definitions, Trends and the Future*, by J. P. Conrad and R. A. Myren (U.S. Department of Justice, September 1979).

For an interesting and helpful "behind the scenes" look at how many criminologists came to be criminologists, how they selected the kinds of theories and research interests that they are known by, and what their present attitudes are (as well as the public's attitudes) toward crime and criminology—especially who supposedly causes crime—see *Criminology in the Making: An Oral History*. This is based on outstanding interviews recorded by John H. Laub (New England University Press, 1983). You would also enjoy a more formal discussion of selected criminologists found in *Criminological Thought Pioneers Past and Present* by Randy Martin, R. J. Mutchnick, and W. T. Austin (Macmillan, 1990). See especially chapter 15 on the life and ideas of Richard Quinney.

ISSUE 3

Is Criminal Behavior Biologically Determined?

YES: C. R. Jeffery, from "Criminology as an Interdisciplinary Behavioral Science," *Criminology* (August 1978)

NO: Tony Platt and Paul Takagi, from "Biosocial Criminology: A Critique," *Crime and Social Justice* (Spring/Summer 1979)

ISSUE SUMMARY

YES: Florida State University criminologist C. R. Jeffery argues that physiological and chemical imbalances are frequently precipitants of criminal behavior. Therefore, research into causes and possible cures might be better placed in the hands of medical researchers.
NO: *Crime and Social Justice* editors Tony Platt and Paul Takagi, characterizing Jeffery's proposals as ridiculous and dangerous, contend that his ideas suffer from a poor understanding of biology, history, and criminology.

The "bad blood" theory of crime has held appeal for both the public and experts alike. What could be more logical than "like father, like son," or "like mother, like daughter"? According to this thinking, criminal traits *must* be genetic since so many criminals have relatives who are also criminals. The origins of crime were sometimes attributed biologically to flawed genes, physiological deficiencies, or other inherited defects. Experts frequently argued that particular ethnic groups and/or races had a "predominance" of such criminogenic traits.

Proponents of this biological theory, which accounted for both general and criminal behavior, often ignored socioeconomic factors, race, discrimination, and the like; late nineteenth-century criminologists took for granted that biology contributed to criminal behavior. In the 1920s, the field of eugenics became very popular. *Eugenics* means "good genes." It was assumed that some groups were biologically superior to others. Therefore, "imbeciles" and the like ought to be controlled, and "controls" at that time included involuntary sterilization.

The inherent irrationalities and cruelties within the eugenics movement were generally overlooked until the 1940s when one logical consequence, or so some contended, was manifested in Hitler's Germany and its insistence upon building a "master race" through the annihilation of the "unter-menschen" (inferior people), based on their assumption of Aryan racial superiority. After the horrors of the Holocaust, explanations of human behavior that drew on genetic origins were labeled racist and have since been unacceptable scientifically and politically to most social scientists until the past ten years or so.

C. R. Jeffery contends that just as scientists are about to make major breakthroughs in understanding human behavior (including criminal behavior), and possibly changing it through their new understanding, we are returning to an irrational, punitive, "lock them up and hang them high" mentality. For Jeffery, former president of the American Society of Criminology, the focus should be on the biological, physiological, and medical aspects of human behavior in order to understand better why criminals are as they are.

Continuing a long-standing and acrimonious debate with Jeffery, radical criminologists Takagi and Platt assert that in spite of his claims to being a heretic, C. R. Jeffery's ideas frequently fit into mainstream criminology. Takagi and Platt in many articles have dismissed current criminology, which they argue Jeffery is representative of, as "new realism." In essence, to them this means an applied, atheoretical criminology that supports the state in its efforts of repression. They contend that Jeffery's variant of conservative criminology reflects just such an applied, funded, policy-oriented approach that serves to legitimize state repression of the poor and oppressed.

They claim that it is not just coincidence that Jeffery's biological criminology control strategies apply only to street criminals, who consist mainly of poor and minority groups, and argue that he purposefully ignores white-collar crimes, organized crimes, and political crimes.

YES

C. R. Jeffery

CRIMINOLOGY AS AN INTERDISCIPLINARY BEHAVIORAL SCIENCE

As Radzinowicz (1977) reminds us, the failures of criminology and criminal justice are found in such facts as (a) we have more people in custody in the United States than any other country reporting, (b) we have more people in custody than at any time in history, (c) we are experiencing a 60%–70% recidivism rate, (d) we have no evidence that punishment and deterrence are solutions to the crime problem, and (e) we have no theory of behavior in criminology that stands close scrutiny.

The growth of a psychological model of treatment a la Freud resulted in the failure of psychology and psychiatry to help the crime problem (Lewis and Balla, 1976). At the same time, there were many violations of the legal rights of those supposedly in treatment (Kittrie, 1971). The merger of law and psychiatry created such tragic problems as exemplified by the Patuxent Institution. When Patuxent was closed in 1976, many criminologists regarded it as the end of a bold experiment in the use of psychology as a rehabilitative tool (American Academy, 1977).

The failure of psychiatry and psychology during the 1920–1950 era is matched by the failure of the sociological model as found in the war against poverty in the 1960 era. The notion that the opportunity structure could be altered through education and job training, thus altering poverty and delinquency, was also a total disaster (Jeffery, 1977; Radzinowicz, 1977). The failure of criminology as a science of the individual offender was matched by its failure as a science of the social offender.

The failure of the treatment model in criminology—that is, the failure of criminology—led to the LEAA* program of the 1970s with an emphasis on law and order, punishment, and bigger and better prisons. We are told we

*[*Law Enforcement Assistance Administration. Important provision of the Omnibus Crime Control and Safe Streets Act, passed by Congress in 1968 to curb crime. Heavily criticized for misuse of funds by various police agencies that received LEAA monies.*—ED.]

From C. R. Jeffery, "Criminology as an Interdisciplinary Behavioral Science," *Criminology*, vol. 16, no. 2 (August 1978). Copyright © 1978 by The American Society of Criminology. Reprinted by permission.

cannot know the causes of criminal behavior. We are told we cannot prevent crime. This is the Martinson "nothing works" era. The experts of the 1970s, such as Wilson, Morris, Fogel, and Von Hirsch, are advocating a return to punishment and prisons, to the use of fixed sentences, to sentences based on the crime and not the criminal. This philosophy does not allow for discretion, and it depends on larger police departments and more prisons to solve the crime problem (Jeffery, 1977; Serrill, 1976a). Involuntary treatment is not allowed, but we do allow the executions of criminals or their confinement to snake pits for life. In the 1970s the legal view that man cannot be treated but must be punished comes once again into full bloom.

We have given up the treatment model at a time when the behavioral sciences are about to make a major contribution to our knowledge of human behavior. It is ironic that in the 1970s, when we are returning to an eighteenth-century punishment model of crime control, twenty-first century breakthroughs are occurring in our understanding of human behavior.

A NEW MODEL: BIOSOCIAL CRIMINOLOGY

Elements of the New Model

The new model must contain several basic elements now absent in criminology: (1) It must move from deterrence, punishment, and treatment to *prevention*. (2) It must move from a social to a *physical environment*. (3) It must move from a social to a *biosocial* model of learning.

Crime Prevention

By crime prevention we mean those actions taken before a crime is committed to reduce or eliminate the crime rate. The public health model of medical care is a prevention model. Today medicine is more concerned with the prevention of heart disease and cancer than with the treatment and institutionalization of those already afflicted.

The present criminal justice model waits for the crime to occur before responding. The LEAA and federal government response has been to increase the capacity of the criminal justice system. The more police we have, the more arrests: the more arrests, the more courts and lawyers; the more courts, the more prisons; the more prisons, the more people who will return to prisons.

Behavior is the product of two sets of variables: a physical environment and a physical organism in interaction. Crime prevention must be based on a social ecology which recognizes the interaction of man and environment as complementary physical systems in interactions.

On January 3, 1978, there was a special on medicine in America on NBC news. In this program the Delta Health Center in Mississippi was discussed in detail. The Delta project was established by a community health group at Tufts University to prevent disease among the rural poor of the Delta. They were concerned with such variables as diet, sanitary conditions, food supplies, inoculations, preventive physical care, and preventive medicine in general. The disease rate dropped immediately, and the clinics and hospitals for the sick were almost empty. Then Washington and the federal government decided that monies would not be available for disease control, but only for the treatment of those already diseased. Payments were made for X-rays, surgery, medications, hospital costs, and other expenses connected with being ill.

Within a few months the hospitals in the Delta were again filled with sick people, with people standing in long lines all day long in hope of getting some medical care.

The more hospitals and mental institutions we build, the more sick people we have. The more prisons and courts we build, the more criminals we have. We have made the "Delta Plan" national policy.

The Physical Environment

Criminology must move from Sutherland, Shaw, and McKay, from the cultural conflict perspective, to a physical environment perspective (Jeffery, 1976). Crime rates are highly correlated with the physical features of the environment, such as buildings, streets, parks, automobiles, and highways. Most areas of the urban environment are crime-free; crime is very selective in where it occurs. Some blocks have many murders and robberies, others have none. Crime prevention involves the design of physical space. This is a joining of urban design, environmental psychology, and social ecology into a meaningful relationship.

Last year I was in a gymnasium on the Florida State campus to watch a dance review, and my daughter had to use the bathroom facilities which were located in the basement. At that time I remarked how this was a perfect environment for a mugging and/or rape. Within a month a rape occurred there, one of many on the campus. On January 15, 1978 two coeds were murdered and three brutally attacked on the campus. The intruder gained entrance to a sorority house by means of an unlocked door. The police are now spending thousands of dollars and thousands of man-hours on the case, the politicians want to execute the bastard, and yet this predictable response has not helped the dead girls or their families and friends, nor has it reduced the level of hysteria and fear on this campus. As I am writing this article, there is another radio account of an attempted rape on campus over the weekend.

Biosocial Criminology

The new criminology must represent a merging of biology, psychology, and sociology. It must reflect the hierarchies of sciences as found in systems analysis.

Behavior reflects both genetic and environmental variables. The equipotentiality environmentalism of the past must be replaced with a model which clearly recognizes that each and every individual is different genetically (except perhaps for MZ* twins). Williams (1967), a biochemist and past president of the American Chemical Society, argues that only 15% of the population has what is termed normal anatomical features. If our noses varied as much as our hearts and kidneys and hormonal systems, some of us would have noses the size of beans, others would have noses the size of watermelons.

The sociologist/criminologist often assumes that if behavior is learned, then learning in no way involves biology or psychology. This argument ignores the fact that learning is a psychobiological process involving changes in the biochemistry and cell structure of the brain. Learning can only occur if there are physical changes in the brain. The process is best summarized as a system of information flow from environment to organism:

[identical—Ed.]

Genetic code × Environment =
Brain code × Environment = Behavior

Genetic codes and brain codes are of a biochemical nature, involving the biochemical structure of genes and of neural transmission in the brain. The types of behavior (response) exhibited by an organism depends on the nature of the environment (stimulus) and the way in which the stimulus is coded, transmitted, and decoded by the brain and nervous system. This is what is meant by the biological limitations on learning (Jeffery, 1977).

We do not inherit behavior any more than we inherit height or intelligence. We do inherit a capacity for interaction with the environment. Sociopathy and alcoholism are not inherited, but a biochemical preparedness for such behaviors are present in the brain, which, if given a certain type of environment, will produce sociopathy or alcoholism.

The brain contains a center for emotion and motivation, based on pleasure and pain, a center for reason and thought, and a center for the processing of information from the environment. This is almost a Freudian model put within the context of modern psychobiology, as suggested by Pribram and Gill (1976) in their work on the new Freud. The concept of social control is a neglected theory in criminology, although it is to be found in Reckless, Nye, Hirschi, and others. Certainly biosocial learning theory, as I have presented it, is control theory. In summary, what biosocial control theory holds is that behavior is controlled by the brain. Behavior involves biochemical changes in the neurons which then activate muscles and glands. An incoming impulse or experience from the social environment must be encoded, stored, acted upon,

and decoded by the brain before it comes out as social behavior. Social behavior, be it conforming or deviant, must go into a brain and come out of a brain. G. H. Mead made this a basic part of his social behaviorism, but this has been totally neglected by the symbolic interactionists.

Emerging Issues in Criminology

If one regards behavior as a product of the interaction of a physical organism with a physical environment, then one must be prepared to find different sorts of things in criminology in the near future, assuming the courage to look for them. Gordon (1976) and Hirschi and Hindeland (1977) have in recent articles suggested a link between low intelligence and delinquency. Mednick and his associates found that 41.7% of the XYY* cases identified in Denmark had a history of criminal careers, compared to 9% of the XY population. They also found that the link between XYY and criminality was not aggression and high testosterone but rather low intelligence. They also found that criminals from the XY population had low intelligence. Since genes interact with one another, this suggests the possibility that the Y chromosome is involved in those biochemical processes labeled intelligence (Mednick and Christiansen, 1977).

Intelligence is related to both genetics and environment (Oliverio, 1977; Halsey, 1977; Stine, 1977). This means the impact of poverty and social class on crime rates must be reinterpreted in terms of intelligence, as well as influencing intelligence. To take one example, protein intake is a crucial variable in brain devel-

*[Chromosomal abnormality has been researched as a cause of crime, especially crimes of violence. Males are a combination of XY, and females are XX. A male with a surplus chromosome is XYY.—ED.]

opment and thus intelligence. Protein intake is also very dependent on the educational and socioeconomic background of the parents. The link between poverty and crime is intelligence and protein intake, at least as one of several interacting variables.

Criminal and delinquent behaviors have also been related to learning disabilities, hypoglycemia, epilepsy, perceptual difficulties, and sociopathy (Hippchen, 1978; Lewis and Balla, 1976; and Kalita, 1977).

The new model of treatment emerging in biological psychiatry is one involving the biochemistry of the brain (Rosenthal and Kety, 1968; Brady, et al., 1977; Maser and Seligman, 1977; Van Praag and Bruinvels, 1977; Hamburg and Brodie, 1975). The genetic factor in mental disorders is now well recognized. Dopamine and norepinephrine levels in the brain are related to behavioral disorders; the more norepinephrine, the greater the level of excitation, as in schizophrenia; the lower the norepinephrine level, the lower the level of excitation, as in sociopathy and depression.

The use of drugs in the treatment of behavioral disorders has resulted in a dramatic decrease in institutionalization for schizophrenics. Chlorpromazine (thorazine) is the major drug used in the United States (Julien, 1975). Lithium to treat depression has received widespread publicity because of its use in the case of Tony Orlando, the popular television star. Lithium and thorazine act to block the norepinephrine postsynaptic sites, thus reducing the amount of norepinephrine available for the neurochemical transmission of information. As noted, behavior depends on the encoding and decoding of information by the brain.

A Private Criminal Justice System

The future of crime control must depend on the development of a crime prevention program involving both the physical organism and the physical environment. The environmental design aspects of crime control must be addressed within the structure of federal policy concerning housing and urban design. The more crucial issue, as far as implementation of policy is concerned, is at the level of the individual offender.

In order to implement a biosocial approach to crime prevention, we must have early diagnosis and treatment of neurological disorders. This means experimentation and research. It will mean brain scans and blood tests. It will mean tests for learning disabilities and hypoglycemia. All of this involves medical examinations, intrusions into the privacy of the individual, and controversial and experimental surgeries and/or drug therapies. Under such circumstances, and with as much opposition as exists today to the control of human behavior by the state system, it will be difficult if not impossible to turn biomedical research over to a federal agency.

Because of the major failures of the federal government with health, education, and welfare problems, including crime, and because of the great dangers attendant upon the use of behavioral control systems by the state, it is recommended that a private treatment system be set up to parallel or to replace the present criminal justice system. The treatment of behavioral disorders, including those labeled as crime, must be removed *from the political arena*. The lawyer and politician are so committed to a given view of human nature and justice that an impossible gap has been created between the behavioral sciences and the criminal justice system. The administration of LEAA in the Department of Justice is a beautiful example of what happens to crime control policy in the political arena.

A private treatment system would be established at two or three major research centers, hopefully associated with major medical research centers. At such a clinic a complete medical and behavioral history would be taken, including a complete neurological work-up as described by Lewis in her book on the New Haven clinic. Treatment would flow from a total assessment of the behavioral state of the individual. Such services would be on a voluntary basis, as it is for cancer, kidney disorders, and heart disease.

Since such clinics would be expensive, private funds must be sought. A new policy must be established wherein public funds could be transferred to such clinics if they accept cases from the current criminal justice system. The state would save a great deal of money by transferring cases to the private sector. This would be established as a part of the existing legal doctrine of "right to treatment." Under such a doctrine no one would be denied needed medical care, including medical attention for brain disorders. Mental illness has been redefined as physical illness by biological psychiatry, and it should have the same legal status as a heart attack or cancer of colon. We worry about not providing counsel for a defendant before we send him to the electric chair or to prison, but we do not show the same amount of concern for placing neurologically disordered people in prison. We worry about the insanity defense and all the nonsense it has produced about behavioral disorders, but we do not ask why the definitions of insanity do not include those

found today in biological psychiatry. We would rather put Charles Manson in prison or Gary Gilmore before a firing squad than spend the time and money needed to find out why they become what they became.

It has been proposed for years that a voucher system be created by the state for its educational system. Such a system would allow students to select the elementary or high schools they want to attend, and they would then buy their education. In this way the school becomes directly responsible to the client. In the same way I propose a voucher system for criminal justice.

Each defendant could spend his voucher where he wanted. If he was not helped by the clinic, then the clinic would have failed him. Unsuccessful treatments would be driven out of existence once we make those engaged in treatment responsible for the outcome of the treatment.

It goes without saying that a major research effort is needed to join biology, medicine, psychology, criminology, and criminal law into a new crime prevention model. We must approach the crime problem as a behavioral problem and not as a political problem. We must recognize that the police, courts, and corrections cannot handle a genetic defect, hypoglycemia, or learning disabilities any more than they can handle cancer or heart disease.

I realize that this paper is caught in the winds of an era powered by fixed sentencing and punishment with justice. The denial of the rehabilitative and medical model for criminology is such today that my plea for a behavioral criminology is unlikely to receive a very warm reception. However, this is nothing new to me, and I have patience and faith in history and in the human animal.

For those who insist on being on the stormy water of criminology, as I do, I offer the following:

A ship in Harbor is Safe
But That is Not What
A Ship is Made For

REFERENCES

American Academy of Psychiatry and the Law (1977). "Patuxent Institution." Bulletin 5: 116–271.

Bell, G. (1977). "Memorandum for the President: the Law Enforcement Assistance Administration." November 21.

Brady, J. P. (1977). Psychiatry. New York: Spectrum.

Gordon, R. (1976). "Prevalence: the rare datum in delinquency," in M. Klein (ed.) The Juvenile Justice System. Beverly Hills, CA: Sage.

Halsey, A. H. (1977). Heredity and Environment. New York: Free Press.

Hamburg, D. and H. Brodie (1975). American Handbook of Psychiatry, Vol. 6: New Psychiatric Frontiers. New York: Basic Books.

Hippchen, L. (1978). The Ecologic-Biochemical Approaches to Treatment of Delinquents and Criminals. New York: Van Nostrand Reinhold.

Hirschi, T. (1969). The Causes of Delinquency. Berkeley: Univ. of California Press.

_____ and M. Hindelang (1977). "Intelligence and delinquency." Amer. Soc. Rev. 42: 571–586. Behav. Scientist 20: 149–174.

Jeffery, C. R. (1977). Crime Prevention Through Environmental Design. Beverly Hills, CA: Sage.

_____ (1976). "Criminal behavior and the physical environment." Amer. Behav. Scientist 20: 149–174.

_____ (1967). Criminal Responsibility and Mental Disease. Springfield, IL: Thomas.

_____ (1965). "Criminal behavior and learning theory." J. of Criminal Law, Criminology, and Police Sci. 56: 294–300.

_____ (1956). "The structure of American criminological thinking." J. of Criminal Law, Criminology, and Police Sci. 46: 658–672.

Julien, R. (1975). A Primer of Drug Action. San Francisco: Freeman.

Kitterie, N. (1971). The Right To Be Different. Baltimore: Johns Hopkins Press.

Klein, M., K. Teilmann Styles, S. Lincoln, and Labin-Rosensweig (1976). "The explosion of police diversion programs," in M. Klein (ed.) The Juvenile Justice System. Beverly Hills, CA: Sage.

Klir, G. (1972). Trends in General Systems Theory. New York: John Wiley.

Kuhn, A. (1975). Unified Social Science. Homewood, IL: Dorsey.

Lewis, D. and D. Balla (1976). Delinquency and Psychopathology. New York: Grune & Stratton.

Loehlin, J., G. Lindzey, and J. Spuhler (1975). Race Differences in Intelligence. San Francisco: Freeman.

Maser, J. and M. Seligman (1977). Psychopathology: Experimental Models. San Francisco: Freeman.

Mednick, S. and K. O. Christiansen (1977). Biosocial Bases of Criminal Behavior. New York: Gardner.

Michael, J. and M. J. Adler (1933). Crime, Law and Social Structure. New York: Harcourt, Brace.

Mueller, G. O. W. (1969). Crime, Law and the Scholars. Seattle: Univ. of Washington Press.

Nettler, G. (1978). Explaining Crime. New York: McGraw-Hill.

Newman, G. (1978). The Punishment Response. Philadelphia: Lippincott.

Oliverio, A. (1977). Genetics, Environment, and Intelligence. New York: Elsevier.

Packer, H. L. (1968). The Limits of the Criminal Sanction. Stanford, CA: Stanford Univ. Press.

Pribram, K. and M. Gill (1976). Freud's Project Re-Assessed. New York: Basic Books.

Radzinowicz, L. (1977). The Growth of Crime. New York: Basic Books.

NO

Tony Platt and Paul Takagi

BIOSOCIAL CRIMINOLOGY: A CRITIQUE

The sharp polarization in criminology has recently taken a new twist with the revival of biological and sociobiological theories. There is of course a long and notorious history of biologically-oriented theory in criminology. Though such a perspective had its heyday in the late nineteenth and early twentieth centuries, (Fink, 1962), it has always retained a respectable foothold in academic circles from Ernest Hooton's anthropological treatise on "criminal stock" in the 1930's, to chromosomal research on the XYY syndrome and studies on the relationship between criminal violence and brain damage in the 1960's, to the investigations by Jose Delgado and Ralph Switzgebel into psychosurgery and biotechnology in the 1970's (Moran, 1978). In Europe, the theoretical expression of this "school" is centered around the work of Eysenck in England and Mednick and Christiansen (1977) in Denmark.

Biological research on criminality is increasingly acceptable in the United States. The 1979 Southern Conference on Corrections, for example, included a whole panel on "A Biological Perspective on the Criminal Justice System," as well as other papers on XYY research and a "psychobiological analysis" of Synanon and People's Temple. The "biosocial" perspective on crime has received a new impetus and respectability in this country from the recent writings of C. Ray Jeffery. For a long time a major figure in American criminology, with a prolific list of publications and awards, Jeffery was president of the American Society of Criminology in 1977–78 and he made full use of this platform to advocate the development of a "biosocial criminology."

In his lead article for the special issue of *Criminology*, (devoted to "Criminology: New Concerns and New Directions," 1978), Jeffery argues that a "new criminology," a *biosocial* criminology must be articulated as the first priority of research. As the title of his article indicates, he believes that criminology must be an interdisciplinary behavioral science, representing a merger of biology, psychology and sociology, as well as reflect the hierarchies of sciences as found in "systems analysis."

From Tony Platt and Paul Takagi, "Biosocial Criminology: A Critique," *Crime and Social Justice*, vol. 11 (Spring/Summer 1979). Reprinted by permission of *Crime and Social Justice*, P.O. Box 40601, San Francisco, CA 94140.

Critical of the present clamor by the leading "experts" for more prisons and fixed sentences, Jeffery instead calls for a major research effort intended to [bring] biology, medicine, psychology, criminology and criminal law into a new crime control model. Prevention techniques, starting at the prenatal period, not punishment and deterrence after the fact, is Jeffery's departure point. Biosocial criminology, not criminal justice, must be turned to for solutions.

Jeffery argues that since criminality involves behavior, the scientific understanding of "deviance" and "norm violations" first requires the articulation of a basic theory of behavior, in particular learning theory as derived from biology and psychology. He rejects the argument that every individual possesses the same potentiality for learning behavior in a given environment and proposes instead that genetic differences must be recognized: not the social environment, but the physical one is the primary determinant.

In support of this perspective, Jeffery points to recent studies which claim that a linkage exists between low intelligence, the XYY chromosome, and criminality. Hence "the impact of poverty and social class on crime rates must be reinterpreted in terms of intelligence"; and "the link between poverty and crime is intelligence and protein intake, at least as one of several interacting variables." Criminal and delinquent behavior is also said to be related to learning disabilities, hypoglycemia, epilepsy, etc.

While Jeffery's work departs in some important respects from the typical concerns of the new "realists," we think that he shares a great deal of political and scientific unity with his leading criminological colleagues. Despite his self-assessment as a renegade and his relentless and somewhat unique emphasis on *biosocial* criminology, his political ideology is very much in the mainstream of the new conservative tendency.

Jeffery is motivated like the "realists," by the crisis in liberal penology and the ineffectiveness of the criminal justice apparatus in controlling crime. He supports their proposals which call for "target hardening," "defensible space," and the use of experimental psychology to test the deterrent effects of specific punishments. But while he shares the "realists' " emphasis on utilitarian models of penal discipline he argues that crime can only be fully controlled through *preventive strategies*. Jeffery's solution is crime prevention through a combination of environmental design and a "biosocial model of learning." By crime prevention, he says, "we mean those actions taken before a crime is committed to reduce or eliminate the crime rate." The way to control crime is to regulate the environment by the "science and technology of behavior," especially physiology and psychopharmacology (Jeffery, 1971: 184).

Jeffery's model of crime control assumes that people are not purposeful, conscious, and self-actualizing social beings. Since there are no criminals, only criminogenic conditions, people are not accountable or responsible for their actions. Aside from this mechanistic and static view of social relations, Jeffery at least implies that "scientists" are not only capable of being effective "environmental engineers," but also that they are above and beyond the law. With prevention the goal, the adversary system and the niceties of due process are simply abandoned. While we of course recognize that bourgeois justice is an imperfect instrument—to say the least—for protecting the rights of working people, we do however think that it provides some measure of defense against arbitrary actions by the state. Constitutional rights represent hard-won concessions to the working class, as well as a practical weapon to defend political and labor organizing. Under Jeffery's proposal, as under fascism, such rights would apparently not exist.

As we noted earlier, the "realists" focus "almost exclusively on those crimes which are either specific to or concentrated primarily within the working class" (Platt and Takagi, 1977). In this respect, Jeffery is no different: the "crime problem" is synonymous with "street" crime. In his article for *Criminology* and in his address to the ASC, Jeffery simply ignores other kinds of crime. "Environmental engineering," "biosocial criminology," cybernetics, psychopharmacology, etc., are reserved exclusively for working class criminals.

Lumping together "crimes involving morality, political corruption, and financial violations," Jeffery (1971: 221) argues that they are basically different from ordinary criminality because they do not primarily involve harm against individuals. Consequently, "the control of crime in these categories is not possible through the traditional techniques . . . or through science, technology, and urban design" (Ibid.). While Jeffery believes that some "victimless crimes, especially those involving alcohol and other drugs can be controlled by biochemical or conditioning therapy" (Ibid.: 229), he is not sure that business crime is a legitimate concern of criminology. "Perhaps organized and white-collar crime should be regarded not as problems in criminology but as problems of politics and economics" (Ibid.: 231).

In other words, "street" crime is a behavioral problem which can be disassociated from the political economy, whereas business crime is primarily a political-economic problem which cannot be controlled behaviorally; "street" crime is committed against individuals, whereas business crime is committed against the "general public"; "street" criminals can be controlled by penal sanctions before and after they commit crimes, whereas the "criminal sanction is not the proper one for organized and white-collar crime"; and "street" crime can be controlled by a "merging of biology, psychology, and sociology" (Jeffery, 1978a), but not history, economics and political science. Such is the word magic and definitional gymnastics which Jeffery employs to explain, for example, why corporate criminals should be exempt from biochemical and genetic therapies. In the same way that there is one law (civil) for the bourgeoisie and another (criminal) for the working class, Jeffery similarly organizes his scientific frame of reference on the basis of class distinctions.

There are several different levels at which Jeffery's work can be criticized. We could, for example, hold his version of sociobiology up to close scrutiny and demonstrate his inaccurate understanding of genetics, biology and social psychology. Like other scientists who have ventured outside their fields of expertise to develop a theory of behavior or society, Jeffery demonstrates that a little knowledge can be irresponsible as well as dangerous.

But even if Jeffery had a profound and sophisticated grasp of, for example, genetics, we would find his explanation of criminality no more scientific and no less reactionary. The problem lies not so much in his shoddy scholarship as in the scientific and ideological premises which motivate his scholarship. The theoretical underpinnings of Jeffery's proposals are to be found in his address to the ASC (1978). Here, Jeffery brings to bear an impressive inventory of research findings from biology, psychology, biochemistry and genetics to argue why punishment, as currently practiced, is not a deterrent to crime. Jeffery argues that a theory of punishment must be based upon behavioral genetics and psychobiology.

Jeffery's psychobiology as well as the debate surrounding Edward O. Wilson's sociobiology (1975) deserve close reading and critical analysis. Their concept of a *biosocial man* in a theory of human behavior needs to be assessed on scientific grounds. It would be a serious error to dismiss psychobiology as simply a revival of Lombrosian criminology.

In the specific area of Jeffery's concern, we are told that "each individual is different in terms of brain structure, past experience, genetic inheritance, and present environmental conditions." This is a way of saying that individuals have certain fixed propensities and if we can develop a *formula* which captures these elements, then we can determine that "punishment works under certain conditions for certain individuals" (Jeffery, 1978b: 18). Jeffery suggests that we should look into his big black box to discover the formula.

His empiricist-positivist paradigm takes individuals as the basic units of analysis and abstracts human beings from their social conditions of existence and their dynamic potential for change and development. He paradoxically ignores what we have learned from the physical and biological sciences: the atom, once thought to be eternal and indivisible, has been dissolved and even its constituent particles are not fundamental in any absolute sense. Science teaches us that they too come into being, undergo several transformations, and pass away. Similarly, people are not things, units, or fixed entities, nor can they be summed up in a mechanistic formula and isolated from ongoing social processes.

Jeffery's psychobiology, despite its scientific trappings, is metaphysics. He hypothesizes some *ultimate* constituent in human behavior, be it the gene structure or the brain code. For example, he identifies intelligence as an emerging issue in criminology—as in the proposed link between low intelligence and delinquency, or education and class mediated by intelligence, or between protein intake and brain development. Jeffery, however, fails to recognize that IQ is not an observable *thing*. Intelligence, as measured by paper and pencil tests, is a reification, a mechanistic construct which assumes that cognitive ability is a fixed attribute. Even after everything has been learned about genes and the structure of the brain, bourgeois science will surely fantasize some other mechanism to explain human behavior.

Central to Jeffery's and others' positivist philosophy is a view of science as antithetical to ideology and scientists as non-participants in politics. While many positivists readily concede that this is not a reality, they nevertheless claim that it is both desirable and possible. Like many "traditional" intellectuals, to use Gramsci's term, Jeffery professes to be an independent, value-free criminologist. In fact, one of the issues which motivates his crusading urgency is his concern that criminology has become too politicized in recent years, too tied to governmental interests, and too practically oriented. Criminology, he says, "must shift from a service orientation to a scientifically based *research* orientation."

Jeffery is very much opposed to the government giving millions of dollars to government agencies. This collusion, he says, between government and agencies corrupts effective crime control. Instead, "we would do better granting the money to three or four research centers which would be responsible for a five-to-ten-year research program in crime and criminal justice. The centers would be attached to universities, independent of any governmental agency, and the research emphasis would be determined by the scientists, not by the governmental bureaucracy" (Ibid: 273–74). Aside from the self-serving aspect of this recommendation, why does Jeffery believe that intellectuals would be any less corruptible or contaminated than criminal justice professionals? How could these research centers be "independent" if they are funded by the state at taxpayers' expense?

The theme of intellectual neutrality appears again and again in the writings of the new "realists." It is certainly not monopolized by Jeffery. Donald Cressey, another leading criminologist, criticizes both the "realists" and radicals for allowing ideology and emotion to overwhelm rationality. Cressey (Cressey, 1978) argues that "criminologists should not abandon science to become policy advisers. . . . Neither should they retreat into broad intellectualizing, accompanied by political proselytizing."

As a model for what criminologists should be doing Cressey refers us to *The New Criminology*, written by Max Schlapp and Edward Smith in 1928. Subtitled *A Consideration of the Chemical Causation of Abnormal Behavior*, this book is representative of the "scientific racism" genre of the 1920's. Schlapp, a professor of neuropathology at the New York Graduate Medical School, and Smith, a mystery writer, proposed that crime is caused by glandular disturbances which result from chemical imbalances in the blood and lymph of the criminal's mother during pregnancy (Schlapp and Smith, 1928: 103–15).

Schlapp and Smith's policy recommendations include compulsory treatment for defectives, euthanasia, registration of delinquents, sterilization, and forced labor (Ibid.: 271–81). They argue for the inferiority of women and against social equality: "In spite of the howls of the demons, mankind probably must go back to some sort of caste system founded on productiveness, upon ability, upon service to the state" (Ibid: 287).

While Cressey makes it clear that he rejects Schlapp and Smith's glandular theory of criminality, he defends their "new criminology" for being "based on the scientific principle that crime control should depend on knowledge rather than on defense and terror." He admires their "empirical criminology" and their efforts to develop "positive, constructive programs." He urges contemporary criminologists to follow their exemplary scientific methodology and ideological neutrality (Cressey, 1978: 188).

CONCLUSION

The strenuous revival and defense of bourgeois positivism, which characterizes so much of the recent criminological literature, can perhaps be understood as a part of the counter-offensive against radical social science in general and interest in Marxism in particular. It is not by accident that Jeffery's call for an inter-disciplinary criminology exempts only those disciplines which are at the heart of Marxism—history, politics and economics. The writings of the "realists," Jeffery's biosocial criminology, and the right-wing tendency among criminologists are not only an indication of the crisis and bankruptcy of liberalism, they also reveal a conscious unwillingness to even consider the scientific merits of Marxism. Whatever the petty internal squabbles among the old boys' club which dominates the American Society of Criminology, they are united in their hostility to historical materialism.

Jeffery's biosocial criminology and the "realists" quest for scientific neutrality are examples of the confusion and utopianism of petty bourgeois intellectuals. Stripped of a veneer of scientific rhetoric, it becomes clear that the "realists" and their allies are not more "independent" than the corporate foundations, government agencies, and boards of trustees who finance and regulate their work. Jeffery and the other leaders of the American Society of Criminology may genuinely believe that they are still sitting on the fence, but we have no doubt that objectively their ideas and practice locate them squarely in right field.

REFERENCES

Ann Arbor Science for the People Collective, 1977. Biology as a Social Weapon. Minneapolis: Burgess Publishing Co.

Bravermann, Harry, 1974. Labor and Monopoly Capital. New York: Monthly Review Press.

Cressey, Donald R., 1978. "Criminological Theory, Social Science, and the Repression of Crime." Criminology 16 (August): 171–91.

Criminology, 1979. Volume 16 (February).

Engels, Frederick, 1972. The Origin of the Family, Private Property and the State. New York: International Publishers.

Fink, Arthur E., 1962. Causes of Crime: Biological Theories in the United States, 1800–1915. New York: A. S. Barnes.

Galliher, John F., 1978. "The Life and Death of Liberal Criminology," Contemporary Crises 2 (July): 245–63.

Harris, Marvin, 1968. The Rise of Anthropological Theory. New York: Thomas Crowell.

Jeffery, C. Ray, 1971. Crime Prevention Through Environmental Design. Beverly Hills: Sage Publications.

1978a "Criminology as an Interdisciplinary Behavioral Science." Criminology 16 (August): 149–69.

1978b "Punishment and Deterrence: A Psychobiological Statement." Unpublished paper presented to annual meeting of American Society of Criminology in Dallas (November).

Mednick, Sarnoff and Karl O. Christiansen, 1977. Biosocial Bases of Criminal Behavior. New York: Gardner Press.

Moran, Richard, 1978. "Biomedical Research and the Politics of Crime Control: A Historical Perspective." Contemporary Crises 2 (July): 335–57.

Platt, Tony and Paul Takagi, 1977. "Intellectuals for Law and Order: A Critique of the New 'Realists.'" Crime and Social Justice 8 (Fall-Winter): 1–16.

Quadagno, Jill S., 1979. "Paradigms in Evolutionary Theory: The Sociobiological Model of Natural Selection." American Sociological Review 44 (February): 100–09.

Rhodes, Robert P., 1977. The Insoluble Problems of Crime. New York: John Wiley.

Sahlins, Marshall, 1977. The Use and Abuse of Biology: An Anthropological Critique of Sociobiology. Ann Arbor: University of Michigan Press.

Schlapp, Max G. and Edward H. Smith, 1928. The New Criminology: A Consideration of the Chemical Causation of Abnormal Behavior. New York: Boni and Liveright.

Schwendinger, Herman and Julia R. Schwendinger, 1974. The Sociologists of the Chair: A Radical Analysis of the Formative Years of North American Sociology (1883–1922). New York: Basic Books.

Society, 1978. Volume 15 (September-October).

The Criminologist, 1979. Volume 3 (January).

Washburn, S. L., 1978. "Animal Behavior and Social Anthropology." Society 15 (September-October).

Wilson, E. O., 1975. Sociobiology: The New Synthesis. Cambridge, Belknap.

Wilson, James Q., 1977. Thinking About Crime. New York: Vintage.

POSTSCRIPT

Is Criminal Behavior Biologically Determined?

One of the most important contributions from a structural/sociological perspective reflected generally in sociology, anthropology, and psychology has been that crime is largely *learned* behavior that results from both the cultural environment and individual interactions. Social scientists dismissed the rough biological explanations of late nineteenth-century criminologists as they consistently found that sociocultural factors, such as the values of a particular group, socialization patterns, poverty levels, and population density, were all much better predictors of crime rates than race, ethnicity, and even family membership per se.

Sociobiological criminology is a very emotional issue—one in which remaining neutral is difficult. Thus far, the literature seems conclusive that there are chemical and other physiological differences among individuals. Period. Some crimes of violence are caused by chemical imbalances. Fortunately or unfortunately, in spite of the glib "objective" conclusions found in books such as *Born to Crime: The Genetic Causes of Criminal Behavior*, by Lawrence Taylor (Greenwood Press, 1984), there are few real feasible policy changes thus far to be made from insights provided by this approach to crime and criminal justice.

One of the most interesting exchanges to appear over the past decade or so is the one between Robert Bonn and Alexander B. Smith opposing Richard J. Herrnstein, coauthor with James Q. Wilson of *Crime and Human Nature*. Bonn and Smith survey the field and warn against policy proposals that might allow biological indicators in judicial decision-making. Herrnstein attacks their comments and defends his and Wilson's thinking. Bonn and Smith provide a rejoinder followed by a bitter rebuttal by Herrnstein. See *Criminal Justice Ethics* (Winter/Spring 1988), pp. 1–19.

A good summary of the broader implications of sociobiology is found in A. L. Caplan's *The Sociobiology Debate* (Harper and Row, 1978). Two recent edited books dealing with biological applications to criminology that partially parallel elements within both Jeffery's and Platt and Takagi's thinking are *Biology, Crime and Ethics*, edited by F. Marsh and J. Katz (Anderson, 1985), and *The Causes of Crime: New Biological Approaches* (Cambridge University Press, 1987). These works examine in depth modern variants of the old issue.

For current articles that are much more sympathetic to sociobiological criminology, see D. H. Fishbein's "Biological Perspectives in Criminology," *Criminology* (vol. 28, no. 1, 1990); for an acrimonious debate involving a leading Canadian proponent of the alleged race-crime connection, J. Phillipe Rushton, see the *Canadian Journal of Criminology*—especially J. V. Roberts and T. Gabor's "Lombrosian Wine in a New Bottle: Research on Crime and Race" (April 1990).

ISSUE 4

Is Street Crime More Serious Than White-Collar Crime?

YES: James Q. Wilson and Richard J. Herrnstein, from *Crime and Human Nature* (Simon & Schuster, 1985)

NO: Jeffrey H. Reiman, from *The Rich Get Richer and the Poor Get Prison*, Second Edition (Macmillan, 1984)

ISSUE SUMMARY

YES: UCLA professor James Q. Wilson and Harvard psychologist Richard J. Herrnstein argue that the focus of crime study ought to be on persons who "hit, rape, murder, steal, and threaten."

NO: American University professor Jeffrey Reiman contends that a focus on street crimes is little more than a cover-up for more serious crimes such as pollution, medical malpractice, and dangerous working conditions that go uncorrected.

By now, from your course and the readings in this volume, it is probably clear to you that scholars and the general public differ intellectually, ideologically, and politically in their definitions of crime as well as why it exists. Liberal, conservative, or radical ideologies are likely to generate different definitions and explanations of crime.

One aspect of American society is its extremely heavy emphasis on economic success. Apparently for many who desire the material benefits that "the haves" take for granted but who are thwarted by lack of training or skills or by discrimination, their only recourse is to engage in predatory street crimes. Others are able to "make it" financially because they know how to and are allowed fully to participate: They can attend good schools, join a solid corporation, work their way up the ladder, not to mention speak proper English and wear the right clothes. Probably very few of these business executive types would dream of holding up someone, breaking into a house, attacking someone in a rage.

Yet in certain companies, the pressure to succeed, to keep corporate profits up, and to fulfill the expectations of managers and administrators drives many to commit white-collar crimes. No one knows for sure how many street crimes occur each day (many are not reported). Nor do we know how many white-collar crimes occur each day. The latter are much more likely to be carefully hidden and their consequences delayed for months or even years. Moreover, white-collar crimes are far more likely to be dismissed as "just another shrewd business practice by an ambitious executive in order to keep ahead of competitors." Most of us never directly see the results of white-collar crimes, nor do we know many people who are visibly harmed by them. By contrast, many of us have been victims of street crimes or know such victims. Sometimes we see their suffering the results of a physical assault, or we comfort them while they are still trembling following the discovery of a burglarized home or a stolen car.

But how should we view those who shiver in the cold because their utility bills were hiked illegally, forcing them to keep their thermostats under 60°? Or those robbed of health because of lung infections contracted while they worked in unsafe mines or around unsafe chemicals? Are they usually thought of as the victims of criminals? Are those Americans killed in traffic accidents because their automobiles left the factory in unsafe condition—with the factory's full knowledge and approval—thought of as murder victims?

Frequently, both the general public and criminologists concentrate on street crimes, their perpetrators and victims, while ignoring white-collar crimes. But beginning with the seminal work of Edwin Sutherland, *White Collar Crime*, some criminologists have been concerned with this form of violation.

However, as you will see in the debate that follows, it remains problematic as to not only what crime is and what its most adequate scientific explanations are but also which crimes are the most harmful and dangerous to members of society.

YES

James Q. Wilson and
Richard J. Herrnstein

CRIME AND HUMAN NATURE

CRIME AND ITS EXPLANATION

Predatory street crimes are most commonly committed by young males. Violent crimes are more common in big cities than in small ones. High rates of criminality tend to run in families. The persons who frequently commit the most serious crimes typically begin their criminal careers at a quite young age. Persons who turn out to be criminals usually do not do very well in school. Young men who drive recklessly and have many accidents tend to be similar to those who commit crimes. Programs designed to rehabilitate high-rate offenders have not been shown to have much success, and those programs that do manage to reduce criminality among certain kinds of offenders often increase it among others.

These facts about crime—some well known, some not so well known—are not merely statements about traits that happen occasionally, or in some places but not others, to describe criminals. They are statements that, insofar as we can tell, are pretty much true everywhere. They are statements, in short, about human nature as much as about crime.

All serious political and moral philosophy, and thus any serious social inquiry, must begin with an understanding of human nature. Though society and its institutions shape man, man's nature sets limits on the kinds of societies we can have. Cicero said that the nature of law must be founded on the nature of man (*a natura hominis discenda est natura juris*). This book is an effort to set forth an understanding of human nature by examining one common, if regrettable, manifestation of that nature—criminality. We could have chosen to understand human nature by studying work, or sexuality, or political activity; we chose instead to approach it through the study of crime, in part out of curiosity and in part because crime, more dramatically than other forms of behavior, exposes the connection between individual dispositions and the social order.

The problem of social order is fundamental: How can mankind live together in reasonable order? Every society has, by definition, solved that problem to some degree, but not all have done so with equal success or without paying a high cost in other things—such as liberty—that we also value. If we believe that man is naturally good, we will expect that the problem of order can be rather easily managed; if we believe him to be naturally wicked, we will expect the provision of order to require extraordinary measures; if we believe his nature to be infinitely plastic, we will think the problem of order can be solved entirely by plan and that we may pick and choose freely among all possible plans. Since every known society has experienced crime, no society has ever entirely solved the problem of order. The fact that crime is universal may suggest that man's nature is not infinitely malleable, though some people never cease searching for an anvil and hammer sufficient to bend it to their will.

Some societies seem better able than others to sustain order without making unacceptable sacrifices in personal freedom, and in every society the level of order is greater at some times than at others. These systematic and oft-remarked differences in the level of crime across time and place suggest that there is something worth explaining. But to find that explanation, one cannot begin with the society as a whole or its historical context, for what needs explanation is not the behavior of "society" but the behavior of individuals making up a society. Our intention is to offer as comprehensive an explanation as we can manage of why some individuals are more likely than others to commit crimes.

THE PROBLEM OF EXPLANATION

That intention is not easily realized, for at least three reasons. First, crime is neither easily observed nor readily measured. As we shall see later in this chapter, there is no way of knowing the true crime rate of a society or even of a given individual. Any explanation of why individuals differ in their law-abidingness may well founder on measurement errors. If we show that Tom, who we think has committed a crime, differs in certain interesting ways from Dick, who we think has not, when in fact both Tom and Dick have committed a crime, then the "explanation" is meaningless.

Second, crime is very common, especially among males. Using interviews and questionnaires, scholars have discovered that the majority of all young males have broken the law at least once by a relatively early age. By examining the police records of boys of a given age living in one place, criminologists have learned that a surprisingly large fraction of all males will be arrested at least once in their lives for something more serious than a traffic infraction. Marvin Wolfgang found that 35 percent of all the males born in Philadelphia in 1945 and living there between the ages of ten and eighteen had been arrested at least once by their eighteenth birthday.[1] Nor is this a peculiarly American phenomenon. Various surveys have found that the proportion of British males who had been convicted in court before their twenty-first birthday ranged from 15 percent in the nation as a whole to 31 percent for a group of boys raised in London. David Farrington estimates that 44 percent of all the males in "law-abiding" Britain will be arrested sometime in their lives.[2] If committing a crime at least once is so commonplace, then it is quite likely that there will be few, if any, large differences between those who never break the law and those who break it at least once—even if we had certain knowledge of which was which. Chance events as much as or more than individual predispositions will determine who commits a crime.

Third, the word "crime" can be applied to such varied behavior that it is not clear that it is a meaningful category of analysis. Stealing a comic book, punching a friend, cheating on a tax return, murdering a wife, robbing a bank, bribing a politician, hijacking an airplane—these and countless other acts are all crimes. Crime is as broad a category as disease, and perhaps as useless. To explain why one person has ever committed a crime and another has not may be as pointless as explaining why one person has ever gotten sick and another has not. We are not convinced that "crime" is so broad a category as to be absolutely meaningless—surely it is not irrelevant that crime is that form of behavior that is against the law—but we do acknowledge that it is difficult to provide a true and interesting explanation for actions that differ so much in their legal and subjective meanings.

To deal with these three difficulties, we propose to confine ourselves, for the most part, to explaining why some persons commit serious crimes at a high rate and others do not. By looking mainly at serious crimes, we escape the problem of comparing persons who park by a fire hydrant to persons who rob banks. By focusing on high-rate offenders, we do not need to distinguish between those who never break the law and those who (for perhaps chance reasons) break it only once or twice. And if we assume (as

we do) that our criminal statistics are usually good enough to identify persons who commit a lot of crimes even if these data are poor at identifying accurately those who commit only one or two, then we can be less concerned with measurement errors.

THE MEANING OF CRIME

A crime is any act committed in violation of a law that prohibits it and authorizes punishment for its commission. If we propose to confine our attention chiefly to persons who commit serious crimes at high rates, then we must specify what we mean by "serious." The arguments we shall make and the evidence we shall cite in this book will chiefly refer to aggressive, violent, or larcenous behavior; they will be, for the most part, about persons who hit, rape, murder, steal, and threaten.

In part, this limited focus is an unfortunate accident: We report only what others have studied, and by and large they have studied the causes of what we call predatory street crime. We would like to draw on research into a wider variety of law-violating behavior—embezzlement, sexual deviance, bribery, extortion, fraud—but very little such research exists.

But there is an advantage to this emphasis on predatory crime. Such behavior, except when justified by particular, well-understood circumstances (such as war), is condemned, in all societies and in all historical periods, by ancient tradition, moral sentiments, and formal law. Graeme Newman . . . interviewed people in six nations (India, Indonesia, Iran, Italy, the United States, and Yugoslavia) about their attitudes toward a variety of behaviors and concluded that there is a high—indeed, virtually universal—agreement that certain of these behaviors were wrong and should be prohibited by law.[3] Robbery, stealing, incest, and factory pollution were condemned by overwhelming majorities in every society; by contrast, abortion and homosexuality, among other acts, were thought to be crimes in some places but not in others. Interestingly, the characteristics of the individual respondents in these countries—their age, sex, education, social class—did not make much difference in what they thought should be treated as crimes. Newman's finding merely reinforces a fact long understood by anthropologists: Certain acts are regarded as wrong by every society, preliterate as well as literate; that among these "universal crimes" are murder, theft, robbery, and incest.[4]

Moreover, people in different societies rate the seriousness of offenses, especially the universal crimes, in about the same way. Thorsten Sellin and Marvin E. Wolfgang developed a scale to measure the relative gravity of 141 separate offenses. This scale has been found to be remarkably stable, producing similar rankings among both American citizens and prison inmates,[5] as well as among Canadians,[6] Puerto Ricans,[7] Taiwanese,[8] and Belgian Congolese.[9]

By drawing on empirical studies of behaviors that are universally regarded as wrong and similarly ranked as to gravity, we can be confident that we are in fact theorizing about *crime* and human nature and not about actions that people may or may not think are wrong. If the studies to which we refer were to include commercial price-fixing, political corruption, or industrial monopolization, we would have to deal with the fact that in many countries these actions are not regarded as criminal at all. If an American business executive were to bring all of the nation's chemical industries under his control, he would be indicted for having formed a monopoly; a British business executive who did the same thing might be elevated to the peerage for having created a valuable industrial empire. Similarly, by omitting studies of sexual deviance (except forcible rape), we avoid modifying our theory to take into account changing social standards as to the wrongness of these acts and the legal culpability of their perpetrators. In short, we seek in this book to explain why some persons are more likely than others to do things that all societies condemn and punish.

To state the same thing a bit differently, we will be concerned more with criminality than with crime. Travis Hirschi and Michael Gottfredson have explained this important distinction as follows. *Crimes* are short-term, circumscribed events that result from the (perhaps fortuitous) coming together of an individual having certain characteristics and an opportunity having certain (immediate and deferred) costs and benefits. . . . *Criminality* refers to "stable differences across individuals in the propensity to commit criminal (or equivalent) acts."[10] The "equivalent" acts will be those that satisfy, perhaps in entirely legal ways, the same traits and predispositions that lead, in other circumstances, to crime. For example, a male who is very impulsive and so cannot resist temptation may, depending on circumstances, take toys from his playmates, money from his mother, billfolds from strangers, stamps from the office, liquor in the morning, extra chocolate cake at dinner time, and a nap whenever he feels like it. Some of these actions break the law, some do not.

THE CATEGORIES OF EXPLANATION

Because we state that we intend to emphasize individual differences in behavior or predisposition, some readers may feel that we are shaping the argument in an improper manner. These critics believe that one can explain crime only by beginning with the society in which it is found. Emile Durkheim wrote: "We must, then, seek the explanation of social life in the nature of society itself."[11] Or, put another way, the whole is more than the sum of its parts. We do not deny that social arrangements and institutions, and the ancient customs that result from living and working together, affect behavior, often profoundly. But no explanation of social life explains anything until it explains individual behavior. Whatever significance we attach to ethnicity, social class, national character, the opinions of peers, or the messages of the mass media, the only test of their explanatory power is their ability to account for differences in how individuals, or groups of individuals, behave.

Explaining individual differences is an enterprise much resisted by some scholars. To them, this activity implies reducing everything to psychology, often referred to as "mere psychology." David J. Bordua, a sociologist, has pointed out the bias that can result from an excessive preference for social explanations over psychological ones.[12] Many criminologists, he comments, will observe a boy who becomes delinquent after being humiliated by his teacher or fired by his employer, and will conclude that his delinquency is explained by his "social class." But if the boy becomes delinquent after having been humiliated by his father or spurned by his girl friend, these scholars will deny that these events are explanations because they are "psychological." Teachers and employers are agents of the class structure, fathers and girl friends are not; therefore, the behavior of teachers and employers must be more important.

We believe that one can supply an explanation of criminality—and more important, of law-abidingness—that begins with the individual in, or even before, infancy and that takes into account the impact on him of subsequent experiences in the family, the school, the neighborhood, the labor market, the criminal justice system, and society at large. Yet even readers who accept this plan of inquiry as reasonable may still doubt its importance. To some, explaining crime is unnecessary because they think the explanation is already known; to others, it is impossible, since they think it unknowable.

Having taught a course on the causes of crime, and having spoken to many friends about our research, we have become acutely aware that there is scarcely any topic—except, perhaps, what is wrong with the Boston Red Sox or the Chicago Cubs—on which people have more confident opinions. Crime is caused, we are told, by the baby boom, permissive parents, brutal parents, incompetent schools, racial discrimination, lenient judges, the decline of organized religion, televised violence, drug addiction, ghetto unemployment, or the capitalist system. We note certain patterns in the proffered explanations. Our tough-minded friends blame crime on the failings of the criminal justice system; our tender-minded ones blame it on the failings of society.

We have no *a priori* quarrel with any of these explanations, but we wonder whether all can be true, or true to the same degree. The baby boom may help explain why crime rose in the 1960s and 1970s, but it cannot explain why some members of that boom became criminals and others did not. It is hard to imagine that both permissive and brutal parents produce the same kind of criminals, though it is conceivable that each may contribute to a different kind of criminality. Many children may attend bad schools, but only a small minority become serious criminals. And in any case, there is no agreement as to what constitutes an incompetent school. Is it an overly strict one that "labels" mischievous children as delinquents, or is it an overly lax one that allows normal mischief to degenerate into true delinquency? Does broadcast violence include a football or hockey game, or only a detective story in which somebody shoots somebody else? Economic conditions may affect crime, but since crime rates were lower in the Great Depression than during the prosperous years of the 1960s, the effect is, at best, not obvious or simple. The sentences given by judges may affect the crime rate, but we are struck by the fact that the most serious criminals begin offending at a very early age, long before they encounter, or probably even hear of, judges, whereas those who do not commit their first crime until they are adults (when, presumably, they have some knowledge of law and the courts) are the least likely to have a long or active criminal career. Racism and capitalism may contribute to crime, but the connection must be rather complicated, since crime has risen in the United States (and other nations) most rapidly during recent times, when we have surely become less racist and (given the growth of governmental controls on business) less

capitalist. In any event, high crime rates can be found in socialist as well as capitalist nations, and some capitalist nations, such as Japan and Switzerland, have very little crime. In view of all this, some sorting out of these explanations might be useful.

But when we discuss our aims with scholars who study crime, we hear something quite different. There is no well-accepted theory of the causes of crime, we are told, and it is unlikely that one can be constructed. Many explanations have been advanced, but all have been criticized. What is most needed is more research, not better theories. Any theory specific enough to be testable will not explain very much, whereas any theory broad enough to explain a great deal will not be testable. It is only because they are friends that some of our colleagues refrain from muttering about fools rushing in where wise men, if not angels, fear to tread. This question of whether it is useful to think systematically about the causes of crime is so important that we devote a large part of the next chapter to a discussion of it.

But there is one version of the claim that explaining crime is impossible to which we wish to take immediate exception. That is the view, heard most frequently from those involved with criminals on a case-by-case basis (probation officers and therapists, for example), that the causes of crime are unique to the individual criminal. Thus, one cannot generalize about crime because each criminal is different. Now, in one sense that argument is true—no two offenders are exactly alike. But we are struck by the fact that there are certain obvious patterns to criminality, suggesting that something more than random individual differences is at work. We think these obvious patterns, if nothing else, can be explained.

PATTERNS IN CRIMINALITY

Crime is an activity disproportionately carried out by young men living in large cities. There are old criminals, and female ones, and rural and small-town ones, but, to a much greater degree than would be expected by chance, criminals are young urban males. This is true, insofar as we can tell, in every society that keeps any reasonable criminal statistics.[13] These facts are obvious to all, but sometimes their significance is overlooked. Much time and effort may be expended in trying to discover whether children from broken homes are more likely to be criminals than those from intact ones, or whether children who watch television a lot are more likely to be aggressive than those who watch it less. These are interesting questions, and we shall have something to say about them, but even if they are answered satisfactorily, we will have explained rather little about the major differences in criminality. Most children raised in broken homes do not become serious offenders; roughly half of such children are girls, and . . . females are often only one-tenth as likely as males to commit crimes. Crime existed abundantly long before the advent of television and would continue long after any hint of violence was expunged from TV programs. Any worthwhile explanation of crime must account for the major, persistent differences in criminality.

The fact that these regularities exist suggests that it is not impossible, in principle, to provide a coherent explanation of crime. It is not like trying to explain why some people prefer vanilla ice cream and others chocolate. And as we shall see . . . there are other regularities in criminality beyond those associated with age, sex, and place. There is mounting evidence that, on the average, offenders differ from nonoffenders in physique, intelligence, and personality. Some of these differences may not themselves be a cause of crime but only a visible indicator of some other factor that does contribute to crime. . . . [W]e shall suggest that a certain physique is related to criminality, not because it causes people to break the law, but because a particular body type is associated with temperamental traits that predispose people to offending. Other individual differences, such as in personality, may directly contribute to criminality.

There are two apparent patterns in criminality that we have yet to mention, though they are no doubt uppermost in the minds of many readers—class and race. To many people, it is obvious that differences in social class, however defined, are strongly associated with lawbreaking. The poor, the unemployed, or the "underclass" are more likely than the well-to-do, the employed, or the "respectable poor" to commit certain kinds of crimes. We are reluctant, however, at least at the outset, to use class as a major category of explanations of differences in criminality for two reasons.

First, scholars who readily agree on the importance of age, sex, and place as factors related to crime disagree vigorously as to whether social class, however defined, is associated with crime. Their dispute may strike readers who have worked hard to move out of slums and into middle-class suburbs as rather bizarre; can anyone seriously doubt that better-off neighborhoods are safer than poorer ones? As John Braithwaite has remarked, "It is hardly plausible that one can totally explain away the higher risks of being mugged and raped in lower class areas as a consequence of the activities of middle class people who come into the area to perpetrate such acts."[14]

We have much sympathy with his view, but we must recognize that there are arguments against it. When Charles R. Tittle, Wayne J. Villemez, and Douglas A. Smith reviewed thirty-five studies of the relationship between crime rates and social class, they found only a slight association between the two variables.[15] When crime was measured using official (e.g., police) reports, the connection with social class was stronger than when it was measured using self-reports (the crimes admitted to by individuals filling out a questionnaire or responding to an interview). This conclusion has been challenged by other scholars who find, on the basis of more extensive self-report data than any previously used, that crime, especially serious crime, is much more prevalent among lower-class youth.[16] Michael J. Hindelang, Travis Hirschi, and Joseph G. Weis have shown that self-report studies tend to measure the prevalence of trivial offenses, including many things that would not be considered a crime at all (e.g., skipping school, defying parents, or having unmarried sex).[17] Even when true crimes are reported, they are often so minor (e.g., shoplifting a pack of gum) that it is a mistake—but, alas, a frequently made mistake—to lump such behavior together with burglary and robbery as measures of criminality. We agree with Hindelang et al., as well as with many others,[18] who argue that when crime is properly measured, the relationship between it and social class is strong—lower-class persons are much more likely to have committed a serious "street" crime than upper-status ones. But we recognize that this argument continues to be controversial, and so it seems inappropriate to begin an explanation of criminality by assuming that it is based on class.

Our second reason for not starting with class as a major social factor is, to us, more important. Unlike sex, age, and place, class is an ambiguous concept. A "lower-class" person can be one who has a low income, but that definition lumps together graduate students, old-age pensioners, welfare mothers, and unemployed steelworkers—individuals who would appear to have, as far as crime is concerned, little in common. Many self-report studies of crime use class categories so broad as to obscure whatever connection may exist between class and criminality.[19] And studies of delinquency typically describe a boy as belonging to the class of his father, even if the boy in his own right, in school or in the labor force, is doing much better or much worse than his father.[20] By lower class one could also mean having a low-prestige occupation, but it is not clear to us why the prestige ranking of one's occupation should have any influence on one's criminality.

Class may, of course, be defined in terms of wealth or income, but using the concept in this way to explain crime, without further clarification, is ambiguous as to cause and effect. One's wealth, income, status, or relationship to the means of production could cause certain behavior (e.g., "poor people must steal to eat"), or they could themselves be caused by other factors (impulsive persons with low verbal skills tend to be poor and to steal). By contrast, one's criminality cannot be the cause of, say, one's age or sex. As we proceed through our analysis in the chapters that follow, we shall take up the various possible components of social class, such as schooling and labor-market experiences, to see what effect they may have on individual differences in criminality. But we shall not begin with the assumption that we know what class is and that it can be only the cause, and never the consequence, of criminality.

Race is also a controversial and ambiguous concept in criminological research. Every study of crime using official data shows that blacks are heavily overrepresented among persons arrested, convicted, and imprisoned.[21] Some people, however, suspect that official reports are contaminated by the racial bias of those who compile them. Self-report studies, by contrast, tend to show fewer racial differences in criminality, but these studies have the same defect with respect to race as they do with regard to class—they overcount trivial offenses, in which the races do not differ, and undercount the more serious offenses, in which they do differ.[22] Moreover, surveys of the victims of crimes reveal that of the offenders whose racial identity could be discerned by their victims, about half were black; for the most serious offenses, two-thirds were black.[23] Though there may well be some racial bias in arrests, prosecutions, and sentences, there is no evidence . . . that it is so great as to account for the disproportionate involvement of blacks in serious crime, as revealed by both police and victimization data and by interviews with prison inmates.[24]

Our reason for not regarding, at least at the outset, race as a source of individual differences in criminality is not that we doubt that blacks are overrepresented in crime. Rather, there are two other considerations. First, racial differences exist in some societies and not others, yet all societies have crime. Though racial factors may affect the crime rate, the fundamental explanation for individual differences in criminality ought to be based—indeed, must be based, if it is to be a general explanation—on factors that are common to all societies.

Second, we find the concept of race to be ambiguous, but in a different way from the ambiguity of class. There is no reason to believe that the genes determining one's skin pigmentation also affect criminality. At one time in this nation's history, persons of Irish descent were heavily overrepresented among those who had committed some crime, but it would have been foolish then to postulate a trait called "Irishness" as an explanation. If racial or ethnic identity affects the likelihood of committing a crime, it must be because that identity co-varies with other characteristics and experiences that affect criminality. The proper line of inquiry, then, is first to examine those other characteristics and experiences to see how and to what extent they predispose an individual toward crime, and then to consider what, if anything, is left unexplained in the observed connection between crime and racial identity. After examining constitutional, familial, educational, economic, neighborhood, and historical factors, there may or may not be anything left to say on the subject of race. . . .

ARE THERE TYPES OF CRIMINALS?

We are concerned mainly with explaining criminality—why some people are more likely than others to commit, at a high rate, one or more of the universal crimes. But even if the behaviors with which we are concerned are alike in being universally regarded as serious crimes, are not the *motives* for these crimes so various that they cannot all be explained by one theory? Possibly. But this objection assumes that what we want to know are the motives of lawbreakers. It is by no means clear that the most interesting or useful way to look at crime is by trying to discover the motives of individual criminals—why some offenders like to steal cash, others like stolen cash plus a chance to beat up on its owner, and still others like violent sex—any more than it is obvious that the best way to understand the economy is by discovering why some persons keep their money in the bank, others use it to buy tickets to boxing matches, and still others use it to buy the favors of a prostitute. The motives of criminal (and of human) behavior are as varied as the behavior itself; we come to an understanding of the general processes shaping crime only when we abstract from particular motives and circumstances to examine the factors that lead people to run greater or lesser risks in choosing a course of action.

To us, offenders differ not so much in what kind of crimes they commit, but in the rate as which they commit them. In this sense, the one-time wife murderer is different from the persistent burglar or the organized drug trafficker—the first man breaks the law but once, the latter two do it every week or every day. . . . [T]he evidence suggests that persons who frequently break universal laws do not, in fact, specialize very much. A high-rate offender is likely to commit a burglary today and a robbery tomorrow, and sell drugs in between.

Explaining why some persons have a very high rate and others a low one is preferable, we think, to the major alternative to this approach: trying to sort offenders and offenses into certain categories or types. Creating—and arguing about—typologies is a major preoccupation of many students of crime because, having decided that motives are what count and having discovered that there are almost as many motives as there are people, the only way to bring any order to this variety is by reducing all the motives to a few categories, often described as personality types.

For example, a common distinction in criminology is between the "subcultural" offender and the "unsocialized" or "psychopathic" one. The first is a normal person who finds crime rewarding (perhaps because he has learned to commit crimes from friends he admires) and who discounts heavily the risks of being punished. The second is abnormal: He commits crimes because he has a weak conscience and cares little about the opinions of friends. Now, as even the authors of such distinctions acknowledge, these categories overlap (some subcultural thieves, for example, may also take pleasure in beating up on their victims), and not all offenders fit into either category. But to us, the chief difficulty with such typologies is that they direct attention away from individual differences and toward idealized—and abstract—categories.

Crime is correlated, as we have seen, with age, sex, and place of residence, and it is associated . . . with other stable characteristics of individuals. Understanding those associations is the first task of criminological theory. Our approach is not to ask which persons belong to what category of delinquents but rather to ask whether differences in the frequency with which persons break the law are associated with differences in the rewards of crime, the risks of being punished for a crime, the strength of internalized inhibitions against crime, and the willingness to defer gratifications, and then to ask what biological, developmental, situational, and adaptive processes give rise to these individual characteristics.

NOTES

1. Wolfgang, 1973.
2. Farrington, 1979c,9$_{25}$, 1981.
3. Newman, G., 1976.
4. Hoebel, 1954.
5. Sellin and Wolfgang, 1964; Figlio, 1972.
6. Akman and Normandeau, 1968.
7. Valez-Diaz and Megargee, 1971.
8. Hsu, cited in Wellford, 1975.
9. DeBoeck and Houschou, cited in Wellford, 1975.
10. Hirschi and Gottfredson, 1984.
11. Durkheim, 1964, p. 102.
12. Bordua, 1962.
13. Radzinowicz and King, 1977; Archer, Gartner, Akert, and Lockwood, 1978.
14. Braithwaite, 1981.
15. Tittle, Villemez, and Smith, 1978.
16. Elliott and Ageton, 1980; Elliott and Huizinga, 1983.
17. Hindelang, Hirschi, and Weis, 1979, 1981.
18. For example, Kleck, 1982.
19. Johnson, R. E., 1979.
20. Braithwaite, 1981.
21. For example, Wolfgang, Figlio, and Sellin, 1972.
22. Hindelang, Hirschi, and Weis, 1979, 1981; Berger and Simon, 1982.
23. Hindelang, Hirschi, and Weis, 1979, p. 1002; Hindelang, 1978.
24. Blumstein, 1982; Petersilia, 1983.

NO

Jeffrey H. Reiman

A CRIME BY ANY OTHER NAME

WHAT'S IN A NAME?

If it takes you an hour to read this chapter, by the time you reach the last page, two of your fellow citizens will have been murdered. *During that same time, at least 4 Americans will die as a result of unhealthy or unsafe conditions in the workplace!* Although these work-related deaths could have been prevented, they are not called murders. Why not? Doesn't a crime by any other name still cause misery and suffering? What's in a name?

The fact is that the label "crime" is not used in America to name all or the worst of the actions that cause misery and suffering to Americans. It is primarily reserved for the dangerous actions of the poor.

In the March 14, 1976 edition of the *Washington Star,* a front-page article appeared with the headline: "Mine Is Closed 26 Deaths Late." The article read in part:

> Why, the relatives [of the 26 dead miners] ask, did the mine ventilation fail and allow pockets of methane gas to build up in a shaft 2,300 feet below the surface? . . .
>
> [I]nvestigators of the Senate Labor and Welfare Committee . . . found that there have been 1,250 safety violations at the 13-year-old mine since 1970. Fifty-seven of those violations were serious enough for federal inspectors to order the mine closed and 21 of those were in cases where federal inspectors felt there was imminent danger to the lives of the miners working there.[1] . . .

Next to the continuation of this story was another, headlined: "Mass Murder Claims Six in Pennsylvania."[2] It described the shooting death of a husband and wife, their three children, and a friend in a Philadelphia suburb. This was murder, maybe even mass murder. My only question is, why wasn't the death of the miners also murder?

Why do 26 dead miners amount to a "disaster" and 6 dead suburbanites a "mass murder"? "Murder" suggests a murderer, while "disaster" suggests the work of impersonal forces. But if over 1000 safety violations had been found in the mine—three the day before the first explosion—was no one

Reprinted by permission of Macmillan Publishing Company from *The Rich Get Richer and the Poor Get Prison: Ideology, Class, and Criminal Justice, Second Edition,* by Jeffrey H. Reiman. Copyright © 1979, 1984 by Jeffrey H. Reiman.

responsible for failing to eliminate the hazards? Was no one responsible for preventing the hazards? And if someone could have prevented the hazards and did not, does that person not bear responsibility for the deaths of 26 men? Is he less evil because he did not want them to die although he chose to leave them in jeopardy? Is he not a murderer, perhaps even a mass murderer?

These questions are at this point rhetorical. My aim is not to discuss this case but rather to point to the blinders we wear when we look at such a "disaster." Perhaps there will be an investigation. Perhaps someone will be held responsible. Perhaps he will be fined. But will he be tried for *murder*? Will anyone think of him as a murderer? *And if not, why not?* Would the miners not be safer if such people were treated as murderers? Might they not still be alive? . . . didn't those miners have a right to protection from the violence that took their lives? *And if not, why not?*

Once we are ready to ask this question seriously, we are in a position to see that the reality of crime—that is, the acts we label crime, the acts we think of as crime, the actors and actions we treat as criminal—is *created:* It is an image shaped by decisions as to *what* will be called crime and *who* will be treated as a criminal.

THE CARNIVAL MIRROR

It is sometimes coyly observed that the quickest and cheapest way to eliminate crime would be to throw out all the criminal laws. There is a thin sliver of truth to this view. Without criminal laws, there would indeed be no "crimes." There would, however, still be dangerous acts. And this is why we cannot

really solve our crime problem quite so simply. The criminal law *labels* some acts "crimes." In doing this, it identifies those acts as so dangerous that we must use the extreme methods of criminal justice to protect ourselves against them. But this does not mean that the criminal law *creates* crime—it simply "mirrors" real dangers that threaten us. And what is true of the criminal law is true of the whole justice system. If police did not arrest or prosecutors charge or juries convict, there would be no "criminals." But this does not mean that police or prosecutors or juries create criminals any more than legislators do. They *react* to real dangers in society. The criminal justice system—from lawmakers to law enforcers—is just a mirror of the real dangers that lurk in our midst. *Or so we are told.*

How accurate is this mirror? We need to answer this in order to know whether or how well the criminal justice system is protecting us against the real threats to our well-being. The more accurate a mirror, the more the image it shows is created by the reality it reflects. The more misshapen a mirror is, the more the distorted image it shows is created by the mirror, not by the reality reflected. It is in this sense that I will argue that the image of crime is created: The American criminal justice system is a mirror that shows a distorted image of the dangers that threaten us—an image created more by the shape of the mirror than by the reality reflected. What do we see when we look in the criminal justice mirror?

On the morning of September 16, 1975, the *Washington Post* carried an article in its local news section headlined "Arrest Data Reveals Profile of a Suspect." The article reported the results of a study of crime in Prince George's County, a suburb of Washington, D.C. It read in part that

The typical suspect in serious crime in Prince George's County is a black male, aged 14 to 19 . . .[3]

This report is hardly a surprise. The portrait it paints of "the typical suspect in serious crime" is probably a pretty good rendering of the image lurking in the back of the minds of most people who fear crime. . . . [T]he portrait generally fits the national picture presented in the FBI's *Uniform Crime Reports* for the same year, 1974. In Prince George's County, "youths between the ages of 15 and 19 were accused of committing nearly half [45.5 percent] of all 1974 crimes."[4] . . . In 1980, this age group made up 39.0 percent of Index Crime* arrests.[5] . . . In 1980, blacks made up 11.7 percent of the nation's population and 32.8 percent of Index Crime arrests.[6] This, then, is the Typical Criminal, the one whose portrait [former] President Reagan has described as "that of a stark, staring face, a face that belongs to a frightening reality of our time—the face of a human predator, the face of the habitual criminal. Nothing in nature is more cruel and more dangerous."[7] This is the face that we see in the criminal justice mirror. Whose face is it? Let us look more closely.

He is, first of all, a *he*.[8] Second, he is a *youth*—most likely under the age of 20. Third, he is predominantly *urban*—although increasingly suburban.[9] Fourth, he is disproportionately *black*—blacks are arrested for Index Crimes at a rate three times that of their percentage in the national population. And finally, he is *poor*. . . .

[Index Crimes are homicide, forcible rape, robbery, assault, burglary, larceny, and auto theft.—Ed.]

This is the Typical Criminal feared by most law-abiding Americans. His crime, according to former Attorney General John Mitchell (who is by no means a typical criminal), is forcing us "to change the fabric of our society," "forcing us, a free people, to alter our pattern of life," "to withdraw from our neighbors, to fear all strangers and to limit our activities to 'safe' areas."[10] These poor, young, urban (disproportionately) black males comprise the core of the enemy forces in the war against crime. They are the heart of a vicious, unorganized guerrilla army, threatening the lives, limbs, and possessions of the law-abiding members of society—necessitating recourse to the ultimate weapons of force and detention in our common defense. They are the "career criminals" President Reagan had in mind when he told the International Association of Chiefs of Police, assuring them of the tough stance that the Federal Government would take in the fight against crime, that "a small number of criminals are responsible for an enormous amount of the crime in American society."[11]

And how do we know who the criminals are who so seriously endanger us that we must stop them with force and lock them in prisons? . . .

The reality of crime as the target of our criminal justice system and as perceived by the general populace is not a simple objective threat to which the system reacts: *It is a reality that takes shape as it is filtered through a series of human decisions running the full gamut of the criminal justice system*—from the lawmakers who determine what behavior shall be in the province of criminal justice to the law enforcers who decide which individuals will be brought within that province.

Note that by emphasizing the role of "human decisions," I do not mean to suggest that the reality of crime is voluntarily and intentionally "created" by individual "decision-makers." Their decisions are themselves shaped by the social system, much as a child's decision to become an engineer rather than a Samurai warrior is shaped by the social system. Thus, to have a full explanation of how the reality of crime is created, we have to understand how our society is structured in a way that leads people to make the decisions that they do. In other words, these decisions are part of the social phenomena to be explained—they are not the explanation. . . .

It is to capture this way of looking at the relation between the reality of crime and the real dangers "out there" in society that I refer to the criminal justice system as a "mirror." Who and what we see in this mirror is a function of the decisions about who and what are criminal, and so on. Our poor, young, urban, black male, who is so well-represented in arrest records and prison populations, appears not simply because of the undeniable threat he poses to the rest of society. As dangerous as he may be, he would not appear in the criminal justice mirror *if* it had not been decided that the acts he performs should be labeled "crimes," *if* it had not been decided that he should be arrested for those crimes, *if* he had access to a lawyer who could persuade a jury to acquit him and perhaps a judge to expunge his arrest record, and *if* it had not been decided that he is the type of individual and his type of crime that warrants imprisonment. *The shape of the reality we see in the criminal justice mirror is created by all these decisions.* What we want to know is how accurately the reality we see in this mirror reflects the real dangers that threaten us in society. . . .

The acts of the Typical Criminal are not the only acts that endanger us, nor are they the acts that endanger us the most. We have a greater chance (as I show below) of being killed or disabled, for example, by an occupational injury or disease, by unnecessary surgery, by shoddy emergency medical services than by aggravated assault or even homicide! Yet even though these threats to our well being are graver than that posed by our poor, young, urban, black males, they do not show up in the FBI's Index of serious crimes. And the individuals who are responsible for them do not turn up in arrest records or prison statistics. *They never become part of the reality reflected in the criminal justice mirror, although the danger they pose is at least as great and often greater than those who do!*

Similarly the general public loses more money *by far* . . . from price-fixing and monopolistic practices, and from consumer deception and embezzlement, than from all the property crimes in the FBI's Index combined. Yet these far more costly acts are either not criminal, or if technically criminal, not prosecuted, or if prosecuted, not punished, or if punished, only mildly. . . . *Their faces rarely appear in the criminal justice mirror, although the danger they pose is at least as great and often greater than those who do. . . .*

The criminal justice system is like a mirror in which society can see the face of the evil in its midst. But because the system deals with some evil and not with others, because it treats some evils as the gravest and treats some of the gravest evils as minor, the image it throws back is distorted like the image in a carnival mirror. Thus, the image cast back is false, not because it is invented out of thin air, but because the proportions of the real are distorted. . . .

If criminal justice really gives us a carnival-mirror image of "crime," we are doubly deceived. First, we are led to believe that the criminal justice system is protecting us against the gravest threats to our well-being when, in fact, the system is only protecting us against some threats and not necessarily the gravest ones. We are deceived about how much protection we are receiving and thus left vulnerable. But, in addition, we are deceived about what threatens us and are, therefore, unable to take appropriate defensive action. The second deception is just the other side of the first one. If people believe that the carnival mirror is a true mirror—that is, if they believe that the criminal justice system simply *reacts* to the gravest threats to their well-being—they come to believe that whatever is the target of the criminal justice system must be the greatest threat to their well-being. . . .

A CRIME BY
ANY OTHER NAME . . .

Think of a crime, any crime. Picture the first "crime" that comes into your mind. What do you see? The odds are you are not imagining a mining company executive sitting at his desk, calculating the costs of proper safety precautions, and deciding not to invest in them. Probably what you see with your mind's eye is one person physically attacking another or robbing something from another on the threat of physical attack. Look more closely. What does the attacker look like? It's a safe bet he (and it is a *he*, of course) is not wearing a suit and tie. In fact, my hunch is that you—like me, like almost anyone in America—picture a young, tough, lower-class male when the thought of crime first pops into your head. You (we) picture someone like the Typical Criminal described above. And the crime itself is one in which the Typical Criminal sets out to attack or rob some specific person.

This last point is important. What it indicates is that we have a mental image not only of the Typical Criminal, but also of the Typical Crime. If the Typical Criminal is a young lower-class male, the Typical Crime is *one-on-one harm*—where harm means either physical injury or loss of something valuable or both. If you have any doubts that this is the Typical Crime, look at any random sample of police or private eye shows on television. How often do you see Jim Rockford or Matt Houston investigate consumer fraud or failure to remove occupational hazards? . . . [E]ven when a TV show such as "Columbo" specializes in crimes by the well-to-do in the California "castle circuit," the crimes they commit are basically the same as those that occupy the Hill Street cops on grubby urban sidestreets: crimes of one-on-one harm. A recent study of TV crime shows by The Media Institute in Washington, D.C., indicates that, while the fictional criminals portrayed on television are on the average both older and wealthier than the real criminals who figure in the FBI Uniform Crime Reports, "TV crimes are almost 12 times as likely to be violent as crimes committed in the real world."[12] In short, TV crime shows broadcast the double-edged message that the "one-on-one" crimes of the poor are the typical crimes of all and thus not uniquely caused by the pressures of poverty; *and* that the criminal justice system pursues rich and poor alike—thus when the criminal justice system happens mainly to pounce on the poor in real life, it is not out of any class bias.

It is important to identify this model of the Typical Crime because it functions like a set of blinders. It keeps us from calling a mine disaster a mass murder even if 26 men are killed, even if someone is responsible for the unsafe conditions in which they worked and died. In fact, I argue that this particular piece of mental furniture so blocks our view that it keeps us from using the criminal justice system to protect ourselves from the greatest threats to our persons and possessions.

What keeps a mine disaster from being a mass murder in our eyes is the fact that it is not one-on-one harm. What is important here is not the numbers but the *intent to harm someone.* An attack by a gang on one or more persons or an attack by one individual on several fits the model of one-on-one harm. That is, for each person harmed there is at least one individual who wanted to harm that person. Once he selects his victim, the rapist, the mugger, the murderer, all want this person they have selected to suffer. A mine executive, on the other hand, does not want his employees to be harmed. He would truly prefer that there be no accident, no injured or dead miners. What he does want is something legitimate. It is what he has been hired to get: maximum profits at minimum costs. If he cuts corners to save a buck, he is just doing his job. If 26 men die because he cut corners on safety, we may think him crude or callous but not a killer. He is, at most, responsible for an *indirect harm,* not a one-on-one harm. For this, he may even be criminally indictable for violating safety regulations—but not for murder. The 26 men are dead as an unwanted consequence of his (perhaps overzealous or undercautious) pursuit of a legitimate goal. And so, unlike the Typical Criminal, he has not committed the Typical Crime. Or so we generally believe. As a result, 26 men are dead who might be alive now if cutting corners of the kind that leads to loss of life, whether suffering is specifically intended or not, were treated as murder.

This is my point. Because we accept the belief . . . that the model for crime is one person specifically intending to harm another, we accept a legal system that leaves us unprotected against much greater dangers to our lives and well-being than those threatened by the Typical Criminal . . .

According to the *FBI Uniform Crime Reports,* in 1980 there were 23,040 murders and nonnegligent manslaughters. During that year, there were 654,960 reported cases of aggravated assault. "Murder and nonnegligent manslaughter" includes "all willful felonious homicides as distinguished from deaths caused by negligence." "Aggravated assault" is defined as "assault with intent to kill or for the purpose of inflicting severe bodily injury by shooting, cutting, stabbing, maiming, poisoning, scalding, or by the use of acids, explosives, or other means."[13] Thus, as a measure of the physical harm done by crime in 1980, I will assume that reported crimes led to roughly 23,000 deaths and 650,000 instances of serious bodily harm short of death. As a measure of property loss due to crime, we can use $8,628,330,000 —the total value of property stolen in 1980 according to the UCR.[14] Whatever the shortcomings of these reported crime statistics, they are the statistics upon which public policy has traditionally been based. Since it is my aim to analyze the difference between public policy regarding crime and that regarding other dangers, it is appropriate to use the reported figures. Thus I will consider any actions that lead to loss of life, physical harm, and property loss comparable to the figures in the UCR as actions that pose grave dangers to the community comparable to the threats posed by crimes. . . .

WORK MAY BE DANGEROUS TO YOUR HEALTH

Since the publication of *The President's Report on Occupational Safety and Health*[15] in 1972, numerous studies have documented both the astounding incidence of disease, injury, and death due to hazards in the workplace *and* the fact that much or most of this carnage is the consequence of the refusal of management to pay for safety measures and of government to enforce safety standards.[16]

In that 1972 report, the government estimated the number of job-related illnesses at 390,000 per year and the number of annual deaths from industrial disease at 100,000.[17] In *The Report of the President to the Congress on Occupational Safety and Health* for 1980, these estimates were rather sharply reduced to 148,900 job-related illnesses and 4950 work-related deaths.[18] Note that the latter figure is not limited to death from occupational disease but includes all work-related deaths including those resulting from accidents on the job.

Before considering the significance of these figures, it should be mentioned that all sources including the just-mentioned report as well the U.S. Department of Labor's *Interim Report to Congress on Occupational Diseases* indicate that occupational diseases are seriously under-

reported. *The Report of the President* states that "recording and reporting of illnesses continue to present measurement problems, since employers (and doctors) are often unable to recognize some illnesses as work-related. The annual survey includes data only on the visible illnesses of workers. To the extent that occupational illnesses are unrecognized and, therefore, not recorded or reported, the illness survey estimates may understate their occurrence.[19] . . .

For these reasons, plus the fact that OSHA's* figures on work-related deaths are only for workplaces with 11 or more employees, we must supplement the OSHA figures with other reported figures. One study conservatively estimates the number of annual cancer deaths attributable to occupational factors at 17,000.[20] Richard Schweiker, [former] U.S. Secretary of Health and Human Services, states that "current estimates for overall workplace-associated cancer mortality vary within a range of five to fifteen percent."[21] With annual cancer deaths at 400,000, that translates into between 20,000 and 60,000 cancer deaths per year associated with the workplace. A report for the American Lung Association estimates 25,000 deaths a year from job caused respiratory diseases.[22] None of these figures include deaths from heart disease, America's number one killer, a substantial portion of which are likely caused by stress and strain on the job.[23] Thus even if we discount the OSHA's 1972 estimate of 100,000 deaths a year due to occupational disease, we would surely be erring in the other direction to accept the figure of 4950. We can hardly be overestimating the actual toll if

*[Occupational Health and Safety Administration.— Ed.]

we set it at 25,000 deaths a year resulting from occupational disease.

As for the OSHA estimate of 148,000 job-related illnesses, here too there is reason to assume that the figure considerably underestimates the real situation. One study suggests that it may represent no more than half of the actual number.[24] However, since this figure is probably less inaccurate than the figure for job-related deaths, it will suffice for our purposes. Let us assume, then, that there are annually in the United States approximately 150,000 job-related illnesses and 25,000 deaths from occupational diseases. How does this compare to the threat posed by crime? Before jumping to any conclusions, note that the risk of occupational disease and death falls only on members of the labor force, while the risk of crime falls on the whole populations, from infants to the elderly. Since the labor force is less than half the total population (96,800,000 in 1980, out of a total population approaching 230,000,000), to get a true picture of the *relative* threat posed by occupational diseases compared to that posed by crime we should *halve* the crime statistics when comparing them to the figures for industrial disease and death. Using the 1980 statistics, this means that the *comparable* figures would be:

	Occupational Disease	Crime (halved)
Death	25,000	11,500
Other physical harm	150,000	325,000

If it is argued that this paints an inaccurate picture because so many crimes go unreported, my answer is this. First of all, homicides are by far the most completely reported of crimes. For obvious reasons, the general underreporting of crimes is not equal among crimes. It is much easier or tempting to avoid reporting a rape or a mugging than a corpse. Second, aggravated assaults are among the better-reported crimes, although not the best. Based on victimization studies, it is estimated that 54 percent of aggravated assaults were reported to the police in 1980, compared to 26.9 percent of thefts.[25] On the other hand we should expect more—not less—underreporting of industrial than criminal victims because diseases and deaths are likely to cost firms money in the form of workdays lost and insurance premiums raised, occupational diseases are frequently first seen by company physicians who have every reason to diagnose complaints as either non-job-related or malingering, and many occupationally caused diseases do not show symptoms or lead to death until after the employee has left the job. . . . In sum, both occupational and criminal harms are underreported. Consequently, it is reasonable to assume that the effect of underreporting is probably balanced out, and the figures that we have give as accurate a picture of the *relative* threats of each as we need.

It should be noted further that the statistics given so far are *only* for occupational *diseases* and deaths from those diseases. They do not include death and disability from work-related injuries. Here too, the statistics are gruesome. The National Safety Council reported that in 1980, work-related accidents caused 13,000 deaths and 2.2 million disabling work injuries; 245 million man-days lost during that year because of work accidents, plus another 120 million man-days that will be lost in future years because of these accidents; and a total cost to the economy of $30 billion.[26] This brings the number of occupation-related deaths to 38,000 a year. If, on the basis of these additional figures, we recalculated our chart comparing occupational to criminal dangers, it would look like this:

	Occupational Hazard	Crime (halved)
Death	38,000	11,500
Other physical harm	2,350,000	325,000

Can there be any doubt that workers are more likely to stay alive and healthy in the face of the danger from the underworld than in the face of what their employers have in store for them on the job? If any doubt lingers, consider this. Lest we falter in the struggle against crime, the FBI includes in their annual *Uniform Crime Reports* a table of "crime clocks," which graphically illustrates the extent of the criminal menace. For 1980, the crime clock shows a murder occurring every 23 minutes. If a similar clock were constructed for occupational deaths—using the conservative estimate of 38,000 cited above and remembering that this clock ticks only for the half of the population that is in the labor force—this clock would show an occupational death about every 14 minutes! In other words, in roughly the time it takes for one murder on the crime clock, two workers have died *just from trying to make a living.*

To say that some of these workers died from accidents due to their own carelessness is about as helpful as saying that some of those who died at the hands of murderers asked for it. It overlooks the fact that where workers are careless, it is not because they love to live dangerously. They have production quotas to meet, quotas that they themselves do not

set. If quotas were set with an eye to keeping work at a safe pace rather than to keeping the production-to-wages ratio as high as possible, it might be more reasonable to expect workers to take the time to be careful. Beyond this, we should bear in mind that the vast majority of occupational deaths result from disease, not accident, and disease is generally a function of conditions outside a worker's control. Examples of such conditions are the level of coal dust in the air (about 10 percent of all active coal miners have black lung disease),[27] or textile dust (some 85,000 American cotton textile workers presently suffer breathing impairments due to acute byssinosis or brown lung, and another 35,000 former mill workers are totally disabled with chronic brown lung),[28] or asbestos fibers (a study of 632 asbestos-insulation workers between 1943 and 1971 indicates that 11 percent have died of asbestosis and 38 percent of cancer; two doctors who have studied asbestos workers conclude "we can anticipate three thousand excess respiratory, cardiopulmonary deaths and cancers of the lung—three thousand excess deaths *annually* for the next twenty or thirty years"),[29] or coal tars ("workers who had been employed five or more years in the coke ovens died of lung cancer at a rate three and a half times that for all steelworkers"; coke oven workers also develop cancer of the scrotum at a rate five times that of the general population).[30] . . .

To blame the workers for occupational disease and deaths is simply to ignore the history of governmental attempts to compel industrial firms to meet safety standards that would keep dangers (such as chemicals or fibers or dust particles in the air) that are outside of the worker's control down to a safe level.

This has been a continual struggle, with firms using everything from their own "independent" research institutes to more direct and often questionable forms of political pressure to influence government in the direction of loose standards and lax enforcement. . . .

Over and over again, the same story appears. Workers begin to sicken and die at a plant. They call on their employer to lower the level of hazardous material in the air, and their employer responds first by denying that a hazard exists. As the corpses pile up, the firm's scientists "discover" that some danger does exist but that it can be removed by reducing the hazardous material to a "safe" level—which is still above what independent and government researchers think is really safe. At this point, government and industry spar about "safe" levels and usually compromise at a level in between—something less dangerous than industry wants but still dangerous. This does not mean that the new levels are met, even if written into the law. So government inspectors and compliance officers must come in, and when (and if) they do, their efforts are too little and too late:

• Federal officials cited the Beryllium Corporation for 26 safety violations and 5 "serious violations" for "excessive beryllium concentration in work place areas." Fine: $928. The corporation's net sales for 1970 were $61,400,000.[31]
• On request from the Oil, Chemical and Atomic Workers Union, OSHA officials inspected the Mobil Oil plant at Plausboro, New Jersey. Result: citations for 354 violations of the Occupational Health and Safety Act of 1970. Fine: $7350 (about $20 a violation).[32]

• In 1972, a fire and explosion at the same Mobil plant killed a worker. Fine: $1215.[33] . . .
• "In 1981, a Labor Department study found nearly 2 million Americans were severely or partially disabled from an occupational disease; the lost income is estimated at $11.4 billion. Yet, the study found, only 5 percent of the severely disabled received workers' compensation."[34]
• "OSHA recently offered to reduce the penalties against the operator of a grain elevator in Galveston, where an explosion killed 18 workers, and injured 22, from $126,000 to $8000—a mere $444 for each employee killed."[35]

And things seem to be getting worse rather than better. The Reagan administration [gave] every indication that it believe[d] that OSHA's regulatory activity [was] too aggressive and should be toned down! Under the new administration, OSHA "has announced yet another policy change that should please most employers. OSHA will no longer automatically inspect a company accused of violating safety or health codes. Instead, OSHA will limit its inspections to companies that are accused of 'violations which pose physical harm or imminent danger' to employees. . . . Minor complaints will be resolved by registered letter. . . . Murray Seeger, a spokesman for the AFL-CIO said, 'Fewer inspections mean more danger on the job.' "[36] . . .

And so it goes on.

Is a person who kills another in a bar brawl a greater threat to society than a business executive who refuses to cut into his profits in order to make his plant a safe place to work? By any measure of death and suffering the latter is by far a greater danger than the former. But because he wishes his workers no harm, because he is only indirectly responsible for death and disability while pursuing legitimate economic goals, his acts are not called *crimes*. Once we free our imagination from the irrational shackle of the one-on-one model of crime, can there be any doubt that the criminal justice system does *not* protect us from the gravest threats to life and limb? It seeks to protect us when danger comes from a young, lower-class male in the inner city. When a threat comes from an upper-class business executive in an office, the criminal justice system looks the other way. And this in the face of growing evidence that for every American citizen murdered by some thug, two American workers are killed by their bosses.

HEALTH CARE MAY BE DANGEROUS TO YOUR HEALTH

. . . On July 15, 1975, Dr. Sidney Wolfe of Ralph Nader's Public Interest Health Research Group testified before the House Commerce Oversight and Investigations Subcommittee that there "were 3.2 million cases of unnecessary surgery performed each year in the United States." These unneeded operations, Dr. Wolfe added, "cost close to $5 billion a year and killed as many as 16,000 Americans."[37] . . .

> a Congressional committee earlier this year [1976] estimated that more than 2 million of the elective operations performed in 1974 were not only unnecessary—but also killed about 12,000 patients and cost nearly $4 billion.[38]

Since the number of surgical operations performed in the United States rose from 20 million in 1975 to 23.8 million in 1979 (from 95.6 per 1000 population to 110.5 per 1000),[39] there is every reason to believe that at least somewhere between 12,000 and 16,000 people a year still die from unnecessary surgery. In 1980, the FBI reported that 4212 murders were committed by a "cutting or stabbing instrument."[40] Obviously, the FBI does not include the scalpel as a cutting or stabbing instrument. If they did, they would have had to report that between 16,212 and 20,212 persons were killed by "cutting or stabbing" in 1980—depending on whether you take *Newsweek's* figure or Dr. Wolfe's. No matter how you slice it, the scalpel may be more dangerous than the switchblade. . . .

WAGING CHEMICAL WARFARE AGAINST AMERICA

One in four Americans can expect to contract cancer during their lifetimes. The American Cancer Society estimated that 420,000 Americans would die of cancer in 1981, up from 412,000 in 1980, and 404,000 in 1979. "A 1978 report issued by the President's Council on Environmental Quality (CEQ) unequivocally states that 'most researchers agree that 70 to 90 percent of cancers are caused by environmental influences and are hence theoretically preventable.' "[41] This means that a concerted national effort could result in saving 300,000 or more lives a year and reducing each individual's chances of getting cancer in his or her lifetime from 1-in-4 to 1-in-12 or less. If you think that this would require a massive effort in terms of money and personnel, you are right. But how much of an effort would the nation make to stop a foreign invader who was killing a thousand people a day and bent on capturing one-quarter of the present population? . . .

The evidence linking *air pollution* and cancer, as well as other serious and often fatal diseases, has been rapidly accumulating in recent years. During 1975, the epidemiological branch of the National Cancer Institute did a massive county-by-county analysis of cancer in the United States, mapping the "cancer hotspots" in the nation. The result was summed up by Dr. Glenn Paulson, Assistant Commissioner of Science in the New Jersey Department of Environmental Protection: "If you know where the chemical industry is, you know where the cancer hotspots are."[42] What distinguishes these findings from the material on occupational hazards discussed above is that NCI investigators found higher death rates for *all* those living in the "cancer hotspots"—not just the workers in the offending plants. . . .

In 1970, Lester B. Lave and Eugene P. Seskin reviewed over 50 scientific studies of the relationship between air pollution and morbidity and mortality rates for lung cancer, nonrespiratory tract cancers, cardiovascular disease, bronchitis, and other respiratory diseases. They found in every instance a *positive quantifiable relationship*. Using sophisticated statistical techniques, they have concluded that a 50 percent reduction in air pollution in major urban areas would result in:

• A 25 percent reduction in mortality from lung cancer (using 1974 mortality rates, this represents a potential saving of 19,500 lives per year).

• A 25 percent reduction in morbidity and mortality due to respiratory disease (a potential saving of 27,000 lives per year).

• A 20 percent reduction in morbidity and mortality due to cardiovascular disease (a potential saving of 52,000 lives per year.)[43] . . .

A more recent study, done in 1978 by Robert Mendelsohn of the University of

Washington and Guy Orcutt of Yale University, estimates that air pollution causes a total of 142,000 deaths a year.[44] A government study released in February, 1981 indicates that "sulfates and other air pollutants, just from coal-fired power plants, may help cause the deaths of 8000 people a year in Ohio."[45] . . .

And as with OSHA, the Reagan administration [showed] every sign of slowing down enforcement of EPA and FDA (Food and Drug Administration) regulations rather than making them more aggressive. . . .

And so the chemical war goes on. No one can deny that we know the enemy. No one can deny that we know the toll it is taking. Indeed, we can compute the number of deaths that result from every day that we refuse to mount an offensive. Yet we still refuse. And thus for the time being the only advice we can offer someone who values his life, is: If you must breathe our air, don't inhale. . . .

The average American consumes *one pound* of chemical *food additives* per year.[46] Speaking on the floor of the United States Senate in 1972, Senator Gaylord Nelson said:

People are finally waking up to the fact that the average American daily diet is substantially adulterated with unnecessary and poisonous chemicals and frequently filled with neutral, nonnutritious substances. We are being chemically medicated against our will and cheated of food value by low nutrition foods.[47]

A hard look at the chemicals we eat and at the federal agency that is empowered to protect us against eating dangerous chemicals reveals the recklessness with which we are being "medicated against our will."

Beatrice Hunter has taken such a hard look and reports her findings in a book aptly titled *The Mirage of Safety.* Her book is a catalogue of the possible dangers that lurk in the foods we eat. But more than this, it is a description of how the Food and Drug Administration, through a combination of lax enforcement and uncritical acceptance of the results of the food industry's own "scientific" research, has allowed a situation to exist in which the American food-eating public is the real guinea pig for nearly *three thousand* food additives. As a result, we are subjected to chemicals that are strongly suspected of producing cancer,[48] gallbladder ailments,[49] hyperkinesis in children,[50] and allergies[51]; to others that inhibit "mammalian cell growth" and "may adversely affect the rate of DNA, RNA, and protein synthesis"[52] and to still others that are capable of crossing the placental barrier between mother and fetus and are suspected causes of birth defects and congenital diseases.[53] . . .

Based on the knowledge we have, there can be no doubt that air pollution, tobacco, and food additives amount to a chemical war that makes the crime wave look like a football scrimmage. Quite conservatively, I think we can estimate the death toll in this war as at least a quarter of a million lives a year—*more than ten times the number killed by criminal homicide!*

POVERTY KILLS

. . . We are prone to think that the consequences of poverty are fairly straightforward: Less money equals less things. And so poor people have fewer clothes or cars or appliances, go to the theater less often, and live in smaller homes with less or cheaper furniture. And this is true and sad, but perhaps not intolerable. I will argue that one of the things poor people have less of is *good health.* Less money means less nutritious food, less heat in the winter, less fresh air in summer, less distance from other sick people, less knowledge about illness or medicine, fewer doctor visits, fewer dental visits, less preventive health care, and above all, less first-quality medical attention when all these other deprivations take their toll and a poor person finds himself seriously ill. What this means is that the poor suffer more from poor health and die earlier than do those who are well off. Poverty robs them of their days while they are alive and then kills them before their time. A prosperous society that allows poverty in its midst is guilty of murder. . . .

A comparison of the health and mortality of blacks and whites in America yields further insight into the relationship of health and mortality to economic class. In 1981, about 1 out of every 3 blacks lived below the poverty level, as compared to 1 out of every 11 whites. Black unemployment is consistently double that of whites. As of October, 1982, 20.2 percent of blacks were unemployed compared to 9.3 percent of whites. . . .

In 1978, black mothers died in childbirth at a rate *four times* that of white mothers. Black infant mortality was 23.1 per thousand live births compared to 12.0 for whites.[54] In 1979, the figure for blacks was down to 21.8, and the figure for whites was 11.4[55] In short, black mothers lose their babies within the first year of life nearly twice as often as white mothers. In the face of this situation, the Reagan administration . . . reduced funding for maternal and child health programs by more than 25 percent and attempted to reduce support of immunization programs for American children.[56] . . .

ONCE AGAIN, OUR INVESTIGATION LEADS to the same result. The criminal justice system does not protect us against the gravest threats to life, limb, or possessions. Its definitions of crime are not simply a reflection of the objective dangers that threaten us. The workplace, the medical profession, the air we breathe, and the poverty we refuse to rectify lead to far more human suffering, far more death and disability, and take far more dollars from our pockets than the murders, aggravated assaults, and thefts reported annually by the FBI. And what is more, this human suffering is preventable. A government really intent on protecting our well-being could enforce work safety regulations, police the medical profession, require that clean air standards be met, and funnel sufficient money to the poor to alleviate the major disabilities of poverty. But it does not. Instead we hear a lot of cant about law and order and a lot of rant about crime in the streets. It is as if our leaders were not only refusing to protect us from the major threats to our well-being but trying to cover up this refusal by diverting our attention to crime—as if this were the only real threat. But as we have seen, the criminal justice system is a carnival mirror that presents a distorted image of what threatens us. . . . All the mechanisms by which the criminal justice system comes down more frequently and more harshly on the poor criminal than on the well-off criminal take place *after* most of the dangerous acts of the well-to-do have been excluded from the definition of crime itself. The bias against the poor within the criminal justice system is all the more striking when we recognize that the door to that system is shaped in a way that excludes in advance the most dangerous acts of the well-to-do.

NOTES

1. *The Washington Star*, March 14, 1976, pp. A1, A9.
2. Ibid., p. A9.
3. *The Washington Post*, September 16, 1975, p. C1.
4. Ibid.; see also The Maryland-National Capital Parks and Planning Commission, *Crime Analysis 1975: Prince George's County* (August 1975), p. 86.
5. *UCR-1980*, P. 200.
6. *Stat Abst-1981*, P. 26, Table No. 29; and *UCR-1980*, p. 204.
7. Speech to International Association of Chiefs of Police, September 28, 1981.
8. Out of 1,289,524 persons arrested for FBI Index Crimes in 1974, 1,043,155, or over 80 percent were males. See *UCR-1974*, p. 190. In Prince George's County, males "represented three of every four serious crime defendants." *Crime Analysis 1975: Prince George's County*, p. 3.
9. Out of 1,474,427 persons arrested for FBI Index Crimes in 1974, 1,267,955 were "city arrests" and 420,682 were "suburban" (suburban arrest figures include arrests in suburban cities, and thus overlap with statistics for city arrests). *UCR-1974*, p. 180.
10. John N. Mitchell, "Crime Prevention: Citizen Participation," speech delivered before the Conference on Crime and the Urban Crisis of the National Emergency Committee of the National Council on Crime and Delinquency, San Francisco, California, February 3, 1969, in *Vital Speeches of the Day*, XXXV, No. 10 (March 1, 1969), p. 290.
11. See note 7, above.
12. *The Washington Post*, January 11, 1983, p. C10.
13. *UCR-1980*, pp. 7, 20, and 38.
14. *UCR-1980*, p. 179.
15. *The President's Report on Occupational Safety and Health* (Washington, D.C.: U.S. Government Printing Office, 1972).
16. See, for instance, Joseph A. Page and Mary-Win O'Brien, *Bitter Wages: Ralph Nader's Study Group Report on Disease and Injury on the Job* (New York: Grossman, 1973); Rachel Scott, *Muscle and Blood* (New York: E. P. Dutton, 1974); and Jeanne M. Stellman and Susan M. Daum, *Work Is Dangerous to Your Health* (New York: Vintage Books, 1973). See also Fran Lynn "The Dust in Willie's Lungs," *The Nation*, 222, No. 7 (February 21, 1976), pp. 209–212; and Joel Swartz, "Silent Killers at Work," *Crime and Social Justice*, 3 (Summer 1975), pp. 15–20.
17. *President's Report on Occupational Safety and Health*, p. 111.

18. *Report of the President to the Congress on Occupational Safety and Health, 1980* (August 4, 1981), p. 86; reporting on deaths and illnesses for 1979.

19. Ibid., p. 91. Robert Johnson, who has conducted extensive interviews with present and former textile workers suffering from brown lung, indicates that another reason for the underreporting of occupational diseases is that workers are often hesitant to admit symptoms for fear of being seen as "defective" or "worn out" and therefore losing their jobs (personal communication).

20. Richard Doll and Richard Peto, "The Causes of Cancer: Quantitative Estimates of Avoidable Risks of Cancer in the United States Today," *Journal of the National Cancer Institute 66*, No. 6 (June 1981), p. 1245.

21. Letter from Schweiker to B.J. Pigg, Executive Director of the Asbestos Information Association, dated April 29, 1982.

22. Thomas C. Brown, *Occupational Respiratory Disease—A Statistical Overview for the American Lung Association Occupational Health Task Force*, April 1980, p. 1.

23. "An unknown, but quite possibly substantial, proportion of the 75% of heart disease risk which is presently unaccounted for could be related to work and its attendant hazards, particularly stress" (Nicholas Ashford, *Crisis in the Workplace: Occupational Disease and Injury* [Cambridge, Mass.: MIT Press, 1976], p. 93). Note that heart disease is responsible for 750,000 deaths a year, almost twice the toll from cancer.

24. P. Derr, R. Goble, R. E. Kasperson, and R. W. Kates, "Worker/Public Protection: The Double Standard," *Environment* 23, no. 7 (September 1981), p. 9.

25. U.S. Department of Justice, *Bureau of Justice Statistics Technical Report: Criminal Victimization in the U.S.* (July 1982), p. 3.

26. National Safety Council, *Accident Facts*, 1981 edition, pp. 23–24.

27. Page and O'Brien, *Bitter Wages*, p. 16.

28. Testimony of Peter Henle, Deputy Assistant Secretary for Policy Evaluation and Research, given before the Labor Standards Subcommittee of the House Committee on Education and Labor, 96th Congress, First Session, May 26, 1979. Chronic brown lung is a severely disabling occupational respiratory disease. For a description of its impact on its victims, see Robert Johnson, "Labored Breathing: Living with Brown Lung," paper presented at the Annual Meeting of the American Society of Criminology, Fall 1982, Toronto, Canada. See also, Page and O'Brien, *Bitter Wages*, p. 18.

29. Page and O'Brien, p. 23; and Scott, *Muscle and Blood*, p. 196.

30. Scott, pp. 45–46; cf. Page and O'Brien, p. 25.

31. Scott, *Muscle and Blood*, pp. 35–36.

32. Ibid., pp. 109, 111.

33. Ibid., p. 112.

34. Joann Lublin, "Workplace Perils: Occupational Diseases Receive More Scrutiny Since the Manville Case," *Wall Street Journal*, December 20, 1982, p. 1.

35. George Miller (Democratic representative from California), "OSHA Sure is Backsliding," *The Washington Post*, January 30, 1982, p. A21.

36. "OSHA Shift Means Cutback in its Inspections," *The Washington Post*, February 3, 1982, p. A21.

37. *The Washington Post*, July 16, 1975, p. A3.

38. *Newsweek*, March 29, 1976, p. 67. Lest anyone think this is a new problem, compare this passage written in a popular magazine about 30 years ago:

> In an editorial on medical abuses, the *Journal of the Medical Association of Georgia* referred to "surgeons who paradoxically are often cast in the role of the supreme hero by the patient and family and at the same time may be doing the greatest amount of harm to the individual."
>
> Unnecessary operations on women, stemming from the combination of a trusting patient and a split fee, have been so deplored by honest doctors that the phrase "rape of the pelvis" has been used to describe them. The American College of Surgeons, impassioned foe of fee-splitting, has denounced unnecessary hysterectomies, uterine suspensions, Caesarian sections. [Howard Whitman, "Why Some Doctors Should Be in Jail," *Colliers*, October 30, 1953, p. 24.]

39. *Stat Abst-1981*, Table no. 180.

40. *UCR-1980*, p. 12.

41. Lewis Regenstein, *America the Poisoned* (Washington, D.C.: Acropolis Books, 1982), pp. 246–247.

42. Quoted in Stuart Auerbach, "N.J.'s Chemical Belt Takes Its Toll: $4 Billion Industry Tied to Nation's Highest Cancer Death Rate," *The Washington Post*, February 8, 1976, p. A1.

43. Lester B. Lave and Eugene P. Seskin, "Air Pollution and Human Health," *Science*, 169, No. 3947 (August 21, 1970), pp. 723–733, especially p. 730. The source for the 1974 mortality rates for lung cancer, respiratory disease (excluding cancer), and cardiovascular disease is the Department of Health, Education and Welfare.

44. Robert Mendelsohn and Guy Orcutt, "An Empirical Analysis of Air Pollution Dose-Responsive Curves," *Journal of Environmental Economics and Management* (June 1979), pp. 85–106; cited in Regenstein, *America the Poisoned*, p. 194.

45. Regenstein, *America the Poisoned*, p. 195.
46. Hunter, *The Mirage of Safety*, p. 4.
47. Quoted in Hunter, p. 2.
48. Hunter, pp. 40–41, 64–65, 85, 148–151, *inter alia*.
49. Ibid., p. 119.
50. Ibid., pp. 123–124.
51. Ibid., pp. 127–140.
52. Ibid., pp. 102–103.
53. Ibid., pp. 162–176.
54. *Stat Abst-1981*, p. 73, Table #111.
55. Rich, "Study Finds . . ."
56. Anthony Robbins, "Can Reagan Be Indicted . . .?," pp. 12–13.

POSTSCRIPT

Is Street Crime More Serious
Than White-Collar Crime?

American society is currently in the throes of disdain, if not out-and-out hate, for street crimes and the people who commit them. Yet, according to Reiman and others, street thugs are not nearly as dangerous or harmful to life and limb as are corporate criminals. Ironically, many political candidates have made a partial career out of attacking street criminals while at the same time generously borrowing some of their verbal mannerisms. For instance, on more than one occasion, then-president Reagan challenged drug dealers and the like to give him the opportunity to "stomp them" or, in his inimitable vernacular, to "make my day."

Similarly to Wilson and Herrnstein, Paul Tappan, in "Who Is the Criminal," *American Sociological Review* (February 1947), insists that white-collar criminals and the like are not really the concerns of criminologists—at least not until laws are passed prohibiting certain acts. Otherwise, to attack corporations simply because we may disagree with their standards and/or efforts to make a profit is to dilute our definition of crime. Others are more provocative on this controversial subject. Nancy Frank wrestles with it in "Unintended Murder and Corporate Risk Taking: Defining the Concept of Justifiability," *Journal of Criminal Justice*, vol. 16, no. 1 (1988).

For a fresh look at the issue of corporate crimes being more dangerous than street crimes, see the highly controversial *Poisoning for Profit: The Mafia and Toxic Waste in America*, by A. A. Block and F. R. Scarpitti (William Morrow, 1985), and Marshall B. Clinard's *Corporate Corruption* (Praeger, 1990). A good discussion of the important and controversial issue of legal control of organized crime is the symposium "Reforming RICO. . . " in *Vanderbilt Law Review* (April 1990). Also, the *Corporate Crime Reporter,* published weekly since 1987 and edited by Russell Mokhiber, is an invaluable source.

You may find interesting a study that weaves concern over an alleged "street crime" with the antics of corporate thugs, H. Kohn's *Who Killed Karen Silkwood?* (Summit, 1981). Other works that focus directly on official deviancy and white-collar crime are J. Douglas and J. M. Johnson's, *Official Deviance* (Lippincott, 1977); M. D. Ermann and R. J. Lundman's *Corporate and Government Deviance* (Oxford University Press, 1982); also, the winter 1985 issue of the *American Criminal Law Review,* which is devoted to the problem of white-collar crime, its definitions and extent.

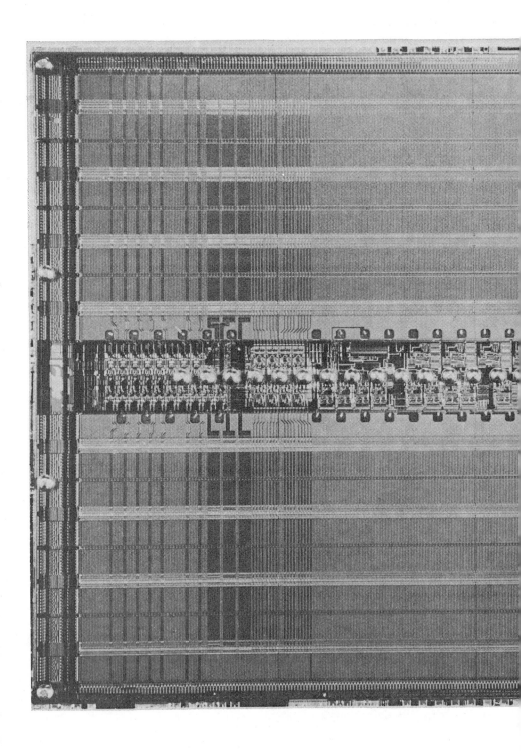

IBM Corporation

PART 2

Measuring Crime

*In the late 1960s when victimization
surveys began to be made throughout the
United States, it was discovered that
frequently twice as many people were crime
victims as were reported on official records.
Many people, even victims of very serious
crimes such as rape, robbery, and assault,
did not report crimes to the police. The
most important statistics by far for
criminologists and criminal justice scholars
are official ones (that is, those crimes
known to the police and compiled annually
as the Uniform Crime Reports). Yet many
contend that those statistics are so badly
flawed as to be close to worthless. An
equally important issue pertains to whether
crimes are increasing or decreasing. Also
problematic is how to take the measure of a
prison system, and how to assess criminal
justice practices in countries other than
one's own.*

Are Official Statistics Meaningful?
_____

Is Crime Getting Worse?
_____

Are Dutch Prisons Superior to Others?

ISSUE 5

Are Official Statistics Meaningful?

YES: A. Keith Bottomley and Ken Pease, from *Crime and Punishment: Interpreting the Data* (Open University Press, 1986)

NO: Bruce Jackson, from *Law and Disorder: Criminal Justice in America* (University of Illinois Press, 1984)

ISSUE SUMMARY

YES: British criminologists A. Keith Bottomley and Ken Pease, while acknowledging problems with official statistics, nonetheless maintain that they are extremely useful for both analyzing crime and generating a more humane criminal justice system.

NO: Social critic Bruce Jackson disagrees, claiming that official statistics are virtually worthless for understanding the types, rates, or distributions of crime.

> There are three kinds of lies—
> lies, damn lies, and statistics.
> —*Benjamin Disraeli* (1867)

> while you and i have lips and voices which
> are kissing and to sing with
> who cares if some one-eyed son a bitch
> invents an instrument to measure Spring with?
> —*e e cummings*

Next to defining and explaining crime, measuring crime is a major problem for criminology and criminal justice students and scholars. It is also a controversial area as researchers clash over the appropriate measurements to determine the rates and trends of crimes.

Traditionally, official statistics produced by law enforcement agencies have been the primary source of data on crime rates. Although various individual precincts and jurisdictions have been collecting statistics on crimes for over one hundred and fifty years (New York City collected data on court dispositions in the late 1820s), a national data pool in the United States did not begin until the early 1930s. This was the result of Congress empowering the Federal Bureau of Investigation to collect and compile crime statistics. This compilation has become known as the Uniform Crime Reports (UCR), which is published annually in *Crime in the United States*.

Approximately 15,000 agencies report crimes to the FBI. This is 98 percent of all law enforcement agencies, and thus the UCR is by far the most comprehensive source of crime statistics in this country. It is divided into crimes that are known to police and crimes that result in arrests. Critics traditionally argue that there are sharp disagreements as to which crime category certain crimes fall into, which results in ambiguous reporting.

The surprising fact that apparently most victims of crimes do not report them was first documented in 1965 in a study ordered by the President's Commission on Law Enforcement and Administration of Justice. It was found that Americans surveyed indicated that they were victims of serious crimes, including rape, attempted murder, and aggravated assault, at rates of up to five times more than crime rates reflected in official statistics. Since then, annual victimization surveys conducted under the title of the National Crime Survey (NCS) continue to reflect large discrepancies between victim reports and official crime data. The NCS has been conducted since 1981 by the Bureau of Justice Statistics.

Another important source of crime statistics in the United States that directly attempts to uncover the hidden rate of crime are studies of self-reported crimes, which began in the late 1940s. It has been consistently discovered on these self-reported crime questionnaires that people from every level of society have committed serious crimes at one time or another. Recently, specific populations such as incarcerated drug abusers have been surveyed. The findings frequently show that many of these criminals have committed several dozen or more serious crimes that are either never reported and/or never solved. This source, then, also shows real discrepancies between crime rates and official statistics.

Another set of important crime statistics deals with court dispositions. In addition, recidivism rates are vitally important for a better understanding of the results of sentencing and imprisoning inmates, even though the meaning and interpretation of recidivism rates remain highly problematic.

These are only some of the controversial issues pertaining to official statistics raised by Bottomley, Pease, and Jackson in the readings that follow.

YES

A. Keith Bottomley
and Ken Pease

EVALUATING CRIMINAL JUSTICE
BY NUMBERS

Some would argue that crime statistics are biassed, partial and often misleading because of the perceived significance of crime and punishment for the social and moral fabric; in the face of real or imagined threats to personal safety and security, official statistics are naturally turned to for information and reassurance. More specifically, it is commonly expected that they should be able to indicate whether the crime problem is under control, and how effective the law enforcement and penal processes are in combatting it. We would go further, to argue that any form of information-gathering cannot be accurate in any absolute way, but only usable for a purpose or set of purposes. Certainly the way in which data are collected and organized depends on what you want to do with them. This is a difficult point to recognize until a novice researcher comes to analyse a first major data-gathering exercise.

Although what follows is implicit or explicit in much of what went earlier, we should end . . . with some brief reflections on the role of official statistics in evaluating criminal justice policy and practice. It will be concluded that the regularly published criminal statistics provide few, if any, significant answers to many of the important traditional questions of evaluation. The fact that many of the available statistics *appear* to provide such answers means that extra caution is needed in their interpretation. On the other hand, criminal justice statistics are informative in a variety of ways, and should not be discarded as meaningless, as has sometimes been their fate. Let us then look at some typical questions to which it might quite sensibly be thought that criminal statistics would provide answers. . . .

HESITANT QUESTIONS AND TENTATIVE ANSWERS

. . . . As far as the police are concerned, the basic question is perhaps about how successful they are in clearing up the crimes which become known to them; for sentencing, the basic question has often been taken to concern the relative reconviction rates of those given different sentences. Both questions bring with them untested assumptions about objectives and methods.

. . . [M]any crimes are automatically solved by the very fact of becoming known to the police, in many crimes against the person the offender is immediately identifiable; in consequence much of the variation between the clear-up rate of different police forces is attributable to the crime mix of the area. . . .

These conclusions not only have direct implications for the interpretation of variations between police forces. They also raise serious doubts about the extent to which any clear-up rate, whether local or national, should be used as a measure of police work outcomes. The basic invalidity of this statistic for the purpose of internal or external monitoring is fully recognized by the police. . . .

A recent review of research into the relationship between police work and crime, by Clarke and Hough (1984), confirms that clear-up rates bear little relationship to the realities of detective work and are not an appropriate measure of police effectiveness. Most detective work is concerned with relatively routine burglary and theft, where the investigation is either straightforward (because the offender is caught red-handed or directly implicated from the start) or very unpromising (Clarke and Hough 1984, p. 9). Available research suggests that 'increases in detective manpower and technological improvements yield only marginal gains in clear-up rates'. It seems much more likely that trends in clear-up rates are directly affected by changes in the balance between *prima facie* detectable and undetectable crimes amongst those recorded by the police (Clarke and Hough 1984, pp. 11–12).

Widening the consideration of police effectiveness from clear-up rates to the generally assumed crime preventive function of police patrol does not enable any more optimism about the appropriateness of the statistics to the performance of police work. After a thorough review of the research evidence, from Britain and overseas (especially North America), on the effectiveness of both general and specialized police patrols, of criminal investigation and community policing, Morris and Heal (1981) concluded—'At the risk of some over-simplification the message most obviously to be drawn from this review is that it is beyond the ability of the police to have a direct effect on a good deal of crime' (Morris and Heal 1981, p. 49). Similarly, Clarke and Hough (1984) agree that there is little evidence that increasing the number or frequency of foot or car patrols actually reduces crime. . . . The apparent failure of traditional measures of police effectiveness to reflect any direct impact by the police on crime levels has led to a reassessment not only of the adequacy of the measures themselves but of the appropriateness of a monolithic view of the police function in simple crime control terms. Thus, among the legitimate and desirable roles for the police in this broader conception of their crime-related task, Morris and Heal emphasized police responsibility for alleviating the community's *fear of crime* 'which in practice may be only loosely related to the actual level of crime occurring, and is possibly more socially harmful,' and also their important role in *victim support*, since for the victim 'the aftermath of the incident may well be more distressing than the incident itself' (Morris and Heal 1981, p. 52). . . . The material that has already come from the British Crime Survey on public perceptions of crime risk and the actual rates of crime victimization provides a good example of the way regular statistics could be used to produce a different 'consumer-oriented' angle upon overall police effectiveness and public satisfaction. . . .

Information on the proportion of offenders proceeded against each year for breach of court order is of some significance in its own right, because it shows how 'successful' sentencers are in selecting offenders who will abide by statutory conditions and/or how 'successful' probation officers appear to be in inducing clients to behave in accordance with expected norms of behaviour. It does however introduce a somewhat unfortunate comparative or competitive dimension vis-à-vis the breach rate of different measures, *as if* identical offenders are given each sentence, so that any difference in outcome can be attributed to the merits or deficiencies of the particular measure and the way in which it is administered, like medicine to a group of clones. This comparative obsession also ignores the 'negotiable' element inherent in most breach proceedings, as well as the different statutory criteria that can count as grounds for proceedings. . . . The most that can be said of breach statistics is that they superficially monitor some aspects of the officially recognized misbehaviour of those on whom court orders are made or licences granted. Beyond that, speculation unfettered reigns.

A similar situation obtains with respect to the Prison Department's statistics of reconvictions of those who have served sentences of imprisonment. The central point that bears repetition here is that the value and proper use of statistics depend wholly on what *purposes(s)* the

user has in mind. Most of those who are interested in reconviction rates want to be able to see whether one sentence is 'better' than another in this respect, or whether the 'success rate' of a particular type of sentence has changed over time. There is no way in which the information currently available in regularly published statistics can provide adequate answers to these questions. The dedicated enquirer must delve into special research studies or other 'one-off' Home Office analyses, and will only then begin to discern the complexities of the problem and the essential tentativeness of the conclusions. . . .

Continued doubts about research methods in this area, and an increased fashion for retribution as a penal purpose, has resulted in widespread scepticism in many quarters about the capacity of any sentence to change the future behaviour of an offender significantly more or less than any other sentence. Thus, the current edition of *The Sentence of the Court* (3rd edn. 1978), after summarizing the results of this evaluative research, concludes that 'research studies have almost unanimously failed to show that any one type of sentencing measure is more likely to achieve reform than any other' (Home Office 1978a, para 291). We think such a conclusion is overstated, and that a much more open-minded approach is necessary. The 'nothing works' pessimism of the 1970s was premature. On matters methodological, at least one extremely good prediction instrument (see Nuttall *et al.* 1977) based on sixteen criminal history-social background variables is in current use in the administration of the parole scheme, and has wider applicability (Sapsford 1978). On substantive grounds, *both* Home Office studies of the reconviction of paroled prisoners (Nuttall *et al.* 1977, Home Office 1978) *suggest* that parole may reduce the likelihood of reconviction. This is not conclusive, since explanations other than the effect of supervision and threat of recall to prison are possible, which well-designed research should address. . . . Most fundamentally, we have been much too inclined to behave in evaluation as though all prisons, all probation officers and all community service tasks had the same impact on people. Greater differentiation among sanctions in the same nominal category is necessary. . . .

Research has continued into patterns of reconviction, albeit generally in ways which do not address the question of the effectiveness of sanctions in reducing reconviction. There has been an interesting shift of focus towards a 'criminal career' perspective. Although this perspective is unlikely to become incorporated as a regular feature of official statistics, which are largely *offence* oriented rather than *offender* oriented, there are signs of a developing interest within the Home Office that might result in regular supplementary criminal career data being produced, in a similar way to that in which British Crime Survey data are being published in parallel with data on officially recorded crime. It is certainly significant that the Home Office Statistical Department is now geared up to consider criminality in this way. Home Office Statistical Bulletin 7/85 examined the criminal careers of those born in 1953, 1958 and 1963. It confirmed that the reconviction rate of those who were first convicted at an early age was generally higher than that of those first convicted later in life, but suggested that the conventional use of a 2-year follow-up period for purposes of reconviction should be reconsidered in the light of evidence

that reconviction rates *after 8 years* were often more than 50% higher than after 2 years (Home Office 1985b, para 19). To this our answer is—it all depends on what you want to use them for. If the *relative* risks of reconviction of different groups are the same at 2 years as at 8, there is only a restricted range of purposes for which 8-year rates are preferable.

Reconviction rates of juveniles were found to vary according to the type of sentence imposed, but many of these differences disappeared when the nature of the offence was taken into account. The below average reconviction rates of those fined or given conditional/absolute discharges were found to be attributable to a significant extent to type of offence, but the above average rates for those given supervision were not. Those convicted of burglary were generally more likely to be reconvicted whatever the sentence than those convicted of other types of offence. . . .

A novel feature of this Home Office analysis was its examination of the relationship between the type of first conviction as a juvenile and the probability and type of any second conviction within two years. This information is of direct significance and importance to sentencers, as it enables them to answer such questions as: 'What chance is there of this juvenile offender being convicted of this type of offence within the next two years? What chance is there of his being reconvicted for a different type of offence within the next two years?' . . .

The development of the kind of criminal career information contained in Statistical Bulletin 7/85 provides a valuable model for application to other decision stages in the process which also involve predictive assumptions. These may occur upstream in the process, as in bail/remand in custody decisions, or 'downstream', as in parole decisions (Pease 1985b).

ALTERNATIVE EVALUATIONS OF CRIMINAL JUSTICE

The findings of research into the effectiveness of policing and sentencing have wide implications. They do far more than simply showing the inadequacy of statistics of clear-up rates and patterns of reconviction. When considered alongside the findings of criminological research into the apparent causes and correlates of crime, they offer a crucial insight. This is that criminal justice policy and practice has a strictly limited effect on rates of crime. Increasingly, it is coming to be recognized by those who work in or study the penal services that the impact of the criminal justice system upon crime is marginal. Further, this would continue to be true of any realistically attainable state of criminal justice policy under any tenable theory of criminal behaviour. The problem of what to do about crime and the problem of what to do with convicted criminals are for most practical purposes different problems with different answers. . . .

This conclusion could be seen as having a liberating effect upon those involved in the criminal justice process or concerned about how it ought to be evaluated. No longer need one feel guilty about the inability to interpret the technicalities of reconviction rates and follow-up periods, or the convoluted mathematics of North American studies of the general deterrent effect of sentencing. If it were seen as comforting, the reader should pause. A

criminal justice system stripped of utilitarian purpose might in fact end up a system bereft of humanity. And a recognition that the treatment of criminals is largely irrelevant to the amount of crime is different from an assertion that treating criminals in ways which would make the marginal differences should not be a penal purpose. . . .

The role of criminal statistics in the evaluation of these alternative objectives or criteria varies. Any assessment of the *humanity* of the criminal justice process must ultimately remain a matter of values, but the state of affairs disclosed by many descriptive statistics may have a considerable influence on any public debate about the humanity of the process. Examples of the kind of statistics which are likely to be very relevant in this debate include the general level of the use of custody as a penal sanction, and the degree of security imposed upon those imprisoned; the extent of overcrowding and cell-sharing in prisons; the use of discipline and prescribed drugs in prison; the sanctions for breaching the non-offence conditions of sentences or statutory licences (e.g. recall of parolees or life sentence prisoners); the length of time awaiting trial, and so on.

Similarly, the concept of '*fairness*' must inevitably rest on perceptions and principles. This has given rise to the wide-ranging philosophical, ethical and empirical controversy about what is entailed in a criminal justice system that claims to reflect a 'justice-model' approach. Once again, however, data from official sources can provide a helpful starting point for fundamental questions about fairness and consistency to be raised. In fact there is the probability that any debate about justice will be sterile which is not informed by information about extant inequalities and their determination as justified or unjustified. There are many examples of disparity and variation in the criminal justice process, which suggest *prima facie* evidence of unfairness. They invariably require more detailed research to test initial impressions. Among the most significant variations, of which many have been discussed in earlier chapters, are those related to the grant of bail by police and magistrates courts, the police decision to caution or prosecute, the grant of legal aid, entering guilty pleas, conviction, sentence and release from custody. While statistics of these decisions can rarely be conclusive proof of unfairness or injustice when taken alone, they can often suggest areas for further enquiry. . . .

Information on the relevant *economic costs*, both direct and indirect, of different penal sanctions, can be found scattered around a number of Government publications, but rarely in a form that enables easy comparisons. A short-lived attempt was made by the Home Office to bring together some limited comparative data on the relative expenditure on the four areas of criminal justice for which it is responsible, in a valuable series of statistical publications that was discontinued after only two years—on economic grounds! (see Home Office 1979b). This analysis showed that throughout the period 1971/2 to 1977/8 the police accounted for about three-quarters of all Home Office expenditure on the criminal justice system; prisons accounted for about 15% of total expenditure; and the administration of justice for about 8%. Total expenditure on the probation service was much smaller than for any of the other three services (Home Office 1979b, pp. 73–77). . . .

HAVE CRIME STATISTICS A FUTURE?

In view of the constant criticisms levelled against official statistics by politicians, practitioners, and, not least, academics, this question does need to be asked, if only for us to put on record our unequivocal belief in the importance of *more* routine statistical information, not less, and the wider (which also means cheaper) dissemination of what is published to the public, in whose name the criminal justice system exists and to which that system ought to be directly accountable. Putting the question another way, what would future debate on criminal justice policy and practice be like *without* routine statistics? In England and Wales we have an array of official statistical publications that, despite their limitations, provide an unrivalled basis on which to develop a more informed climate of public debate and political action. Although some would argue that we had to wait far too long for the first national crime victimization survey, there is no doubt that with its eventual arrival in 1982 the British Crime Survey has added a new dimension to our knowledge about crime, victimization, police recording practice and public attitudes towards and perceptions of crime. . . .

Simple descriptive studies can sometimes have a powerful influence that their lack of technical or theoretical complexity may at first belie—consider, for instance, the important effect upon public attitudes towards capital punishment of basic information about the 'typical' murderer as someone caught up in a stressful domestic situation to which no other solution is seen but a tragic murder—suicide attempt, or the important message from research that most house burglaries involve only quite modest financial losses and no violence by the burglar, and happen during the day. These episodes are completely unlike the stereotype of media reports and pub conversation.

As we have seen, statistics of decision-making in criminal justice can often stimulate further investigation into apparent disparities, which can in turn be measured against a variety of possible yardsticks such as fairness, humanity or effectiveness. Decisions are made by people and are about people—which the form in which statistics are collected tends to conceal—hence the welcome which should be accorded to perspectives in which the *person* is the central unit of analysis, as in data on criminal careers, victimization surveys, and studies of the fear of crime. Just as we should not allow statistics to make us forget the people behind the numbers, neither should we allow ourselves to forget the primacy of objectives, principles and policies. The value of statistical information can only be assessed against the objectives it is meant to reach and the principles and policies which inform its scope and focus. At virtually every stage of the criminal process, the final stumbling block to a coherent evaluation of current practice is that objectives and principles remain unarticulated. However the very existence of routine information allows one to infer these partially, and to challenge their areas of ambiguity. Until principles are fully clarified, the task of full assessment remains impossible, and any search for consistency can achieve only the empty shell of unprincipled uniformity.

NO

Bruce Jackson

CRIMINAL NUMBERS

INDICATORS

All public institutions and all private corporations ratify their legitimacy with entries in account books designed to indicate to the bill payers or stockholders that a fine job is being done by all. Corporations have a simple indicator of success: does the bottom line of the account book show a profit or a loss? Public institutions develop indicators of success based on changing definitions of needed services. Their business is process, not product, and there is no bottom line to a process.

Their indicators of performance are sometimes dubious inventions. One reason, as I shall discuss in more detail later, is that the definition of function imposed on public institutions from without is often totally unmeasurable within, so the managers have no way to link worker performance with outside goal. What they do, therefore, is work very hard at developing institutional behaviors that *are* measurable. Not infrequently, they try to prove to outsiders that those internally measured behaviors mean something. A public institution comes into being because of a perceived social problem or need. Often, there is no way for an institution to measure accurately its absolute effectiveness. The one thing the institution can measure perfectly is its level of being busy. It then tries to conceptualize its mission in terms of its measurable busy-work.

At the heart of all public institutional budgets is the annual statistical accounting of work done, of services rendered. . . .

Three sets of numbers turn up in most discussions of crime, law enforcement, and corrections: the crime rate (or crimes known to police), crimes cleared by arrest (the CBA), and recidivism rates. These purport to describe the amount of criminal predation upon society, the effectiveness of police,

From Bruce Jackson, *Law and Disorder: Criminal Justice in America* (University of Illinois Press, 1984). Copyright © 1984 by the University of Illinois Press. Reprinted by permission.

and the effectiveness of corrections. The numbers or rates form the basis of most law enforcement appropriations; their apparent pattern forms the basis for most changes in the criminal law. Law enforcement and correctional officials, and opponents of law enforcement and correctional agencies and institutions, regularly use these numbers and rates as the bases of their arguments.

Few criminal justice workers or administrators believe those numbers and rates mean anything at all. They are merely something one offers in an argument, something one includes in an appeal or an explanation or a description. They are not taken seriously because each number or rate is subject to enormous variation based not on changes in behavior of crooks, changes in success by cops, or changes in effectiveness by correctional agencies but, rather, on changes in fashion, mood, interest, time, money, politics, and convenience. . . .

Citizens' groups, newspapers, politicians—none of them wants to deal with complexities, ambiguities, multivariate analyses; they want *results*. They want a bottom line. Crimes rates, crimes cleared by arrest, recidivism rates—these appear to be results. They may be as close to results as the criminal justice agencies can claim to get.

For criminal justice agents, long-term solutions to the kinds of problems that create crime are impractical. They can't influence them. A change in the bank robbery rate is more a function of the number of branch banks and ease of parking near the branches than a change in proclivity of thieves to hit banks in the first place. A doubling of auto theft reports may mean people are more likely to steal cars, but it also reflects the fact that there are more cars on the road to be stolen and more people in the age group most likely to steal cars. The police can do nothing about the opportunity aspect of crime except keep score.

Some preventive measures can be taken, but their effects stabilize very quickly, and crime continues. Streets may be given better lighting, citizens may be encouraged to purchase and use burglar alarms, autos may be built with steering wheel locks, and citizens who leave keys in unattended cars may be subject to heavy fines. There is little evidence that such preventive measures decrease the number of criminals running around or the total number of crimes going on. The only thing that can be said for sure is that when such measures are put into effect, the criminals tend to steal something or somewhere else. . . .

The most important statistic to a police agency is the one describing crimes cleared by arrest, not the crimes reported. The number of crimes reported has little to do with what the police do; reporting depends on other matters, other concerns. The way one knows the police are doing their job is by looking at how many crooks get caught. The police need crooks to prove to themselves and others that they are doing a worthwhile job. . . .

We still believe in the notion that the marshal's real job is getting the bad guy. Even though only a fifth or less of a modern police department's time and effort goes to crime control (the rest goes to various service functions), it is the crime rate that gets the public excited and the crime clearance rate the police use to assuage that excitement. . . .

Crime statistics—crimes known to police, crimes cleared by arrest, recidivism—are only occasionally unambiguous descriptions of human behavior. They are always political statements.

CRIME RATES

Crime rates—for a city, county, state, region, or the country as a whole—are generally based on the seven "Index" offenses tallied annually by the FBI. These are homicide, robbery, burglary, aggravated assault, forcible rape, larceny $50 and over, and motor vehicle theft. These are selected not because they accurately reflect the amount of crime going on—they don't—but because FBI statisticians decided they are the crimes most likely to be reported to police by citizens, and most likely to be reported to the FBI by local police.

Arson is one of the most costly property crimes in America now, but it doesn't appear in the Index at all.* There are too many variables for it to be of interest. The amount of arson known to police depends on the kind of communication between police and fire inspectors. . . .

"Knowing a fire was caused by arson is easy," said one fire investigator. "You can usually tell that just by looking at it. And knowing that there is just one person or group of persons standing to profit from the arson is easy to find out too. But if we don't catch one of them with a can of gasoline or something like that, we don't have a case. They say, 'Somebody hated me and burned down my building.' And the insurance company has to pay." Most arson investiga-

*[Arson has been included as Part I offenses in the UCR along with homicide, rape, robbery, assault, burglary, larceny, and motor vehicle theft. We appreciate Dr. Richard A. Wright of the University of Scranton for pointing out this omission in the first edition.—Ed.]

tions, for that reason, are terminated early, and the police stay out of them. Arson is widespread, expensive, and dangerous, but it doesn't affect the appearance of criminal behavior given by any of the major criminal justice indicators.

What distinguishes the FBI's Index crimes more than anything else is that they can be counted. The total crimes reported and the crime rates derived from those reports do not represent actual crime rates—they merely represent crime reporting rates. A number of surveys have demonstrated that the range of discrepancy between actual crimes and crimes reported can be extensive.

The FBI statisticians depend on accurate and honest reporting of crimes by local police agencies, since those agencies are the source of the numbers tabulated in the *Uniform Crime Reports*. To get some idea of how representative were the *UCR* indicators, the 1966 President's Commission on Law Enforcement and Administration of Justice requested victimization studies by the National Opinion Research Council. Some of the differences in victimization rates were significant. . . .

The NORC study was based on individuals reporting their own victimizations, so there are no homicide victims; the respondents gave the information to interviewers who selected them at random, so the NORC responses include individuals who elected for whatever reason *not* to report their victimization to police. The FBI's estimate of crimes against property differed from NORC's by a factor of 26 percent. More startling is the difference in crimes against the person: 124 percent. NORC interviewers found a rape rate almost three times the rate derived from local police reports.

Other victimization studies have produced different dimensions of discrepancy, but all indicate a larger number of unreported crimes. . . .

Police say all crimes should be reported. Even if they can't do anything about the immediate injury, the patterns of information developed might help them do preventive work, or might be useful in prosecutions resulting from cases in which the offenders were identified. Victims who don't report their victimization to the police don't take the police rationale for reporting seriously—and the law enforcement people are themselves largely to blame for that. Police have worked hard attempting to prove that Supreme Court decisions such as *Miranda* have "handcuffed" them, and many citizens have come to believe their claims of inefficacy.

Often, previous experiences reporting incidents to police result in a decision to avoid future reports except when insured property is involved. (A report to the police is a requirement for submitting a claim to the insurance company.) . . .

Balancing the changing reasons people have for not reporting crimes against the changing reasons they have for reporting them is difficult. Police think that the incidence of rape has increased significantly in the past few decades, for example, but they think that the incidence of *reporting* rape has increased at an even greater rate. Women, they say, are now more willing than ever before to seek criminal sanctions against their attackers. They ascribe the change to the women's movement, which has taken much of the stigma off the victim, and also to changing sexual mores. . . .

The evidence for the increase in rape *reporting* is only impressionistic. Surveys directed toward discovering unreported crime, in fact, show relatively little difference in rape reporting over the past decade. . . . Are more rapes happening or are more rapes being reported? Are more rapes being reported or are more rape reports being recorded? There is, presently, no way to document accurately the degree or even the direction of change.

It's not all relative, it's not all a matter of statistical manipulation: real crimes occur, large numbers of citizens are hurt and suffer personal and financial loss. In 1981 the FBI listed 13,290,256 Index crimes: 22,516 murders, 81,536 forcible rapes, 575,134 robberies, 643,720 aggravated assaults, 3,739,821 burglaries, 7,154,541 larceny-thefts, and 1,073,988 motor vehicle thefts (*UCR—1981*:39). The 1981 murder rate per 100,000 persons was 9.8 (in 1976 it was 8.8). . . .

In theory, these numbers tell us how vulnerable we are to crime or to certain kinds of crime. In fact, they tell us nothing of the kind.

Consider murder, which is a fairly unambiguous event. Though a few murders go undetected, most authorities insist that the number of undetected murders is small. Hiding a body is difficult, and few people have the technical expertise to kill someone and make it look accidental or natural. Such things happen, but not often. Police are not likely to underreport murders. A rape may enter the records as an assault, a robbery as a larceny, a motor vehicle theft as nothing at all. But a body with a gunshot wound to the back of the head is hard to downgrade. Gangland killings in which bodies are hidden forever in lonely fields or on the bottom of the sea in cement blocks occur more often in fiction than in real life. With all the spouses and lovers killing one another, the drinking buddies killing other drinking buddies, and the petty thugs shooting down liquor store or corner market clerks, organized criminals just don't figure significantly in the murder rates.

According to the *UCR*, 9.8 out of every 100,000 Americans died of murder in 1981—or, to avoid partial persons, about one person in every 10,000 was a murder victim. That does not mean *you* have one chance in 10,000 of dying by murder. If you are a young black male, the odds against you are far worse; if you are a middle-aged white female, the odds against you are far better. The death-by-murder rate for nonwhite males 30 years of age in 1981 was 123.2; the rate for white females of the same age was 3.8: the black male was 32 times more likely to die of murder in that year than the white female. . . .

Of all murders, 42.4 percent are *known* to have resulted from arguments. The other situations involve robbery (17.2 percent), drugs (10.4 percent), sex (1.4 percent), other felonies (3.6 percent), suspected felonies (5.5 percent); there is no information at all about the other 20 percent. If the same distribution holds as for the known cases, then more than half of all murders result from arguments.

The relationship of the murderer to the victim was not known in 29.6 percent of the cases. Of the others, family members were the killers 21 percent of the time and acquaintances were the killers 37.9 percent of the time; strangers were the killers only 15.5 percent of the time (*UCR—1981*:11–12). . . .

What does all this mean in practical terms? First, it tells us that most murders cannot be prevented by police work, since the killers are rarely nefarious thugs but are instead drinking pals, wives, children, co-workers. Second, it tells us that the paranoia many middle-class whites feel about rising murder rates is misplaced: they are far more at risk from the cake of soap in their shower or their family automobile than they are from any of the imaginative army of killers they've learned about while watching television.

One can qualify murder rates even further. Some observers are convinced that blacks and Latin-Americans have been underreported in censuses for many years. Some Texas census takers, for example, were instructed to list as white any individuals they knew about but did not see. If they got information that a family not available for interview contained five members, the five were entered as whites unless the source of information identified them as nonwhites. All parents and children in mixed marriages, unless an informant offered specific contradictory information, were listed as whites. Such underreporting has obvious political consequences: court orders requiring equal opportunity hiring and school access are often based on the assumed ethnic makeup of a community. A shift of 10 percent of the blacks and Mexican-Americans into the white column in Texas makes a 20 percent difference in the hiring and busing equations. It also significantly *increases* the crime rates in the black and Mexican-American communities. If the census reports 100,000 blacks in a community where there are really 125,000 blacks, the black crime rate is inflated by 20 percent. Right now, no one knows how many blacks and other nonwhites live in America, so none of the crime rates ascribed to them are reliable—not even the apparently obvious rate for murders.

Rates over a period of time might not tell us very much either. Murder rates increased in the 1960s and the first half of the 1970s; then they held steady for a while, and in 1981 and 1982 they declined steadily. Does this mean that Americans were more violent for a while and then became less violent? Probably not—at least not if one checks out population statistics for the same years. . . . The surge and subsequent decline in violent crime were paralleled by a surge and decline in the portion of the population in the age groups most likely to perpetrate and suffer violent crime. In the same period changes in the economy further complicated the distributions. . . .

What all this suggests is that among the population most at risk for death by homicide or most likely to commit homicide, the actual rate may *not* have been increasing at all. Presently, no one knows for sure. The only numbers that are clear and unambiguous in relation to murder, the most clear and unambiguous of the Index crimes, are the broad overall tallies—the deaths by homicide broken down by geography, season, sex, age, and race of victim, and sometimes of the killer as well. All the other rates are also subject to clarification, argument, refinement, and question. The information necessary to make those rates meaningful is rarely available, and the information that is available doesn't tell us much. The most striking thing about the available information, the only certain thing about it, is its availability.

The largest single category of offense in the Index is Larceny-Theft. Its frequency began to decline in the early 1980s; before that it had increased consistently for four decades. From 1972 to 1976 it increased 51 percent. The 1976 total of 6,270,800 offenses represented a net increase of 4.9 percent over 1975, and the rate of 2,921.3 represented an increase of 4.2 percent over 1975; by 1981 the total of offenses had reached 7,154,541 and the rate of victimization was 3,122.3. Clearly a crime on the rise. Or is it?

If we take 1967 as a base year with a cost of living of $100 per month, the cost of living was $116.3 in 1970 and $246.8 in 1980 (according to *Standard and Poor's Statistical Service*, 1980). In 1980, $247 provided approximately the same lifestyle as did $100 per week in 1967. The price of most things—food, cars, silverware, rings, books—more than doubled, but the lower level of thefts included by the FBI in this Index category remained $50. Thefts that would have been petty larceny in constant dollars became grand larceny because of inflation. A significant portion of the rising crime rate was created by the increase in the cost of living, not by any increase in absolute value of goods stolen or by any increase in criminal activity. Some states have taken cognizance of the change and have increased the lower limit for grand larceny—New York now sets it at $250—but the state's law enforcement agencies still forward to the FBI reports of thefts of goods valued at more than $50. If the crime rates in this category were defined in terms of constant dollars, we might have some sense of the real rate of theft increase. Instead, government statistics imply that a man who steals $50 in 1983 is committing a more serious offense than a man who stole $49 in 1935. The decreasing value of $50 in constant terms has increased the range of thefts fitting the "larceny-theft over $50" category. . . .

The editors of *Sourcebook—1981* offered an estimate of vehicle theft rates based on numbers of vehicles in service. They used theft data from the FBI (even though all victimization studies indicate that *UCR* reports underestimate actual theft rates), registration data from the Federal Highway Administration, and information analyses prepared by the Insurance Information Institute. Their figures show a steady *decline* in the national auto theft rate based on 100,000 vehicles: 813 in 1969, 811 in 1971, 713 in 1973, 719 in 1975, 651 in 1977. There was a slight rise to 688 thefts per 100,000 vehicles in 1979 (*Sourcebook—1981*:323), but the rate seems to have dropped again in 1980 and 1981.

Rates of arrest for motor vehicle crimes aren't much help either. Most auto thieves are under 18 (*Sourcebook—1981*: 341), but the arrest rates are not corrected for population bulges. We don't know if the individuals responsible for most car thefts—kids joyriding—are doing it more or less frequently. We don't know if certain segments of the juvenile offender population are more likely than others to engage in this particular crime, and therefore we don't know if the same kind of distortion Silberman argues is introduced by the increase in lower-income children is responsible for the increase in motor vehicle thefts. The *UCR* numbers don't tell us how many stolen vehicles are returned an hour or day later and how many are stripped for parts.

Even if criminal activity had not increased in recent years, certain technological changes would have produced the appearance of increasing rates anyway. One crime that has increased significantly is assault connected with domestic disputes—a couple fights, police are called, someone is arrested. How much of that increase is based on increased household violence and how much on better police access? The introduction of the 911 calling system in New York in 1969, which gave immediate access to police dispatchers to anyone with a phone and a dime (some public phones didn't even require the dime), certainly increased reporting rates. Equally—or more—important is the increase in the number of private telephones. In 1945 there were 1,964,000 private telephones in New York; in 1960 there were 6,088,000; and by January 1980 the number had risen to 9,461,938—an increase of 55 percent over 1960 and 382 percent over 1945. The impact of that increase in household telephones on the apparent crime rate is profound.

Without a telephone, reporting a household fight or a suspicious person required that one drive or walk to a telephone to call the police. . . . It wasn't until the mid-1950s that all police cars had two-way radios, so the police dispatcher would have to send a car all the way from the police station, or wait for a patrol office to call in from a box and ask if anything needed doing. . . . If the police came, they were as likely to find the participants sitting around the kitchen table having a beer and tending their wounds as anything else. The prowler might have drifted far away.

These are not unimportant calls. Police say that domestic disputes are their most dangerous assignments; some think more policemen are killed and injured answering them than any other kind of call. (Actually, most police deaths occur on robbery calls; "disturbance" calls are second. *Sourcebook—1981*:326.) The rate of policemen killed on the job has also gone up in the past 40 years. How much of the increase in domestic violence is a real increase in violent behavior and how much merely reflects the increase in police accessibility? Does the rising number of policemen killed answering such calls reflect an increase in America's violence or an increase in the number of policemen arriving on the scene before the violence that has always been there has had time to work itself out? The introduction of New York's central 911 system was accompanied by increases in reported robberies of 400 percent and in reported burglaries of 1,300 percent (Glaser, 1975:23). Surely the crooks didn't kick into overdrive to celebrate the new communications network.

Some changes in Index crime rates reflect changing attitudes within criminal justice agencies toward certain ethnic or economic groups. In earlier years the victimization of the poor was generally underreported, in part because the police didn't much care and in part because the poor didn't bother calling for help they were sure would not come. . . .

Some increases may represent nothing more than a shifting of criminal activity to areas of increasing opportunity. Bank robberies rose 59 percent between 1977 and 1981 (UCR—1981:17): more people were robbing more banks, obviously. But the meaning of the increases is not so obvious. Banks, as Willie Sutton used to say, are where the money is. The shift in America to a credit card economy has reduced the likely haul in many places that a decade ago could be counted on to have a good deal of cash on hand at the end of a business day. Motels and gas stations may have a small fortune in signed credit slips but very little green money in the cash register; delivery trucks carry no cash, bus drivers often can't change a dollar. Liquor stores still have money, and so do neighborhood grocery stores and banks—and these three businesses have experienced the greatest rise in robberies. The physical nature of banks has changed, making them more attractive to thieves. Instead of large imposing institutions located in the heart of town, most banks now are small places, located in shopping centers with convenient parking lots and easy access to nearby roads and highways. . . .

The Index crimes, curiously, give no sense at all of the real magnitude of the financial costs of crime in America. Losses of the kind reported in the Index are the smallest portion of criminal take-offs. Storeowners lose far more every year to employee pilferage than they do to armed robbers or check forgers; the public loses more money every year because of industrial price fixing than it does because of junkie crime. One white-collar criminal or one moderately unethical executive can take off more in one deal than a dozen competent and dedicated safecrackers can in a lifetime. We know a fair amount about the costs of the physical injuries received in violent crimes, but we know very little about the costs in human health of poisoning by illegal dumpers of toxic wastes.

The 1966 President's Crime Commission estimated the annual loss to robbers at $27 million, and the annual loss to burglars at $271 million (*Crime and Its Impact—An Assessment*, 1967:46), but the estimate for the cost of fraud was $1.3 *billion*, the cost of illegal gambling $7 *billion*, and the annual estimated loss because of drunk driving was set at $1.8 billion (p. 43n).

The crime rates don't tell us where the money is being lost, and they don't tell us where the dangers really lurk. They tell us precious little about the kinds of risks really out there. They are compendious and specific, they are expensive to produce and fearful to read. But they are, by and large, documents in default: they are collected, collated, published, and distributed not because of what they have to say but because no one yet knows where to go for the information that really does need saying. Crime occurs, citizens are worried, officials feel they must say something. The crime statistics are what they say. They are a lot of sound, a lot of fury, and only rarely do they signify anything at all.

POSTSCRIPT

Are Official Statistics Meaningful?

Do Bottomley and Pease lose the argument about the scientific validity of criminological and criminal justice statistics to the caustic Bruce Jackson? Few criminologists are about to abandon their use of statistics because they are simply too important to ignore. In spite of its merits, to embrace Jackson's thinking would be "to throw the baby out with the bath water."

There are many who agree with Jackson's pessimism but who still try to milk statistical crime data as much as possible. For instance, Kevin Wright's third chapter, "Confusing Crime Statistics," in *The Great American Crime Myth* (Greenwood Press, 1985) parallels Jackson's concerns.

Most criminologists and criminal justice researchers, however, are considerably more sympathetic toward official data. Efforts are made to refine and strengthen official data analysis. Leslie T. Wilkins, a preeminent statistician and criminologist, argues in several books and articles for refining official statistics in order to make better national and international comparisons. Among his most recent work is his "Criminal Statistics: National and International," published in *Critique and Explanation*, edited by R. A. Silverman and T. F. Hartnagel (Transaction Books, 1986).

Other works attempt to identify deficiencies in existing crime statistics in order to correct them. *The Use, Nonuse, Misuse of Applied Social Research in the Courts,* edited by M. J. Saks and C. H. Baron (ABT Books, 1978), is a good example of this genre. Gordon P. Waldo, editor, addresses other, more technical problems in his *Measurement Issues in Criminal Justice* (Sage, 1983), as do Michael Gottfredson and Travis Hirschi in their article "Methodological Adequacy of Longitudinal Research on Crime," *Criminology* 25:5 (August 1987). Longitudinal research is studying over time certain aspects of crime or criminals instead of the more common cross-sectional research done at one point in time.

R. M. O'Brien et al. in "Empirical Comparison of the Validity of UCR and NCS Crime Rates," *Sociological Quarterly* (Summer 1980), provide a fairly typical study of this kind. Others focus on a specific problem area and voice real concerns about data such as found in Joel Best's "Missing Children, Misleading Statistics," *Public Interest* (Summer 1988).

Classic texts that are helpful in many courses include Hans Zeisel's *Say It with Figures* (Harper & Row, 1957) and D. Huff's humorous *How to Lie with Statistics* (Norton, 1955). A current textbook that will help you to separate the wheat from the chaff in both official and other criminological and criminal justice statistics and reports is *Research Methods and Statistics: A Primer for Criminal Justice and Related Sciences*, by R. J. Hy, D. G. Feig, and Robert M. Regoli (Anderson, 1983). See also *Measuring Crime: Large Scale, Long-Range Effects*, edited by D. L. Mackenzie et al. (State University of New York Press, 1990). A vital resource for you in your journey into criminal justice scholarship and an eventual career is the massive Bureau of Justice Statistics reports. These are outstanding surveys of most areas of criminal justice, and they are mailed free of charge. Get on their list and begin requesting studies by writing to the U.S. Department of Justice, Bureau of Justice Statistics, Box 6000, Rockville, MD 20850.

ISSUE 6

Is Crime Getting Worse?

YES: Elliott Currie, from *Confronting Crime: An American Challenge* (Pantheon, 1985)

NO: Kevin N. Wright, from *The Great American Crime Myth* (Greenwood Press, 1985)

ISSUE SUMMARY

YES: University of California criminal justice researcher Elliott Currie compares the U.S. rate of violent crimes with those of other industrial nations and concludes that both the reality and the threat of crime are escalating.
NO: State University of New York criminal justice administration professor Kevin N. Wright counters that the so-called crime wave is a creation of the mass media and that the claim of an increasing rate of crime is a major myth of criminology.

Criminologists and criminal justice researchers have known all along that "crime waves" are often manufactured, sometimes accidentally, sometimes deliberately. For instance, the installation of telephones in an impoverished neighborhood that formerly had few or no telephones could result almost instantaneously in tripling crime rates—simply a consequence of the greater ease of calling in a complaint.

A new beat patrol officer who has less tolerance for neighborhood gambling could double the arrests simply by "cracking down" on activities that previous officers had ignored. The insistence of a new precinct captain that *all* citizen complaints be recorded could easily double the number of crimes in that precinct. In each of these cases, the "real" crime rate probably has not changed at all but the introduction of a new technology, an eager officer, or even a new bookkeeping system can create the impression of rapidly rising crimes.

But crime rates do vary over time, sometimes increasing in certain categories and sometimes decreasing. Frequently, the changes are due to social factors over which the criminal justice system has no control. For example, demographic shifts (such as a decrease in the population between the ages of 15 and 25 or an increase in the number of residents of urban areas) could account for changes. Even a downshift in the economy could result in crime increases.

Naturally, the actual rates of crime can be, and almost always are, problematic. In researching any category of human behavior, social scientists and criminologists must also take into account both the subjective perceptions and the objective conditions underlying behavior. That is, even if a crime rate is steady, if people *perceive* it as increasing and see the streets as more dangerous at night, then criminal justice administrators have to act accordingly. Thus, the criminologists have the double task of trying to ascertain what the "real rates" of crime are and in what directions they might be going, then to determine the community's perceptions of crime trends. Frequently, the two do not overlap at all. For example, most people have a far greater risk of being assaulted or murdered by someone they know even though they are convinced that most murderers slay strangers.

University of California researcher Elliott Currie argues that both the liberal and conservative approaches to solving the crime problem in the United States have failed. His position is that crime rates have increased significantly within the United States. In addition, he contends that these increases can be controlled and eventually reduced.

Criminologist Kevin Wright dismisses the claims of Currie and many other "nay sayers." After conducting his own careful research as well as reviewing the literature, Wright proposes that the much-broadcasted crime wave lamented by Currie and others is little more than a carefully constructed creation of the mass media.

YES

Elliott Currie

RETHINKING CRIMINAL VIOLENCE

This book is about why there is so much crime in America and what we can do about it. No one living in a major American city needs much convincing that despite more than a decade of ever-"tougher" policies against crime, the United States remains wracked by violence and fear. Criminal violence is woven deeply into our social fabric—a brutal and appalling affront to any reasonable conception of civilized social life.

In recent months, these incidents took place in the United States: In Illinois, armed marauders attacked travelers on an interstate highway, robbing the occupants of two cars and killing a twelve-year-old boy. In Florida, a passing motorist's intervention barely saved a young woman from attack by a crowd of nearly a hundred men. In New York, gangs of youths robbed and beat participants in a charity walkathon in Central Park. In Fort Lauderdale, Florida, a bandit held up an entire church congregation during an evening service. Not far away, near Pompano Beach, two intrepid men broke *into* a prison and robbed two inmates. A United States senator and his companion, on their way to dinner with the mayor of New York, were mugged by two men just down the street from the mayor's mansion. In Los Angeles, eleven people died in a single weekend in episodes of youth-gang violence, while the home of the chief of the Los Angeles Police Department was burglarized—twice.

The public response to criminal violence has become correspondingly bitter and even desperate. Three-fifths of the American public expressed their support for a self-styled vigilante who shot down four young black men after they asked him for five dollars in a New York subway; respected commentators urge people living in cities to "adopt the tough attitudes of an embattled population."

To live in the urban United States in the 1980s is to feel that the elementary bonds of society are badly frayed. The sense of social disintegration is so pervasive that it is easy to forget that things are not the same elsewhere. Violence on the American level comes to seem like a fact of life, an inevitable feature of modern society. It is not. Most of us are aware that we are worse off, in this respect, than other advanced industrial countries. How *much* worse, however, is truly startling.

Criminal statistics are notoriously tricky, and comparisons of one country's statistics with another's even more so. But the differences in national crime rates—at least for serious crimes of violence, which we rightly fear the most—are large enough to transcend the limitations of the data. In recent years, Americans have faced roughly seven to ten times the risk of death by homicide as the residents of most European countries and Japan. Our closest European competitor in homicide rates is Finland, and we murder one another at more than three times the rate the Finns do.

These differences are sometimes explained as the result of America's "frontier" ethos or its abundance of firearms. Both of these are important, but neither even begins to explain the dimensions of these international differences. With similar frontier traditions, Australia and Canada have murder rates that are, respectively, less than a fourth and less than a third of ours. Though their numbers are roughly the same, Californians are murdered almost six times as often as Canadians. Nor does this simply reflect the relative ease with which Americans can obtain handguns: more Californians are killed with knives alone than Canadians are by *all* means put together. And Canada ranks fairly high, internationally, in homicide rates.

What holds for homicide also holds for other serious crimes of violence. Here the comparisons are more chancy, because of greater problems of definition and measurement. But careful research reveals that Americans are more than three times as likely to be raped than West Germans, and six times as likely to be robbed. These rates were derived from police statistics, which are known to be subject to strong biases. But similar results come from "victimization" studies, which calculate crime rates by asking people whether, and how often, they have been the victims of crime.

In the first English study of this kind, the British Home Office (using a sample of eleven thousand respondents) estimated that the British robbery rate in 1981 was about twenty for every ten thousand people over age sixteen in 1981. In the same year, a comparable American survey by the Bureau of Justice Statistics estimated a robbery rate nearly four times higher. The British study turned up not one rape and only a single attempted rape: the American survey estimated an overall rape rate of about ten per ten thousand (three completed, seven attempted). And Britain is by no means one of the most tranquil of European countries: rates of serious criminal violence in Denmark, Norway, Switzerland, and the Netherlands are lower still.

In the severity of its crime rates, the United States more closely resembles some of the most volatile countries of the Third World than other developed Western societies; and we won't begin to understand the problem of criminal violence in the United States without taking that stark difference as our point of departure. Its consequences are enormous. If we were blessed with the moderately low homicide rate of Sweden, we would suffer well under three thousand homicide deaths a year, thereby saving close to sixteen thousand American lives—nearly three times as many as were lost in battle annually, on average, during the height of the Vietnam War.

The magnitude of the contrast between the United States and most other developed societies is often ignored as we scrutinize the fluctuations in our own crime rates from year to year. We watch the state of the public safety, like that of the economy, with a kind of desperate hopefulness. Just as the economy has "recovered" several times in recent years, so we have periodically "turned the corner on crime." And indeed, by the mid-1980s, the level of violent crime had fallen off from the disastrous peak it had reached at the start of the decade. That respite was certainly welcome; but it should not obscure the more troubling general upward trend since the sixties. From 1969 through 1983, the rate of violent crime—as measured by police reports—rose nationwide by 61 percent. Rape went up 82 percent, robbery 44 percent, and homicide 14 percent (the first two figures are almost certainly inflated because of changes in reporting, the third probably not). Measured this way, the more recent declines have only returned us to the already horrendous levels of the late 1970s, just before we suffered one of the sharpest *increases* in criminal violence in American history. Still more disturbingly, reported rapes and aggravated assaults *rose* again in 1984—at the fastest pace since 1980. Criminal victimization surveys offer a somewhat different but scarcely more encouraging picture, indicating virtually no change in crimes of violence for the past decade, with a slight decline in many violent crimes in 1983—but a slight *rise* in others in 1984.

The recent dip in crime, moreover, has been ominously uneven. Between 1982 and 1983; the murder rate in the economically depressed states of Illinois and Michigan rose by 10 percent; reported rapes shot up by 20 percent in Michigan and 27 percent in Wisconsin. Detroit's murder rate jumped 17 percent from 1981 to 1983; that of East St. Louis, Illinois, by an astonishing 96 percent. Drug-related gang wars helped boost the homicide rate in Oakland, California, by 17 percent between 1983 and 1984. The national crime rate, in short, may have improved—but the situation in some ' of America's inner cities was worsening.

What makes all this so troubling is that our high crime rates have resisted the most extraordinary efforts to reduce them. Since 1973, we have more than doubled the national incarceration rate—the proportion of the population locked up in state and federal prisons and in local jails. By 1983, the prison inmates alone would have filled a city the size of Atlanta, Georgia; including the inmates of local jails (a number that jumped by more than a *third* between 1978 and 1982 alone) would have swollen the "city" to the size of Washington, D.C. And this number doesn't include those confined in juvenile detention facilities, military prisons, and psychiatric facilities for the criminally insane.

Nor is this all. We have not only put a record number of offenders behind bars; we have also drastically changed our daily behavior and escalated the level of social resources we devote to defending ourselves against crime. In 1969, the National Commission on the Causes and Prevention of Violence made a gloomy prediction of what urban life would be like if America did not take immediate and fundamental measures to attack the root causes of crime. Central business districts would be surrounded by zones of "accelerated deterioration," largely deserted at night except for police patrols. The affluent would huddle together in what the commission called "fortified cells," high-rise apartment houses and residential compounds protected by increasingly elaborate security devices and private guards. Homes would be "fortified by an array of devices from window grilles to electronic surveillance equipment," and the affluent would speed from these fortified homes to their fortified offices along heavily patrolled expressways that the commission, in a revealingly military euphemism, called "sanitized corridors." People with business in the central cities would require access to indoor garages or valet parking; schools and other public facilities would be patrolled by armed guards. The ghetto slums would be "places of terror" that might be out of police control altogether after dark.

The commission, writing in a more hopeful time, found this prospect of a society in which the haves were forced to defend themselves ever more vigilantly against the have-nots foreign to the American experience and abhorrent to American values. Yet what is striking is that, in the eighties, much of the commission's indignant vision seems almost old-hat. Most of the changes they feared have taken place, and though their scenario doesn't accurately describe *every* American city, it does describe many. Virtually every big-city police department now possesses a sophisticated armory—from the ubiquitous police helicopter to the armored personnel carrier recently acquired by the Los Angeles police. More generally, we have changed the way we live and go about our daily business in ways that would have seemed appalling and unacceptable in the sunnier sixties. In 1984, a New York Appellate Court justice, speaking for an association of judges calling for still more severe prison sentences in that state, declared that the climate of fear suffusing

New York "would have been unthinkable" a generation before. "If then someone had said that in 1984 hundreds of thousands of apartment windows in New York City would be covered with metal gates," said Justice Francis T. Murphy, Jr., "and that private security guards would patrol the lobbies, hallways, and rooftops of apartment buildings, we would have thought him insane." Like the unprecedented increase in incarceration, this new defensiveness might have been expected to do something substantial about the crime rate. With the possible exception of declines in burglary resulting from more elaborate "hardware," it did not.

Our devastating levels of criminal violence, moreover, have also proved to be remarkably resistant to the effects of a benign demographic change. The frightening rise in violent crime in the late 1970s and early 1980s came just when the most volatile segment of the population—young adult and teenaged men—was growing smaller relative to the population as a whole. Between 1975 and 1982, the proportion of young men aged fourteen to twenty-one in the population fell by 10 percent. Other things being equal, as many criminologists argued, this should have brought down the crime rate. But other things weren't equal, for though the decline in the youth population may have kept the crime rate lower than it would have been otherwise, other forces were clearly keeping it up.

What progress we've made against our uniquely high crime rate seems disturbingly small given our massive attempts to control it. The disparity between effort and results tells us that something is clearly wrong with the way we have approached the problem of violent crime in America, and few are happy with the results. But there is no consensus on how we might do better. . . .

If we are serious about rethinking the problem of crime, we need to engage the issues on that higher level of moral and political values. It is always easier, as R. H. Tawney once observed, to "set up a new department, and appoint new officials, and invent a new name to express their resolution" to do things differently. "But unless they take the pains," Tawney cautioned, "not only to act, but to reflect, they end by effecting nothing."

All societies suffer from predatory and brutal behavior. But not many of them—and no other advanced industrial societies (except perhaps South Africa, a revealing but not inspiring example)—suffer it to the extent we do in America. This tells us that the unusual dangerousness of American life is not simply the result of fate or of human nature, but of forces which, within broad limits, are subject to social action and control. We have the level of criminal violence we do because we have arranged our social and economic life in certain ways rather than others. The brutality and violence of American life are a signal—and a particularly compelling one—that there are profound social costs to maintaining those arrangements. But by the same token, altering them also has a price; and if we continue to tolerate the conditions that have made us the most violent of industrial societies, it is not because the problem is overwhelmingly mysterious or because we do not know what to do, but because we have decided that the benefits of changing those conditions aren't worth the costs.

Not all of those changes will be easy. To be sure, some of them are much less difficult than we have lately been led to believe. But others involve reversing institutional patterns whose origins lie far back in our history. I am not suggesting that this could be a simple task, but I hope to show that it is within our means to build a society that is less brutal, less fearful, and more cohesive. Whether we do so is up to us.

NO

Kevin N. Wright

THE OVERDRAMATIZATION
OF CRIME IN AMERICA

To begin unraveling the mystery of crime in the United States, we should consider how public opinion is shaped. Who is responsible for producing information about crime? Some people form their opinions based on actual experiences. They have been attacked, or some possession has been stolen. Yet surveys indicate that fewer than 10 percent of the population report criminal offenses of any kind against them.[1] Americans for the most part draw on secondary sources of information to know how bad crime really is.

The press—in newspapers, television, and magazines—keeps us apprised of the seriousness of the crime problem. A big-city daily newspaper rarely publishes an issue without at least one article about some violent crime committed the previous evening. Syndicated news services, such as the Associated Press (AP) and the United Press International (UPI), allow newspapers to carry not only local stories but also reports of violence throughout the nation.

The broadcasting industry also engages in vigorous crime reporting. During the evening news, viewers are often taken to the scene of a violent crime. Remote capabilities allow us to see a victim being loaded into an ambulance or the police outline on the pavement. Reporters interview investigators, witnesses, and even victims. By bringing violence right into American homes, such dramatic portrayals make crime seem less remote. Beyond the continuing barrage of reports of violent crimes, what may shape public opinion most are the editorials and review articles in which the press informs the public that crime and senseless violence are nearly out of hand. These reports often claim that the dangers on streets and in our homes are greater now than ever before. For example, *Time's* "The Curse of Violent Crime" appeared behind a cover that depicted a surrealistic violent face.[2] And a *Newsweek* cover that had viewers staring into a barrel of a handgun contained an article that said 1981 was the "year that mainstream America rediscovered violent crime," that "people feel it [crime] as an epidemic come to crisis point," that "crime rates have replaced mortgage rates as the favored topic of concern," and that "life now seems pitifully cheap."[3] Even special-topic magazines, which traditionally give no space to crime, now carry stories about the problem. The fashion and glamour magazine *Mademoiselle* published an article entitled "Crime in America: Living Scared."[4] *Glamour*[5] and *McCall's*[6] had similar pieces. The message in these articles rings clear: Violent crime in America has risen to a crisis point. There is no adequate explanation for what is happening, and few pragmatic solutions to the problem exist. . . .

CRIME BOOMS

If these reports leave you with the impression that the nation is on the brink of catastrophe, you should realize it is not the first time that message has been delivered to the American public. The United States has been through supposedly major crime waves every twenty years or so, and more than once Americans have been told that the social order hangs in trembling peril. Speeches by politicians and officials, and the news articles, of the 1920s, the latter part of the 1940s, and the mid-1960s, are identical to those of today. Contemporary news magazines need not employ reporters to write about the present crime wave. They can simply reprint stories written in the 1920s. The titles alone bear striking similarity to those of today:

"Accounting for the Crime Wave" (*Literary Digest*, August 21, 1921)
"The Carnival of Crime in the United States" (*Current History*, a monthly magazine of the *New York Times*, February 1922)
"Cities Helpless in the Grip of Crime" (*Literary Digest*, April 22, 1922)
"What Shall We Do to Stop Crime?" (*Current History*, September 1922)

"The Rising Tide of Crime" (*Literary Digest*, August 15, 1925)

Even the cartoons are similar. One shows Uncle Sam facing a hoodlum labeled "Crime"; the caption states simply "Day After Day."[7] In another, a choking Uncle Sam holds a poison bottle labeled "Crime Record"; the caption reads "Quick, somebody, an antidote!!"[8] But best of all is a cartoon captioned "A New Yorker Starts to Business" in which a wife and daughter, each packing a revolver, bid the well-dressed but heavily armed father good-bye as he leaves for the office.[9] . . .

A growing concern about the problem led the American Bar Association (ABA) at its 1920 convention to appoint a special committee to investigate violence and law enforcement. After a year of study the committee reported: "Since 1890 there has been, and continues, a widening, deepening tide of lawlessness in this country, sometimes momentarily receding, to swell again into greater depth and intensity. At intervals this tide billows into waves that rise and break, but only for a time attracting public attention."[10] . . . The *St. Paul Pioneer Press* stated, "The truth is that the United States is approaching a condition somewhat resembling anarchy, and that unless something practical is done pretty soon it may be too late."[11]

. . . Most large cities—including Indianapolis, Detroit, and Boston—had serious crime problems.[12] One description of life in New York City sounds remarkably similar to what one might read today:

Never before has there existed in this city such a situation as exists today. Never before has the average person, in his place of business, in his home or on the streets, had cause to feel less secure. Never before has a continuous wave of crime given rise to so general a wave of fear.

New York is becoming a community of gun-toters because everybody knows that the police administration has completely broken down, and because the record of crimes of violence is fast growing longer, and murder and robberies are rapidly increasing. . . .

The security of life and the security of property are equally a gamble. If the citizen is lucky he may not be robbed, if he remains lucky he may not be murdered, but it is all a matter of chance.[13]

A frequent complaint of the period was the lack of adequate statistics on the seriousness of the problem, but there was enough information to lead many to conclude that the situation in the United States was the worst in the world. Crimes of violence as well as the number of criminals incarcerated in this nation far exceeded those in France, Germany, England, and Wales. Comparing the crime situation in Chicago with the crime situation in all of Canada, which has a population three times greater, the ABA's Special Commission on Law Enforcement found that Chicago experienced twice as many burglaries and four times as many robberies. . . .[14]

After the 1920s, the scourge of the Great Depression and the weight of World War II temporarily diverted attention from the crime problem. But as veterans returned and Americans tried to reestablish their lives, crime resurfaced as a major urban problem. The 12.4 percent increase in crime in 1945[15] was the largest in history, yet it paled beside the increase of almost twice that in 1946.[16] The situation was described by reporters as the "worst ever" and the "blackest picture." . . .

As Americans settled into the routine of the 1950s, they became accustomed to the postwar levels of crime. Threats from foreign sources overshadowed any worry about domestic public safety. Not until the early 1960s did Americans discover again that they faced a significant crime problem. Crime surged into public consciousness as never before:

"By every measure, America is on the brink of a major crisis in crime." (U.S. News & World Report, August 26, 1963)

"City streets now are more unsafe than ever." (U.S. News & World Report, August 9, 1965)

Observers noted that crime was taking on new features in the 1960s. For the first time it was no longer confined to slums and deprived areas; it had invaded the suburbs.[17] Traditionally protected middle and upper classes faced a danger that had formerly been a disturbing but distant phenomenon. And public parks and transportation systems were no longer safe.[18] . . .

Within its historical context, the current crime problem does not appear to be so new or so frightening. So we see that Crime Myth 1, "Crime is becoming quantitatively and qualitatively worse," is not valid. Others in the past have been quick to predict the imminent destruction of American culture resulting from crime and lawlessness. Given this tendency, we must reevaluate the situation today. Is the crime problem as bad as we think? The United States appears to have gallantly survived other periods when crime supposedly ran wild, public streets became jungles, and violence was rampant. Given this history, one might be justified in suggesting that the mass media are overdramatizing the crime situation.

HOW THE MEDIA DISTORT CRIME INFORMATION

One need not closely scrutinize media reports to find numerous examples of distortions and exaggerations in crime reporting. Newspaper and magazine articles, as well as the evening news, offer illustration after illustration. A few examples will make it clear that overdramatization is the norm rather than the exception in modern crime reporting.

The media distorts its presentation of crime patterns by selecting particular incidents to report. Unusual, bizarre, violent, and macabre incidents receive more media attention. A recent review of research about patterns of crime reporting found that "without exception, violent individual crimes—particularly murders—are represented disproportionately in news media presentations." This was true in Minneapolis; St. Louis; Houston; Chicago; Oslo, Norway; Ontario, Canada; England; and the Netherlands. Typical of these findings is an analysis of the 1976 crime news appearing in the *Chicago Tribune*: "Murder accounted for 26 percent of the specific crimes mentioned; robbery, assault, and rape together accounted for another 20 percent. In contrast, common property crimes (burglary and larceny/theft) accounted for less than 6 percent of the crimes mentioned. Tax cheating, embezzlement, and drunken driving accounted for only 3 percent." These percentages bear no relationship to the percentage of the total number of crimes each actually represents.[19]

Television's prime-time dramatic programming also distorts its image of crime. Between 1958 and 1977, shows featuring crime and law enforcement claimed one-fourth to one-third of prime-time television programming. Other programs, not primarily crime dramas, often portrayed such events. Murder, assault, and armed robberies accounted for 60 percent of the offenses depicted.[20] . . .

Unfortunately, when the media report official statistics, crime seems worse than it actually is. An article by Ted Gest in *U.S. News & World Report* exemplifies how this is done:

> Figures released by the Federal Bureau of Investigation give only a hint of the problem. They show violent crime rising 11 percent in 1980 over 1979. For a true perspective, it is necessary to look back further.
>
> Since 1960, the number of violent crimes in America has more than quadrupled.
>
> In 1980, 23,000 people died at the hands of murderers, up from 9,000 from two decades earlier.
>
> The same year, 82,000 women were raped, up from 17,000 reported in 1960; more than half a million people were robbed, up from 108,000 and 165,000 plus were assaulted, up from 154,000.
>
> During the same 10 years, crimes against property—burglary, larceny and car theft—tripled, causing billions of dollars in losses.[21]

This presentation either reflects a serious misunderstanding of crime statistics or it reflects an attempt to distort information. The use of absolute numbers rather than rates conveys a more pessimistic message about the magnitude of crime. To read that 23,000 murders were committed in 1980 is far more frightening than being told that one person in 10,000 was murdered. Because it reflects population size, a rate is a better indicator of the chances of victimization, yet the author of the article chose to use absolute numbers. He also failed to adjust his statistics for population increases. Even if the rate of victimization remained unchanged because the population grew 25 percent since 1960, the absolute number of crimes would increase by the same proportion. These differences can be of some magnitude. The figures in the article make it appear that murders increased by two and a half times, but in fact the proportion of the population murdered only doubled.[22] Such growth is not comforting, but the article's failure to account for population increases did little to still fears.

Several other issues make the comparison of 1960 figures and 1980 figures difficult. Gest is citing official statistics generated by the FBI each year and reported annually in the Uniform Crime Reports (UCR). Since 1933 the agency has compiled information about criminal offenses reported to local, county, and state law enforcement agencies. Records are maintained for eight primary serious crimes often referred to as Index crimes: murder and non-negligent manslaughter, forcible rape, robbery, aggravated assault, burglary, larceny-theft, motor vehicle theft, and arson. According to the FBI, the figures include all reported crimes "received from the victims, officers who discovered the infraction and other sources" and reflect "actual offenses known regardless of whether anyone was arrested for the crime, the stolen property is recovered, or prosecution is undertaken." When complaints are determined to be unfounded or false, they are deleted from the total count. Monthly reports from local agencies are scrutinized for accuracy and the quality of the data.[23]

During the early 1960s, several articles critical of the FBI were published.[24] Variation in the methods used by different law enforcement agencies across the nation to gather and compile data was found. The data was found to be incomplete. The Uniform Crime Reporting Program responded by improving its reporting methods, thereby producing a more complete set of statistics. The effect was significant. In New York City from 1965 to 1966, the rate of offenses known to the police jumped by 72 percent, but the true increase was estimated to be 6.5 percent.[25] Experts argue that an actual increase in crime occurred during the late 1960s and early 1970s, but they attribute much of the fluctuation in the UCR data to improvements in crime measurement technology. Therefore, when 1960 data and 1980 data are compared, some of the observed growth does reflect an actual increase, but improved reporting accounts for a significant proportion of the increase. Ted Gest did not make his readers aware of this.

Changes in willingness to report crimes also contributed to an increase that was more apparent than real. Efforts to integrate the poor, particularly blacks and other minorities, into mainstream society during the past two decades encouraged a group of citizens who in the past did not report crime to do so. Sociologist Albert Biderman described the phenomenon: "As people who once felt they were outside of the society feel more and more that they are a part of it, and as our law enforcement officials come to judge them by the same standards and give them the same protection as the middle class, we shall go through a period of decreasing crime but of increasing crime statistics. There will not be new crimes, but more recorded crime."[26] Any increase in willingness to mobilize the police to enforce community conduct will be reflected in the FBI data because the UCR records *reported* crime. Ted Gest also failed to make note of this facet of crime data.

The interpretations added to stories also distort the image of crime. *Senseless violence* will be reported as increasing, yet there is no official statistical category for "senseless violence." This kind of media interpretation is usually supported by graphic descriptions of gruesome murders for which no motives seem to exist. Such presentations encourage the conclusion that such crimes are a recent development and suggest that criminals are becoming less rational and more ruthless.

There is no basis for such arguments. History is replete with violent atrocities. The book *Bloodletters and Badmen* by Jay Nash documents this unfortunate aspect of our history. From Burton Abbott, the mild-mannered man executed for the murder of a fourteen-year-old girl, to Abwar Zwillmen, syndicated gangster, Nash recounts a national legacy of "outlaws, thieves, brothel keepers, gangsters, arsonists, rapists, kidnappers, murderers, forgers, embezzlers, bombers, assassins, bank robbers, and hijackers" who have punctuated American history with mayhem since colonial times. Our violent tradition was initiated by John Billington, who became America's first murderer when he ambushed a fellow pilgrim with whom he was feuding. The atrocities today are not worse than the deeds of ax murderess Winnie Ruth Judd in the early 1930s; or Edward Gein, who retained various anatomical parts as trophies of his numerous murders and engaged in cannibalism during the late 1940s and 1950s; or Herman Webster Mudgett, who became America's most prolific murderer by taking the lives of more than two hundred victims in the late nineteenth century.[27]

So senseless violence is not new. Americans have a lengthy history with such bloody acts. In fact, careful inspection of UCR statistics reveals that senseless violence may be decreasing. Stranger-to-stranger murders reported in 1976 accounted for 18.4 percent of the total murders, but by 1981 the percentage had dropped to 15.5 percent. This change suggests that random acts of savagery in which an unknown victim's life is taken are declining.[28]

The mass media tend to impose a negative image of the situation on the public, as sociologist Michael Fisherman documents. The process begins with a series of similar news stories, for instance, a rash of bank robberies or offenses against the elderly. If these incidents are selected for reporting, a pattern may appear. The events need not be unique or indicate an actual change in incidence rates. The key factor is their selection for reporting. Once the stories have appeared, the media need only suggest that there may be a crime wave. At this point, the response of politicians and law enforcement officials becomes important in establishing the trend. Authorities may "augment, modify, or deny a burgeoning crime wave" by their public statements. Since journalists rely on police accounts of crime, officials actually control the raw material of the crime wave. By selectively releasing information, they have the power to make news. The interplay between law enforcement officials and the news media is the key in producing a crime wave.[29]

The publication of the FBI's Uniform Crime Reports each year provides an excellent example of this process. The statistics, which are gathered, analyzed, and presented by the law enforcement establishment, provide the statistical basis on which assertions may be made. The media turn to the elite members of the law enforcement establishment to substantiate their claims. Big-city police chiefs, nationally recognized judges, and prosecutors are interviewed to confirm the trends. In this way, the media extend to law enforcement officials the opportunity to legitimize the trends established by the crime statistics they produce. As we will see . . . , law enforcement agencies, like the national news media, distort crime data to fit their particular needs. The information from the UCR is used to show that crime is increasing or decreasing, depending on current political demands. To date, neither the law enforcement establishment nor the media questions the validity or accuracy of the other's use of crime information, thereby promoting a symbiotic if not collusive relationship between the two.

NOTES

1. William J. Chambliss, "The Crime Menace in the Hands of Politics" (Working paper, Department of Sociology, University of Delaware, 1983), p. 6.

2. Ed Magnuson, "The Curse of Violent Crime—A Persuasive Fear of Robbery and Mayhem Threatens the Way America Lives," *Time*, March 23, 1981, pp. 16–30.

3. Aric Press et al., "The Plague of Violent Crime," *Newsweek*, March 23, 1981, pp. 46, 47, 48.

4. "Crime in America—Living Scared," *Mademoiselle*, August 1981, p.34.

5. Hugh C. McDonald, "Violent Crime: How to Save Your Own Life," *Glamour*, January 1982.

6. "How Fear Is Changing Our Lives," *McCall's*, March 1981, pp. 43–44.

7. "The Rising Tide of Crime," *Literary Digest* 86 (August 15, 1925): 5. Cartoon by Kirby, first appearing in the *New York World*.

8. Ibid., p. 7. Cartoon by Sykes, first appearing in the *Philadelphia Public Ledger*.

9. "Cities Helpless in the Grip of Crime," *Literary Digest* 73 (April 22, 1922): 10. Cartoon by Kirby, first appearing in the *New York World*.

10. Report of the Special Commission on Law Enforcement presented at the meeting of the American Bar Association in San Francisco, August 10, 1922, reprinted in William B. Swaney, "What Shall We Do to Stop Crime?" *New York Times Current History* 16 (September 1922): 924.

11. Quoted in "The Rising Tide of Crime," p. 5.

12. "Cities Helpless in the Grip of Crime," pp. 10–11.

13. Ibid., p. 11. Quotation from the *New York World*.

14. Report of the Special Commission on Law Enforcement, p. 923.

15. "Crime: Every 20 Seconds," *Newsweek*, April 1, 1946, pp. 24–25; and "Crime Goes Booming Along," *Collier's*, May 18, 1946, p. 98.

16. "Rise in Crime in U.S.," *U.S. News & World Report*, May 17, 1946, pp. 30–31.

17. "Crime Goes On and Gets Worse," *U.S. News & World Report*, September 9, 1963, p. 76.

18. "Crime Runs Wild," p. 64.

19. James Garofalo, "Crime and the Mass Media: A Selective Review of Research," *Journal of Research in Crime and Delinquency* 18 (July 1981): 319–350.

20. Ibid.

21. Ted Gest, "Our Losing Battle Against Crime," *U.S. News & World Report*, October 12, 1981, p. 39.

22. Federal Bureau of Investigation, *Crime in the United States—Uniform Crime Reports, 1980* (Washington, D.C.: Government Printing Office, 1981), pp. 7–13.

23. Ibid., p. 2.

24. For example, see Thorsten Sellin, "Crime in the United States," *Life* 48 (September 9, 1957): 48.

25. Harold E. Pepinsky, "The Growth of Crime in the United States," *Annals of the American Academy of Political and Social Service* 423 (January 1976): 27.

26. Albert D. Biderman, "Social Indicators and Goals," in Raymond A. Bauer, ed., *Social Indicators 1966* (Cambridge, Mass.: MIT Press, 1966), p. 125.

27. Jay Robert Nash, *Bloodletters and Badmen* (New York: M. Evans & Co., 1973).

28. Federal Bureau of Investigation, *Crime in the United States—Uniform Crime Reports, 1976 and 1980* (Washington, D.C.: Government Printing Office).

29. Michael Fisherman, "Crime Waves as Ideology," *Social Problems* 25 (June 1978): 531–543.

POSTSCRIPT

Is Crime Getting Worse?

Wright and Currie probably battled to a draw. At times, though, they are talking about slightly different things. Currie is clearly more interested in predatory street crimes of violence. Some crimes are increasing, but there are reductions as well. However, what is most important, as both Wright and Currie admit, is that, for whatever reasons, the fear of crime is probably increasing much faster than crime itself.

Charles Murray makes just this point. In "Crime in America," *National Review* (June 10, 1988), he bemoans the anxiety and fear that so many Americans are subjected to daily. A much more technical paper, "Some New Evidence on the Seriousness of Crime," by Mark A. Cohen, in *Criminology* (May 1988), concurs. A typical mass-consumption magazine piece featuring just the kind of news writing that is ridiculed by Kevin Wright is found in Ed Magnuson's "The Curse of Violent Crime: A Persuasive Fear of Robbery and Mayhem Threatens the Way Americans Live," *Time* (March 23, 1981).

A very different level of concern is found in the 1988 exposé of official crimes, ranging from the Contragate affair of Oliver North to the debatable legal and ethical activities of former attorney general Edwin Meese. Also, heading the list for many is the disclosure of the FBI's attempt to obtain information on what books library patrons were ordering and reading (for example, Nat Hentoff's, "The FBI in the Library," *Washington Post*, July 23, 1988).

Others, however, suggest that both crimes of officials as well as other forms of crime are either tapering off or were always a figment of the media's imagination. In a classic article, Daniel Bell wisely discussed "The Myth of Crime Waves: The Actual Decline of Crime in the U.S." in his book *The End of Ideology* (Free Press, 1960).

More recent reports include the January 12, 1988, interview with Ronald C. Goldstock in *Law Enforcement News* ("the mob will be unrecognizable in the next five to ten years") and J. S. Gossezux and D. J. Curran's moderately optimistic study based on current events in Philadelphia, "The Team Approach to Curtailing White-Collar Crime," *The Police Chief* (August 1988).

For an excellent discussion of why ten different nations from all over the world do not have America's crime problem, you will want to consult Freda Adler's (editor) *Nations Not Obsessed with Crime* (Rothman, 1983).

ISSUE 7

Are Dutch Prisons Superior to Others?

YES: David Downes, from *Contrasts in Tolerance: Post-war Penal Policies in The Netherlands and England and Wales* (Oxford, 1988)

NO: Herman Franke, from "Dutch Tolerance: Facts and Fables," *British Journal of Criminology* (Winter 1990)

ISSUE SUMMARY

YES: Editor and university professor of criminology David Downes concludes from his extensive comparative research that the Dutch prison system is fairer and more humane than others, and he holds it up as an ideal for other industrialized nations.

NO: Editor and University of Amsterdam criminologist Herman Franke ridicules Downes's research methodology, interpretations, and conclusions. He argues that Downes, like many others, has been fooled by Dutch propaganda into falling for the "myth" of their penal superiority.

With the publication of Karl Mannheim's classic work *Ideology and Utopia* (1936), and, more recently, with Peter Berger and Thomas Luckmann's *Social Construction of Reality* (1967), sociologists and criminologists have become more sensitive to the importance of myths and how they can overshadow and distort one's research. The pervasiveness of this myth-making, or symbolic reality construction, is now well known. Yet, as the issues in this volume continuously reveal, understanding social realities, including criminological ones, is highly problematic, and arriving at "the facts" a difficult undertaking.

One of the most important tasks of criminologists (and all scientists) is to separate, as much as is possible, empirical fact from false belief. Unfortunately, neither rational discourse nor objective research is easy when the issue challenges or threatens people's dearest values, beliefs, or fears.

Criminologists, too, take such elementary conceptions very seriously. In spite of their commitment to truth they are probably as likely as anyone to become aroused when someone violates their own strongly held concepts and beliefs. One characteristic of western scholars, some academic critics claim, is their 'reverse ethnocentrism.' That is, they see elements of other societies and cultures as superior to their own or at least tend to view others systems through rose-colored lenses. Whether Downes makes this error, as Franke claims, is difficult to resolve.

The excerpt here from Downes's book is necessarily highly condensed. The book itself is rich with in-depth discussions of not only Dutch prisons and inmates' attitudes but of the whole enterprise of comparative criminology itself. Clearly, no good research is ever *not* comparative. Something is always, however implicitly, being compared with something else (for example, "control" and "experimental" groups). Downes, for example, not only goes considerably beyond most comparative criminology discussions by pointing out both the strengths and weaknesses of comparative criminology (and thereby seeming to anticipate Franke's attacks), but he also links his specific comparisons with criminal justice policy implications. Most important, as you will see from his article, he actually *does* comparative analysis of English and Dutch prisons.

This debate reflects several conflicting intellectual and political currents. First, both British and U.S. politicians, if not their criminologists, know that prison populations cannot be lowered when crime rates are increasing. Clearly, the rate of crime in the United Kingdom has been rising steadily and the rate in the Netherlands somewhat more sporadically. Yet in the latter, decreasing rates of incarceration have been the norm, while in England (as in the United States), incarceration is significantly increasing. A broad intellectual question, then, is, how is it possible to reduce incarceration in the Netherlands with no discernable effect on rates of crime? A corollary question with political implications is, why are Dutch inmates treated so much more humanely (if indeed they are) and yet they do not recidivate at rates nearly as high as those in either the United States or the United Kingdom?

At the present time, most British administrators, like their North American counterparts, are in a definite "get tough" mode. Moreover, a growing number of scholars, including some criminologists, are not only defending get-tough crime control policies but are also challenging the image of maximum security prisons as degrading and harmful (see the Postscript of this issue). Downes, Franke claims, is grinding his axe in opposition to changing British penal policies.

Certainly since World War II, the avowed official policies of both Great Britain and the Netherlands have been rehabilitation of inmates over punishment (as was also true until recently in the United States). For instance, article 26 of the 1951 Principles of Imprisonment Act in the Netherlands reflects this, as does the 1948 Criminal Justice Act in Britain. Downes asserts that England has never lived up to this ideal, while the Dutch do.

Should prisons be "tolerant"? Does it really make any difference how prisoners are treated? After all, they broke the law. Can one really measure "humane treatment" and prison "tolerance"? Aren't all prisons really the same? And if not, shouldn't they be? Which elements of either the Dutch or English and Welsh systems do you think might be helpful in our system? How and why?

YES

David Downes

POST-WAR PENAL POLICY IN THE NETHERLANDS AND ENGLAND AND WALES

THE CRIMINAL JUSTICE SYSTEMS
OF THE NETHERLANDS AND ENGLAND

Comparative criminology is nothing new. In their broadest sense, of contrasting institutional arrangements and/or forms of conduct between whole societies, comparative studies have long been an invaluable, though underused, resource in historical and socio-economic studies. Travels abroad can be as influential as journeyings at home in the realm of criminal and penal policies. . . .

The problem with 'abroad' is that the demand of governments for precise answers to limited questions—for example, how to deal with 'soccer hooliganism'—rarely shows more than the broad correspondence of other societies' concerns with our own, and limited forays which simply reveal greater complexity become difficult to justify. For the complexities of a methodological character in comparative work are formidable. Categories and definitions of seriousness and specific crimes may vary; what counts as a 'penal' institution in one country may be labelled differently in another; and persons diverted from the criminal justice system at various stages may be regarded for some purposes as 'sentenced', for others not. The process of attempting to ensure that like is being compared with like is protracted and often imprecise. . . .

In the case of the English penal system, . . . 'high-cost squalor' is [one] cogent phrase for a system that combines great costs with enormous waste and considerable inhumanity, where staff and prisoners alike, though in contrasting ways, suffer a measure of indignity and oppressiveness that shows every sign of increasing rather than waning. It embodies undue variations of discomfort and privation, with some jails being relatively

From David Downes, *Contrasts in Tolerance: Post-war Penal Policy in The Netherlands and England and Wales* (Clarendon Press, 1988). Reprinted by permission. Notes omitted.

humane—by and large the training prisons into which proportionally more resources are sunk . . . while others invite metaphors such as pressure-cookers, 'cattle-pens', and the like to capture the reek of overcrowding and subjugation endemic in the local prisons. Reforms are tried and found wanting—parole, suspended sentences, community service orders—in the pursuit of a reduced prison population. . . .

The question 'Does it have to be so?' entails comparative study. . . .

The prison systems of England and The Netherlands, are not entirely dissimilar. A point-by-point comparison would prove unwieldy but some principal similarities are:

1. Both systems are differentiated to some degree: prisons in this country between local and training prisons, the former for remand and short-sentence prisoners, the latter for longer term prisoners. Specific prisons may be run on specialist lines (e.g. Grendon Underwood's psychiatric regime). In The Netherlands, prisons are broadly divided into closed, semi-closed, and open. . . .

2. Comparable forms of age and gender grading are employed in both countries. Women are held in separate prisons, though in The Netherlands only one such prison exists. Some 23 per cent of Dutch prisoners are under 23 years of age, some 29 per cent of English prisoners are under 21, making the English prisoners relatively, though not dramatically, younger. . . .

3. In terms of sheer material environment, the age range of Dutch prisons is similar to that in England, with a number of nineteenth-century establishments of panopticon design. . . . [T]wo-thirds of the cells in the closed prisons in The

Netherlands remain unsewered, though the figure for England is almost 90 per cent. Even so, ready access to toilet facilities is the norm in Dutch prisons.

The differences between the two systems are far more notable than the similarities. . . . Some striking dissimilarities are:

1. One prisoner to a cell is the almost invariable rule in Dutch prisons. . . . No such constraint on the use of capacity exists in England. In 1982, for example, some 16,000 prisoners were sharing cells designed for one prisoner—11,000 sharing two to a cell, 5,000 three to a cell. Prison overcrowding has become the single most potent issue in penal policy over the past two decades. . . . This difference between the ratios of prison population to prison capacity is the most striking surface constast between the Dutch and English systems. . . .

2. The proportion of remand (unconvicted and unsentenced) prisoners to the total is far higher in The Netherlands than in England in 1980, over 60 per cent and 15 per cent respectively. . . .

3. The size of Dutch prisons is much smaller on average than those in England. In The Netherlands in 1985, some 4,500 prisoners were held in 45 institutions with an average capacity of 100, ranging in capacity from 20 to some 150. . . . In England, some 150 establishments held roughly 46,000 prisoners in 1985 (a peak of 48,111 was reached in mid-July of that year), an average of 300 or so in each institution, with a range from under 50 in a few juvenile remand centres to over a thousand in nine local prisons, one or two exceeding 1,500 on occasion (e.g. Liverpool, Manchester). Thus, the average English prison establishment holds three times as many prisoners as those in The Netherlands, and

some hold ten times as many as the largest Dutch prison. Such different orders of magnitude have immense implications for social relations within prison. . . .

4. In one major respect, English prisons are less militaristic. In closed prisons in The Netherlands perimeter guards are armed. British prison officers remain wholly (and British police largely) unarmed by comparison with those in The Netherlands, and indeed the rest of the world.

5. Automatic remission of part of the sentence was abolished in The Netherlands in 1951. Remission of one-third of any sentence of over five days is automatic in England, except for those forfeiting some part of the time remitted as penalty for offences committed in prison, and for those serving life sentences. Far more extensive use is made in The Netherlands than in England of the 'pardon'. For example, in 1983, of 6,176 requests for pardon, 1,793 (29 per cent) were entirely or partially granted. . . .

6. A final major difference between the two systems concerns the disposals available to offenders deemed mentally ill, disordered or psychopathic. In both countries, the use of special hospitals for such offenders has the character of a semi-indeterminate sentence, though in The Netherlands it is termed a 'measure' and those so detained are not commonly counted as part of the prison population. . . . *Terbeschikkingstelling van der Regering* (TBR) or 'placement at the disposal of the government' is not, however, equivalent to 'detention at Her Majesty's pleasure' or life imprisonment, since the case is reviewed judicially every two years. . . .

THE DEPTH OF IMPRISONMENT: AN EXPLORATORY STUDY OF THE NETHERLANDS AND ENGLAND

They treat you like a human being. They say, 'Enjoy your meal', .'Good morning'. They treat you like a man, they let you do things the way you like, they're not always looking . .'. for drugs, they don't guard you when you see the governor, with two warders either side. Even when you go to solitary, you take yourself there. You think, 'It can't be true, there must be a catch.' But there isn't. I just can't believe they don't despise you because you're a criminal. In England, they punish you for being a criminal. . . . (English prisoner in a Dutch closed prison)

Dutch prisons are much better, especially at thinking how to bring prisoners back to the normal life. There is home leave every weekend or so—here there is no way you can get that experience. . . . (Dutch prisoner in English training prison)

Penal reformers, from John Howard onwards, have long preferred the Dutch penal system to that of England. Prisons in The Netherlands have traditionally been smaller, cleaner, and run in a more humane fashion than in England. . . . Is the actual experience of imprisonment in the two systems as distinctively different as penal theory implies?

To go some way towards answering that question, and as part of the broader enquiry into post-war Dutch penal policy, I interviewed a small number of prisoners in each system, some of who had experience of *both*. Interviews were carried out in June and July of 1985 with 12 British (and one Irish) prisoners in 5 Dutch jails, and 14 Dutch prisoners in 4 English jails. . . .

In England, the Prison Department assembled the list of four prisons where Dutch prisoners were held in custody, and it was left to me to contact the appropriate member of staff to arrange the most appropriate time. Prisoners were asked, in advance of my arrival, if they wished to take part in the interviews and none refused. In The Netherlands I was allowed to contact *any* prison at which British prisoners were held, and asked to write a letter to the prisoners outlining the purpose of the interviews. . . . Another difference in the interviewing lay in the constraints which governed the time they could take. In the Dutch prisons, once entry had been gained, there was no particular time limit set to the interview beyond the interviewee's own wishes. In English prisons, strict time limits—usually those of the hours of visiting—were adhered to in all but one case. All interviews in The Netherlands were in private, and in all but one prison in England this was also the case. Interviews were tape-recorded with the prisoners' permission. . . .

The interviews were of a frankly exploratory nature. The main focus was explicitly on the prisoners' experience of the criminal justice system in general and of imprisonment in particular, and it was thought useful to ask for such perceptions even where they had no experience of their own system. Where they had such experience, they were asked about the similarities and differences between the two systems, again in terms of their own experience.

The contrast between the British and Dutch penal systems is usually drawn in terms of the *length* of sentences of imprisonment. The average Dutch sentence—three months or so—is far shorter than the average British sentence of roughly ten months, a difference which principally accounts for the much smaller proportionate size of the Dutch prison population relative to that of Britain. The two sets of prisoners interviewed were, however, closer to each other in terms of sentence length than the average. The British prisoners in Dutch jails were typically in prison for hard drug offences, mainly dealing and trafficking in cocaine, and in three cases for heavy crimes of violence: armed robbery, attempted murder, and murder. Their average length of sentence of 25 months was several times the Dutch average, compared with an average sentence of 39 months for the Dutch prisoners in English jails, which is still four times the average for this country. The principal offence committed by the Dutch prisoners was 'soft' drug smuggling, typically large consignments of cannabis, though in five cases cocaine or heroin was involved. In practice, parole etc. would reduce each average term by one-third, to 16 months for British prisoners in The Netherlands and 26 months for Dutch prisoners in England.

Important as this magnitude of difference is for the individuals concerned, and for the operation of the system as a whole, the main contrast in the interviews between the two systems was couched in terms of the *depth* rather than the length of imprisonment. In a variety of ways, some gross, some nuanced, prison in The Netherlands is experienced as a far less damaging and repressive phenomenon than in Britain. Another way of putting it is to say that even the less unpleasant end of the prison system in Britain holds few positive features for the prisoners. The main impact of the system here, even the training prisons, is to blunt sensibilities rather than—as in the Dutch system in general—making some attempt to preserve or even sharpen them. This sense of a contrast in terms of psychological invasion by the prison was expressed on a variety of levels: relations with staff; relations with other prisoners; rights and privileges; material standards and conditions; and a sense of the overall quality of life which the prison regime made possible or withheld. . . .

Relations with Staff

As the first of the accounts implied . . . relations with staff were among the more unexpected as well as welcome features of prison life in The Netherlands, particularly for prisoners who had experience of the British system . . . British jails were regarded as unnecessarily oppressive. Some saw this difference as lodged in system and broader societal terms:

> The main difference is the attitude of your fellow prisoners and staff. . . . The whole atmosphere was different. The staff seemed to treat you as a human being, whereas the staff in Britain would treat you as, well 'animal' is too strong a word, basically with a lack of any humanity. The way that going to the toilet is arranged, the lack of showers, the way staff would shout at people continually, that wouldn't work in Holland, they'd go on strike or something. It's basically alien to the Dutch character to have that sort of divide between people.

Other prisoners were less constrained in describing their experience of the British local prisons in particular: 'barbaric', 'inhuman', 'degrading', and 'makes you an animal because it treats you like one' were commonly employed. Even the least critical made such points as 'guards here are more human, you can joke with them; in England, guards are more strict'. The Dutch attitude was summed up by one English prisoner: 'They've got

your liberty and that's enough. They don't have to make your life complete hell.' . . .

[What some] have termed the 'normalization' of the prison is much enhanced by the presence of women staff. Women do not serve as guards in men's prisons in The Netherlands but as governors, social workers, and secretaries, as well as psychologists and teachers; their presence is now taken for granted. They are abused neither physically nor verbally: 'nobody has ever tried anything on'. Indeed, their presence is said to lower the aggressive atmosphere that builds up in all-male environments: 'If there are men and women in prison, you relate to them as human beings. If there are only men, you relate to them only as men', as one prisoner put it. . . .

Relations with Other Prisoners

Relations with other prisoners were not, in general, experienced as a problem by British prisoners in Dutch jails. The one-to-a-cell system made for privacy when it was wanted, and the relatively generous amount of time allowed for association and recreation did not make isolation the other side of the coin. Dutch prisoners in English jails tended to feel under constant pressure from the conflicts arising in part from the deprivations of prison life, in part from over-crowding even in the less congested end of the penal system. Only one British prisoner in The Netherlands, in a remand prison, felt cell-sharing was less onerous than enforced privacy, for the company it provided. The rest, who often called their cell their 'room', valued the one-to-a-cell arrangement. . . .

Rights, Privileges, and Conditions

Rights, privileges, and conditions were almost overwhelmingly regarded as far superior in Dutch prisons by comparison with those in England by both sets of prisoners. The major exception to this picture concerned remand prisoners at the pre-trial, or at least the investigative, stage of their confinement in police and prison cells. 'What was not so good was that after arrest I was kept incommunicado in Zutphen for three months, and for a few weeks my wife and family didn't know where I was.' Another prisoner saw the pre-trial remand system in Britain as '10 times better' than that in The Netherlands. . . .

What all prisoners agree upon is that, once the investigative stage is over in The Netherlands, things dramatically improve for the prisoners; and once conviction is secured in Britain, things rapidly change for the worse.

Accommodation

Accommodation provides the basis for much that differentiates the two systems' standards. . . . The commitment to the one-to-a-cell rule was sharply expressed by a senior member of staff in an Amsterdam prison who was willing to resign if it was abandoned: 'If two to a cell, I go.' The closed prisons allow for more individualization of cell furnishing and decoration. . . . TV can be rented at a cost well within the weekly pay budget, floors can be carpeted, 'one man even has an aquarium in his cell'. Here you can control the lighting system in your room, so you can read [at night] if you want to—that's not so in England—very small things make a big difference.' . . .

Food and Clothing

Clothing was left to the prisoners' choice in The Netherlands, not so in England:

few chose to comment on this, but those that did preferred choice, and it is clearly the most visible signifier of prisoner status. . . . In England, food was 'dumped on disgusting plastic plates'; real plates were used in The Netherlands. Washing and toilet facilities were clearly superior in the Dutch prisons. Prisoners could have four showers a week, and could in general leave their cells to use the toilet where cells had no integral flushing toilets. . . .

Work and Pay

Work and pay are basic determinants of the experience of prison. Work offers a break from the cell, a chance to socialize, and at best some form of training that offers a marketable skill on release. The two systems were not so very different as far as foreign prisoners were concerned, though Dutch prisoners in Dutch jails were said to have better training opportunities than British prisoners in British jails. Pay, however, differed greatly between the two systems, with the prisoners in The Netherlands earning roughly £12 a week, compared to a *maximum* £2.98 a week in England. . . .

Communication with the Outside World

The depth of imprisonment is most graphically conveyed by the rules governing letters, phoning, and visits. It is here, for foreign prisoners ineligible for home leave, that the differences between the two systems were most starkly inscribed. 'Prisons are certainly more comfortable here [in The Netherlands] than in Britain. But comfort is beside the point—the main thing is more letters, visits, and so on. There is no reason to deny any number of letters. But in England I had to ask my girl-friend to write fewer letters.' In Dutch prisons, there is no limit to the number of letters prisoners can write or receive. . . .

Use of the phone could vary even more between the two systems. In The Netherlands it was taken for granted that prisoners have the right to make at least one free foreign call a week, two or possibly more by permission of the governor on welfare or other grounds. . . . In England, phoning was unusual, either abroad or domestically. It is very much a privilege, to be granted only on application to the governor. . . .

Visits are the most fundamental of prisoners' rights, the main way in which the prison's hold over the prisoner is temporarily reduced by the presence of family, friends, or other contacts from the outside world. But even here the prison can and does intrude via the host of variables that make up the context in which visits take place, the degree of monitoring that pervades them, the length of time they are allowed to last, and so on. The character of visits is therefore a prime determinant of the depth of imprisonment. At its most developed, in the long-term closed prisons, the Dutch system allows three visits of up to three hours weekly, plus one 'private visit' a month, with extra visits if the case can be made. . . . The frequency of visits in English training prisons was markedly less, one visit of up to two hours being allowed only once fortnightly. . . .

[T]he relative infrequency and lack of privacy in visiting arrangements in British prisons combined with the much more restrictive rules governing letters and telephoning markedly diminish the prisoners' social bonds with the outside world, and correspondingly deepen those within the world of the prison.

Welfare

Welfare considerations loom larger in the Dutch than in the British system. When asked about the chief differences between the two, one English prisoner in The Netherlands replied that it lay in a 'lot of emphasis on rehabilitation', though . . . this was regarded as applying mainly to Dutch rather than to foreign prisoners. 'If you want rehabilitation, they will do anything for you.' . . . In England, the attitude is "once a criminal, always a criminal". Here, they think maybe next time you'll be different.' . . .

Discipline

Discipline was clearly more severe in English than in Dutch prisons, and less subject to rights of appeal. 'There is no democracy inside the prison [in England]. Every prison officer is like God. No complaints are possible. In The Netherlands, if the governor says no, and you think you have a right, you can appeal to a Commission one of whom has to be a jurist, and you might get your right.' . . .

Discussion

The experience of imprisonment varies in terms of depth as well as length. Comparative work on the subject has tended to concentrate on length, in part because it lends itself to quantitative analysis. Recent work on social control trends has focused on its *breadth*, ways in which the 'carceral society' is generated by the permeation of disciplinary modes of supervision by 'penal agents' throughout non-custodial community-based forms of correction. . . .

In conclusion, all prisoners interviewed expressed a clear and strong preference for the Dutch system over that of England. . . . The depth of imprisonment in The Netherlands is markedly shallower than that in Britain; the length of prison sentences is substantially shorter . . . and the breadth of imprisonment remains prima facie less developed than that in Britain. If the prisoners' voice counts for anything in the debate on crime and punishment, it is at one with those who argue that the benefits of reductionist policies tangibly outweigh the as yet undemonstrated costs. . . .

CONTRASTS IN TOLERANCE: CRIMINAL JUSTICE POLICIES IN THE NETHERLANDS AND ENGLAND

. . . The Dutch can act more repressively than the British: their police are armed and employ tear gas and water cannon to disperse 'riotous assemblies'; perimeter guards of their top security prisons are armed. But in almost every other respect, their prisons demonstrate that genuinely humane containment is possible, and that is an important lesson. The means to that end seem to be several rather than one. The drastic shortening of sentences to custody is the major route, but other measures are needed for a properly co-ordinated response. These would include setting limits to the size of the penal estate; introducing minimum and legally enforceable standards for prison conditions; conditionally diverting petty offenders, with their consent, from prosecution; experimenting with victim restitution in suitable cases; co-ordinating crime prevention, occupational surveillance, and youth employment measures; and resisting the use of imprisonment for petty offenders when persistence rather than the gravity of offences constitutes a problem. . . .

The Dutch judiciary have shown great courage in insisting on humane standards and the minimum use of pain in the dispensation of criminal justice. It is to be hoped they can keep their nerve in the face of adverse criticism. It is also to be hoped that we find sufficient nerve to follow their example.

NO

Herman Franke

DUTCH TOLERANCE: FACTS AND FABLES

Well over two hundred years ago, John Howard paid visits to prisons in The Netherlands. Compared to the misery and filth he had seen in England and in other countries on the Continent, he found the Dutch prisons extremely clean and comfortable—a commendation the Dutch were only too ready to accept. In fact, they still proffer Howard's judgement as evidence of the tradition of mildness and tolerance in their country. The British criminologist David Downes, in his study *Contrasts in Tolerance* on post-war penal policy in The Netherlands and England and Wales (Downes 1988), quotes Howard too, and adds a great number of positive assessments of his own regarding the prison system and criminal policy in The Netherlands. For this reason his book will no doubt rank high on the Dutch national scale of sources cited.

As a Dutch criminologist, I read Downes's study with great pleasure. Generally, however, I think that he has contributed more to national myth-making than to a deepening of criminological insight into the post-war reality in The Netherlands. This critical judgement is founded not only on what Downes studied and wrote about, but also on what he *failed* to study and write about. This article, then, is about what I read and what I did not read in his book. . . .

DEFINITION OF THE PROBLEM, METHOD OF RESEARCH, AND SOURCES OF KNOWLEDGE

It is difficult to make a judgement as regards the contents of Downes's study without knowing the problem he defined, the methods he applied, and the sources he used, so let me begin by briefly summarizing them.

Downes gives a clear definition of the problem. He asserts that, shortly after the Second World War, a strikingly higher proportion of the population was imprisoned in The Netherlands than in England. It is a pity that he fails to state that at that time the prison population in The Netherlands was extremely high on account of criminality related to the occupation by the Nazis (e.g. the black market, illegal slaughter of cattle, evasion of rationing

From Herman Franke, "Dutch Tolerance: Facts and Fables," *British Journal of Criminology*, vol. 30, no. 1 (Winter 1990). Copyright © 1990 by The Institute for the Study and Treatment of Delinquency. Reprinted by permission of Oxford University Press. Notes omitted.

and other war-related crime). In fact, the immediate post-war figures for The Netherlands are unnecessary to his case: it is sufficient to note that in 1957 the detention rates were approximately equally high in The Netherlands and in England, yet by 1975, four times as many people were imprisoned per 100,000 population in England than in The Netherlands. The difference later became smaller, but around 1985 England still had proportionately three times as many prisoners.

Even without the inflated differences of the 1940s and 1950s, this development calls for an explanation. Why did The Netherlands experience a process of decarceration that within a few decades led to one of the very lowest detention rates in the world, whereas in England and Wales in the same period the detention rate increased considerably? To this fascinating question Downes tries to find an answer. He also tries to find an explanation for the change around 1975, when for the first time for a long time the detention rate in The Netherlands started to rise again. Soon after this change, some serious offenders had to be released from remand in custody because of lack of cell space, causing outraged reactions among the public at large.

Downes was surely hindered in his research by his lack of knowledge of the Dutch language, though he does not acknowledge this in so many words. He tried to overcome this impediment by having a fellow worker who could read Dutch summarize some publications and source material, but the effect is not the same: Downes's lack of command of Dutch is apparent throughout the book. Dutch words are misspelt, but that is a small part of the problem: a number of important sources have apparently not been studied—criminological and penitentiary journals, the governmental *Prisonnotes* of 1964, 1976, and 1982, and influential reports . . .

Apart from a few exceptions, Downes bases his study almost entirely on articles by Dutch lawyers and criminologists written or translated into English. His selection of literature was determined not by what he wanted to know, but rather by what was available in English. With the exception of some volumes of conference papers, this consists for the most part of publications from the Research Centre of the Ministry of Justice (WODC). . . . A similar criticism applies to a great number of the people interviewed by Downes during the twelve visits he paid to The Netherlands in the early 1980s: other than some academic criminologists, they were all people who made their living within the judicial machinery.

Downes distilled his view of post-war developments in The Netherlands from the stories, anecdotes, interpretations, and knowledge gleaned from these sources. Accordingly his book therefore does not present an analysis of Dutch society, but a description of how Dutch judges, public prosecutors, officials, and fighters against crime see themselves, and how they portray the recent history of their occupations. By virtue of its sources, such an account must necessarily be biased. . . .

Downes's uncritical acceptance of Van Dijk's analysis, which also underlies government policy plans, illustrates the way he trusted his interviewees. It is clear that many of them told him little more than what they themselves had read in newspapers, periodicals, and some handbooks. Thus, Downes repeatedly argues that new prisons are built mainly to maintain the humane principle of one prisoner in one cell—something that some smart promoter of the government's *Samenleving en Criminaliteit**, must have made him believe. To the minister of justice's frequent attempts to undermine this principle, in response to severe pressure from Parliament, Downes pays no attention (or perhaps he was not informed of it?). The most important objection to all this is that by adopting what I would like to call the ordinary first-order constructs of the situation made by most of his respondents, he hardly succeeds in forming second-order constructs of his own, sociological making.

On the first page of the first chapter, he calls his study a form of *comparative criminology*. Indeed, he compares the penal policy and the judicial system in The Netherlands to that in England and Wales. In a separate section on 'salient differences' between both legal frameworks, he points to the absence of trial by jury in The Netherlands and to the extremely powerful position of the public prosecution service, and in particular the public prosecutors themselves. With regard to both prison systems, he points to the fact that in England and Wales around 1986 about 11,000 prisoners had to share one cell between two, and about 5,000 among three. In The Netherlands, prisoners generally do not share cells at all.

Such information indicates once more that comparisons between the two countries are not straight-forward, but Downes does not go on to make this a comparative study in the sense that knowledge of different societies is used in order to

understand the problems of these societies better. In the remainder of the book Downes does little more than tell his fellow countrymen what he has seen and heard in The Netherlands. When he writes about England (which he rarely does) he often uses 'we'. He does not use his knowledge of English society to attain a better understanding of the characteristics of Dutch society; rather he just uses his knowledge of Dutch society to severely criticize the criminal policy in his own country. This gives the impression that Downes visited The Netherlands to collect ammunition for a struggle against England's law-and-order policy, its overcrowded prisons and harsh judicial reactions. Again and again he repudiates arguments against criminal reforms in England by citing that such reforms have long been put into practice in The Netherlands without the crime level being any higher. Apart from the question of whether elements of one society can be transferred to another quite so simply, the importance Downes attaches to this knowledge raises strong doubts about the detachment of his perception. I am convinced that the polemic he is explicitly (and implicitly) conducting with English policy-makers has biased his view of developments in The Netherlands and made him far too clamorous in their praise.

DETAILS OF THE DEFINITION OF THE PROBLEM

The gradual decrease in the detention rate in The Netherlands between 1945 and 1975 as compared to the increase in England at this time could of course be connected with the relative level of criminality. . . . Downes shows quite convincingly that differences in crime figures

*[Samenleving en Criminaliteit, "Society and Crime," is the Dutch government's policy plan—ED.]

and hidden sanctions explain no more than 40 per cent of the smaller number of prisoners in The Netherlands. . . . Consequently, the strong decrease in the prison population of The Netherlands must be attributed mainly to a more restrained penal policy, meaning fewer prison sentences and shorter sentences. Even towards the end of the 1970s, when the sentences in The Netherlands had begun to lengthen remarkably, the mean time served in England amounts to approximately five months and in The Netherlands to less than two months. About 1980 the mean time served amounted to 173 days in England and 83 days in The Netherlands. . . . Downes concludes that a veritable revolution would be required to bring the English detention rate down to that of The Netherlands. Once again, Downes wonders how such a 'silent revolution' has come to pass in The Netherlands since the 1950s. . . .

In The Netherlands . . . the Fick Committee dealing with the further development of the prison system had established the humane principle of one prisoner to a cell as early as 1947. That, Downes continues, made the 'limits of penal capacity' a more compelling theory for The Netherlands. 'The sources of that self-imposed constraint are not, however, at all apparent', he adds. . . .

I am convinced that Downes could have found these sources in history. A better knowledge of the history of Dutch prisons could have taught him that the committee did not really establish the principle of one prisoner to a cell, and in a certain sense actually broke it. From 1886 until the new Principles of Imprisonment Act was introduced in 1953, prisoners in The Netherlands were held one to a cell because the experts considered this would be the most effective. Isolation was thus maintained more severely in The Netherlands than in England and most other West European countries: in fact, the Dutch prison system was among the most rigid in the West. Every contact with fellow-prisoners was prohibited. Disciplinary action was taken even against singing or whistling. Many a prisoner suffered from mental disturbances or attempted suicide. The Fick Committee eventually rejected the system of solitary confinement, partly because of the psychological misconceptions on which it was founded. . . . Instead of permanently being alone in their cells, prisoners were now allowed to meet one another outside the cells. The committee did not advocate the principle of one prisoner to a cell, but a combination of common and solitary confinement. The fact that in the post-war period in The Netherlands group cells have always been considered undesirable is not so much a matter of humane intentions but a continuation of the long history of solitary confinement. In other words, it was the unintended result of historical developments and not of humane principles, stated explicitly. In the system of solitary confinement, group cells were considered even more pernicious than the common dormitories, where immorality was rampant. Even so, in 1953 about 600 prisoners were held in two- and three-man cells in detention centres, and over 800 prisoners were transferred to dormitories. . . . The spectacular fall in the prison population in the first decade after the war therefore cannot be ascribed, as Downes seems to suggest, to subscription to the humane principle of one prisoner to a cell: it was due solely to the disappearance of war-related criminality.

THE DUTCH TOLERANCE

. . . According to Downes, Dutch tolerance springs from 'a long tradition of relative leniency towards, and acceptance of, deviants, minority groups, and religious dissent'. . . . From this point in his book, Downes not only definitely decides on a development of his problem in terms of the humane and tolerant intentions of those stubborn Dutchmen, but he also strongly contributes to a dubious mythologization around Dutch tolerance.

This mythologization is well served by the fact that Downes is not familiar with or does not mention the horrors of the solitary confinement which was introduced on a small scale as early as 1851 and was only abolished in 1951, and also by the obscuring of historical data incompatible with that traditional mildness. Thus, Downes claims that in The Netherlands death penalties and corporal punishments were abolished in 1870, much earlier than in other West European countries. As regards the death penalty this is correct, but public corporal punishments (which were abolished not in 1870 but in 1854) had been applied longer in The Netherlands than in the neighbouring countries; moreover, a national variant—the scourging of the bare back until the blood flowed—gave The Netherlands a further unfavourable distinction. Only someone who is not familiar with the history of The Netherlands can write that Dutch colonialism 'did not rest' on racism or racial feelings of superiority. . . .

Annoyance about the way in which this mythical Dutch tolerance is used to account for complicated processes in society is increased by the ease with which Downes rejects competing explanations.

In another section, he goes into explanations in which the mild Dutch penal climate is regarded as the result of unintended social developments. Downes rejects these explanations merely on the basis of some remarks by Hulsman in an English publication . . .; he fails to realize that the post-war developments might be understood as a reaction to the old-fashioned pre-war cell system, and in the perspective of a discussion that ranged for more than a hundred years in The Netherlands about the efficacy of prison sentences. He does not have an eye for long-term processes at all—that is to say, apart from the age-long tradition of tolerance.

History is thus not Downes's forte. His interest clearly lies in the present and the recent past. In the present, the differences between the two countries as regards the treatment of prisoners are so striking that they indeed require explanation. The passages in which Downes tries to find an explanation in the recent past are the most successful and convincing. I quite liked his assumption that law-and-order sentiments have played a minor part in Dutch politics through till the 1980s because the various socio-political groups necessitated coalitions, compromises, and moderation, unlike in England where there was normally one-party government. . . .

With much approval, I read his observation to the effect that a small number of professionals—lawyers, judges, and criminologists—with hostile views about prison dominate penal policy in The Netherlands and are capable of shutting out popular sentiments due to the absence of a jury of laymen. Such critical attitudes are coherent with their knowledge of criminological literature and the fact that they make more frequent visits to prison than their English colleagues do. Also, the social distance between judges and suspects would be less than in England, and Dutch judges go more deeply into the suspect's personality and circumstances. While Downes again runs the risk here of taking the nice self-image of our Dutch lawyers as gospel, this typically Dutch 'culture of the judiciary' cannot be denied a certain role. Downes finds to his astonishment that abolitionists like Hulsman and Bianchi were even members of government commissions.

The descriptions . . . of the unique and very influential group of scholars which formed the 'Utrechtse' school at the University of Utrecht (the criminologists Rijksen and Kempe, the professor of criminal law Pompe, and the psychiatrist Baan) are very worthwhile reading. It is hard to understand the strong position that the resocialization ideal has occupied in The Netherlands without reference to this school. Nearly thirty years after publication of Rijksen's *Meningen van gedetineerden* (Opinions of prisoners) in 1958, it is still being pointed out to Downes as an 'event of major importance'. Many people he talked with seem to have told him that his book defined their attitude towards imprisonment, but obviously no one added that the Green Book, as it was called, had been castigated in the press, chiefly for the unscientific rousing of public sentiment. This proves how much Downes relies on what people thought of the Utrecht school in retrospect; the shortcomings of this approach are clear when one considers how many Dutch people now claim to have manned the barricades together with the Provos in the 1960s, whereas in reality they saw the Provos as little more than scum. The problem, of course, is the Utrecht school being both

symbol and cause of the mild spirit of the 1950s and 1960s. Downes finds a clever way out of seeking the influence of the school 'in the maintenance of the impetus towards reductionism' in that period. . . . I agree with his criticism that Baan and his successor Roosenburg pushed too hard for treatment, but altogether in his analysis Downes does not exceed an image of social developments as the work of powerful and kind chaps who have been doing better than they do at home. The concluding sentences in the book provide a particularly clear illustration: 'The Dutch judiciary have shown great courage in insisting on humane standards and the minimum use of pain in the dispensation of criminal justice. It is to be hoped they can keep their nerve in the face of adverse criticism. It is also to be hoped that we find sufficient nerve to follow their example'. . . .

THE RECENT HARDENING OF THE PENAL CLIMATE

Downes's inability to analyse social developments in terms of unintended consequences is even more obvious when he tries to account for, or rather, explain *away*, the recent hardening of the Dutch penal climate and the substantial extension of prison capacity. Due to the upward trend in crime figures (which he almost literally links . . .) to a weakening of social control, altered relations of the authorities, and the removal of traditional religious and socio-political barriers, as the Roethof Committee and Van Dijk have put it and the release of criminals on account of cell shortages. The Netherlands would have been faced with a public demand for harsh punishments and measures for the first time.

This demand, Downes explains in a long chapter on the Amsterdam drugs policy, . . . was also stimulated by the inconvenience of hairy junkies and drug-related crime in the large cities. He typifies the drugs policy in the terms of WODC-research worker Ed Leuw: a transition from 'limitless tolerance' to 'controlled tolerance'. The famous tolerance had reached its limits. Civilians and authorities insisted on severe measures. Most criminologists in The Netherlands regard the government's *Samenleving en Criminaliteit* (Society and criminality) as a concession or even an incentive to that demand—which is obvious, for the plan is full of alarming statements on the endangered constitutional state. Besides the building of five new prisons, a drastic reduction of non-suspended dismissals and a severe suppression of organized crime are announced. Downes, however, tries to make his (English) readers believe that the plan is specifically aimed at maintaining reductionism (the striving for less prison sentences), as opposed to the attraction of a more severe policy and more severe judicial actions. More prisons would be the price that has to be paid for the maintenance of the principle of one prisoner to a cell. . . . Again, some smart policy-maker must have told him this, but more important is Downes's missing an opportunity here to show how much power relations and interests, perhaps under the cover-up of Dutch tolerance and beautiful feelings, obstructed the introduction of group cells. For example, prison directors and warders who had been suffering stress for years, because of cut-backs for example, mainly saw problems of discipline and safety. For this reason they (and their trade-unions) expressed their solidarity with protesting and striking prisoners.

Unions of ex-convicts, scholars, and the Coornhert-Liga for penal reform also protested against group cells. Partly due to this unanimous resistance, the minister of justice had to abandon his plans for group cells, although a large majority in Parliament would have supported him. Criticism of the building of new prisons was thus regarded as antisocial, and accordingly died down. In other words, the true picture of the recent hardening was thus quite different from that of a tolerant government bravely resisting society's demand for more severe punishment.

In his last chapter, 'Contrasts in Tolerance', . . . Downes even goes a little further in his ode to the Dutch way of dealing with *Samenleving en Criminaliteit*. Probably because this chapter is directed at the English at home, he wonders what 'we' can learn from the Dutch. As opposed to the English policy of more severe judicial reactions, Downes describes the Dutch policy as being mainly aimed at social measures against crime. He depicts the plan as a model of sociological analysis and criminological profundity, and as such sharply contrasted with the English policy-plans, devoid of any view at all. . . .

In England, Downes writes in his concluding analysis, the criminal problems are not exposed to the view of the outside world because all the 'problems' are piled up in the overcrowded prisons. In The Netherlands, in contrast, the problems are exposed to public view because of the release of suspects of serious offences in the early stages of the criminal process. Consequently these problems have become a community problem and aroused public attention. . . . That is a nice observation, but in assuming that Dutch society has reacted unanimously to the criminal problems by endorsing *Samenleving en Criminaliteit* in order to preserve its achievements of tolerance, Downes is taking things much too far. He uses such conclusions to slate the English policy. If I understand him properly, England hardly has a criminal policy worthy of the name and is messing about with concepts of retaliation and deterrence which The Netherlands have long considered outdated. With overcrowded prisons, the failure of the English system is manifested in the lives of the prisoners in group cells. According to Downes's arguments the Dutch prison system is a miracle of humanity, to which observation he adds that the crime rate in The Netherlands is becoming lower rather than higher. I would like to go further into the humanity of that prison system.

THE HUMANE PRISON SYSTEM?

. . . Downes surveys in detail the humane characteristics of the Dutch prisons. He is not short of superlatives. They are 'far less oppressive institutions' . . . than in England; in England, warders still maintain an atmosphere of intimidation and violence, and prisoners, lacking an institution like the Dutch prisoners' right to complain, are completely powerless. . . .

By means of interviews with English prisoners in The Netherlands and Dutch prisoners in England, Downes shows convincingly that the prisoners share his opinion. They unambiguously prefer the Dutch prison system as regards relations with warders, communication with the world outside, recreation facilities, discipline, labour, clothing, food and other elements of life in prison. Only during pre-trial detention would suspects be treated better in England than in The Netherlands, where the system of restrictions might lead to complete solitary confinement. In The Netherlands, serving one's time is infinitely more bearable. 'They've got your liberty and that's enough. They don't have to make your life complete hell,' an Englishman summarized his opinion. . . . 'It's not just bull . . . for Holland. The prisons there are really better—stay in there for two days or so and you'll see,' someone else said. . . .

Yet I have difficulty with the image of Dutch prisons that emerges from Downes's book. The prisoners he talked to were able to compare and express their preference. The Dutch in English prisons regarded it as hell and claimed to be treated like beasts. The English in Dutch prisons found they were treated like humans. The superlatives used by Downes, however, give the impression that the stay in the Dutch prisons involves little grief. That would be a serious misunderstanding. Prisoners in The Netherlands usually do not judge their suffering relative to what it would be like in prisons abroad. They compare their situation to the freedom outside. The gap between life in prison and life outside might be a better yardstick for measuring the grief endured than the generous treatment compared to prisons elsewhere. And it is precisely that gap that might have widened after the Second World War, as social life was becoming both more free and less hierarchical, as well as more democratic. As the individual in society became more self-assured, prisoners too they were less submissive. Many privileges in Dutch prisons were introduced because prisoners would no longer accept the old authoritative relations, as prison riots in the early 1970s revealed. It is not necessary to be an experienced cynic to realize that it was problems of discipline rather than humane intentions that resulted in increased participation and privileges being granted in the prisons. Yet the facilities and privileges notwithstanding, the lack of freedom, the regimen which minimizes the control one has over one's own life, and the dependence on prison functionaries bear heavily on many prisoners.

There are even indications that, for certain prisoners in The Netherlands, imprisonment is too hard to bear. Casually, in my opinion too casually, Downes goes into that. He calls the rising suicide figures in Dutch prisons a phenomenon 'that should worry the authorities more than it appears to'. . . . According to Downes, between 1971 and 1982 the number of suicides rose from two to eight a year: this is 'several times' higher than in English prisons, 'despite a more humane regime and better medical facilities'. . . . Other dismal figures may be added: . . . it appears that the suicide rate in Dutch prisons is about ten times higher than outside. The number of suicide attempts and serious self-injuries (auto-mutilations) has also increased considerably in the last decades: from 39 in 1965 to 225 in 1985, on an average population of approximately 4,500 prisoners. Hundreds of prisoners run into psychological problems and according to the Mulder Committee 'are pining away', or are a burden to themselves and others by their aggressive behaviour. . . . The latter run a great risk of finishing up in isolation or punishment cells. On the frequency of the use of these solitary places, which a professor of criminal law, C. Kelk, called 'the black of darkness' . . . Downes did not collect any

figures. Since 1973 these figures have disappeared from the prison statistics too. To put it briefly, there is a lot of grief about which no one within the prison system is well informed. Some suffering may even be linked up with the liberalization of the Dutch regime, because prisoners in The Netherlands have more frustrating and painful contacts (tantalization) with their family and friends 'outside' than in England.

These are all reasons for not taking eulogies like Downes's too literally. The figures on suicide, auto-mutilation, and psychological disturbances confirm that the absence of freedom is a very severe punishment, even if the bars are made of gold. But I realize that with such comments on Dutch prison life, Downes would have alienated himself from the English audience. Thus, after all, the title of his book is confirmed precisely by my critical remarks.

POSTSCRIPT

Are Dutch Prisons Superior to Others?

In traditional penology, especially within the United States, the primary philosophical concern has centered around the functions of prisons. Should they be for deterrence, incapacitation, retribution, or rehabilitation? Historically the last factor is remarkably novel as a correctional goal, even though some will argue that rehabilitation as a goal has been consciously abandoned by many administrators and criminologists in the past ten years. Others say that it has not been abandoned but rather that rehabilitation simply did not work. While still others contend that in the United States rehabilitation has not failed at all, it simply has not really been attempted!

From an American perspective, the Franke-Downes controversy is intriguing. The core concern is whether or not Dutch prisons are more *humane* than those in the United Kingdom. Both authors assume that at least at the broadest political and public levels, and certainly in the abstract, prisons *ought* to be humane. By contrast, many and perhaps most American criminologists and criminal justice scholars worry about what they consider far more pragmatic aspects of prison processes: What are their costs and their recidivism rates? What kinds of gangs emerge and how can they be controlled? What are the proportions of white, black, and Hispanic inmates? What programs bring about behavioral changes in inmates while they are incarcerated and after they are released? While these are important issues, rarely if ever is penological research in the United States linked to broader theoretical and/or policy issues. Thus, the Franke-Downes debate raises our level of discourse and analysis.

For generally high-quality research on the United Kingdom's prison system, see the *Howard Journal of Criminal Justice*. It is edited by the preeminent British criminologist Leslie Wilkins. Tom Gitchoff defends the Dutch system in "Crime and Corrections in Holland: A Commentary," in the *International Journal of Offender Therapy and Comparative Criminology* (April 1989).

David Downes responds to Herman Franke's criticisms in *British Journal of Criminology* (Winter 1990). An excellent edited book on comparative law and corrections in Europe is *Abolitionism: Toward a Non-Repressive Approach to Crime*, edited by H. Bianchi and R. van Swaaningen (Free University Press, 1986). Among the many outstanding works on British prisons, see V. Stern's highly critical *Bricks of Shame: Britain's Prisons* (Penguin, 1987).

For a major comparison of public attitudes toward punishment in different countries, see David Fogel's *On Doing Less Harm: A Survey of Western European Attitudes Toward Incarceration* (Office of International Criminal Justice, 1988). An interesting examination of Dutch tolerance toward minority groups and others is P. Scheepers, A. Feeling, and J. Peters's "Ethnocentrism in the Netherlands," *Ethnic and Racial Studies* (July 1989).

PART 3

Social Control and the Criminal Justice System

Specific problems endemic to the criminal justice system as well as possible solutions to crime problems are important. Is the system racist, as most criminologists as well as political activists have claimed for generations? Is the juvenile system too lenient on young criminals, who come close to commiting the bulk of certain crimes in the United States? If it is too lenient, exactly how hard should we crack down on youthful offenders? Other important areas of concern include plea bargaining, the issue of selective incapacitation as a viable crime reduction strategy, and capital punishment. Last, we examine the issue of domestic violence and arrest as a means of deterrence.

Is the Criminal Justice System Racist?

ISSUE 8

Is the Criminal Justice System Racist?

YES: Adalberto Aguirre, Jr., and David V. Baker, from "Empirical Research on Racial Discrimination in the Imposition of the Death Penalty," *Criminal Justice Abstracts* (March 1990)

NO: William Wilbanks, from *The Myth of a Racist Criminal Justice System* (Brooks/Cole, 1987)

ISSUE SUMMARY

YES: University of California, Riverside, criminologist Adalberto Aguirre, Jr., and Riverside Community College professor David Baker insist that in the most crucial prison sentence possible—the imposition of the death penalty—racial discrimination remains a fact of life.

NO: Florida International University criminologist William Wilbanks raises several important issues in his defense of the U.S. criminal justice system. While acknowledging that there are racist police officers, district attorneys, and judges, he contends that, overall, criminal justice is fair.

Long before the U.S. Supreme Court in the early 1970s wrestled with the constitutionality of capital punishment because of the arbitrary manner in which it was applied, many social critics contended that all levels of the criminal justice system were racist. Historically, in many states but especially in the South, blacks were far more likely to be sentenced to death than whites. In the antebellum South, there were sometimes even different types of death penalties set aside for blacks (for example, being burned at the stake). And in many Southern states, there were far more capital crimes for blacks than for whites.

Capital offenses, however, were not the only areas in which blacks were thought to be treated grossly unfairly. Studies have revealed that blacks were more likely to be harassed by police, arrested, brought to trial, given prison sentences rather than probation, given longer prison sentences, less likely to receive parole, and to have more severe guidelines for parole when parole was granted. Within courtrooms in the South and in some midwestern and even northern states, judges would use different forms of address for blacks whether they were witnesses or defendants. In Alabama, for instance, as late as 1968, both prosecuting and defense attorneys had the right to refer to a black witness as "Auntie" or "Missy." Black males, no matter what their earned titles or status within the community, were likely to be called "Boy" or "Uncle." Such demeaning terms served to minimize the credibility of the black witness or defendant.

Even in northern states, blacks were unlikely to be represented within most levels of the criminal justice system, especially in higher positions. Until the past few decades, district attorneys, judges, wardens, and police administrators were rarely black. Blacks were also systematically excluded from jury duty in many counties, especially in major cases. Thus, black defendants were denied the right to be tried by their peers.

On the streets, blacks were frequently subject to dragnets within their communities—a practice that was not uncommon through the early 1970s. When the police suspected a black of having committed a crime, especially involving a white victim, they would routinely go into black neighborhoods, round up any and all black males over fourteen, and take them to the police station. There, without being informed of their rights or even what crimes they were suspected of committing, they would be placed into a lineup.

White patrolmen with beats in black communities would also freely insult blacks. White lawyers often did not feel obligated to provide black clients with first-rate defenses. Within the prison community, until the 1960s, blacks had even fewer privileges and benefits than white inmates. Wardens and guards were more likely to turn control of blacks over to certain black inmates, who could be as cruel or crueler to blacks than racist white guards.

Statistically, blacks currently comprise approximately 12 percent of the U.S. population. However, it does seem evident that they represent a disproportionately large percentage of certain serious crimes. In the 1980s, blacks accounted for over one-fourth of those arrested for burglary, 61 percent of those arrested for robbery, about 45 percent of those arrested for homicide, and 46 percent of those charged with forcible rape. In other areas (for example, occupational and white-collar crimes), they have been significantly underrepresented. On self-reported crime surveys, black adolescents tend to indicate higher rates of involvement in serious violent crimes. However, blacks are often much more likely to be the victims of crime. For instance, currently in the United States, a black male is about six times as likely to be murdered as a white male.

When socioeconomic *class* is taken into account, many of these variations in criminal offenses by *race* disappear.

Issue 9 refocuses the controversy. Aguirre and Baker go to considerable pains to maintain the traditional view that our legal system is racist. Their discussion is penetrating, and they do much to document their claim: "It appears [for] the court that racism is a legitimate penological doctrine." Florida International University criminologist Wilbanks, in a novel reinterpretation of arrest and conviction statistics, presents an unorthodox perspective. He argues that the system is not really racist after all.

YES

Adalberto Aguirre, Jr.,
and David V. Baker

EMPIRICAL RESEARCH ON RACIAL DISCRIMINATION IN THE IMPOSITION OF THE DEATH PENALTY

The U.S. Bureau of Justice Statistics (1985) reports that between 1930 and 1984 there were 3,891 prisoners executed under civil authority in the United States. Of these figures, 2,067 (53.1%) were black, 1,773 (45.5%) were white and 42 (1.0%) were of other races. There were 1,640 (48.7%) blacks and 1,686 (50.8%) whites executed for murder. Racial disparity in imposing the death penalty becomes even more clearly defined among executions for rape. Of the 455 executions for rape during this period, 89% (405) were of blacks and 10.5% (48) were of whites. The South executed 98.3% (398) of all blacks executed for rape. While the north central region of the country executed the remaining seven blacks executed for rape, the western and northwestern sections have never executed a black for rape. The District of Columbia, Virginia, West Virginia, Mississippi, Louisiana and Oklahoma have never executed a white for the crime of rape.

Given that blacks have consistently represented about 11% of the total American population since 1930, these statistics overwhelmingly indicate that the death penalty has been disproportionately applied to blacks. Blacks have been executed for murder at over five times the rate of executions for whites, and blacks have been executed for rape at about nine times the execution rate than whites. These statistics alone do not show that racial discrimination has characterized the imposition of the death penalty to blacks. But a number of empirical studies have shown that in the case of blacks, disproportionality in the application of the death penalty amounts to racial discrimination. The purpose of this paper, then, is to review the empirical studies that have established rather pervasive evidence that the death penalty has not only been disproportionately applied to blacks convicted of rape and murder, but that the death penalty has been imposed on black prisoners in a discretionary and discriminatory manner. This review

From Adalberto Aguirre, Jr., and David V. Baker, "Empirical Research on Racial Discrimination in the Imposition of the Death Penalty," *Criminal Justice Abstracts*, vol. 22, no. 1 (March 1990). Reprinted and condensed by permission of *Criminal Justice Abstracts*, published by Willow Tree Press, P.O. Box 249, Monsey, NY 10952.

will clearly illustrate that racial discrimination has become so well entrenched and routinized in imposing the penalty of death on blacks that it has developed into a "systematic pattern of differential treatment" of blacks.

Many studies have documented evidence of racial discrimination in the imposition of the death penalty on blacks. These studies will be reviewed in relation to whether they were conducted before, during the interim, or after the United States Supreme Court decisions in *Furman v. Georgia* (1972) and *Gregg v. Georgia* (1976). The *Furman* decision basically held that all death penalty statutes in the United States were unconstitutional because they permitted capital punishment to be applied in a discretionary and discriminatory manner amounting to "cruel and unusual punishment" in violation of the Eighth Amendment of the U.S. federal Constitution. The *Furman* decision did not abolish capital punishment in the United States; the court argued that the death penalty "in and of itself" does not constitute cruel and unusual punishment, but, the capricious manner in which the penalty had been applied in the cases before the court at the time of *Furman* was held unconstitutional. In the *Gregg* decision, the court attempted to curb the extent to which the death penalty was applied to blacks in a discretionary and discriminatory manner by providing for guided discretion in capital sentencing. The court affirmed the death sentences of the cases under review in *Gregg* because the states from which the cases had originated, in their capital statutes, had directed attention to the circumstances of the crimes and provided for consideration of mitigating factors designed to protect against arbitrary imposition of the death penalty.

PRE-*FURMAN* STUDIES

The earliest study of black-white differentials in the administration of justice was completed by Brearley in 1930. Brearley found that among 407 homicide cases in South Carolina between 1920 and 1926, 52% of the accusations resulted in guilty verdicts. Of these convictions, 64% involved black defendants and 32% involved whites. Brearley . . . attributes this finding to "such factors as race prejudice by white jurors and court officials and the Negro's low economic status, which prevents him from securing 'good' criminal lawyers for his defense" . . .

As early as 1933, Myrdal reported that in ten southern states: "The Negro constitutes less than thirty percent of the population in these states, but has more than twice as many death sentences imposed. Actual executions make the racial differential still greater, for 60.9% of the Negro death sentences were carried out as compared with 48.7% of the white" . . .

In 1940, Mangum studied racial disparities in imposing the death penalty in several southern states. In his book *The Legal Status of the Negro*, Mangum reports that for the years 1920 to 1938, 74% of the blacks and 50% of the whites sentenced to death were executed. . . ..

Allredge (1942) reported that conviction rates for criminal homicide dramatically differed for blacks and whites in several regions of the South from 1940 to 1941. Allredge found that 89% of the blacks accused of murdering whites were convicted; 67% of the blacks accused of killing blacks were convicted; 64% of the whites accused of murdering whites were convicted; and only 43% of the whites accused of murdering blacks were convicted. . . .

Johnson (1957) studied rape cases resulting in the application of the death penalty in North Carolina between 1909 and 1954. He found that 56% of all persons executed during this period were black, and 43% were white. Johnson's study concluded that blacks were far more likely to suffer the death penalty for rape than whites convicted of rape.

The Florida Civil Liberties Union reported similar findings from a study conducted in that state in 1964. In Florida between 1940 and 1964, 54% (45) of the black males who raped white women, but none of the eight white males convicted of raping a black female, received the death penalty. . . .

Kleck (1981), who has critically evaluated the studies on racial discrimination in the use of the death penalty conducted prior to the *Furman* decision, makes two observations about these various studies. First, he argues that while there are conclusive patterns of racial discrimination against blacks in the use of the death penalty, these patterns are mostly restricted to the imposition of the death penalty in southern states. On this point, however, Kleck is incorrect. While racial disparities in imposing the penalty of death are more pronounced in the South, studies by the Ohio Legislative Service Commission (1961), Wolfgang et al. (1972), Zimring et al. (1976), Carter and Smith (1969), Kalven (1969), Bowers and Pierce (1980), Bedau (1964, 1965), and Gross and Mauro (1984, 1989) have shown that patterns of racial discrimination in presentencing, sentencing, and postsentencing decisions are not simply restricted to southern jurisdictions. . . . Gross and Mauro (1984), in fact, have commented on Kleck's conclusion. They note that "(t)o say there is no racial discrimination in capital sentencing, except in the South, is a bit like saying that there is no housing discrimination in a

metropolitan area, except in the major residential district." . . .

The second observation made by Kleck is that black defendants who murder black victims are the least likely defendant-victim category associated with the death penalty outside of the South. This observation has substantial merit, as noted above. In attempting to explain the apparently lenient treatment of black defendants convicted of murdering a black victim, Kleck suggests that "interracial crimes . . . are considered by [the] predominantly white social-control agents to be less serious offenses, representing less loss or threat to the community than crimes with white victims." . . .

Review of pre-*Furman* studies on capital punishment demonstrates that the death penalty was systematically applied to black defendants in a discretionary and discriminatory manner. We have seen that this practice has not simply been relegated to the South, but that racial discrimination in the use of the death penalty has been a national characteristic. Moreover, these various studies illustrate the extent to which racism has permeated the criminal justice institution in the United States. . . .

THE INTERIM PERIOD (POST-*FURMAN*, PRE-*GREGG*)

Several studies have been conducted on racial discrimination during the interim period after *Furman* was decided by the U.S. Supreme Court in 1972, but before the court handed down its decision in *Gregg* in 1976. One of the most important studies conducted during this period compared the racial composition of offenders under the sentence of death in December 1971 (pursuant to pre-*Furman* capital statutes) with offenders under the sentence of death as of December 1975 (pursuant to mandatory and discretionary post-*Furman* capital statutes). Riedel (1976) not only found that the racial disparities affecting death row inmates in the pre-*Furman* era remained unchanged in the post-*Furman* period, but also that black defendants-white victims was the racial category with the highest rate of death sentences imposed. Riedel reported that 53% of the death row inmates in December 1971 were nonwhite, and that this figure rose to 62% in December 1975. While the racial disparity of death row populations in the South had declined from 67% to 63% during this period, the western region of the United States increased its degree of racial disparity of black/white death row inmates from 26% to 52%. From these figures, Riedel concluded that the statutes enacted before and after the *Furman* decision produced the same degree of racial disproportion in death sentences.

Riedel also found that 87% of the death sentences were for white-victim murders, and 45% were for the murder of white victims by black defendants. The degree of racial disparity in death sentences is even more pronounced in this period (1971–1975), and the white victim-black defendant category comprised the smallest proportion of the total number of murder cases.

In a study of first-degree murder prosecutions in Dade County, Florida, from 1973 to 1976, Arkin (1980) reported that black defendants who murdered whites were more likely to be sentenced to death than white defendants. Arkin's data reveal that black offenders who killed whites were convicted of first-degree murder about four times more often than blacks who killed blacks. While the black offender/white victim category of criminal offense comprised only 21% of the 350 murder cases prosecuted, 50% of the cases resulting in death penalty sentences came from that category of offender. . . .

In sum, these studies show that the *Furman* decision had little or no diminishing effect on the extent to which black capital offenders were subjected to racial discrimination in imposition of the death penalty. As noted, the *Furman* decision ruled that discrimination in applying the death penalty is blatantly unconstitutional. These studies show, however, that the death penalty was still used as a mechanism by which to protect a specific class of individuals—namely whites— from criminal victimization. Black defendants whose victims were white were overwhelmingly convicted and sentenced to death when compared to other racial categories of defendant-victim. *Furman* had no demonstrable effect on the manner in which the death penalty was being applied in this country.

POST-*GREGG* STUDIES

In *Gregg,* the U.S. Supreme Court upheld the constitutionality of the death penalty for murder. The court affirmed the convictions because the states from which the capital cases originated had provided for: bifurcated trials (one trial to establish the guilt of the defendant, and another trial to determine an appropriate sentence); consideration of mitigating circumstances of the defendant and the crime; and appellate review of capital sentences. These guidelines were affirmed by the court because they were specifically designed to prevent arbitrary and discriminatory imposition of the death penalty. . . .

Within the past few years, empirical analyses have revealed that the guidelines established in *Gregg* have failed to eliminate racial disparities in capital cases. One of the most extensive studies analyzing data collected after the *Gregg* decision was conducted by Bowers and Pierce (1980). Bowers and Pierce examined patterns of death sentencing in Florida, Texas, Ohio, and Georgia from 1972 to 1977. . . . Basically, Bowers and Pierce found that the decision to execute in these states reflects the same arbitrariness and discrimination that has characterized the imposition of the death penalty in the past (before the *Furman* and *Gregg* decisions). In each of these states, Bowers and Pierce found that killers of whites were more likely to be sentenced to death than killers of blacks, and that black defendants with white victims were more likely to receive the death penalty than white defendants with black victims. In Florida, black defendants with white victims were found to have a 22% chance of being sentenced to death; white defendants with white victims had a 20% chance; and black defendants with black victims had a .6% chance. It should be noted that in Florida, no white was sentenced to death for the killing of a black. Georgia and Texas had somewhat lower rates of death sentences according to defendant-victim categories, but the pattern of racial discrimination in imposing the death penalty in particular defendant-victim racial combinations still prevailed. . . . More specifically, black defendants with white victims were eight times more likely to be sentenced to death than black defendants with black victims. In addition, Florida prosecutors overcharged non-felony homicide cases involving black killers of white victims as felony homicides. Bowers and

Pierce have pointed out that the data on felony homicides suggests that "in black offender/white victim cases, prosecutors may have alleged felony circumstances to enhance their plea bargaining positions or as a demonstration of concern for the kinds of crimes the community finds most shocking." . . . Likewise, in Florida and Georgia, appellate review of capital sentences did not correct for patterns of racial discrimination in imposing death to blacks. Thus, the guidelines established in *Gregg* have "become the instruments of arbitrariness and discrimination, not their cure." . . .

Radelet (1981) examined whether race remains a significant factor in the processing and outcome of post-*Furman* homicide cases in 20 Florida counties in 1976 and 1977. He discovered that blacks accused of murdering whites were more likely to be sentenced to death than blacks accused of murdering blacks. This trend is explained by Radelet as due primarily to higher probabilities that blacks accused of murdering whites would be indicted for first-degree murder. . . . Thus, Radelet's study tends to indicate that racial discrimination is alive and well in Florida's criminal justice system to the extent that a lower value is placed on the lives of blacks than on the lives of whites. . . .

Using data on 1,400 homicide cases in some 32 Florida counties between 1973 and 1977, Radelet and Pierce (1985) examined disparities between police reports and court records on "felony," "possible felony" and "non-felony" homicides. Among racial combinations of defendant-victim, black defendants who killed white victims were considerably more likely to have their cases upgraded to a felony charge and least likely to have their cases downgraded to a lesser charge as they moved through the judicial process. . . .

In South Carolina, Paternoster (1983) found that when the race of the offender and of the victim are considered together a clear pattern of racial disparity in prosecutors' decisions to seek the death penalty is evidenced. . . . The race of the victim appears to be a more important consideration of public prosecutors than is the race of the offender, concludes Paternoster. Hence, post-*Furman* capital punishment statutes fail to remedy the problem of racial discrimination influencing imposition of the death penalty in capital cases. . . .

Gross and Mauro . . . conducted a very extensive study of sentencing under post-*Furman* death penalty laws in Arkansas, Florida, Georgia, Illinois, Mississippi, North Carolina, Oklahoma and Virginia. . . . While the data permitted separate analyses for Georgia, Florida and Illinois, death sentences for the states of Arkansas, Mississippi, North Carolina, Oklahoma and Virginia were analyzed collectively. In Georgia, Florida and Illinois, Gross and Mauro . . . found that while blacks and other racial minorities comprised a larger percentage of homicide victims than whites, the risk of a death sentence was far lower for suspects charged with killing blacks than for defendants charged with killing whites. For the state of Georgia, defendants who killed whites were almost ten times more likely to be sentenced to death than defendants whose victims were blacks; in Florida, the killers of whites were eight times more likely to be sentenced to death; and in Illinois, killers of whites were about six times more likely to be sentenced to death.

When controlling for the race of the victim, Gross and Mauro found that blacks who killed whites were far more likely to be sentenced to death than whites who killed whites. . . .

McCLESKY V. KEMP (1987)

In 1978, Warren McClesky, a black man, was convicted in Fulton County, Georgia of murdering a white police officer during an armed robbery of a furniture store. The conviction was in keeping with the Georgia statute, under which a jury cannot sentence a defendant to death for murder without a finding that the crime was aggravated by at least one of ten particular circumstances. McClesky failed to present any mitigating evidence to the jury and was subsequently sentenced to death.

On appeal to the U.S. Supreme Court, McClesky claimed that the Georgia capital sentencing process is administered in a racially discriminatory manner in violation of the eighth amendment protection against "cruel and unusual punishment," and that the discriminatory system violates the fourteenth amendment guarantee to the "equal protection of the law." McClesky proffered the results of the Baldus et al. . . . study in support of his claim. In 2,484 murder and non-negligent manslaughter cases in Georgia between 1973 and 1979, defendants who killed whites were sentenced to death in 11% of the cases, while defendants who killed blacks were sentenced to death in only 1% of the cases. Baldus et al. discovered that the death penalty was imposed in 22% of the cases where the defendant was convicted of murdering a white, 8% of the cases with white defendants and white victims, 3% of the cases with white defendants and black victim, and only 1% of the cases involving black defendants and black victims. Baldus et al.

controlled for some 230 non-racial variables and found that none could account for the racial disparities in capital sentences among the different racial combinations of defendant-victim. Killers of whites were 4.3 times more likely to be sentenced to death than killers of blacks, and black defendants were 1.1 times more likely to be sentenced to death than other defendants.

McClesky claimed that race had, therefore, infected the administration of capital punishment in Georgia in two distinct ways. First, "prisoners who murder whites are more likely to be sentenced to death than prisoners who murder blacks," and, secondly, "black murderers are more likely to be sentenced to death than white murderers" (McClesky, 1987:9). McClesky held that he was discriminated against by the Georgia system of imposing the death penalty because he is a black man who killed a white.

On April 22, 1987, the U.S. Supreme Court handed down its decision. . . . The question before the court in McClesky was "whether a complex statistical study that indicates a risk that racial consideration enters into capital sentencing determinations . . . is unconstitutional under the Eighth and Fourteenth Amendments" (McClesky, 1987:1).

Writing for the majority, Justice Powell held that the Baldus study does not prove that the administration of the Georgia capital punishment system violates the equal protection clause of the fourteenth amendment or the eighth amendment's protection against cruel and unusual punishment. The court held that "a defendant who alleges an equal protection violation has the burden of proving 'the existence of purposeful discrimination,' " and that the "purposeful discrimination had a discriminatory ef-

fect on him." That is, McClesky must prove that the jury in his particular case acted with a discriminatory purpose; to establish only that a "pattern" of racial discrimination in imposing the death penalty to a select group of defendants is not sufficient to support a claim of constitutional violation of equal protection of the law. The court further held that McClesky's claim of cruel and unusual punishment also fails because McClesky "cannot prove a constitutional violation by demonstrating that other defendants who may be similarly situated did not receive the death penalty." The Georgia sentencing procedures were found by the court to be sufficient to focus discretion "on the particularized nature of the crime and the particularized characteristics of the individual defendant," and that it cannot, therefore, be presumed that McClesky's death sentence was "wantonly and freakishly" imposed.

The essence of the court's holding in McClesky is that there are acceptable standards of risk of racial discrimination in imposing the death penalty. The court held that the Baldus study simply shows that a discrepancy appears to correlate with race in imposing death sentences, but the "statistics do not prove that race enters into any capital sentencing decisions or that race was a factor in petitioners' cases." The court was also concerned that a finding for the defendant in this case would open other claims that "could be extended to other types of penalties and to claims based on unexplained discrepancies correlating to membership in other minority groups and even to gender."

To Justices Brennan, Marshall, Blackmun, and Stevens, "McClesky has clearly demonstrated that his death sentence was imposed in violation of the Eighth and Fourteenth Amendments," and that "(n)othing could convey more powerfully the intractable reality of the death penalty: 'that the effort of eliminate arbitrariness in the infliction of that ultimate sanction is so plainly doomed to failure that it—and the death penalty—must be abandoned all together". . . . The dissenters argued that whether McClesky can prove racial discrimination in his particular case is totally irrelevant in evaluating his claim of a constitutional violation because the court has long recognized that to establish that a "pattern" of substantial risk of arbitrary and capricious capital sentencing suffices for a claim of unconstitutionality.

The dissenting justices also called into question the effectiveness of the statutory safeguards designed to curb discretionary use of the death penalty. Justice Brennan specifically argued that "(w)hile we may hope that a model of procedural fairness [as that established in *Gregg*] will curb the influence of race on sentencing, 'we cannot simply assume that the model works as intended; we must critique its performance in terms of its results". . . .

CONCLUSIONS

This review has examined several of the more important studies that have been conducted on the extent to which arbitrariness and discrimination characterize the imposition of capital punishment in the United States. Two substantive conclusions emerged. First despite the attempts by the U.S. Supreme Court in *Furman v. Georgia (1972)* and *Gregg v. Georgia (1976)* to thwart racial discrimination in the use of capital punishment, the death penalty continues to be imposed against blacks in a "wanton" and "freakish" manner. Second, the specific find-

ing by many of the studies that blacks who victimize whites consistently have the highest probability of receiving a capital sentence tends to substantiate the claim that capital punishment serves the extralegal function of majority group protection; namely, the death penalty acts to safeguard (through deterrence) that class of individuals (whites) who are least likely to be victimized.

The review has shown that the death penalty continues to be imposed to blacks in a capricious manner. That is, the evidence tends to confirm the hypothesis that arbitrariness is an inherent characteristic of the use of the death penalty. Studies by Riedel (1976) and Arkin (1980) show that the same degree of racial disparity present in pre-*Furman* cases is also prevalent in post-*Furman* cases. Several other studies have also shown that the safeguards for guided discretion in the use of the death penalty have failed to correct for the racial disparities. Specific analyses have shown that as long as individual prosecutors continue to have broad-based discretion to select which cases they will try as capital cases, racial discrimination in application of the death penalty will undoubtedly continue. Racial discrimination in the use of the death penalty has also been found to be perpetuated through appellate review of capital cases. The irony here is that the appellate courts were highly touted in *Gregg* as the foremost safeguard against unguided discretion in the application of the death penalty.

Various studies reviewed in this paper have shown that black defendants with white victims have been overwhelmingly convicted and sentenced to death when compared to other defendant-victim racial categories. . . . These findings clearly show that when whites are the victims of heinous crimes perpetrated by blacks, punishment is much more harsh. The review clearly illustrates that racism has become so well entrenched and routinized in the imposition of the death penalty that it has developed into a systematic pattern of differential treatment of blacks that is specifically designed to protect members of the dominant white group. While a preponderance of contemporary authors and jurists writing on theories of crime and punishment readily cite retribution and deterrence as foremost rationales for imposing the death penalty on those who commit heinous crimes, this review of empirical studies shows that the death penalty serves the extralegal function of protecting whites.

As we have seen in reviewing post-*Gregg* studies, the wrongs of racial prejudice, racial inequality, and caprice in the imposition of the death penalty have not been abolished by the procedural safeguards established in *Gregg*. Capital punishment continues to be imposed in a wanton and freakish and discriminatory manner against black criminal defendants. As Goodman has explained, "the sentencer's choice between life and death increasingly appears inchoate and uncontrollable, a decision more visceral than cerebral." . . . Empirically-based evidence that racial discrimination continues to influence the imposition of the death penalty has literally been ignored by the court in *McClesky*. The proposed safeguards that surround the application of the death penalty amount to no safeguards at all. The only substantive conclusion that can be drawn from this review is that the court has moved from a position of formally recognizing that imposition of the death penalty is imbued with racial prejudice (*Furman*), to a position of sanctioning racial prejudice

as a cost of imposing the penalty (*McClesky*). It appears from the cases handed down from the court that racism is a legitimate penological doctrine. For the advocates of racial and ethnic equality, the death penalty cannot be morally justified on the premise that racial oppression, subjugation, and social subservience are legitimate liabilities of maintaining social order. Social order under these circumstances amounts to social order predicated upon racism.

REFERENCES

Allredge, E. (1942). "Why the South Leads the Nation in Murder and Manslaughter." *The Quarterly Review* 2:123.

Arkin, Steven (1980). "Discrimination and Arbitrariness in Capital Punishment: An Analysis of Post-*Furman* Murder Cases in Dade County, Florida, 1973–1976." *Stanford Law Review* 33:75–101.

Baldus, David C., Charles Pulaski and George Woodworth (1983). "Comparative Review of Death Sentences: An Empirical Study of the Georgia Experience." *Journal of Criminal Law and Criminology* 74(3):661–770.

———— (1985). "Monitoring and Evaluating Contemporary Death Sentencing Systems: Lessons from Georgia," *University of California, Davis Law Review* 18(4):1375–1407.

Bowers, William J. (1974). *Executions in America*, Lexington, MA: D.C. Heath and Company.

———— (1983). "The Pervasiveness of Arbitrariness and Discrimination Under Post-*Furman* Capital Statutes." *Journal of Criminal Law and Criminology* 74(3):1067–1100.

———— and Glenn L. Pierce (1980). "Arbitrariness and Discrimination Under Post-*Furman* Capital Statutes." *Crime & Delinquency* 26(4):563–635.

Brearley, H. (1930). "The Negro and Homicides." *Social Forces* 9(2):247–253.

Carter, Robert M. and LaMont A. Smith (1969). "The Death Penalty in California: A Statistical Composite Portrait." *Crime & Delinquency* 15(1):63–76.

Furman v. Georgia (1976). 408 U.S. 238.

Johnson, Elmer (1957). "Selective Factors in Capital Punishment." *Social Forces* 35(2):165–169.

Kalven, Harry, Jr. (1969). "A Study of the California Penalty Jury in First-Degree Murder Cases. [Preface.]" *Stanford Law Review* 21:1297–1301.

Kleck, Gary (1981). "Racial Discrimination in Criminal Sentencing: A Critical Evaluation of the Evidence with Additional Evidence on the Death Penalty." *American Sociological Review* 46:783–804.

McClesky v. Kemp (1987), Slip Opinion #84–6811.

Paternoster, Raymond (1983). "Race of Victim and Location of Crime: The Decision to Seek the Death Penalty in South Carolina." *Journal of Criminal Law and Criminology* 74(3):754–785.

_____ (1984). "Prosecutorial Discretion in Requesting the Death Penalty: A Case of Victim-Based Racial Discrimination." *Law & Society Review* 18(3):437–478.

Radelet, Michael (1981). "Racial Characteristics and the Imposition of the Death Penalty." *American Sociological Review* 46:918–927.

_____ and Glenn Pierce (1985). "Race and Prosecutorial Discretion in Homicide Cases." *Law & Society Review* 19:587–621.

_____ and Margaret Vandiver (1983). "The Florida Supreme Court and Death Penalty Appeals." *Journal of Criminal Law and Criminology* 73:913–926.

Riedel, Marc (1976) "Discrimination in the Imposition of the Death Penalty: A Comparison of the Characteristics of Offenders Sentenced pre-*Furman* and post-*Furman*." *Temple Law Quarterly* 49:261–287.

Wolfgang, Marvin E. (1974). "Racial Discrimination in the Death Sentence for Rape." In: William J. Bowers ed., *Executions in America*. Lexington, MA: D.C. Heath and Company, 109–120.

_____ and Marc Riedel (1973). "Racial Discrimination and the Death Penalty." *Annals of the American Academy of Political and Social Science* 407:119–133.

_____ and Marc Riedel (1975). "Rape, Race, and the Death Penalty in Georgia." *American Journal of Orthopsychiatry* 45:658–668.

_____, Arlene Kelley and Hans C. Nolde (1962). "Comparison of the Executed and the Commuted Among Admissions to Death Row." *Journal of Criminal Law, Criminology, and Police Science* 53(3):301–311.

Zimring, Franklin, Sheila O'Malley and Joel Eigen (1976). "The Going Price of Criminal Homicide in Philadelphia." *University of Chicago Law Review* 43:227–252.

NO   William Wilbanks

THE MYTH OF A
RACIST CRIMINAL JUSTICE SYSTEM

THE MYTH EXAMINED

White and black Americans differ sharply over whether their criminal justice system is racist. The vast majority of blacks appear to believe that the police and courts do discriminate against blacks, whereas a majority of whites reject this charge. In Dade County (Miami), Florida, for example, a poll by a television station found that 97 percent of blacks believed the justice system to be racist and that 58 percent of whites rejected this charge. This disparity in views between blacks and whites also appears to exist among those who work in the criminal justice system. A supplemental study for the National Advisory Commission on Civil Disorders in 1968 found that 57 percent of black police officers but only 5 percent of white officers believed that the system discriminated against blacks.

Some black critics have suggested that the criminal justice system is so characterized by racism that blacks are outside the protection of the law. Furthermore, many blacks believe that when whites speak of wanting justice, they really mean "just us" (blacks). Another critic finds the criminal justice system to be more criminal than just.

A sizable minority of whites, in contrast, believe that the justice system actually discriminates for *for* blacks in "leaning over backward" for them in reaction to charges of racism from the black community, liberal white politicians, and liberal elements of the news media. . . .

This book is written in the belief that many aspects of the question "Is the criminal justice system racist?" have not been addressed by criminologists and that the issue as a whole has not been addressed in a manner designed for consumers. Both laypersons and those who work in the criminal justice system can find nothing in the current literature to guide them in determining whether the system is racist. This book is intended to fill that void. . . .

I take the position that the perception of the criminal justice system as racist is a myth. . . .

SENTENCING AND RACIAL DISCRIMINATION

There are more empirical studies on discrimination at sentencing than at any other decision point in the criminal justice system. The reason does not appear to be that researchers view judges as those in the system who are most likely to discriminate (most would make that charge against the police); rather, data are more readily available at this point for statistical analysis. Furthermore, sentencing is a popular subject because the judge makes decisions that can result in lengthy prison terms or even death. . . .

Three Major Reviews of the Literature
Three major reviews of the literature in recent years have summarized and critiqued "what we know" about the impact of race on criminal sentencing. The first was in 1974 by Hagan, who reviewed twenty published studies. In 1981 Kleck reviewed fifty-seven studies. And the National Research Council reviewed more than sixty studies in 1983.

Hagan computed a measure of association for seventeen of the studies that he had reviewed and found that (before controls) knowledge of race of offender improved accuracy in predicting the sentence by a maximum of only 8 percent. (Several of them improved predictive ability by less than 1 percent, though the results were statistically significant.) Hagan concluded that the researchers' failure to calculate measures of association and reliance only on tests of statistical significance had left the incorrect impression that race was an important predictor of sentence. Furthermore, those studies that had controlled for type of offense and prior record found that the small relationship between race and sentence was reduced to statistical insignificance.

Hagan found similarly low measures of association in studies of capital sentencing. Even before controlling for type of offense the median measure of association was only .015, indicating that knowing the race of the offender in capital cases increased the accuracy of predicting sentence by only 1.5 percent. Hagan also compared intraracial with interracial cases but found that knowing the race of defendants and victims was important only in capital rape cases in the South (increasing prediction of outcome by 22.6 percent, before controls). He summarized his review with respect to race in the following words:

> Evidence of differential sentencing was found in inter-racial *capital cases* in the southern United States. In samples of *noncapital cases*, however, when offense type was held constant among offenders with no prior record, the relationship between race and disposition was diminished below statistical significance. Holding offense type constant, among offenders with "some" previous convictions, a modest, statistically significant relationship between race and disposition was sustained in two of three studies. The need for stricter control over the *number* of previous convictions was indicated.

Kleck reviewed seventeen studies of the imposition of the death penalty and forty studies of noncapital sentencing. He summarizes his conclusions as follows:

> 1. The death penalty has not generally been imposed for murder in a fashion discriminatory toward blacks, except in the South. Elsewhere, black homicide offenders have been less likely to receive a death sentence or be executed than whites.

2. For the 11 percent of executions which have been imposed for rape, discrimination against black defendants who had raped white victims was substantial. Such discrimination was limited to the South and has disappeared because death sentences are no longer imposed for rape.

3. Regarding noncapital sentencing, the evidence is largely contrary to a hypothesis of general or widespread overt discrimination against black defendants, although there is evidence of discrimination for a minority of specific jurisdictions, judges, crime types, etc.

4. Although black offender-white victim crimes are generally punished more severely than crimes involving other racial combinations, the evidence indicates that this is due to legally relevant factors related to such offenses, not the racial combination itself.

5. There appears to be a general pattern of less severe punishment of crimes with black victims than those of white victims, especially in connection with imposition of the death penalty. In connection with noncapital sentencing, the evidence is too sparse to draw any firm conclusions.

The third major review of the empirical literature on impact of race on sentencing is by the Panel on Sentencing Research, which was established by the National Academy of Sciences on request of the U.S. Department of Justice. The panel itself drew some conclusions and also reported the conclusions of consultants. After reviewing over seventy sentencing studies it concluded:

Our overall assessment of the available research suggests that factors other than racial discrimination in the sentencing process account for most of the disproportionate representation of black males in U.S. prisons, although discrimination in sentencing may play a more important role in some regions, jurisdictions, crime types, or the decisions of individual participants.

We also note, however, that even a small amount of racial discrimination is a matter that needs to be taken very seriously, both on general normative grounds and because small effects in the aggregate can imply unacceptable deprivations for large numbers of people. Thus even though the effect of race in sentencing may be small compared to that of other factors, such differences are important.

Some studies find statistical evidence of racial discrimination; others find none. While there is no evidence of a widespread systematic pattern of discrimination in sentencing, some pockets of discrimination are found for particular crime types, and in particular settings. The studies, however, are vulnerable in varying degrees to a variety of statistical problems that temper the strength of these conclusions.

The panel also addressed the combined impact of the race of the victim and offender. Though it found that ten of the fourteen studies examining the offender's and victim's race did find a race effect, it also pointed out that

the 10 studies finding an effect for offender and victim race either fail to include or only partially control for these dimensions of offense seriousness. Four other studies that do control for factors associated with interracial offenses do not find any effect on sentence for offender and victim race. . . . The suppression of the estimated discrimination effect when controls for these other elements of offense seriousness are included suggests that the biases in the offender/victim race effect are likely to be dominated by overestimates.

The conclusions of the panel's consultants are similar to those above. Two of these articles, however, attempt to explain why some sentencing studies find a race effect and others do not. An article by Hagan and Bumiller points out that the increased tendency in recent (post–1969) studies to control for more legal variables has not resulted in fewer findings of racial discrimination but in more such findings:

> The challenge is to explain why some studies find discrimination while others do not, and why among those studies including controls for legitimized variables the proportion finding discrimination has shown signs of increasing. Our explanation is that with increasing sensitivity, those researchers who find evidence of discrimination have specified for study structural contexts in which discrimination by race is most likely to occur.

Hagan and Bumiller suggest that those "structural contexts" that increase the likelihood of finding a race effect include the death penalty in the South, rural rather than urban courts, politically sensitive crimes like rape, and jurisdictions where probation officers make sentencing recommendations. In contrast, studies in the last decade that did not find discrimination had focused on areas such as large urban courts, which are so highly bureaucratized that they may be too constrained by a lack of time and resources to allow direct discrimination by race.

The second review article that attempts to explain why some sentencing studies find a race effect but others do not is by Klepper, Nagin, and Tierney. The authors argue that "sample selection bias is likely to cause all the studies to underestimate the magnitude of discrimination in sentencing decisions." Sample selection bias refers to the possibility that studies examining only the sentencing stage may underestimate the race effect in sentencing, since the race effect does not occur at the point of sentencing but at earlier decision points (arrest, charging, conviction). They point out, however, that sample selection bias can mask a race effect at sentencing only if there is a demonstrable race effect at one or more earlier points in the system. Their analysis appears to have led the panel to recommend that future research compare black/white ratios by type of crime at each of the intermediate stages of the criminal justice system between arrest and prison. . . .

Differences in Method and Interpretation

The conclusions of the three reviews described above have not gone unchallenged. Austin maintains that Kleck's evidence "shows discrimination to be more widespread than he allows." According to Austin, some studies that Kleck claims showed no discrimination had been improperly interpreted. Also, Kleck is sometimes misread as having concluded that there was *no* evidence of racial discrimination, when he had actually concluded that the evidence was *largely* contrary to the discrimination thesis and that discrimination was not *general or widespread* (not that it did not exist).

Going further, one can find numerous assertions in the literature that "the evidence" clearly indicates widespread racial discrimination at the point of sentencing (a view opposite to that expressed by the three major reviews). Note the following:

> The nature and extent of racial discrimination in criminal sentencing is seldom addressed by legal authorities or dis-

cussed in judicial circles. Yet such discrimination is widely perceived in our communities and clearly supported by statistics.

Numerous studies have shown that African-Americans are more likely to be arrested, indicted, convicted, and committed to an institution than are whites who commit the same offenses, and many others have shown that blacks have a poorer chance than whites to receive probation, a suspended sentence, parole, commutation of a death sentence, or pardon.

Why do the more exhaustive reviews of the literature find little evidence of racial discrimination, whereas individual studies often find evidence of a race effect at the point of sentencing? Kleck maintains that commentators selectively choose studies (from among those with contradictory conclusions) to support their position. But the problem is more than simple bias in the selection of studies. Different models of method and interpretation contribute to the disagreement found in the literature. . . .

What Is Known About Race and Sentencing: A Summary

[I have] attempted to point out the difficulties in proving or disproving the existence of racial discrimination at the point of sentencing by illustrating how different research methods and interpretations lead to different conclusions about a race effect. You should not be left with the impression, however, that these difficulties prevent us from really knowing anything about race and sentencing. Several findings appear to be generally valid across the literature.

1. *Racial discrimination in sentencing has declined over time.* Two reviews of the literature suggest that a race effect was more likely to have been found (and if found more likely to have been greater in magnitude) in studies from the 1960s and earlier. One study that examined burglary and robbery cases in Milwaukee courts for an eleven-year period found that a race effect found for 1967–1968 had disappeared by 1971–1972 and 1976–1977. The authors of that study attributed the "racial neutrality" in later years to changes in the composition of the judiciary, a greater bureaucratization of the prosecutorial and defense bar, and the rise of decision rules that reduced the effect of judicial ideology on outcomes.

2. *Race of defendant does not have a consistent impact across crimes and jurisdictions.* In other words, some studies have found that in some jurisdictions blacks receive harsher sentences for some crimes but more lenient sentences for others. Likewise, although blacks may be more likely than whites to be sent to prison in one state, they may be less likely in another. California and Pennsylvania illustrate this change in the "direction" of the relationship between race and sentence. . . . Also even within a state the extent of a race effect may vary sharply between rural and urban courts.

3. *Race of victim may be a better predictor of sentence than race of defendant.* This is certainly true for death penalty cases, but the research in noncapital cases has seldom included race of victim as a variable, and thus the pattern is less clear. However, studies finding that cases involving white victims received harsher treatment than cases involving black victims also find that white defendants were treated more harshly than black defendants (since much crime is intraracial). Thus if one argues that racial discrimination exists because of favoritism to white victims (that is, by harsher sentences to

offenders against white victims), one should also argue that reverse racial discrimination exists against white defendants because of their tendency to victimize other whites. It is curious that harsher treatment of white defendants is seen as racial discrimination against blacks.

4. *Extralegal variables (for example, race, sex, age, socioeconomic status of defendant) are not as predictive of sentence as legal variables (for example, type of crime, strength of evidence).*

5. *The black/white variation in sentences is generally reduced to near zero when several legal variables are introduced as controls.*

6. *The race effect, even before controls, is not "substantially" significant, in that the predictive power of race is quite low.* Given this result it is difficult to maintain the position that race has a "pervasive" effect on sentences. In other terms, it is difficult to argue from the available evidence that black defendants "always" or even "often" receive harsher sentences (either with respect to the in/out decision or in length of prison term) than whites.

7. *There is no evidence that black judges are less likely than white judges to send blacks to prison or to give them lengthy terms.* The only study comparing sentencing by black and white judges found that all sixteen black judges gave harsher sentences to black defendants than to whites and that the black judges sentenced black defendants more harshly than white judges did. If one argues that racial disparity in sentencing is indicative of racial discrimination, it is clear that black judges are more racist than white judges. The most likely interpretation is that blacks were sentenced more harshly by both white and black judges because of factors other than race that were deemed appropriate to consider. The fact that

there is no evidence that black judges "make a difference" suggests that racial discrimination is not an important factor in criminal sentencing.

8. *Most sentencing studies have a large residual variation, suggesting that the models used did not fit the actual decision-making process of judges.* The large residuals suggest that we know very little about sentencing as a result of the statistical studies that have been conducted.

9. *Since most sentencing studies have not examined the sentences of individual judges, the possibility remains that racial discrimination (both for and against blacks) exists on a rather large scale for individual cases but that the harsher and more lenient sentences by individual judges cancel each other out, thus producing no overall race effect for the court as a whole.*

POSTSCRIPT

Is the Criminal Justice System Racist?

Of the many clashing issues examined in this volume, none is more controversial while at the same time more or less "settled" as part of the received wisdom in criminology than the notion that the criminal justice system is racist. Everyone has always "known" that the police were far more likely to arrest blacks, that citizens were more likely to report blacks for alleged infractions, that courts were more likely to show blacks disrespect, convict them, and then sentence them to longer sentences than whites (or execute them).

Wilbanks's thesis—that while many elements within the criminal justice system remain racist, the system as a whole is no longer that way—fits into mainstream revisionist thinking. Some black sociologists and economists (for example, Thomas Sowell) have argued that blacks are economically deprived because of *class* rather than race. The assumption is that the social, economic, and political systems, for all practical purposes, no longer systematically discriminate against blacks. The reasons, then, for a disproportionately high number of blacks living below the poverty line have to be sought outside of racism.

In 1905, W. E. B. Du Bois predicted that the problem of the twentieth century would be the problem of racial discrimination. As we approach the end of this century, his insight remains uncanny. Looking at crime and criminology alone, we observe that the largest percentage of victms of violent crimes are blacks, that the largest proportion of American citizens arrested are black, and that the largest number of inmates in many prisons are also black and are frequently serving the longest sentences. Crime and color are linked in both official statistics and public perceptions.

Traditionally, America has been a racist society. Blacks, it is well known, were exploited and oppressed in virtually every aspect of social, economic, and political life. Today they are often not thought of as *victims* of crime but as criminals. Many maintain that the political sloganeering of "get tough on crime and drugs" means little more than "crack down on blacks."

Even nonpartisan political commentators feel that George Bush was elected president in 1988 partially on his campaign's successful effort to link Willie Horton with Michael Dukakis. (Horton is the young black male from Massachusetts who had been imprisoned for committing violent crimes. Walking away from a prison furlough he went to Maryland, where he terrorized a white couple and raped the wife. The Bush campaign message was brilliantly conveyed to middle-class white America that if Bush is not elected president, Willie Horton—or someone just like him—might be in your home next.)

Problematic is the extent of racism within the criminal justice system. Thomas Jefferson's assertion that "Error of opinion may be tolerated when reason is left to combat it" seems almost quaint when applied to this problem. If the system is still racist, as Aguirre and Baker insist, then immediate additional actions are clearly needed to remedy this injustice. If, as Wilbanks argues, it is not, then Wilbanks's message should be conveyed to the many liberal criminologists and a significant segment of the black and Hispanic populations who think otherwise.

For further reading, an excellent account of extreme prejudice is told in *Blood Justice: The Lynching of Mack Charles Parker*, by Howard Smead (Oxford University Press, 1985). One of the earlier studies finding evidence somewhat similar to Wilbanks's is Joan Petersilia's *Racial Disparities in the Criminal Justice System* (The Rand Corporation, 1985); see her "Racial Disparities in the Criminal Justice System" as well as opposing viewpoints in the *Crime and Delinquency* issue on "Race, Crime, and Criminal Justice," edited by R. Chilton and J. Galvin (January 1985).

Andrew Hacker provides an insightful discussion of several books on racism in the criminal justice system in "Black Crime, White Racism," *New York Review of Books* (March 3, 1988). For works agreeing with Aguirre and Baker's viewpoint, see "Race and the Death Penalty," by A. G. Amsterdam in *Criminal Justice Ethics* (Winter/Spring 1988); J. Humphrey and T. Fogarty's "Race and Plea Bargained Outcomes," in *Social Forces* (September 1987); and the article in the special issue of *Social Justice*, "Racism, Powerlessness and Justice" (Winter 1989). For a current overview of the tragedy of young black males in the justice system, see M. Mauer's "Young Black Men and the Criminal Justice System," in *Corrections Compendium* (March 1990). A helpful anthology of racism in another culture's legal system is *Ivory Scales: Black Australia and the Law*, edited by K. M. Hazlehurst (New Wales University Press, 1987).

ISSUE 9

Juvenile Justice: Are Kids "Getting Away With Murder"?

YES: Alfred S. Regnery, from "Getting Away With Murder: Why the Juvenile Justice System Needs an Overhaul," *Policy Review* (Fall 1985)

NO: Stephen J. Brodt and J. Steven Smith, from "Public Policy and the Serious Juvenile Offender," *Criminal Justice Policy Review* (March 1987)

ISSUE SUMMARY

YES: Former Office of Juvenile Justice and Delinquency Prevention administrator Alfred S. Regnery says that children commit one-third of all crimes yet are not held accountable for their acts. He calls for a return to the doctrine of deterrence because the old rehabilitation philosophy has clearly failed.

NO: Ball State University criminologists Stephen J. Brodt and J. Steven Smith reject Regnery's view of juvenile delinquency as well as the solutions he proposes, assert that claims of juveniles getting away with murder are greatly exaggerated, and argue that rehabilitation remains a workable ideal.

Adults have regularly complained that kids are running amuck. We cannot know the extent to which adult complaints are mere exaggeration based on misunderstandings or even envy. However, we can be certain that very real changes have taken place within the past century in response to juvenile delinquency.

Historically, in most societies, youths were treated similarly to adult offenders. But by the beginning of the twentieth century as social critics, concerned citizens, and criminologists became aware of serious abuses of juveniles within the criminal justice system, their efforts sparked reforms, and separate courts as well as separate penal institutions for youths emerged in many enlightened cities and towns in the United States.

A new legal and criminological theory developed vis-à-vis juvenile delinquents. The assumption was that the criminal justice system should work to help youngsters, not to humiliate or punish them. In many parts of the country, youths who were accused of crimes or who were identified by authorities as in need of supervision, went before juvenile masters and magistrates instead of judges. Trials were replaced by hearings and conferences, the ostensible purpose of which was to ascertain the best way to help a youth, not to determine his or her guilt. Structurally, components of the criminal justice system began to include youth service bureaus, social workers, counselors, and other professional youth workers.

Unfortunately, as the proverb observes, "the road to hell is paved with good intentions," and there were serious unanticipated negative consequences to these early twentieth-century reforms in the treatment of youthful offenders. Among the several negative consequences were those that resulted from the reconceptualization of what constituted a "crime" as applied to juveniles.

A brand new concept called "status offenders" was created. Offenses came into being for children that, if committed by adults, would not elicit official responses. These included truancy, running away from home, and "being sassy," among others. Children suspected of committing these offenses would no longer be called criminals or even juvenile delinquents. Instead, a new label, something such as "children in need of supervision," was applied.

Since reform schools existed to help, not punish, youths, it was assumed that there was nothing wrong with sentencing youths *indefinitely* to training schools. Thus, with little more than a murmur, the legal rights of youths in the United States at local levels were almost eliminated. Very few even had lawyers to represent them at their "hearings," let alone any recourse after being placed in a reform school. An 11-year-old runaway, truant, or "mouthy kid" might be placed in such a school and kept there until 18 or even 21 in some states.

Well-meaning judges and social workers seldom considered the fact that juvenile correctional schools might be almost as barbaric as adult prisons, nor did they recognize that such schools had little or no discernible effect on reducing juvenile crime and/or "rehabilitating" incarcerated youngsters.

It was not until the 1950s and 1960s, following the growing popularity of labeling theory, that many criminologists began to worry about the wisdom of spreading the criminal justice net over youths who were not being helped once they became part of the system and, in fact, were probably permanently harmed by being labeled "delinquent." By the late 1960s, the many problems of the juvenile justice system had been thoroughly documented.

In the 1970s, the juvenile justice system, attempting perhaps to remedy earlier mistakes and to follow the theoretic implications of the labeling approach, often did everything possible to keep juveniles from being incarcerated. The result as now perceived by many members of the criminal justice system, including the police, and by the general public is that "kids are getting away with murder." But some criminologists, such as San Diego State University criminologist Tom Gitchoff, argue that youth remain America's most precious asset. Therefore, it behooves us as a society to do everything possible to help, not punish, them.

YES

Alfred S. Regnery

GETTING AWAY WITH MURDER

WHY THE JUVENILE JUSTICE SYSTEM NEEDS AN OVERHAUL

Children commit nearly one-third of serious crime in America. Our system of rendering justice for their crimes, however, is antiquated and largely incapable of dealing with the offenses they commit. Disliked by the public, by those who work in it, and even by many offenders, the juvenile justice system, which is supposed to act only in the "best interests of the child," serves neither the child, his victim, nor society. Juvenile crime rates since the 1950s have tripled, yet the theories and policies we use to deal with such crime fail to hold offenders accountable and do not deter crime. At best, they are outdated; at worst, they are a total failure, and may even abet the crimes they are supposed to prevent.

Some people still refuse to accept the fact that juveniles commit crimes. Prevailing social theory during much of the 20th century has been based on the belief that children under 18 do not have the mental capacity to distinguish between right and wrong, and thus should not be held accountable for their behavior, as are adults. Those who administer this social policy even use different language to enunciate the difference between children and adults. In the jargon of the juvenile court, children do not commit crimes, but "acts of delinquency." They are not found guilty by the court, but are "adjudicated delinquent." After adjudication, they are not punished, but are "treated." If secure confinement is necessary, it is not a jail or prison, but in a "detention center" or a "training school." When juveniles get out—usually not when they have completed a sentence, but when a social worker finds them "cured"—their records do not become part of the active police records, but are sealed to all the world.

Despite attempts by some to treat juvenile crimes as trivial indiscretions committed by misguided youth, the statistics suggest something different—a grave problem on a national scale. There are currently about 15 million Americans between 14 and 17, or about seven percent of the entire U.S.

From Alfred S. Regnery, "Getting Away with Murder: Why the Juvenile Justice System Needs an Overhaul," *Policy Review,* the quarterly publication of the Heritage Foundation (Fall 1985). Copyright © 1985 by the Heritage Foundation. Reprinted by permission.

population; but about 30 percent of all people arrested for serious crimes are juveniles—a total of some 1.5 million arrests per year. (Police generally estimate that there are at least five offenses for each arrest.) The violence and intensity of these crimes is staggering. Of those arrests, 2,000 were for murder, 4,000 were for rape, and 34,000 were for aggravated assault. Despite the beliefs of certain social theorists, juveniles do commit crimes at a rate significantly higher than the rest of the population. In fact, 16-year-old boys commit crimes at a higher rate then any other single age group. These are criminals who happen to be young, not children who happen to commit crimes.

INSTITUTIONAL JARGON

Traditional juvenile justice policy could be said to have been inspired by Jean-Jacques Rousseau, the French philosopher who argued some 200 years ago that human beings are incapable of evil unless they are corrupted by the institutions of bourgeois society. And if society is the problem, it can also be the solution: Rousseau believed that properly structured government could inculcate goodness and virtue in man. Many juvenile justice professionals take this seriously; they believe that no matter how heinous the crimes committed by young people, no matter what pathological symptoms they demonstrate, they do not pose a threat to society; they should not be locked up but simply "brought into line" with the mainstream of society—in other words, they should be educated in civic virtue.

In a paper issued by the Carter Administration Justice Department in 1979, for example, youth crime was attributed to the effect of "large impersonal institutions—schools, juvenile justice systems, employment channels, public and private human service agencies, and others—on the development of young people, especially low income and minority youth." The paper concluded that all too often the "policies and practices of these institutions tend to inhibit the satisfactory development of young people. Many of the youth then turn to patterns of delinquency and crime."

The main solution advocated was development programs which, in the words of another Carter Administration Justice Department report, would seek the "cultivation of the three human social responses: the sense of confidence, the sense of belongingness, and the sense of usefulness." The report went on to suggest that youth should be offered "mechanisms which offer them the communication, coping, and decision-making skills they need to enter the mainstream of society; value clarification experience; opportunities for artistic self-expression; meaningful work experience; and involvement in community service and community decision making."

But these buzzwords (and they are little more than that) hardly come to terms with the reality of juvenile crime. A New York policeman recently profiled for me a typical candidate for juvenile arrest. Fourteen years old, the boy has already been arrested a dozen times. He dropped out of school years ago and cannot read or write; he has no job skills nor any hope of getting them. He is most likely black, possibly Hispanic, born to an unwed teenaged mother on welfare, living in public housing or a tenement, and has more than five siblings. A series of men have lived in his mother's house;

the boy has not developed a rapport with any, and has tended to be regarded as a nuisance by the adults. He has been physically abused since early childhood, and he has spent a good deal of time living on the street. His only way of getting anything of value is either by theft or by going on welfare. This boy will survive, for most of his life, at the taxpayer's expense.

The bulk of our crime—probably 75 percent of all serious offenses—is committed by someone like our profiled youngster. Known as chronic offenders, these people comprise fewer than 10 percent of the population; in the case of juveniles, probably closer to seven percent. Yet because of the high rate at which they commit felonies, sometimes as many as 100 or more a year, they are responsible for a great proportion of robberies, burglaries, muggings and aggravated assaults, car thefts, rapes, and even a significant number of murders.

A University of Pennsylvania research project found that seven percent of the juvenile population committed over 70 percent of all the serious juvenile crime. The research also revealed that there was an 80 percent certainty that boys arrested more than five times would continue to be arrested, again and again, well into their adult years.

PROFILES IN CARNAGE

Such children present problems to the juvenile justice system which evade all philosophical notions about crime. They present a problem which neither the social theorists, nor the police and prosecutors who would like to lock them up, can hope to alleviate more than temporarily. Chronic offenders pose the greatest threat to society and the greatest challenge to juvenile justice programs across the country.

Consider, for example, two typical juvenile cases, which appeared recently in Miami's juvenile courts. The first involves "Lester," a 15-year-old recently "adjudicated" by the court for burglary. Lester is black and has been arrested 12 times. His mother abandoned him at an early age, and he grew up in the streets of Miami, with occasional stops for a hot meal at a grandmother's house.

His record shows he has been placed in 20 shelter homes, and has run away from each of them. He commonly breaks into homes, steals cars, and hustles, then robs, homosexuals. He has rarely gone to school, is illiterate, and had been in and out of Florida's court system since he was 11. The first criminal charge was brought against him when he was 12. He was arrested for loitering, prowling, and finally burglary, for which he was sentenced to be "rehabilitated" in the state training school for six months. He was declared rehabilitated, but two weeks after returning to Miami, Lester was back in court for grand larceny.

Lester has been counselled, analyzed, rehabilitated, and trained. He has undergone therapy, and been placed in foster homes, state schools, socializing programs, and virtually every other sort of service available. None have made much difference. In 1981, his psychiatrist described Lester as an emotionally disturbed youngster who responded to his deficits by becoming distrustful, by decreasing verbal communication, and by increasing use of fantasy. The therapist concluded that all Lester was seeking was a warm and lasting relationship with an adult.

In 1982, a psychologist found him charming, affable, and fairly bright (he was found to have an IQ of 93) and just trying to survive. In 1983, a teacher at the state training school described him as disruptive and totally lacking in motivation.

The second Miami case involves a Hispanic male, 15 years old, recently convicted of armed robbery. Call him Marco. He has been arrested 12 times, is a member of a housing project gang, and is actively involved in drugs, burglary, and robbery. He has been described by his social workers as easygoing and with considerable potential, but is said to defy all efforts to socialization. He has also been analyzed as envisioning himself as a desperado, modeled after Al Pacino's role in *Scarface*. His father disappeared years ago, but his mother remarried, and his stepfather is presently serving a jail sentence in New Jersey for robbery. His mother is on welfare, and has seven children. Marco, who is slight for his age, cries whenever he is first locked up, but soon starts to thrive within the training school. As soon as he is released, he goes on a drug binge.

Marco has been in at least half a dozen programs, and in each case he promptly rises to a leadership position; as soon as he is released, he is back on drugs, and is shortly rearrested for breaking into a house or stealing a car. His stepfather has consistently helped Marco in his criminal undertakings, but also beats Marco unmercifully when something goes wrong. After the last beating, Marco notified the F.B.I. of his stepfather's whereabouts, resulting in his arrest and conviction.

Sadly, the juvenile justice system has shown little ability either to help such youngsters or to protect society from their crimes. In most of our major cities (where most serious juvenile crime ex-

ists), there is virtually no chance that juveniles who are first or second offenders will be punished. The lesson that the system provides to the offender is that he can continue to commit such acts because there is no penalty. The criminal's punishment is limited to listening to the psychobabble of social workers and therapists.

FOLLY OF REHABILITATION

Rehabilitation has been the premise of the juvenile court system throughout the 20th century, but it has failed miserably. The late Robert Martinson reviewed the results of over 200 separate efforts to measure the effects of programs designed to rehabilitate convicted adult offenders. Martinson concluded, in what has become one of the most quoted phrases in modern criminology, that "with few and isolated exceptions, the rehabilitative efforts that have been reported so far had no appreciable effect on recidivism." Martinson did his review in the late 1960s; since that time, rehabilitation has sunk further in esteem, both in the eyes of the public and the professionals. The criminal justice system has all but given up on the concept. Virtually no successful juvenile programs—those that reduce recidivism to an appreciable degree—rely on rehabilitation.

Knowing what we do about the young people who finally wind up in correctional institutions, it is little wonder that we are unable to turn them back into good little boys (which they probably never were in the first place). As Harvard professor James Q. Wilson has said:

> It requires not merely optimism but heroic assumptions about the nature of man to lead one to suppose that a per-

son finally sentenced after (in most cases) many brushes with the law, and having devoted a good part of his youth and young adulthood to misbehavior of every sort, should, by either the solemnity of prison or the skillfulness of a counselor, come to see the error of his ways and to experience a transformation of his character. We have learned how difficult it is by governmental means to improve the educational attainments of children or to restore stability and affection to the family, and in these cases we are often working with willing subjects in moments of admitted need. Criminal rehabilitation requires producing equivalent changes in unwilling subjects under conditions of duress or indifference.

Some advocates of rehabilitation thought a better idea would be to build a society so devoid of evil that young people would not be inclined to do wrong. If crimes are committed because of societal forces beyond the control of the individual offender, the logic runs, then remove those forces and change society. What better way to do so than to use the power, and the money, of the federal government?

A report issued by the Justice Department in 1976 had several recommendations for such changes. It cited three approaches to understanding and tackling juvenile crime. First, the individual approach, which "focuses on the pathology of the individual . . . including the identification of the emotional, motivational, and attitudinal factors that could explain delinquency." The solutions recommended were "psychotherapy, social casework, individual counselling, or behavior therapy as a means by which clients would be able to resolve their personality conflicts and assume a positive orientation towards society."

Second, the environmental approach "views situational conditions as the dominant factor in stimulating and perpetuating delinquent activity." Solution? "Remodeling and reorganizing the community so that potential offenders can find positive alternatives to delinquent activity. Programs using this approach attempt to deal with significant social institutions like the school or family and illegitimate institutions like gangs, street corner groups, and pool halls."

Finally, there is the theoretical approach, which "considers most delinquency programs harmful as well as ineffective . . . fundamental to this approach is the observation that delinquents are frequently not different from nondelinquents. Virtually all youth in the community have at some time been guilty of delinquent misconduct. Singling out only some of those delinquents may contribute to their behavior, however." Recommendation: "Prevention activities must avoid the effects of labeling and should strive for a universality of application to all children." In other words, everyone is a delinquent.

Notably absent from all of this is the deterrent approach, which views punishing the criminal as the best way to prevent future violations, protect the community, and achieve justice. Such notions are anathema to the social theorists, much of whose work has been a vain search for the institution which excuses abhorrent behavior by young people. Thus poverty, racism, sexism, frustration from any number of problems, failure to do well in school, learning disabilities, inability to accept love, child abuse and neglect, adverse peer pressure, and a desire to be different have been identified as causes for children going astray.

Obviously, some of these are contributory factors. But the criminal justice system, adult as well as juvenile, must realize that ultimately crime is a matter of choice. It is not always true that criminals make conscious calculations that the benefits of crime exceed the risks. Yet there is a calculus of risks and rewards in the criminal mind, evidenced by the fact that as society diminished the certainty and duration of punishment for crime in the last few decades, crime rates soared.

VALUE OF DETERRENCE

What can be done to ameliorate the problem of juvenile crime? First, the deterrent approach should be the main focus of the justice system. This does not mean that we should not continue to look for rehabilitation programs that actually work, even if the record does not give us grounds for optimism. It does mean that rehabilitation should not be a substitute for justice.

For the past 85 years, the courts have been making decisions about juveniles based almost exclusively on "what is in the best interests of the child." Ironically, the remedies proposed have not measurably helped children's interests. Our juvenile courts should continue to act for the benefit of children, but they should also seek justice and consider the rights of the victims of crime.

The juvenile justice system should abandon its practice of sealing the records of young criminals when they become adults. The rationale for this practice was the idea that these youths should have "learned their lesson" by the time they turned 18, and should be permitted to begin their new life as

adults without previous errors being held against them. The only problem is that the most fertile age for crime, statistics show, is between 16 and 24. Thus many juvenile criminals are just getting started on a career of crime. To seal their records is to conceal from the police and prosecutor their previous actions, and crime prevention becomes more difficult.

Nor is it obvious that sealing juvenile records helps the juveniles themselves. As Charles Murray points out in *Losing Ground*:

> By promising to make the record secret, or even more dramatically, by actually destroying the physical record, the juvenile justice system led the youth to believe that no matter what he did as a juvenile, or how often, it would be as if it had never happened once he reached his 18th birthday. Tight restrictions on access to the juvenile arrest and court records radically limited liability for exactly that behavior—chronic, violent delinquency—that the population at large was bemoaning.

So not only do police find it tougher to identify crime subjects, but juveniles enter adulthood under the illusion that they can get away with criminal behavior—get away with murder, so to speak. To their shock, many of them discover that this is not the case after age 18.

Another step that juvenile justice professionals should consider is reducing the traditional distinction between juveniles and adults. Criminals should be treated as criminals. It is true that environmental factors may contribute to some juvenile crimes, but this is also true of adult crimes. Society may wish to be lenient with first offenders, particularly for lesser crimes, but there is no reason that society should be more lenient with a 16-year-old first offender than a 30-

year-old first offender. Anyone familiar with the nature of juvenile crime will not make the argument that juvenile crimes differ in their magnitude or brutality than adult crimes; in many cases the reverse is true. So the current approach, which makes a radical distinction between criminals under 18 and those over 18, is often counterproductive.

LOCAL INITIATIVES

Various states are experimenting with innovative approaches to controlling juvenile crime. Many large cities, for example, are beginning to focus their resources on chronic offenders, who commit most violent crime. Techniques include improved record keeping, specialized crime analysis techniques, and "vertical prosecution"—where one prosecutor sticks with a case from arrest through sentencing.

The results are encouraging. In Cook County, Illinois, 400 juveniles with four arrests each for serious crimes were tried according to this approach in a 10 month period; 90 percent were convicted and sentenced. Assuming that the juveniles committed five crimes for each arrest, a conservative estimate, the 360 convicted youths had already committed 7,200 serious crimes. It's about time they were stopped.

Another promising state initiative is restitution, a program in which property offenders are required to reimburse their victims. This has the advantage of giving the community back some of the goods it loses through theft and vandalism, but it also helps teach accountability and responsibility to the offender. Prince Georges County, Maryland, collected over $750,000 for victims of juvenile offenders in the past three years, at a cost to the county of about five cents on the dollar.

The juvenile system also needs to rely more on the private sector, as well as on volunteer citizens to assist young offenders, instead of placing total reliance on government and professionals. A number of privately owned and operated correctional programs now exist, for example, usually at substantially lower costs than public institutions; these programs are often more responsive to the needs of both the offender and society, and are much more innovative than public programs. The private sector is also increasing its role and influence in probation services, either by assisting public systems, or by actually running probation on a contract basis. These programs use parents and other volunteers to work with marginally delinquent youth. Yet officials within the system, and public employee unions, often do everything in their power to torpedo such services, usually out of fear that volunteers will displace their salaried positions.

Through the Office of Juvenile Justice and Delinquency Prevention, the federal government has been encouraging these initiatives. The primary responsibility to tackle the problems of juvenile crime rests with state and local governments, though the Justice Department will continue to encourage pilot programs across the country.

But we need the help of juvenile justice professionals, state legislatures, and the public to place justice, reason, and common sense above social experimentation. If we do, the victim, society, and even the offenders themselves will benefit. If we don't, there will be more of the same.

NO

Stephen J. Brodt
and
J. Steven Smith

PUBLIC POLICY AND THE SERIOUS JUVENILE OFFENDER

In the fall of 1985, Alfred S. Regnery, the Administrator of the Justice Department's Office of Juvenile Justice and Delinquency Prevention, proposed a significant change in our country's orientation toward juvenile crime (Regnery, 1985). Citing statistics and "profiles in carnage," he urged that the juvenile justice system focus on chronic juvenile offenders. These individuals, although relatively few in number, comprising only 7.0% of the population, are responsible, according to Regnery, for the bulk of our "serious" offenses. They commit robberies, burglaries, muggings, aggravated assaults, car thefts, rapes and even murders at a rate that is well out of proportion to their number.

Regnery states that the rehabilitation philosophy, "which has been the premise of the juvenile court system throughout the 20th century," has failed to solve the problems which these individuals pose to society. He advocates (1) returning to the deterrent approach; (2) stopping the sealing of court records of juveniles when they become adults; (3) reducing the distinction between juvenile and adult criminals; and (4) experimenting with local programs for controlling juvenile crime.

The implications of such a significant shift in orientation require careful review before steps are taken to implement these ideas. It is our intention to critically review Regnery's proposals, which we believe are representative of those who favor the deterrent approach, with an eye toward suggesting a more effective solution to the problem of juvenile crime. We shall first elaborate on his characterization of chronic offenders and what he sees as needed adjustments in our approach to these individuals.

From Stephen J. Brodt and J. Steven Smith, "Public Policy and the Serious Juvenile Offender," *Criminal Justice Policy Review*, vol. 2, no. 1 (March 1987). Reprinted by permission of *Criminal Justice Policy Review*, Indiana University of Pennsylvania, Indiana, PA 15705.

REGNERY'S CHRONIC OFFENDER

Regnery's chronic offender, who poses "the greatest threat to society and the greatest challenge to juvenile justice programs across the country," has a profile with recognizable characteristics. In addition to the obvious prerequisite of being responsible for numerous felonies, the "typical candidate for juvenile arrest" is described in this way:

> Fourteen years old, the boy has already been arrested a dozen times. He dropped out of school years ago and cannot read or write; he has no job skills nor any hope of getting them. He is most likely black, possibly Hispanic, born to an unwed teenaged mother on welfare, living in public housing or a tenement, and has more than five siblings. A series of men have lived in his mother's house; the boy has not developed a rapport with any, and has tended to be regarded as a nuisance by the adults. He has been physically abused since early childhood, and he has spent a good deal of time living on the street. His only way of getting anything of value is either by theft or going on welfare. This boy will survive, for the most of his life, at the taxpayer's expense. (Regnery: 2)

"Lester," a 15-year-old black male, and "Marco," a 15-year-old Hispanic male, two other "profiles in carnage" which Regnery uses for purposes of illustration, have the same type of life history, the stereotypical background of the delinquent. Poverty and being on welfare are common denominators of their environment. As a result of unstable family lives which provided no adequate role models, these individuals are inadequately socialized. They experience difficulties in school and eventually drop out. Job skills are never developed. Their lives become a continuous revolving door, in and out of a variety of agencies and programs.

According to Regnery, few of the present juvenile justice system's efforts have any positive impact. Juveniles with these problems are not helped and society is not protected from their crimes. Recidivists learn that there is no penalty for their crimes: "The criminal's punishment is limited to listening to the psychobabble of social workers and therapists" (Regnery: 3).

WHO IS THE CHRONIC OFFENDER?

Since the focus of Regnery's proposals is the chronic juvenile offender, it is important that we understand the specific meaning of the term. At one point, Regnery implies that chronic offenders are responsible for "a great proportion" of serious offenses, a category which includes murder, rape, and aggravated assault. These offenses are highlighted in a section of Regnery's paper (Regnery: 1) which emphasizes the violence and intensity of juvenile crime.

However, Regnery's profile of typical chronic offenders, those who "pose the greatest threat to society," does not include references to murder, rape, and aggravated assault. Instead, these are individuals who are likely to be arrested on a frequent basis but primarily for property crimes and occasionally for robbery.

When the quality and quantity of offenses are both taken into consideration, Regnery's chronic offender may be one of three different types of individuals: (1) the individual who commits a violent crime or crimes but does not engage in a string of lesser offenses; (2) the individual who commits a string of lesser offenses but commits few serious offenses;

(3) the individual who is actively involved in both types of offenses.

Since these three categories often contain individuals of very distinct types it seems unreasonable to lump them all under one heading; Regnery almost forces us to choose which type actually deserves the label of chronic offender. We might opt for the individual who commits violent crimes as being the prototype of the chronic offender. However, we must face the fact that there are relatively few juveniles who are chronically violent. Support for this view is provided by a report published in 1985 under the auspices of the OJJDP (Hamparian, et al.), with a foreword by Regnery himself, which states: "Relatively few violent juvenile offenders are repeat violent offenders" (Hamparian, et al., 1985: 8). The authors state that their data cause them to reject the idea, encouraged by public concern and governmental initiatives, that "an increasing number of youthful offenders are 'specializing' in violent crime and that these violent youth are responsible for a significant portion of the most serious crimes" (Hamparian, et al., 1985:8). Of the 1222 individuals in the cohort they analyzed, only 15.4% had been arrested more than once for a violent crime and only 8.1% had been arrested more than once for index violence. Only 24 people in the cohort (2.0%) had two or more arrests for index violent offenses and no other arrests for less serious offenses (Hamparian, et al., 1985: 8).

This leads to the conclusion that Regnery's first type of chronic offender may have committed a serious offense (one involving violence) but is not likely to have committed a number of these offenses. It seems to us that the label, chronic offender, is more justifiably applied to an individual because of his involvement in a string of lesser offenses. Regnery's inclusion of the serious offender in the chronic offender category, is, therefore, misleading. Repeat offenders are generally those involved in offenses of a less serious nature. Policies which are designed to reduce the incidence of juvenile crime must focus on these offenses and the individuals who commit them.

THE FOLLY OF REHABILITATION (REVISITED) OR THE JOYS OF DETERRENCE AND OTHER IDEAS

Regnery declares that rehabilitation, denounced for its repeated failure by Martinson in his indictment of programs designed to rehabilitate adult offenders, is dead as a viable philosophy in the treatment of juveniles: "The criminal justice system has all but given up on the concept. Virtually no successful juvenile programs—those that reduce recidivism to an appreciable degree—rely on rehabilitation" (Regnery, 1985: 3). Furthermore, this lack of success is understandable: "Knowing what we know about the young people who finally wind up in correctional institutions, it is little wonder that we are unable to turn them back into good little boys (which they probably never were in the first place)" (Regnery, 1985: 3).

According to Regnery, the first step toward solving the problem posed by the chronic offender is the substitution of deterrence for rehabilitation as the primary focus of the justice system. Crime is a matter of choice: risks and rewards are calculated in the criminal mind. The fact that in the recent past crime rates "soared" while the certainty and duration of punishment declined is offered as evidence in support of this view. Therefore, Regnery concludes, the appropriate response to crime is obvious: the criminal must believe that punishment will be swift and severe. The perceived potential "pain" associated with the criminal act will need to exceed the perceived potential benefits. Implementation of deterrence is suggested as being "the best way to prevent future violations, protect the community, and achieve justice" (Regnery, 1985: 3).

Regnery believes that the juvenile justice system should cease the sealing of the records of "young criminals" when they reach 18. Since the most "fertile age" for crime is the late teens and early 20s, many "juvenile criminals" are just embarking on a "career of crime." The practice of sealing their juvenile records prevents the police and prosecutor from discovering their past offenses and, therefore, makes crime prevention more difficult.

Another change which Regnery proposes is reducing the "traditional distinction" between adults and juveniles: "Criminals should be treated as criminals" (Regnery, 1985: 3). Leniency is acceptable with first offenders, particularly in the case of lesser offenses. However, he also states, a first offender is a first offender and age should not be a consideration in the sentencing process. The current approach also ignores the fact that juvenile crimes are frequently of a more serious nature than adult crimes.

Regnery's fourth suggestion stems from his belief that state and local governments should be responsible for spearheading the effort to control juvenile crime. He advocates support of innovative programs that use a variety of techniques. He also sees increased reliance on the private sector and on the use of volunteers as beneficial in dealing with juvenile crime.

ON DETERRENCE

Regnery proposes that to ameliorate the problem of juvenile crime the "deterrent approach should be the main focus of the justice system" (Regnery, 1985: 4). Deterrence has been a major focus of the adult system for most of this century. In a recent work, Currie (1985) has analyzed the effectiveness of deterrence in the adult system.

Since 1973 the incarceration rate in the United States has doubled (Currie, 1985: 7), but between 1969 and 1983 the rate of violent crime rose by 61.0% as measured by police reports (Currie, 1985: 6). This would seem to demonstrate that incarceration does not in itself deter violent crime.

Not only have the rates of incarceration remained much higher than those of the other industrialized nations (see Table 1) but the length of time spent in prison, another measure of punishment,

Table 1

1981 Rate of Incarceration	Rate per 100,000
United States	217
Holland	21
Japan	44
Norway	45
Sweden	55
West Germany	60
Denmark	63
France	67
Great Britain	80

Eugene Doleschal and Anne Newton, *International Rates Of Imprisonment*, National Council On Crime And Delinquency. Hackensack, NJ.

is also higher in the United States. The average sentence in the United States in the late 1970s was about 16 months but the average sentence in Holland was 1.4 months and in Britain about 5 months. Currie also notes: "The average maximum sentence for robbery was 150 months in the U.S. federal prisons and 68 months in the state prisons; in the Dutch prisons it was 19 months" (1985: 29).

Current sentencing policies in the United States have provided a test of the deterrence arguments that are so popular now and which form the basis for Regnery's proposition. However, what we find when we look more closely is that deterrence does not reduce crime as its proponents claim. The conclusion to be reached concerning the "get tough" ideas that are currently in vogue is best stated by the following quote:

> Given these huge and growing disparities between our rates of imprisonment and those of otherwise comparable societies, how can anyone argue that our crime rate has undoubtedly resulted from the absence of punishment. (Currie, 1985: 29)

POSING ALTERNATIVES

If we are to categorize deterrence as a failure, what are some alternatives to the "get tough" attitude? To begin a discussion of alternatives to the popular ideology, we should begin with an overview of what we "know" about the needs of youth.

We know, for example, that to raise a child to be a productive citizen in adulthood, the child must have training in morality. There must be someone who takes the responsibility to oversee the mistakes of a child and to correct those mistakes with firmness and consistency.

Children who have such a personal model and guide tend to develop a personal sense of morality that serves to contain their impulses to commit crime.

A moral guide is necessary, but, for the guidance to become important enough to be internalized, the youth must sense a personal commitment on the part of the leader. The permanent commitment of the moral leader must come first. The youth then sees the personal investment and, as a result, feels that the moral guide will invest in the youth's success at moral decisions. Once the youth sees a long-term payoff for his moral decisions, then, and only then, will the youth perceive a reason to behave in a moral fashion.

In addition to guidance and personal commitment on the part of the moral leader, the relationship between the child and the person(s) responsible for the training in moral behavior must be long term. A youth who finds that there is no one willing to invest a significant length of time in his/her future success or failure comes to understand quickly that such lack of commitment indicates that the leader does not feel that the youth will succeed.

This last point is a subtle one because we tend to assign youths who have no volunteer moral guides to professional agencies. Professional moral guides are usually good people who genuinely care about children, but they find themselves in an organization that is of necessity concerned with the production of units of service and unable to insure the permanent availability of staff required if youths are to be expected to follow and internalize the values of the moral leaders.

Without a permanent and personally committed moral leader/guide, a child is left to his own devices to develop a sense of moral behavior. We know that children need moral guidance and we know that they need permanency and a sense of personal commitment to become productive, law-abiding members of our society.

Realizing that youth need long-term supervision, direction, and accountability from people who care about them provides a basis for understanding and research findings which demonstrate that the deterrent to commission of a crime rests in the interpersonal relationships of individuals. These relationships are extra-legal in nature and are rarely utilized by the formal agents of social control. Charles Tittle concluded this 1980 research with the following: "Social control is rooted almost entirely in how people perceive the potential for negative reactions from interpersonal acquaintances" (Tittle: 4). He believed that formal sanctions were largely irrelevant to deterring criminal behavior.

There are many who would argue that the youth of a society need supervision, guidance, accountability, and a genuine sense of being worthy. Traditionally, the family has been the agent to provide these needed qualities through the primary socialization process. There are, however, social forces at work that have undermined the ability of the family to function as the primary socialization agent and the state has been called upon to take over the role of socialization agent.

Technology has created a superabundant economy in which the traditional virtues of thrift, self-denial, and living by the sweat of one's brow seemed not only absurd, but actually dangerous to prosperity. (Flacks, 1979: 23)

Economic and political factors have led to the development of family structures and value systems which are often inadequate to the task of socializing children to the law-abiding behaviors which are desired. Alternatives to the present punishment-oriented policies must begin at the sources of crime and delinquency and provide guidance to the juvenile justice system.

"GETTING TOUGH" WITH THE POOR

Returning to Regnery's "profiles in carnage," we are struck by the obvious racial and class biases which would seem to underlie his analysis and conclusions. When President Richard Nixon declared war on crime, he set in motion an aggressive refocusing of the criminal justice system on apprehending and punishing street crime and poor criminals. Nevertheless, the crime rate remained essentially unchanged. Now Regnery and other deterrence advocates propose the same misguided plan. In practice, getting tough means "let's get tough" with the following groups: (1) blacks; (2) Chicanos; (3) the poor; (4) the uneducated; (5) youth from single parent families; (6) the unemployed; (7) illegitimate youth; (8) welfare families; and (9) abused children. Concerted efforts to rid the society of the "criminal element" that is associated with these groups failed in England during the 1700s and, as noted, were a failure during the Nixon Administration. Consequently, there is no reason to expect success from this most recent attempt.

A get-tough policy is analogous to locking the door after the burglary. Since we know the criminal problems that result from poverty, abuse, and lack of

NO Brodt and Smith / 177

parental guidance, we must ask the question: Why not address those issues and prevent crime? During Reagan's administration we have seen increases in minority unemployment, divorce, school drop-outs (push-outs) and numbers of children in poverty. Coincident with increasing needs, we have seen the present administration cut back on funds for social programs. Increasing needs for assistance, reduced funding for needed services, and now a "get tough" policy against crimes of the street combine to show either a callous disregard for the neediest Americans or an incredibly uninformed national policy.

GOVERNMENT'S ROLE

With demonstrated failure of present governmental policies to reduce the incidence of crime in any reasonable proportion to the amount of expenditures, it is tempting to state that the government has no role to play in the reduction of crime. The case has even been made by many authors and researchers that the government has played a major role in the creation of social policies which tend to produce an environment encouraging to criminal behavior.

> Government can fairly be said to have adopted a pro-crime policy for decades in America. It subsidized the mechanization of agriculture that pushed masses of the rural poor into the cities, simultaneously encouraging the flight of the urban industry and employment. Similarly, it subsidizes the transfer of capital and jobs overseas, and routinely adopts monetary and fiscal policies, in the name of fighting inflation, that create widespread unemployment and its resulting community and family fragmentation. (Currie, 1985: 26)

Governmental policies have an effect on the lives of the citizenry, and policies designed to benefit the corporate structures in the society fail regularly to recognize the needs of the individuals and families which are called upon to serve the corporations. If government policies can work to create the social structures which tend to encourage criminal behaviors, then the policies of the government can be modified to establish social structures that will reduce or inhibit the growth of crime.

Throughout the previous discussion and indeed throughout most of the texts on criminal behavior and delinquency, it is noted that delinquents "tend to share a common set of antecedent problems: poverty, poor schooling, and participation in a delinquent subculture" (Empey, 1982: 515). It is the opinion of the authors that there may well be a place for punishment and incapacitation in the process to deter crime, but only if the youthful offender has viable options or behavioral choices.

"If a juvenile has experienced a decent home life, has attended school, and might be able to find a job, accountability and punishment make sense" (Empey, 1982: 516). Juveniles who find that they have been denied such "habilitating" opportunities are certainly limited in the behavioral choices they are able to make. Illiteracy, abuse, neglect and deprivation limit the choices available to the young man/woman. To impose on such youth an emphasis on the letter of the law and an argument for deterrence through punishment is "bizarre" (Empey, 1982: 516).

The role of the government should be to facilitate the development of social policies and practices that will provide the most vulnerable juveniles with the opportunities to learn in a supportive and challenging environment. This will require the government at the federal, state and local levels to address several different fronts simultaneously: families, schools, employment, and a strong commitment to law abiding behavior.

Developing a program or policy which will support the family is perhaps a Herculean undertaking, given the myriad of different values and family practices in a society as diverse as the United States. There are, however, policies which can go a long way to support parents and children so that they may have the resources and the time to devote to the development of interpersonal relationships which will encourage the "stake in conformity" proposed by criminologists. The government can promote the development of community / neighborhood child care centers operated by people who know the family of the child and can provide the kind of care desired by the parents. The public policy should be to encourage the involvement of the family in neighborhood activities, perhaps centered in the neighborhood recreation centers and in small neighborhood parks which could be maintained by neighborhood youth.

Even with all the right opportunities for growth and support there will undoubtedly be families who lack the ability or the motivation to create and maintain wholesome and nurturing environments for children. These youth who are being victimized by their families need not be further victimized by the juvenile justice system. There are now current programs in operation, some with years of successful experience, that provide wholesome, caring normal living experiences for youth with behavior problems. One of these programs, with a couple of decades of program experience, is the Youth Program of the Menninger Foundation. The program began with The Villages and has now grown into a community-responsive, locally-based, set of self-supporting programs in a number of states. These programs provide a caring, family-based program of service to a wide range of dependent and delinquent youth. The program succeeds because it has incorporated in its practice what we all "know" about raising children: children need supervision, direction, accountability, and someone who is willing to fail or succeed with the child over the long term.

The Menninger Youth program and many others like it are successful and reasonably priced. This is the new direction delinquency programs must take in the future if we are to reduce the incidence of juvenile crime. Greenwood and Zimring (1985), in arguing that rehabilitation remains a viable ideology, cite many other programs which offer promise in reducing juvenile crime through rehabilitative efforts. Such programs, according to Greenwood and Zimring, include: Vision Quest, Headstart, the Oregon Social Learning Center, and the California Conservation Corps. Punishing juveniles does not change behavior. Providing juveniles with intensive supervision and nurturing environments does. It is amazing how little attention we pay to what we know, when a political program repackages an old, failed philosophy.

In conclusion, the following allegory is offered:

Imagine that one morning you wake up, get ready for work and go out to your garage to get your car. To your great surprise, your car is rolling down the driveway and onto the street (you knew the emergency brake needed attention).

There are several actions you can take at this point, all "reasonable" given your particular set of personal or ideological interests.

1. As a neighbor and friend you might run down the street alongside your car and shout to your neighbors and friends that they need to be careful. They should be warned so that they can avoid your car. One might call this the *Education Approach*.

2. You could go back into the house and look in the phone book to find the nearest towing and wrecker service because you "know" that you are going to be needing one. This would be efficient because at the same time you could look up your attorney's phone number; you will probably be needing him/her also. Thus would be the *Legal Approach*.

3. You could also go back in the house and pour another cup of coffee and act surprised when the police knock on your door, the *Laissez-Faire Approach*.

A truly reasonable person would take some action to stop the car before the inevitable crash occurred. Given that many of us have had little practice in stopping runaway cars, we might not do the job correctly. Indeed, there might still be a crash, even with our best effort and our purest intentions. But reason dictates that we act to try to stop what we know will be a tragic situation.

Regnery's "typical candidates for juvenile arrest," Lester, Marco and others, are "runaway cars." We know that given the social processes that are in motion, these young people are headed for trouble. We can take the approaches proposed by the present administration or we can act in a truly responsible way to prevent the disaster, realizing that attempting to "fix" a dangerous situation requires a willingness to face the risk of failure.

Lester, Marco and friends can be dealt with by the Education Approach by funding television programs urging our neighbors to buy deadbolts and carry firearms for their own protection. Bernard Goetz becomes the hero of our model and we can relax with a sense of false security believing that the present administration has taken a "new" approach to solving the problems of juvenile delinquency.

The present administration in Washington has proposed a Legal, Laissez-Faire approach by proposing a program that lets the car run wildly down the street and punishes the responsible party after the disaster. The following statement sums up the present administration's attitude very well:

> Another matter about which the Reagan Administration feels very strongly is the necessity of getting the government out of people's hair sufficiently for them to live their lives the way they wish and solve their problems in their own way. (Regnery, 1985: 43)

When a potential is noted that may lead to serious harm, it is the duty of responsible people to act to the best of their ability to end or reduce the danger, not wait for the worst to happen and then react to the disaster.

BIBLIOGRAPHY

Currie, E., 1985. Confronting Crime: An American Challenge. New York, NY: Pantheon Books.
Empey, Lamar T., 1982. American Delinquency: Its Meaning And Construction. Homewood, IL: The Dorsey Press.
Flacks, R., 1979. Growing up confused. In Socialization And The Life Cycle, Peter Rose (ed.). New York, NY: St. Martin's Press.
Greenwood, Peter and Frank Zimring, 1985. One More Change: The Pursuit Of Promising Inter-

vention Strategies For Chronic Juvenile Offenders. Santa Monica, CA: The Rand Corporation.

Hamparian, D. M., J. M. Davis, J. M. Jacobson, and R. E. McGraw, 1985. The Young Criminal Years And The Violent Few. Washington, D.C.: U.S. Department Of Justice, Office Of Juvenile Justice And Delinquency Prevention.

Doleschal, E., and A. Newton, 1981. International Rates Of Imprisonment. Hackensack, NJ: National Council On Crime And Delinquency.

Regnery, Alfred S., 1985. Getting away with murder. Policy Review, Fall, 34.

Tittle, Charles, 1980. Sanctions And Social Deviance. New York, NY: Praeger Publishers.

POSTSCRIPT

Juvenile Justice:
Are Kids "Getting Away with Murder"?

Criminal Justice administrator Regnery continues the controversy with a rebuttal to Brodt and Smith in "Response to Critique of Brodt and Smith," *Criminal Justice Policy Review* (April 1988). He states that his critics reflect "unsubstantiated sociological bias" in their assertion that deterrence does not work. Regnery also accuses Brodt and Smith of "socialist gibberish" for their claim that capitalism causes poverty and delinquency.

A hard-line approach is rapidly achieving hegemony within the United States. People generally like to hear politicians promise to get tough on criminals, including youthful offenders. This, too, is ironic because, within the past twenty years, both state and local governments have supported many creative and innovative programs for juveniles, including significant alternatives to incarceration. Critics contend that these programs do not work and, in some cases, probably increase the likelihood that kids are getting away with murder.

Two excellent sources that are sympathetic to Brodt and Smith's position are Anthony Platt's *The Child Savers*, 2nd edition (University of Chicago Press, 1977), and I. M. Schwartz's *(In)Justice for Juveniles* (D. C. Heath, 1989).

A more evenhanded and empirical work is the collection of essays by James R. Klugel, *Evaluating Juvenile Justice* (Sage, 1983). However, for a recent Supreme Court ruling affirming many of the concerns of Platt and Schwartz, see the Court's ruling on June 4, 1984, affirming the right of counties and states to hold juveniles in custody before trial. Moreover, the Court has yet to bar executing offenders under 18 years old.

For the best expression of the approach advocated by Regnery, see "Prevention: Families and Schools," chapter 6 of *Understanding and Controlling Crime: Toward a New Research Strategy*, by D. P. Farrington, L. E. Ohlin, and J. Q. Wilson (Springer-Verlag, 1983). An in-between perspective is that of E. Currie's, "Understanding Crime: Families and Children," chapter 6 in his *Confronting Crime* (Pantheon Books, 1986).

Additional helpful sources include James Gilbert's *Cycle of Outrage: America's Reaction to the Juvenile Delinquent in the 1950s* (Oxford University Press, 1986) and *Alternative Treatment for Troubled Youth*, by W. S. Davidson II et al. (Plenum Press, 1990). The classic study by David Matza, *Delinquency and Drift*, has been reissued with a new introduction (Transaction Press, 1990). Two very different kinds of discussions of delinquency in Britain are D. Hebdige's *Subculture: The Meaning of Style* (Methuen, 1979) and J. Pitts's *The Politics of Juvenile Crime* (Sage, 1988).

ISSUE 10

Should Plea Bargaining Continue to Be an Accepted Practice?

YES: Samuel Walker, from *Sense and Nonsense About Crime: A Policy Guide,*
Second Edition (Brooks/Cole Publishing Company, 1989)

NO: Ralph Adam Fine, from *Escape of the Guilty: A Trail Judge Speaks Out
Against Crime* (Dodd, Mead & Co., 1988)

ISSUE SUMMARY

YES: University of Nebraska, Omaha, professor Samuel Walker, while
acknowledging that plea bargaining is an imperfect component of the
criminal justice system, still feels that it is an integral part of both the
courtroom work group and the manufacturing and maintenance of justice.
NO: Wisconsin circuit court judge Ralph Fine argues that criminals are
hardly punished for even the most heinous crimes due to plea bargaining
and, citing some of the same studies that Walker draws from, concludes that
elimination of plea bargaining increases justice.

"Copping a plea," "striking a deal," has been part of the American court
process for at least a century. Curiously, plea bargaining has only been
formally recognized by the higher courts and scholarly research in the past
twenty years or so. Although plea bargaining has occurred since the 1920s
and 1930s, up until the late 1960s most members of the "courtroom work
group" (judges, prosecutors, lawyers) denied its existence. However, everyone knew that many if not most guilty pleas resulted from some concessions
being made between the prosecutor and the defense attorney, frequently
with the judge's approval.

Since *Boykin v. Alabama* (1969), judges are required to question defendants
to show that their guilty pleas are "intelligent and voluntary." In *Santobello v.
New York* (1971), the Court ruled that promises by prosecutors in plea
bargaining cases must be kept.

Currently, approximately 90 percent of all local and state felony cases and
85 percent of federal charges are plea bargained (with sharp variations
between jurisdictions). Thus, plea bargaining is both a fact and a way of life
in the United States. The mechanics can assume many forms. Charge
bargaining is one of the most typical. This results more than likely from the

complexities of our legal system and the practice of "bedsheeting" (over-charging) that exists in some jurisdictions. For instance, in some states there are four or more degrees of assault—from slapping a face to firing a gun at someone. Thus, the more serious assault charge could be reduced in specific cases, or even a different, milder charge (for example, trespass) could be substituted as a consequence of plea bargaining (the defendant pleads guilty to trespass, and the assault charge is dropped). In other states, police and/or prosecutors sometimes overcharge in order to ensure obtaining a guilty plea on at least one count.

The filing of multiple charges is also fairly common (for example, car theft, fleeing an officer, leaving the scene of an accident, attempted vehicular homicide). This, too, gives the state ammunition by which to obtain a guilty plea in order to prevent a trial.

The sentence bargaining is another form. Here the judge may be directly involved in the agreement or the prosecutor simply agrees to make a no-sentence or a light-sentence recommendation. Although, since *Boykin*, judges are required to ascertain if the guilty plea is voluntary and understood, judges are not involved in plea bargaining itself in many states.

While both police and prosecutors benefit from using plea bargaining to get informants to trade information, most police prefer that the original charges stand and if possible that a conviction and jail sentence result.

On the one hand, critics of plea bargaining such as the police and Judge Fine feel that it allows criminals to "walk" or at least to receive very light sentences. Other critics, reflecting a liberal perspective, point out that it is another form of discrimination against America's underclasses; many such defendants cannot post bail after being arrested and will probably lose their jobs and possibly home and family while awaiting trial. Consequently, since they may receive credit for the time already served (frequently several months) after "copping a plea," they may be eligible for immediate release. If they go to trial with the original charges, they may have to remain in jail for several more months and may receive a lengthy prison sentence if found guilty. Thus, they are especially pressured to strike a deal even if they are not guilty of the charges.

Defenders argue that plea bargaining is very efficient in that it reduces the exorbitant cost of trials. Walker and others also feel that it is fair and results in conviction that might not otherwise be obtained.

Curiously, in 1900, there were slightly over 100,000 lawyers in the United States. By 1985, there were over 650,000, and today some law firms have as many as 1,000 attorneys! Yet apparently fewer cases go to trial. If you were wrongly arrested and faced with several months or even years in jail as well as depleting your life savings defending yourself, would you plea-bargain to keep your freedom? If someone you knew had committed a terrible crime but there was insufficient evidence to guarantee conviction at trial, would you allow him or her to strike a deal to much lesser charges in order to get at least one conviction and a mild sentence on the record?

YES

Samuel Walker

CLOSE THE LOOPHOLES

In each jurisdiction there is a general consensus on the going rate for each offense. This is simply an expression of how much a case is worth. In Detroit, for example, crimes involving a gun are worth about five or six years in prison. In California, imprisoned robbers do an average of fifty months of actual time in prison. . . .

The administration of criminal justice is a human process, involving a series of discretionary decisions by people who work together day in and day out. We call them the courtroom work group. It is a sociological truism that such officials develop a shared need to get the work done. Consequently, they need to get along and develop informal understandings about how cases should be handled. Their everyday working language reflects these shared understandings. Prosecutors and defense attorneys agree on the distinction between "heavy" or "serious" cases and the "garbage" . . . ones. They also make the same evaluations of the strength of the evidence. They recognize the "dead-bang" cases, where the evidence is conclusive, and the "weak" cases. Their terminology is a form of shorthand that allows them to classify and dispose of cases quickly.

These shared understandings generate a high degree of cooperation in the courthouse. Conflict between prosecution and defense is the exception rather than the rule. The absence of conflict has led most criminal justice experts to describe our system as administrative rather than adversarial. That is to say, the idea of a truly adversarial system, one in which the question of guilt or innocence is contested, is a notion expressed in the Old Idealism but not found in any American courthouse. . . . Many critics of plea bargaining argue that in a climate of cooperation the defendant is the primary loser. In this view, courthouse officials sacrifice the interests of the defendant for the sake of getting along with each other. Rather than aggressively push for the best possible deal, the defense attorney "sells" the deal to the defendant. This view underpins the recent calls for the abolition of plea bargaining. . . .

ABOLISH PLEA BARGAINING

Plea bargaining has been attacked by both conservatives and liberals. Conservatives hold that it is another loophole that allows criminals to beat the system, either by having charges dropped altogether or by having a serious felony charge reduced to a lesser felony or misdemeanor. Liberals, for their part, believe that plea bargaining is a fundamentally irrational practice by which decisions are made on the basis of expediency rather than according to any factor related to the merits of the case. More troubling to liberals is the belief that bargaining puts a premium on pleading guilty and thereby subtly coerces defendants into waiving their constitutional protection against self-incrimination. Some argue that the practice encourages prosecutors deliberately to "overcharge," to add on more charges to be used as bargaining chips, while the defense attorney becomes more interested in maintaining good relations with other members of the courtroom work group than in vigorously defending his or her client. Thus the rights of the defendant are sacrificed in the name of efficiency. Finally, plea bargains are almost completely unregulated, and their very secrecy is a source of much public suspicion about the criminal justice system.

The standard defense of plea bargaining is based on the argument that it is absolutely essential to the operations of the American criminal courts. It is the only way to dispose of the enormous volume of criminal cases that pour into the system daily. If plea bargaining were abolished, according to this view, the system would collapse immediately. I call this argument the "nightmare defense" of plea bargaining.

For a brief period in the early 1970s there was a lot of talk about abolishing plea bargaining. The National Advisory Commission on Criminal Justice Standards and Goals recommended in 1973 that plea bargaining be abolished within five years. Alaska abolished plea bargaining in 1975. Meanwhile, new sentencing laws restricted plea bargaining for certain offenses in a few states, and some local prosecutors limited bargaining for particular offenses in their jurisdictions. The opponents of plea bargaining, although numerous throughout the country, have never coalesced into an organized movement, as the well-organized opponents of the death penalty have done. Interest in abolition gradually faded.

The Phantom Loophole

Plea bargaining proved to be an extremely elusive target. As an informal process rather than a concrete event, it is simply hard to get hold of. The exclusionary rule, by way of contrast, is a manageable target. Plea bargaining is also a phantom loophole. Hard-core criminals do not routinely use it to beat the system. Abolishing plea bargaining produces results quite irrelevant to our basic goal of reducing serious crime. Public awareness of plea bargaining and outrage against it reached their peak in 1973, when Vice President Spiro Agnew, in perhaps the most famous plea bargain of all time, avoided going to prison on extortion charges by agreeing not to contest a lesser charge. The Agnew case, of course, represents the classic celebrated case. We should be careful not to overreact to such unique events. Rather, we should direct our attention to routine felony cases. . . . [T]he majority of felonies are handled with a profound sense of bureaucratic regulatory. Most bargains are made in open-and-shut cases and little actual bargaining takes place at all.

As far as the control of serious crime is concerned, we can state with confidence: . . . The abolition of plea bargaining will not reduce serious crime.

To UNDERSTAND PLEA BARGAINING AND ITS effect on the crime rate, we should now look at those jurisdictions that have tried to abolish it.

Alaska Bans Plea Bargaining!

In 1975 the attorney general of Alaska banned plea bargaining throughout the state. This action constitutes the single most important experiment in plea-bargaining reform. Alaska is unique in that local prosecutors are appointed by and work under the supervision of the state attorney general. In the continental United States local prosecutors are elected and enjoy almost complete political and administrative independence. Yet none of them have the authority to abolish plea bargaining, or to make any other reforms in prosecutorial operations.

On July 3, 1975, Avrum Gross, Alaska's attorney general, issued a memorandum . . .

The new policy . . . attacked plea bargaining in three ways. . . . [It] abolished the traditional practice of "sentence bargaining"; . . . abolished "charge bargaining"; and . . . established a procedure for formal supervision and allowed possible exceptions to the general policy.

Contrary to popular expectations, Alaska's criminal justice system did not collapse with the end of plea bargaining. The criminal courts in Alaska continued to function much as they had been doing. Surprisingly, defendants pleaded guilty about as often as they had done before. The number of trials increased about 50 percent but the total remained quite small. The percentage of cases that went to trial increased from 6.7 percent to 9.6 percent.

The ban also failed to confirm another common prediction. Norval Morris and others argue that discretion is a fixed quantity in the administration of justice: we can't eliminate it; we succeed only in moving it around. . . .[1] Knowing that prosecutors have less flexibility, cops will be more careful about whom they bring into the system and on what charges. Evidence drawn from evaluations of other reforms indicates that this phenomenon does exist. But it did not appear to be a factor in Alaska's ban on plea bargaining.

One measure of the movement of discretion within the system is the rate of dismissals, either by the prosecutor (in what is called "postarrest screening") or by a judge at some point before trial. In theory, more cases will be dismissed because prosecutors are unable to settle them by bargaining down to a lesser offense. . . . There was some increase in the rate of dismissals of drug and morals cases, but it did not seem to relate to problems of weak evidence. It appeared to be more a function of the fact that prosecutors accorded those cases low priority. . . .

With respect to sentencing, some surprising results were found. Sentences were more severe, but only for offenses not considered serious and for offenders whose records showed only minor infractions, if any. This is the trickle-up phenomenon that has been observed elsewhere. New policies designed to get tough with serious crime exert their primary effect on lesser offenses. Under normal circumstances, persons charged with lesser felonies—the lowest grade of felonious assault or burglary—or with no prior criminal record receive relatively light punishment, usually through plea bargaining. A get-tough policy, such as a ban on plea bargaining, closes off this avenue of mitigation and produces harsher penalties.

The ban did not have the same effect on defendants who were charged with serious crimes or who had substantial criminal records. The researchers who evaluated the Alaska experiment concluded that "the conviction and sentencing of persons charged with serious crimes of violence such as murder, rape, robbery, and felonious assault appeared completely unaffected by the change in policy."[2] These people were not beating the system before plea bargaining was banned. There was no loophole to close. . . .

Other Experiments

Other attempts to ban plea bargaining focus on specific offenses, such as the use of handguns and possession of narcotics. When Michigan enacted a new gun-control law providing mandatory prison terms in 1976–1977 ("One with a gun gets you two"), the Wayne County (Detroit) prosecutor supplemented it with a ban on plea bargaining. Prosecutors would not drop gun-related charges in return for a guilty plea. This was a seemingly important step. A common plea-bargaining tactic is to drop a gun-related charge to a nongun charge: from armed robbery to simple robbery, for example. . . .[3]

An evaluation of the Michigan law found no significant change in minimum sentences for homicide and armed robbery cases. The going rate for armed robbery continued to be about six years in prison. Nor was there any evidence

that Wayne County prosecutors had previously been exceptionally lenient in bargaining with defendants charged with those crimes. . . . Here leniency was not the problem, and getting tough by ending plea bargaining was no solution.

The 1973 New York drug law, widely advertised as "the nation's toughest drug law," also restricted plea bargaining. Persons charged with a Class A-I drug felony (which carried a mandatory penalty of fifteen or twenty-five years to life imprisonment) could not plead to a lesser felony. Persons charged with a lesser drug charge could not plead to a misdemeanor. An extensive evaluation of the New York law found that it was ineffective in reducing either drug use or violent crime. . . .

Meanwhile, in Hampton County, Iowa, a local prosecutor ran for office successfully on a platform of "no deals with dope pushers." The policy only served to push discretion further back in the system. In 1972, before the new policy went into effect, guilty pleas were accepted in 107 out of the 109 drug-sale cases disposed of. Eighty-eight of those 107 defendants pleaded guilty to a reduced charge. By 1974, a year after the policy went into effect, all of the guilty pleas were to the original charge. Yet only 41 drug-sale cases were disposed of (37 by plea and 4 by trial). The number of drug cases disposed of had dropped by more than 60 percent. Only part of this decline can be attributed to outright dismissals. The dismissal rate increased slightly, from 31 percent to 36 percent. More significant was the decline in cases filed in the first place: from 157 in 1972 to 63 in 1974. Getting tough in this instance meant getting tough with far fewer cases, a message that hardly represents getting tough with the original crime problem.

In Search of Bargains

Plea bargaining resists abolition for many reasons. First, as we have seen, the courtroom work group can easily evade the intent of any major change imposed by outsiders. Second, and perhaps more important, plea bargaining simply may not be the problem many people think it is. Peter Nardulli's study of plea bargaining in three states (Illinois, Pennsylvania, Michigan) . . . found a "rather high level of order" in the 7,500 cases he analyzed. The charges were changed significantly in only 15 percent of the cases in which defendants pleaded guilty. In 60 percent of those 5,600 cases, the original charge was not changed at all. . . . In other words, prosecutors were not wheeling and dealing with charges as if the courts were some kind of Middle Eastern bazaar.[4]

Regulation, Not Abolition

The evidence yielded by attempts to abolish plea bargaining confirms our general theory of the criminal justice wedding cake. Prosecutors routinely make moral judgments about criminal cases. Cases that fit a common-sense label of "serious," because of either the nature of the crime or the defendant's prior record, fall into the second layer. Those deemed "not serious" fall into the third layer. The relationship between the offender and the victim is a crucial element in this judgment. Robberies and rapes between people who know each other quickly find themselves in the third layer, where most bargains are to be found. But armed robberies and rapes by strangers are grouped in the second layer, where prosecutors are routinely fairly tough. . . .

Much can and should be done about plea bargaining short of abolishing it. The most reasonable proposals call for regulation. Bargaining should be brought out of the closet, so to speak, through the requirement of a written record. Formal policy guidelines could also establish criteria for reduction of charges and sentence recommendations. Implementation of these proposals would bolster public confidence in the administration of justice. It is the appearance of injustice and arbitrary decision making, as distinct from substantive injustice, that generates so much public cynicism and distrust of the administration of justice. . . .

NOTES

1. Norval Morris and Gordon J. Hawkins, *Letter to the President on Crime Control* (Chicago: University of Chicago Press, 1977), p. 61.
2. Ibid.
3. Colin Loftin and David McDowall, " 'One with a Gun Gets You Two': Mandatory Sentencing and Firearms Violence in Detroit," *The Annals* 455 (May 1981): 150–167.
4. Peter F. Nardulli, Roy B. Flemming, and James Eisenstein, "Criminal Courts and Bureaucratic Justice: Concessions and Consensus in the Guilty Plea Process," *Journal of Criminal Law and Criminology* 76 (Winter 1985): 1103–1131.

NO

Ralph Adam Fine

"PLEA BARGAINING SHOULD BE ABOLISHED"

On average, one of us is murdered every 28 minutes; there is a forcible rape every six minutes, a robbery every minute and a burglary every ten seconds.

There is no doubt about it. We are a nation tormented by crime and the fear of crime. As TV commentator Bill Moyers noted some years ago, crime in America has become a form of terrorism that threatens our way of life. "Desperately we crave victory over it," he said, "occasions on which to embrace one another in the belief that civilization may yet win out. Until then, every compromise with crime is surrender."

Unfortunately, we compromise with crime every day. The major compromise is plea bargaining, the system that gives leniency to criminals in return for a guilty plea. Herbert J. Stern, a former federal judge and prosecutor, calls the practice a "derogation of the spirit of the entire criminal-justice system." While serving as U.S. Attorney in New Jersey in 1973, he put his assistants on notice that he was inflexibly opposed to bargaining just to get guilty pleas. "I see no necessity which would justify us in engaging in such discussions," he wrote, "and thereby turning the processes of justice into a marketplace of bargain and sale."

No Free Rides

Scattered across this nation are others in the legal system who share Judge Stern's and my own view that we should not bargain with criminals. Yet plea bargaining remains common. As a result, courthouses have become places where criminals learn they can get away with crime. The following examples from Wisconsin, where I have been a judge for eight years, are all-too typical.

• One young man admitted to robbing three savings and loan institutions, crimes that carry maximum penalties of 20 years each. His case was plea bargained down to a year at the Milwaukee House of Correction. During this time, he was driven around town by social workers to help him find work. While they thought he was seeking employment, he robbed two more S&Ls. Four days after he was freed, he held up another S&L.

• A man was accused of holding up a gas station and threatening to shoot the operator. The robbery, which carries a maximum sentence of ten years, was plea bargained down to theft. Despite his having served 11½ years for complicity in the murder of a police officer, he was sentenced to only a one-year term. A little over a year later, he was in court again, charged with four armed robberies. The new cases were plea bargained. Released on parole after serving four years, he was later arrested and convicted for selling cocaine to a police officer.

• A defendant who was facing five years' imprisonment on a felony charge of conspiracy to make methamphetamine was allowed to plea bargain on five food-store and pharmacy robberies, three of them while armed with a gun. Four of the robbery charges were dropped in exchange for his guilty plea to the fifth. He pleaded guilty to the drug charge and was sentenced to three years in prison. He received a concurrent five-year sentence on the robbery conviction. In a real sense, he received a pass not only on four of the robberies but on the drug conviction as well. He was paroled after serving about two years.

To deter crime, the criminal-justice system must be credible. Potential criminals must be certain that their crimes will be punished and there will be no free rides. Plea bargaining destroys that credibility. It has made us impotent in our battle against crime.

"Quick Buck"

As far back as 1973 the National Advisory Commission on Criminal Justice warned, "Plea bargaining results in leniency that reduces the deterrent impact of the law." Yet plea bargaining has grown to the point where now roughly 90 percent of felony convictions are the result of guilty pleas, and the majority of those, in my experience, are the consequence of a "deal." The only excuse supporters can offer in defense of a system that is so obviously unfair to victims and unjust to society is expediency—they say it's the system's only way of moving cases through our crowded courts.

Prosecutors like plea bargaining because trials are time-consuming and they usually have heavy caseloads. Some defense lawyers prefer to plead their clients guilty rather than go to trial because it is an easier way to make a living. One defense lawyer put it this way: "A guilty plea is a quick buck." A thousand dollars is a handsome fee for two hours spent making a deal with the prosecutor, but a paltry payment for a four-day trial. And guilty defendants, naturally, like plea bargains because they usually get off lightly.

No judge is required to give the sentence worked out by the prosecution and defense, of course. But most accept plea bargaining because they fear the justice system would bog down without it.

To illustrate the weakness of the reasoning that supports plea bargaining, University of Hawaii professor Kenneth Kipnis compares it with a hypothetical system of grade bargaining in school. The instructors might not want to read term papers, for example, and would be willing to give a B to avoid the task. Many students would know that they have a slim chance for an A and that their papers would likely pull C's or below if graded fairly. The B compromise would permit teachers to "process" more students. But grade bargaining would defeat the aims of education. It is as deeply flawed an approach to criminal justice as it is to academics.

The whole question goes back to fundamental fairness: whether we will, as a civilized society, enforce criminal laws fairly and impartially. . . .

Innocent at Risk

A finely tuned criminal-justice system will punish the guilty and leave the innocent unmolested. . . . Since the Supreme Court's 1978 Hayes decision, the innocent have been at risk. . . . Hayes was a five-to-four decision written by the late Justice Potter Stewart. It permits prosecutors to threaten a more serious charge against defendants who insist on going on trial. This is the other side of plea bargaining; it can pressure innocent defendants into falsely condemning themselves.

When I was assigned to the juvenile division early in my judicial career, a 16-year-old boy was charged with carrying a concealed weapon. His lawyer told me that "they" wished to enter a guilty plea, and in return the prosecutor would recommend probation.

I asked the young man what happened. He said he was sitting on his back stoop peeling an apple with a steak knife. Some friends came by, and they got into a tussle. He put the knife in his boot so nobody would get hurt. A neighbor called the police, who searched everyone, found the knife and arrested him.

The police report confirmed that the knife was part of the family's steak-knife set, so I asked why he was pleading guilty. "My lawyer told me to," he replied. The lawyer's response when I asked him why he advised the guilty plea, given his client's story: "C'mon, judge, they're recommending probation. Let's not take all day."

A concealed-weapon conviction in Wisconsin requires proof that the object was being carried as a weapon and not for some other purpose. If the boy's story were true, he was innocent. I rejected the guilty plea and we went to trial. The evidence supported the boy's story, and he was acquitted. His lawyer left the courtroom grumbling about my "waste of everyone's time."

Kicking the Habit

What would happen if plea bargaining were abolished? Would most defendants stop pleading guilty, demand a trial and cause the system to grind to a screeching halt? The answer is a clear "no."

In 1975, Alaska's attorney general, Avrum M. Gross, abolished plea bargaining statewide. There were to be no sentence concessions or charge reductions in exchange for guilty pleas. After a plea of guilty, Gross permitted his assistants to make sentencing recommendations, but not suggestions for a specific term of incarceration. Gross knew the key to abolishing plea bargaining was the careful screening of cases *before* suspects were charged. He wrote in a memo to his district attorneys, "Charge what you can prove," reminding them that they would have more chance of getting a guilty plea if they made the charge realistic in the first place. He also pointed out that much of his prosecutors' time previously taken up by haggling with defense lawyers would be better spent preparing for cases.

Change wasn't easy. At first Gross received almost no cooperation. Prosecutors and judges were concerned the system would become backlogged. Defense lawyers worried about stiffer sentences for their clients and their own ability to make a living. But since Gross had the power to appoint all the district attorneys under the state's centralized system, he was able to make his program stick. To most people's surprise, it worked.

In 1980 the National Institute of Justice sponsored a study of Alaska's plea-bargaining ban. It concluded that the ban was successful. Cases actually moved more quickly without plea bargaining. In Anchorage, for instance, the disposition time for felonies fell from 192 days to under 90.

CAN OTHERS EMULATE THE ALASKAN EXPErience? In my view they can. Indeed, two jurisdictions—New Orleans and Oakland County, Michigan—have successfully kicked the plea-bargaining habit. . . .

New Orleans and Oakland County have debunked the expediency argument. The criminal-justice system does not need plea bargaining, and we should no longer tolerate this abuse of justice.

POSTSCRIPT

Should Plea Bargaining Continue to Be an Accepted Practice?

As indicated in other issue discussions, plea bargaining (unlike gun control, legalization of drugs, or abortion) has no real grass-roots lobby. While many professional groups and studies have recommended eliminating plea bargaining, there is no real groundswell of public support either in opposition or in favor of it. Meanwhile, plea bargaining remains central to our criminal justice system.

It is interesting to note that both Fine and Walker look at some of the same research findings (for example, the Alaskan modification of plea bargaining) and reach different conclusions. This is sometimes typical in the social sciences, which shows you once again the importance of developing your critical skills so that you will be able to sift through controversial issues to locate the facts and analyze them intelligently. In the final analysis, of course, you have to reach your own conclusions, then be able to defend them rationally.

For general discussions of plea bargaining, its history and changing forms, see A. W. Alschuler's "The Changing Plea Bargaining Debate," *California Law Review,* vol. 69 (1981) and J. B. Sanborn's "A Historical Sketch of Plea Bargaining," *Justice Quarterly,* vol. 3 (1986). Other studies of a more specific nature include "The Abolition of Plea Bargaining in the Coast Guard," by J. England and S. Talrico, *Journal of Criminal Justice,* vol. 11, 1983); D. Champion's "Felony Offenders, Plea Bargaining, and Probation," *Justice Professional,* vol. 2 (1987); R. Parnas's "Empirical Data, Tentative Conclusions, and Difficult Questions About Plea Bargaining in Three California Counties," *Federal Probation,* vol. 44 (1980); M. Rubenstein and T. White's "Plea Bargaining: Can Alaska Live Without It?" *Judicature,* vol. 62 (1979); and P. Nardulli et al., "Criminal Courts and Bureaucratic Justice: Concessions and Consensus in the Guilty Plea Process," *Journal of Criminal Law and Criminology* (Winter 1985).

For an invaluable journey through court decisions and a lucid constitutional critique of plea bargaining, see Malvina Halberstam's "Towards Neutral Principles in the Administration of Criminal Justice: A Critique of Supreme Court Decisions Sanctioning the Plea Bargaining Process," *Journal of Criminal Law and Criminology* (Spring 1982). Two rational decision-making approaches to plea bargaining of interest are G. Grossman and M. Katz's "Plea Bargaining and Social Welfare," *American Economic Review,* vol. 73 (1983) and J. F. Reinganum's "Plea Bargaining and Prosecutorial Discretion," *American Economic Review* (September 1988).

ISSUE 11

Is Selective Incapacitation Just?

YES: Brian Forst, from "Selective Incapacitation: A Sheep in Wolf's Clothing?" *Judicature* (October/November 1984)

NO: Andrew von Hirsch, from "Selective Incapacitation Reexamined," *Criminal Justice Ethics* (Winter/Spring 1988)

ISSUE SUMMARY

YES: Brian Forst, on the faculty of George Washington University, says that we now have the capacity to identify repeat offenders (in his words, "real *convicted* offenders") who pose a threat to society, so we should give them longer sentences, which will keep them off the streets and significantly reduce crime.

NO: Professor of criminal justice Andrew von Hirsch argues that we do not have the ability to identify repeat offenders, nor would it be just to give them longer sentences even if we knew for certain who they were.

As Durkheim tried to make clear in an earlier issue (Issue 1), crime is historically an intrinsic part of all social systems. We might also suggest the theorem that, wherever there has been crime, there have also been efforts to control it.

Early Americans, particularly the Quakers, constructed prisons for the specific purpose of isolating individuals as opposed to torturing them or to temporarily housing them on their way to execution or exile. Isolation or incapacitation of offenders was considered to be a more humane response to crime than simple retribution.

It was assumed that, by being in isolation, criminals would have abundant time to reflect upon and pray for their transgressions. By doing this, it was reasoned, inmates might become "better people." This precursory idea helped form the modern correctional philosophy of rehabilitation. That is, the philosophy whereby the purpose of social control is to help and treat offenders—not to punish them, or to extract revenge, or even to deter others from crime. In addition, if the treatment was successful and the criminal able and willing to refrain from criminal acts subsequent to release, then the community would be better off as a consequence. This, though, was ostensibly *not* the primary function of rehabilitation; to help the individual offender was its avowed aim.

Since the 1950s, at least among enlightened criminal justice administrators and many criminologists, the underlying philosophy of incarceration has been rehabilitation. It was assumed that with the proper classification and diagnosis of inmates, proper treatments could be administered that would successfully reduce or eliminate recidivistic inmates. During this time many technological advances were also made. Prediction tables, for instance, appeared to be more reliable than guesswork in determining the probability that certain offenders would be either a "good" or a "poor" risk for probation or parole. Many criminal justice administrators, wishing to be rational, were willing to draw from "scientific" guidelines in recommending or not recommending that inmates receive early parole or release from custody.

As a consequence of this rehabilitation philosophy, many adjudicated adult offenders were given indeterminate sentences. The idea was that the offender would be rehabilitated, not punished. Therefore, the legal requirement of a specific sentence being given for a specific crime was ignored. Advocates of this thinking felt that for the inmate's sake, he or she would be better off in prison until rehabilitation had taken place. However, throughout the 1970s and 1980s, study after study suggested that prison programs were not rehabilitating anyone. Recidivism rates continued to rise, in some systems reaching as high as 70 percent within 90 days after release! Also, the United States moved into a politically more conservative age in the 1980s, and politicians took up the call for a return to punishment, not rehabilitation, for prisoners. Many criminologists also questioned the practicality and feasibility of rehabilitation within the existing prison systems.

Once again scholars are debating how we should control offenders. Should we imprison them? If so, should it be to rehabilitate them? To deter both the general population and the incarcerated criminal from future crimes? Should it be plainly for retribution—that is, if someone has been found guilty of a crime, should it not be his or her "just deserts" to be punished for the crime?

Others argue that we as a society should not hesitate to imprison criminals simply to keep them from committing crimes while they are in prison. Incapacitation is the best reason for incarceration. Inmates cannot continue to break laws within the community when locked up.

Others go a step beyond this. Their arguments are based on their assumption that we now have the ability to predict future criminal behavior on the basis of former acts. Also, since rehabilitation is to them a failure, then the only logical purpose of incarceration is to rid society at least temporarily of the threat of the imprisoned criminal. Therefore, why not engage in "selective incapacitation"? What is wrong with arresting and incarcerating individuals who have a high probability of eventually breaking the law? Would this not greatly reduce our crime rate?

Brian Forst, well known for his studies disputing the deterrent value of capital punishment, argues that selective incapacitation of dangerous repeat *convicted* offenders can be a useful tool to reduce crime and protect society. Conservative criminal justice scholar Andrew von Hirsch dismisses Forst's proposals.

YES

Brian Forst

SELECTIVE INCAPACITATION: A SHEEP IN WOLF'S CLOTHING?

Despite our inability to predict an offender's future behavior with certainty, selective incapacitation may be a way to confront the twin demons of high crime rates and prison overcrowding.

DEBATE OVER THE BASIC PURPOSE OF SENTENCING HAS SHIFTED SUBSTANTIALLY over the past century. Retribution, the dominant purpose of sentencing until about the 1920s, eventually gave ground to the seemingly more scientific and humane principle of rehabilitation and its associate, the indeterminate sentence. Decades later, the crime rate explosion of the 1960s, combined with prominent studies citing little or no scientific evidence in support of the theory of rehabilitation, induced a widespread perception that rehabilitation was a failure and that the purposes of deterrence and incapacitation would be more effective, and no less humane.[1] Then, by the mid to late 1970s, uncertainty over the effectiveness—and concerns about the appropriateness—of existing crime control strategies led to an emergence of the "just deserts" principle, a humane rendering of the retribution school of sentencing.

The latest prominent principle of sentencing is that of "selective incapacitation."[2] Selective incapacitation, like general incapacitation, involves sentencing with the goal of protecting the community from the crimes that an offender would commit if he were on the street. It differs from general incapacitation in its attempt to replace bluntness with selectivity. Under a strategy of selective incapacitation, probation and short terms of incarceration are given to convicted offenders who are identified as being less likely to commit frequent and serious crimes, and longer terms of incarceration are given to those identified as more crime prone.

CRIME REDUCTION POTENTIAL

An attractive aspect of the selective incapacitation concept is its potential for bringing about a reduction in crime without an increase in prison populations. This reduction could be substantial.

Consider, for example, the 30,000 or so people convicted and sentenced annually in federal courts, about half of whom receive terms of incarceration that average two years. A recent study sponsored by the Department of Justice produced estimates that the most recidivistic half of all convicted federal offenders commits about 15 more nondrug offenses per year "on the street" than the least recidivistic half.[3] Given these figures, the number of serious crimes committed annually by convicted federal offenders that are *potentially* preventable could be as high as 450,000, depending on which ones are selected as the half to be incarcerated. The *actual* number of preventable current crimes is likely to be but a small fraction of 450,000—perhaps only 5 or 10 per cent—since our justice system does not now ignore dangerousness altogether and because we cannot perfectly identify the most dangerous offenders in advance. Moreover, even broad maximum and minimum sentences based on offense seriousness can impose further limits on the crime control potential of a strategy of selective incapacitation; obviously, sentencing judges cannot totally ignore the seriousness of the recent offense for which the defendant is being sentenced.

Preventing thousands of serious crimes annually, in the federal system alone, without increasing prison populations (or reducing prison populations without increasing crime) is, nonetheless, an idea that might warrant further consideration. Extending this logic to the state and local level makes the case even stronger—for every conviction at the federal level, state and local courts convict about 15 felony offenders.

The concept of selective incapacitation is controversial, however, for two basic reasons. First, it represents a departure from the more traditional purposes of criminal sanctions—retribution, deterrence, and rehabilitation—purposes that have solid philosophical, if not scientifically validated, foundations. Selective incapacitation is controversial, secondly, because its effectiveness is based largely on the statistical prediction of criminality, and such prediction is an imperfect science. The courts have had great difficulty acknowledging the acceptability of a policy in which its actions are based on imperfect predictions of human behavior, despite the fact that actions of the courts are routinely based on such predictions already in the absence of any such acknowledgment.[4]

Is selective incapacitation truly an effective and appropriate proposal, an "idea whose time has come," or is it another criminal justice fad, or worse—a proposal that carries with it a potential for injustice?

SELECTIVE INCAPACITATION AND JUSTICE

Beginning with basics, sentencing policy aims typically to ensure that criminal sanctions are just and effective. Unfortunately, a just sentence may not be effective, and an effective one may not be just. The tension between these goals is exemplified by a common dilemma: judges routinely give harsher sentences to the older offender because he tends to have a longer record and hence is presumed to be more "hardened" than the young offender, and in any event old enough to know better. It is generally easy to justify such sentences on grounds of deservedness, but not on grounds of crime prevention.

Studies have repeatedly found that a strategy that is more consistent with the goal of crime control is to take into account both the age and prior record of the convicted person (of course, as well as the seriousness of the current offense) at the time of sentencing.[5] Such a strategy would normally mean a longer sentence for the younger offender than for the older one, since young offenders have been found to be more criminally active than older ones.[6] Longer sentences for younger offenders are hence easy to justify on grounds of crime prevention, but not on conventional grounds of justice.

Another prominent area of conflict between the goals of crime prevention and deservedness centers on the defendant's prior record. To the extent that proponents of the just deserts school of sentencing might use the defendant's prior record at all, the focus is only on prior convictions, under the notion that blame can accumulate, but that the ascription of blame requires a conviction.[7]

A proponent of selective incapacitation, on the other hand, in deciding whether to sentence toward the maximum or minimum end of an incarceration range (a range based on offense seriousness), would include any constitutionally acceptable variable that predicts subsequent dangerousness, including prior arrests that did not end in conviction. The just deserts proponent argues that it is not fair to incarcerate Defendant A rather than Defendant B, when both have been convicted of the same offense, simply because A has a prior arrest. The proponent of selective incapacitation justifies such a practice on the grounds that too many persons who are not dangerous, many with no prior arrests, are currently behind bars; it is neither fair nor a good use of prison space to incarcerate Defendant B rather than Defendant A, both convicted of the same offense—especially when A has a prior arrest record while B does not— simply because the judge incorrectly assesses B to be more dangerous.

SOCIAL JUSTICE AND DETERRENCE

Reserving prison and jail space for the most criminally active offenders may in some instances conflict not only with other norms of legal justice, but with norms of social justice as well. Repeat offenders fall basically into two categories: those who are prone to violence and those who are not. If we reserve the sanction of incarceration only for the dangerous repeat offender, excluding the white collar offender and certain other criminals who pose no serious threat of physical injury to others, we may end up permitting harmful people from the middle class to evade a sanction that less privileged offenders cannot. Some white collar offenders, after all, impose greater costs on society than many dangerous street offenders, and it is clearly unjust to allow the former to pay a smaller price for their crimes than the latter must pay.

One solution is to impose on the white collar offender a short term of incarceration and a fine sufficiently large to deter both the individual offender and others from committing such crimes in the future. If the offender continues to commit crimes that are costly to society after incarceration, even if they do not involve injury, a longer term of incarceration may be in order to accomplish the same crime control objective—incapacitation—that is more commonly sought for the dangerous street offender. Thus, a strategy of selective incapacitation, combined judiciously with a strategy of deterrence, can be implemented in a way that is fully supportive of conventional norms of social as well as legal justice.

For many classes of offenders, a short term of incarceration, indeed, may have a substantially larger crime control impact by way of deterrence than by way of incapacitation. Which offenders? Both empirical evidence and common sense point to the white collar and the property crime offender as the ones who are most deterred by criminal sanctions; the violent offender has been found to be less influenced by the threat of a severe sanction.[8]

As long as the offender is a serious, high crime-rate offender, selective incapacitation must obviously be an effective crime control strategy (ignoring crimes against other inmates), regardless of the color of his collar; but it is likely to be a superfluous crime control concept for the offender who is more prone to being individually deterred by a short and unpleasant experience in jail or prison.

EFFECT ON PRISON POPULATION

What about the prospect of selective incapacitation leading to further prison overcrowding? If, in addition to those who are presently being sent to prison and jail, we were to follow a strategy of incarcerating those with the highest crime-risk profiles, some of whom would not otherwise be incarcerated, then prison and jail populations would indeed be larger than otherwise.

That, however, is not how selective incapacitation works. Under a selective incapacitation strategy, many of those who are currently being incarcerated would receive alternative sanctions— probation with close supervision, the "halfway" house, community service, and so on. Selective incapacitation means reserving prison and jail space for those who are predictably the most criminally active and harmful, subject to maximum and minimum sentence constraints based on offense seriousness. Many who are currently incarcerated would not be under such a strategy. Those who believe strongly in deterrence or just deserts might, indeed, have reason to fear that a strategy of selective incapacitation could cause offenders who they think belong in prison or jail to be released, so that more criminals could go unpunished under that strategy than under other strategies. Thus, larger prison populations might in fact be more closely associated with the deterrence or just deserts strategies than with a selective incapacitation strategy.

It should be obvious that no particular sentencing strategy or mix of strategies is likely to please everyone. Any given prison and jail occupancy level is bound to be too high for some and too low for others. For any given prison population level, however, a selective incapacitation strategy does offer a consistent rationale for attempting to minimize the crime rate.

THE PROBLEM OF PREDICTION

One of the most pervasive criticisms of selective incapacitation is that it is based on the statistical prediction of dangerousness; because such predictions are often erroneous, according to this point of view, they should not be used by the court. This criticism is related to both the nature of the errors and to the use of certain information for predicting a defendant's dangerousness.

Let's first consider the nature of errors in prediction. Prediction usually results in some successes and in two kinds of errors: predicting that a phenomenon such as recidivism will occur when in fact it does not ("false positives") and predicting that it will not occur when in fact it does ("false negatives"). The problem of false positives in sentencing is costly primarily to incarcerated defendants who are not really so dangerous, while false negative predictions impose costs primarily on the victims of subsequent crimes committed by released defendants. In predicting whether a defendant will recidivate or "go straight," the problem of false positives is widely regarded as especially serious, for many of the same reasons that it has been regarded in our society as better to release nine offenders than to convict one innocent person.

Because the false positive problem has been closely associated with statistical prediction, many authorities have been disinclined to base court decisions on such prediction systems. The problem of errors in prediction, however, is not unique to statistical prediction. The false positive risk has been a real problem every time a judge has ever detained a defendant in jail prior to trial based on a subjective assessment of the risk of non-appearance or pretrial crime. Sentencing decisions, too, even when publicly justified on grounds other than a prediction of either individual crime proneness or general deterrence, can easily be based on prediction nonetheless, and thus produce false positives.

Nonstatistical prediction in bail and sentencing decisions has in fact been found repeatedly to produce errors at a *higher* rate than the more scientific approach.[9] Those findings suggest that criteria derived from the application of sound statistical procedures not only do not "cause" false positives where none existed before, but that they generally *reduce* the rate of false positives. If we are truly interested in minimizing the social costs of erroneous prediction in selecting cases for detention, incarceration, or parole release, we should prefer to use such criteria to support those decisions.

A tempting alternative is to reject prediction altogether; obviously, if we do not predict, then no errors of prediction are possible. A flaw in this logic is that, whether we like it or not—indeed, even if we tried to forbid it—criminal justice decisions are now, and surely always will be, based on predictions, and imperfect ones, at that. Attempts to discourage prediction in sentencing may in fact produce the worst of both worlds: the deceit of predictive sentencing disguised as something more tasteful, and inferior prediction as well.

If we are to reserve at least some prison and jail space for the most criminally active offenders, then the prediction of criminal activity is an inescapable task. As long as some false positives and some false negatives are a necessary consequence of such policy, it would seem prudent to keep those errors as small as possible.

USE OF QUESTIONABLE FACTORS

The collective evidence of a variety of studies suggests that the strongest predictors of crime proneness include: age, prior record, use of illegal drugs, one or more recent arrests for burglary or robbery, and employment status.[10] The criminally active offender is more often young than old, typically with a juvenile record and prior adult arrests, a drug user, and unemployed. Under a strategy of selective incapacitation, judges who are used to giving harsher sentences primarily on the basis of the seriousness of the current offense and the existence of prior felony convictions would shift their consideration somewhat to such factors as youthfulness, prior juvenile commitments, prior arrests that did not end in conviction, use of hard drugs, and unemployment. Is this proper?

Needless to say, the consideration of such factors in the sentencing decision must be done in a way that is fully consistent with the defendant's right to due process. The Supreme Court has held that the strict due process provisions that apply to the trial procedure do not apply to sentencing.[11] As a result, presentence investigation reports, used to assist judges in making sentence decisions, often contain information about prior arrests—including those that did not result in conviction—as well as information about juvenile delinquency, drug use, unemployment, and a variety of other factors not generally revealed in the trial proceeding.[12] Such information is subject to a set of rules of disclosure to ensure due process at sentencing generally, and reliability of the information in particular.[13]

The use of such information is especially important, however, to protect defendants—specifically, those who are currently committed to prisons and jails when they do not belong there. Matters could be even worse. If the court were to impose the same set of disclosure restrictions on information used to support the sentencing decision as apply to the trial proceeding, it is safe to say that many more relatively harmless defendants would be incarcerated than at present—especially, persons with no prior arrests, persons who are not heroin addicts, and so on. In the meantime, however, the fact that information about such factors is often, but not consistently made available, and is not systematically used in sentencing and parole release decisions even when available, suggests that our current prison and jail populations may be substantially larger than they need be.

DEALING WITH DEMONS

The idea that current prison and jail populations are larger than necessary is one that might not win the support of a population that has been besieged by crime as long as ours. While declining crime rates since 1980 have undoubtedly helped to reduce the public frenzy over crime, crime rates are still quite high by most standards. Until people can feel safe walking in city parks, they are not likely to take a charitable view of what to do with convicted felons. Reduced public frenzy nonetheless tends to lessen the need to find drastic solutions generally and more draconian criminal sanctions in particular.

This brings us full circle. Selective incapacitation, the latest theory for dealing with crime, is in fact a modest proposal for simultaneously confronting the twin demons of high crime rates and large prison populations. It is less than a universal remedy, first, because our prisons and jails are already populated with many crime prone offenders and, second, because it is not fully consistent with other legitimate reasons to incarcerate some offenders and release others, reasons related primarily to basic principles of justice.

Modest gains, however, are better than none. Continuing frustration with crime on the one hand, and prison and jail overpopulation on the other, suggests a need to exploit modest opportunities whenever they present themselves. Neither the pervasive "career criminal" prosecution programs nor the most touted sentencing guideline systems currently in operation make use of the factors that have been found repeatedly to be associated with repeat criminal behavior. The result is to impose avoidable, and possibly substantial, costs on two groups: offenders who are incarcerated for terms that exceed what can be supported by evidence on how those terms protect the public, and victims of crime committed by released offenders for whom abundant evidence indicates that their release was premature.

It is frequently asserted that the public is foolish to insist, simultaneously, on less crime and less taxes for prisons and jails. In fact, less crime may be compatible with less public expenditures on prisons and jails for a variety of reasons. One is the opportunity for prosecutors, judges, and parole boards to make their decisions with a more informed view of the degree of crime risk presented by each defendant.

NOTES

1. Bailey, *Correctional Outcome: An Evaluation of 100 Reports*, 57 J. OF CRIMINAL L., CRIMIN., AND POLICE SCI. 157 (1966); Martinson, *What Works—Questions and Answers About Prison Reform*, PUBLIC INTEREST 22 (Spring 1974).

2. The elementary idea of protecting society from dangerous offenders by locking them up has, of course, been around perhaps since the time of the castle dungeon. As a fully developed scientific theory, with estimates of crime prevention effects based on individual crime rates and prison capacity levels, the concept of a measurable incapacitation effect came into being in 1973, with the work of Avi-Itzhak and Shinnar, *Quantitative Models in Crime Control*, J. OF CRIM. JUST. 185 (1973). The idea of refining the notion of general incapacitation with the prediction of individual crime rates by type of offender, under the term "selective incapacitation," was reported in 1975 by Greenberg, *The Incapacitative Effect of Imprisonment: Some Estimates*, 9 L. AND SOC'Y. REV. 541 (1975). The selective incapacitation concept received national attention in late 1982, with the publication of two prominent Rand Corporation reports on the subject. Greenwood, with Abrahamse, SELECTIVE INCAPACITATION (Santa Monica, CA: Rand Corporation, 1982); and Chaiken and Chaiken, VARIETIES OF CRIMINAL BEHAVIOR (Santa Monica, CA: Rand Corporation, 1982).

3. Forst, Rhodes, Dimm, Gelman, and Mullin, *Targeting Federal Resources on Recidivists: An Empirical View*, 47 FEDERAL PROBATION 10 (1983).

4. *Selective Incapacitation: Reducing Crime Through Predictions of Recidivism*, 96 HARV. L. REV. 525 (1982); Wilson, *Dealing With the High-Rate Offender*, PUBLIC INTEREST 63 (1983); and Feinberg, *Selective Incapacitation and the Effort to Improve the Fairness of Existing Sentencing Practices*, 12 N.Y.U. REV. OF L. AND SOCIAL CHANGE 53 (1983–84).

5. Boland and Wilson, *Age, Crime, and Punishment*, PUBLIC INTEREST 23 (1978); Williams, SCOPE AND PREDICTION OF RECIDIVISM, (Washington, DC: Institute for Law and Social Research, 1979); Forst, *supra* n. 3.

6. Gottfredson, et al., *The Outcome of Parole According to Base Expectancy Rates*, in Radzinowicz and Wolfgang, eds., CRIME AND JUSTICE, VOL. III: THE CRIMINAL IN CONFINEMENT 382–87 (New York: Basic Books, 1971); Wolfgang, Figlio, and Sellin, DELINQUENCY IN A BIRTH COHORT (Chicago: University of Chicago Press, 1972); Williams, *supra* n. 5; Chaiken and Chaiken, *supra* n. 2; and Forst, *supra* n. 3.

7. Von Hirsch, *The Ethics of Selective Incapacitation: Observations on the Contemporary Debate*, 30 CRIME AND DELINQUENCY 181 (1984).

8. Andenaes, *The General Preventive Effects of Punishment*, 114 U. PA. L. REV. 957 (1966); Zimring and Hawkins, DETERRENCE: THE LEGAL THREAT IN CRIME CONTROL 128–41 (Chicago: University of Chicago Press, 1973); Blumstein, Cohen, and Nagin, DETERRENCE AND INCAPACITATION: ESTIMATING THE EFFECTS OF CRIMINAL SANCTIONS ON CRIME RATES 99–111 (Washington, DC: National Academy of Science, 1978); Forst, *Capital Punish-*

ment and Deterrence: Conflicting Evidence?, 74 J. OF CRIM. L. AND CRIMINOLOGY (1983).

9. Meehl, CLINICAL VS. STATISTICAL PREDICTION (Minneapolis, MN: University of Minnesota Press, 1954); Gough, *Clinical vs. Statistical Prediction in Psychology*, in Postman, ed., PSYCHOLOGY IN THE MAKING 526–84 (New York: Knopf, 1962); Goldberg, *Man versus Model of Man: A Rationale, Plus Some Evidence for a Method of Improving on Clinical Inference*, 73 PSYCHOLOGICAL BULLETIN 422 (1970); Steadman and Cocozza, *Psychiatry, Dangerousness and the Repetitively Violent Offender*, 69 J. OF CRIM. L. AND CRIMINOLOGY 226 (1978); Roth and Wice, PRETRIAL RELEASE AND MISCONDUCT IN THE DISTRICT OF COLUMBIA 61–64 (Washington, DC: Institute for Law and Social Research, 1980); Monahan, PREDICTING VIOLENT BEHAVIOR: AN ASSESSMENT OF CLINICAL TECHNIQUES (Beverly Hills, CA: Sage, 1981); Carroll, et al., *Evaluation, Diagnosis, and Prediction in Parole Decision Making*, 17 L. AND SOC'Y. REV. 199 (1982); Holland, et al., *Comparison and Combination of Clinical and Statistical Predictions of Recidivism Among Adult Offenders*, 68 J. OF APPLIED PSYCHOLOGY 203 (1983); Gottfredson and Gottfredson, "Accuracy of Prediction Models," unpublished manuscript (1984), at 67–69.

10. Wolfgang, *supra* n. 6 at 88; Williams, *supra* n. 5; Forst, *supra* n. 3; Greenwood, *supra* n. 2; Chaiken and Chaiken, *supra* n. 2.

11. Williams v. New York, 337 U.S. 241, 251 (1949).

12. Fennell and Hall, *Due Process at Sentencing: An Empirical and Legal Analysis of the Disclosure of Presentence Reports in Federal Courts*, 93 HARV. L. REV. 1615–97 (1980); Forst and Rhodes, *Structuring the Exercise of Sentencing Discretion in the Federal Courts*, 46 FEDERAL PROBATION 3 (1982).

13. Schulhofer, *Due Process of Sentencing*, 128 U. PA. L. REV. 733 (1980); Fennell and Hall, *id.*

NO

Andrew von Hirsch

SELECTIVE INCAPACITATION REEXAMINED: THE NATIONAL ACADEMY OF SCIENCES' REPORT ON CRIMINAL CAREERS AND "CAREER CRIMINALS"

Prediction research in criminology has had a sixty-year history in this country. From the 1920s until only a few years ago, the research techniques remained much the same. Various facts about convicted criminals would be recorded: previous arrests and convictions, social history, and so forth. It would be identified which of these factors were, statistically, most strongly associated with subsequent offending. The prediction instrument, based on these factors, would then be constructed and tested.[1]

These traditional prediction studies did suggest that a certain capacity to forecast recidivism existed. Generally, they found that certain facts about an offender—principally, his criminal history, drug habits, and history of unemployment—were to a modest extent indicative of increased likelihood of recidivism.[2] Some such studies were put to use: The U.S. Parole Commission's parole-release guidelines, for example, rely in part (albeit not primarily) on a predictive index known as the Salient Factor Score.[3]

The techniques did not, however, try systematically to distinguish serious from trivial recidivism. Moreover, they offered no promise of reduced crime rates; no attempt was made to estimate aggregate crime-prevention effects. Locking up the potential recidivist thus assured only that he or she would be restrained; since other criminals remained at large, it did not necessarily diminish the overall risk of victimization. These limitations tended, by the late 30s, to diminish penologists' interest in traditional prediction techniques.

The present decade has, however, signaled the beginning of a purportedly new approach to prediction research: "selective incapacitation."[4] Surveys of imprisoned offenders found that a small number of such persons admitted responsibility for an unusually large number of serious offenses.[5] Perhaps the criminal careers of these most active and dangerous offenders were

From Andrew von Hirsch, "Selective Incapacitation Reexamined," *Criminal Justice Ethics*, vol. 7, no. 1 (Winter/Spring 1988), pp. 19-35. Copyright © 1988 by *Criminal Justice Ethics*. Reprinted by permission.

NO Andrew von Hirsch / 205

worth close scrutiny. If this minority of high-risk individuals could be identified and segregated, might this not reduce crime rates after all?

The most notable product of this research to date has been a study by a RAND Corporation researcher, Peter W. Greenwood, published in 1982.[6] Greenwood concentrated on *high-rate, serious* offenders—those likely to commit frequent acts of robbery or other violent crimes in future. He developed a seven-factor prediction index, designed to identify such individuals on the basis of their early criminal records, and their histories of drug use and unemployment.[7] He also attempted to project the crime-reduction impact of his technique. If applied in sentencing convicted robbers, he asserted, the technique could reduce the robbery rate by as much as fifteen to twenty percent—without appreciable increases in the numbers of persons confined.[8]

Greenwood's technique sounded like a sensational discovery, and received wide publicity. What could be better than a simple, easy-to-apply forecasting index, capable of leading to large reductions in crime without adding substantially to the populations of already-overfilled prisons? Some penologists seized upon his proposals—most notably, James Q. Wilson in his revised edition of *Thinking About Crime*.[9] The Reagan Justice Department provided enthusiastic advocacy and funding for more research.

But doubts were not long in coming. Several researchers questioned whether Greenwood's scale had any predictive value if officially recorded information available to courts were relied upon, instead of offender self-reports.[10] Others questioned his projections of large reductions in the robbery rate, arguing that

these projections were based on a faulty research design.[11] Still others[12] questioned the fairness of a scheme which would impose wide disparities in the sentences given to robbers on the basis of factors alien to the degree of harmfulness and culpability of their criminal conduct.[13]

It was in this environment—of lively interest in career-criminal research and yet acute controversy about its results— that the National Academy of Sciences established its Panel on Research on Criminal Careers under the chairmanship of Professor Alfred Blumstein of Carnegie-Mellon University. The Panel's stated mission was to evaluate the current research on criminal careers, and measure the potential crime-prevention benefits of incapacitation strategies.[14] Inevitably, the Greenwood research would be a matter of interest—and the Panel commissioned a staff member, Christy Visher, to do a reanalysis of Greenwood's estimates.[15] . . .

SELECTIVE INCAPACITATION: THE EMPIRICAL QUESTIONS

How much do we know about identifying potential serious offenders? And what impact would confining the supposedly dangerous have on crime rates? The Panel's report addresses these issues.

The Greenwood Study

The report contains, not surprisingly, an extensive discussion of Peter Greenwood's study. One topic is the reliability of his prediction scale. The objective of selective incapacitation is to identify the potential high-rate *serious* offenders, and distinguish them from lesser recidivists. To make this distinction, the RAND studies, including Greenwood's, relied upon offender self-reports. A sentencing court, however, is scarcely in a position to obtain the necessary information from the defendant facing sentence. The court would have to rely on officially recorded information about offenders' adult and juvenile records, and existing records make the distinction poorly. When Marcia and Jan Chaiken reanalyzed Greenwood's data to see how well the potential high-risk serious offenders could be identified from information in court records, the results were disappointing. The officially recorded facts—arrests, convictions, and meager information about offenders' personal histories—did not demarcate the potential frequent robbers from the potential burglars and car thieves. The factors in the self-report study that had proved useful, such as early and extensive youthful violence and multiple drug use, were not reflected in official records.[16]

The Panel affirms this criticism. The Greenwood scale cannot be readily operationalized because officially recorded variables do not suffice to distinguish the high risks. In the Panel's words:

There are also questions about the availability of the scale variables for operational use. In Greenwood's analysis, all of the variables, except past convictions for the same charge, are based on self-reports by inmates. Implementation of the scale at sentencing would have to depend on official reports rather than self-reports as the source of data for scale variables. For some of the scale variables, especially those relating to juvenile record, drug use, and employment, this requirement may be more than records can routinely include.[17]

It is conceivable that, with a change in law concerning the confidentiality of juvenile court records, the offender's juvenile record could become available to courts. But this would leave out three of Greenwood's seven factors—those concerning drug use and unemployment—for which obtaining the necessary official records could be a matter of considerable difficulty.[18]

The other major issue is the impact on crime rates. The novelty of Greenwood's study is that it claims to offer a method of reducing the aggregate rate of robberies were the scale to be applied in sentencing decisions. The Panel devotes considerable space to examining the crime reduction claims. It begins by examining Greenwood's calculations themselves. Its reanalysis finds that Greenwood overstated the crime reduction effects. His scenario of imposing short jail terms for "low-rate" robbers and lengthy prison terms for high-rate robbers could not, upon recalculation, produce the 20 percent reduction in the robbery rate for California that Greenwood claimed. The actual estimate drops to a little more than half the amount.[19]

Moreover, even those revised estimates seemed to be unique to California. When applied to another state, Michigan, it was discovered that the prediction scale was less accurate, and that the same proposed sentencing policy might actually *increase* robberies.[20] The Panel thus cautions against generalizing the Greenwood findings to other jurisdictions.

Thus far, the reestimates are based on Greenwood's factual assumptions. But are these correct? Here, there are several problems, which the Panel addresses.

1. Greenwood, some critics had noted, assumes (without supplying supporting

evidence) that his "high-risk" robbers have extremely long, even indefinite, criminal careers. Were criminal careers shorter than he assumed, how much would the crime-reduction estimates shrink? The Panel utilized an analysis by Jacqueline Cohen of the impact of career-lengths estimates.[21] Those calculations are not encouraging. Even an assumed residual robbery career of fifteen years—quite a lengthy period—could reduce the anticipated crime-reduction significantly; cutting the residual career estimate to five years could more than halve the impact.[22]

2. Greenwood assumes that robbery is a single-offender offense. Removing the high-rate robber from circulation would thus eliminate a number of offenses equal to his predicted number of robberies. But this assumption is unrealistic: a substantial proportion of robberies, especially by younger offenders, is committed in groups. Removal of one of the group's members is not likely to terminate the group's activities. The Panel notes:

> The incapacitative effect will be less if the offenses of incarcerated inmates persist in the community, perhaps because the inmate is replaced by a new recruit or because incarceration of some members of offending groups does not disrupt the groups' crimes.[23]

3. Greenwood bases his crime-reduction estimates on the self-reported activities of *incarcerated* robbers, and then extrapolates those estimates to robbers generally. The incarcerated robbers, however, may well have unrepresentatively high rates of criminal activity. (It is like trying to learn about the smoking habits of smokers generally by studying the smoking activity of residents of a lung cancer ward.) Don Gottfredson and I estimated that if this

extrapolation is eliminated, the projected crime-reduction impact could shrink by about a half.[24] The Panel does not address our calculations specifically but recognizes the existence of this problem in its general discussion of the problem of estimating the intensity of robbers' criminal activity.[25]

Where does this leave one? The Panel, understandably, does not supply a single revised crime-reduction estimate after all the foregoing problems are taken into account. But the scaling down would be considerable. Thus one begins with Greenwood's estimated 20 percent robbery reduction for California. Recalculation of the estimates alone reduces this to about 13 percent.[26] Taking career length into account may pare the impact down to only 6 percent.[27] Even *that*, the Panel notes, may be a "best-case" estimate,[28] because the other problems—such as group offending—could result in a further reduction. Were the extrapolation problem considered also, even those scaled-down estimates would need to be halved.[29] At the end, very little indeed can confidently be said of the potential crime reduction effect of the Greenwood prediction technique.

Other Prediction Methods

What of prediction scales other than Greenwood's? The report mentions a few. One is the U.S. Parole Commission's Salient Factor Score. This prediction device, designed to forecast parole recidivism, has been repeatedly revalidated, and the Panel finds that it performs reasonably well for its purpose.[30] The Score, however, is a traditional prediction device. It was designed to distinguish potential recidivists from non-recidivists—without regard to the seriousness and frequency of the recidivism involved. The Panel examined the Score's ability to identify potential frequent offenders. It performed badly; as the Panel notes.

> The [Salient Factor Score] thus appears to discriminate most effectively between persisters and those who do not incur another arrest within three years (which includes mainly offenders who have terminated their criminal careers) *and is less effective in distinguishing frequency rates for active offenders. This finding still leaves a challenge to find adequate predictors of differential frequency rates among those who do persist in their criminal careers after release.*[31]

The Panel report also mentions two other instruments. The Iowa parole-risk scale resembles the Salient Factor Score, save that it has not yet been so carefully validated.[32] A traditional forecasting instrument, it does not try to forecast the frequency of offending. The INSLAW scale attempts to predict "career criminals" using data on federal probationers and parolees. It has not been validated on a sample other than the construction sample.[33]

Prospects for Improving Predictive Techniques

What of the future? Can a breakthrough in selective-incapacitation techniques be achieved with a modest additional effort, or are the problems more serious? The Panel indicates that the task will be far from easy. One obstacle is the kind of research required. Analyses of convicted offenders' criminal activities suffer from the difficulty mentioned already: it is unclear to what extent those persons' activities are representative of the activity of offenders in the community. Samples drawn from the general population are free of such bias, but may contain too small a number of active offenders.[34]

Another obstacle concerns estimating the length of criminal careers. The serious offenders with whom selective incapacitation is concerned generally will be imprisoned in any event: the major policy issue is the duration of their confinement. The strategy is to impose longer terms on the supposed "high risk" offenders, but that assumes they will continue their criminal activities for some time. Little prevention is accomplished if the high risk offenders who are confined are those whose careers shortly will end. The Panel report confirms this point by showing how sensitive crime-prevention estimates are to variations in the assumed duration of residual criminal careers.[35]

This means that selective incapacitation, to succeed, needs not merely to pick out high risk offenders, but *those high risk offenders who are likely to continue offending for an appreciable time.* But how much do we know about forecasting the residual career? At the moment, rather little. The report mentions that there is aggregate data on the relationship of the residual career to age, suggesting that offenders who continue to offend through their thirties remain active for some time thereafter.[36] This, however, is not helpful to the extent that such aggregate data mask differences among the remaining careers of thirty-year-olds and do not help project career length among younger offenders.

The Panel suggests that career termination may depend on new variables— not so much prior criminal record but later events, including steady employment and marriage.[37] Were that so, predicting termination could present practical difficulties. While a court can have offenders' prior records at its disposal, it will not have information about these later events.

Such factors may be ethically trouble-some as well. Aside from the desert con-cerns which are addressed below, many feel it inappropriate to base punishment on matters of social status. Having a steady job is a social-status variable over which the offender may have limited control. Being single or married—or hav-ing a "steady relationship" or not—is a constitutionally protected choice. It would be disturbing if duration of imprison-ment was made to depend on such mat-ters.[38] Even mothers anxious to see their sons wed do not usually think they merit extra years in prison for insisting on bachelorhood.

SELECTIVE INCAPACITATION: THE ETHICAL QUESTIONS

The Problem of Proportionality

Selective prediction strategies—whether of the traditional sort or involving methods such as Greenwood's—seem to conflict with the requirements of proportionality and desert. A deserved sentence should be based primarily on the gravity of the crime for which the offender currently stands convicted. The previous criminal record should have only a secondary role, if considered at all.[39]

With selective risk prediction, the em-phasis shifts *away* from the seriousness of the current offense. Since the aim is to identify the higher-risk individuals from among those convicted of a specified type of crime, the character of the cur-rent crime tends not to have much weight. Traditional prediction indices largely ignored the gravity of the current offense and concentrated on the of-fender's earlier criminal and social histo-ries. The new "selective incapacitation" techniques maintain a similar emphasis.

Of Greenwood's seven predictive factors, three do not measure criminal activity of a serious nature at all but the offender's personal drug consumption and lack of stable employment instead. Of the four other factors, only two measure the of-fender's recent criminal record; and *none* measures the degree of heinousness (for example, the extent of violence) of the offender's current robbery offense.[40]

When one tries to take aggregate pre-ventive impact into account, matters become worse. Selective-incapacitation techniques, by their own proponents' reckoning, are capable of providing sig-nificant crime-reduction effects only if they infringe proportionality require-ments to a *very* great degree. Green-wood's projection of a large reduction in the robbery rate for California is made on the assumption that robbers who score badly on his prediction index would re-ceive about *eight years'* imprisonment, whereas better-scoring robbers would receive only *one* year in jail.[41] This is a huge difference in severity—700 per-cent—in the punishment of offenders convicted of the same offense of robbery, and one that cannot even begin to be accounted for by distinctions in the seri-ousness of the offenders' criminal con-duct. . . .

OTHER ISSUES

In this essay, I have addressed only one of the issues with which the Panel deals—namely selective incapacitation. The Report also contains a discussion of so-called categorial or charge-based inca-pacitation.[42] Elsewhere, I have suggested that such a technique might—with ap-propriate restrictions—be integrated into a desert rationale more readily than se-lective incapacitation could.[43] But the

Panel correctly indicates that categorial incapacitation research is too much in its infancy to warrant any possible present use in sentencing policy[44]—and thus I have not addressed it here. The Report contains, finally, an extended and useful examination of various methodological issues[45] which are beyond the scope of this paper or my competence.

CONCLUSIONS

When the Panel was organized in 1983, selective incapacitation was spoken of by its proponents in strongly optimistic terms. The technique, it was asserted, would permit identification and segregation of "career" criminals involved in violent, repetitive criminality; could have a substantial impact on rates of serious crime if utilized in sentencing decisions; and might even, if so used, permit reduction of prison populations.

The Panel's essential message about selective incapacitation is one of skepticism and caution. While urging further research, the Panel stresses the technique's limitations: Identifying high-risk, serious offenders will be impeded for the foreseeable future by the quality of information available to sentencing courts. The potential impact of selective incapacitation on crime rates is far below proponents' initial estimates, and likely to be quite modest. Considerations of proportionality and desert significantly limit the inequalities in sentence that may fairly be visited for the sake of restraining "high-risk" offenders; and narrowing those permissible inequalities may, in turn, further restrict the technique's impact on crime. The Panel thus confirms that selective incapacitation, far from being the near-panacea some of its advocates have asserted it was—is both

on empirical and ethical grounds a device of limited potential, at best. . . .

Postscript: Greenwood's Follow Up

After this article was written, Peter Greenwood published a new report[46] describing a follow-up of his original prediction study. The results were disappointing. When actual subsequent arrests rather than self-reported crimes were used to measure recidivism, the supposed high-risk offenders recidivated only slightly more often than the low-risk ones. Reconstructing the prediction scale so as to use officially recorded data about offenders also reduced the power of the scale to identify the potential high-rate offenders. The study does not attempt to calculate aggregate crime prevention effects. Greenwood's conclusions, however, are rather pessimistic:

> It is clear that substantial differences in sentence length for the types of chronic offenders studied here cannot currently be justified on selective incapacitation grounds alone, because there are no reliable methods for either measuring or predicting future offense rates.[47]

This new study's results will require further analysis, and prediction techniques other than Greenwood's still merit examination. But the sober tone of this new report, a report written by one of the main former advocates of selective incapacitation, confirms the need for a healthy skepticism concerning predictive sentencing and its supposed benefits.

NOTES

The ideas for this paper grew originally out of a discussion with Norval Morris in November 1986; while I disagree here with some of his thoughts, I found them, as always, greatly stimulating. The paper also underwent substantial revision as a result of comments received from several of my colleagues: Jacqueline Cohen, Douglas Husak, Nils Jareborg, John Kleinig, Marc Miller, Paul Robinson, Michael Tonry, and Martin Wasik.

1. A. Von Hirsch, Past or Future Crimes: Dangerousness and Deservedness in the Sentencing of Criminals 105–06 (1985). The prediction devices did not measure recidivism per se, but rather some official responses to it such as rearrest, reconviction, or parole revocation.

2. *Id.*

3. *Id.* at 105; D. Gottfredson, L. Wilkins & P. Hoffman, Guidelines for Parole and Sentencing ch. 3 (1978).

4. The term originated in Greenberg, *The Incapacitative Effect of Imprisonment: Some Estimates*, 9 Law & Socy's Rev. 541 (1980), and was then popularized by P. Greenwood, Selective Incapacitation (1982).

5. P. Greenwood, *supra* note 4; J. Chaiken & M. Chaiken, Varieties of Criminal Behavior (1982).

6. P. Greenwood, *supra* note 4.

7. Greenwood's scale uses seven factors. The presence of four or more indicates the person is a high risk. The factors are: (1) prior conviction for the instant offense types; (2) incarceration for more than half the preceding two years; (3) conviction before age 16; (4) time served in a state juvenile facility; (5) drug use during preceding two years; (6) drug use as juvenile; (7) unemployed more than half the preceeding two years. *Id.* at 50.

8. *Id.* at 78–79. The calculations do not take victimizations *within* prison into account. Incapacitation, according to its proponents, is designed to protect persons in the community. The justification of disregarding in-prison victimization is seldom even discussed.

9. J. Wilson, Thinking About Crime, chs. 8 & 10 (rev. ed. 1983).

10. A. Von Hirsch, *supra* note 1, 111–12; Chaiken & Chaiken, *Offender Types and Public Policy*, 30 Crime & Delinq. 195 (1984).

11. A. Von Hirsch, *supra* note 1, ch. 10; Von Hirsch & Gottfredson, *Selective Incapacitation: Some Queries about Research Design and Equity*, 12 N.Y.U. Rev. L. & Soc. Change 11 (1983/84).

12. A. Von Hirsch, *supra* note 1, ch. 11.

13. For further recent discussion, *see* Messinger & Berk, "Review Essay: Dangerous People," 25 Criminology 1401 (1987).

14. The Panel's report is set forth in 1 Criminal Careers and "Career Criminals" 1–209 (A. Blumstein, J. Cohen, J. Roth & C. Visher eds. 1986) [hereinafter cited as Panel Report].

15. Visher, *The Rand Inmate Survey; A Reanalysis*, 2 Criminal Careers and "Career Criminals" 161–211 (A. Blumstein, J. Cohen, J. Roth & C. Visher eds. 1986).

16. Chaiken & Chaiken, *supra* note 10.

17. Panel Report, *supra* note 14, at 181.

18. See also text accompanying note 40, *infra*.

19. Panel Report, *supra* note 14, 131–32; Visher, *supra* note 15.

20. Panel Report, *supra* note 14, at 132–33. The report explains the possible reason for this paradoxical effect as follows: "The substantial increase in crime in Michigan would be due to the large reduction in sentences for the many medium- and low-rate offenders; they would serve only one year in jail rather than the average of four or five years in prison under current policy. In addition, few inmates in Michigan would be classified as high-rate offenders—and thus subject to long prison terms—using the same classification scale." *Id.* at 133.

21. Cohen's conclusions are reported in *id.* at 133–35.

22. *Id.*

23. *Id.*, 135. *See also* Reiss, *Co-Offender Influences on Criminal Careers*, in 2 Criminal Careers and "Career Criminals" 121–60 (A. Blumstein, J. Cohen, J. Roth & C. Visher eds. 1986).

24. For a summary of these calculations, *see* Past or Future Crimes, *supra* note 1, 115–23. For the full discussion, *see* von Hirsch & Gottfredson, *supra* note 11, at 22–31, 46–51.

25. Panel Report, *supra* note 14, at 101–04.

26. *See* text accompanying note 22, *supra*.

27. *See* text accompanying notes 24–25, *supra*.

28. Panel Report, *supra* note 14, at 135.

29. *See* text accompanying notes 27–28, *supra*.

30. Panel Report, *supra* note 14, at 181–83.

31. *Id.* at 183 (emphasis added).

32. *Id.* at 183–86.

33. *Id.* at 186–88.

34. *Id.* at 101–04.

35. *See* text accompanying notes 24–25, *supra*.

36. Panel Report, *supra* note 14, at 206.

37. *Id.*

38. Even advocates of predictive sentencing have questioned reliance on factors which are beyond offenders' control or involve constitutionally protected choices. *See* Underwood, "Law and the Crystal Ball: Predicting Behavior with Statistical Preference and Individualized Judgment," 88 Yale L. J. 1408, 1436–38 (1979).

39. *See* A. Von Hirsch, *supra* note 1, ch. 7.

40. For fuller discussion, ch. 11.

41. The Panel Report, *supra* note 14, at 131–32, calculates these durations from the Greenwood study.

42. The idea of "categorial" or charge-based incapacitation was pioneered by Dr. Jacqueline Cohen. She examined the rates of recidivism associated with conviction for various types of crime, and found, in one U.S. jurisdiction, that conviction for robbery was on average associated with more frequent and more serious subse-

quent crimes than conviction for burglary. If true, this means that a policy of incarcerating convicted robbers would have a higher incapacitation effect than that of confining the burglars. Since risk here is defined in terms of conviction offense, the strategy (unlike selective incapacitation) would not involve punishing differently those convicted of similar criminal acts. *See* Cohen, *Incapacitation as a Strategy for Crime Control: Possibilities and Pitfalls*, in 5 CRIME AND JUSTICE: AN ANNUAL REVIEW OF RESEARCH 1–84 (M. Tonry & N. Morris eds. 1983).

43. A. VON HIRSCH, *supra* note 1, ch. 13. I suggest, however, that the strategy would also carefully have to be restricted in such a fashion as to meet also the rank-ordering requirements of ordinal desert. *Id.* at 154–59.

44. PANEL REPORT, *supra* note 14, at 139–40. In its discussion of categorial incapacitation, the Panel assumes that the policy would be implemented by adopting a mandatory minimum sentence for the crimes of convictions found associated with serious subsequent recidivism, such as robbery. Such a policy, as the Panel correctly notes, would raise problems of fairness. Merely imposing, say, a two-year minimum for robbery—without changing other aspects of the penalty structure—does not assure that this offense is punished commensurately with other offenses. The minimum also does not limit the imposition of more severe sentences on some convicted robbers—thus violating parity among convicted robbers. And a rigid minimum would unfairly preclude reduced sentences for robbers whose crimes were committed in extenuating circumstances.

However, these difficulties merely show that the mandatory minimum is too crude a device. One could use the more sophisticated device of presumptive penalties, the format employed in sentencing guidelines such as Minnesota's. Knowledge that conviction for robbery, not burglary, tends to be associated with serious recidivism could be used—not to impose a special penalty for robbery—but to justify drawing the "in-out" line on the sentencing grid between crimes that have robbery's higher seriousness-rating and those that have lower seriousness-ratings such as burglary. Once the line was drawn, other penalties could be scaled proportionately.

Categorically incapacitation would *not* necessarily preclude consideration of mitigating circumstances. In a presumptive penalty scheme, imprisonment could be the normally applicable penalty for robbery and crimes of comparable gravity—but with deviations permitted in extenuating circumstances. With a requirement of "substantial and compelling" reasons, the rate of deviations could be restricted and estimated: the

incidence of the so-called "dispositional departures" has been running about 10% in Minnesota (*see* A. VON HIRSCH, K. KNAPP & M. TONRY, ch. 8). Even though this complicates the estimation somewhat, it should be possible to model the categorial-incapacitation impact of a rule that imposes a given (say, 90%) probability of imprisonment for convicted robbers.

45. *See* PANEL REPORT, *supra* note 14, chs. 2–4 & apps. A and B.

46. P. GREENWOOD & S. TURNER, SELECTIVE INCAPACITATION REVISITED (1987); *see also* another recent Rand study, S. KLEIN & M. CAGGIANO, THE PREVALENCE, PREDICTABILITY, AND POLICY IMPLICATIONS OF RECIDIVISM (1986).

47. P. GREENWOOD & S. TURNER, *supra* note 46, at 49.

POSTSCRIPT

Is Selective Incapacitation Just?

As America grows less and less tolerant of many of its deviants, and especially of offenders who commit violent crimes and drug-related crimes, rehabilitation dims as a viable correctional goal. Incapacitation, deterrence, and retribution are once again acceptable objectives even among many criminological and criminal justice scholars.

Brian Forst feels that we ought to do what is necessary to reduce crime within reason. He has little problem with incarcerating dangerous offenders as long as the evidence is clear that they have a high probability of repeating their offenses. Andrew von Hirsch, probably as interested as any criminal justice scholar in reducing and/or preventing crime, rejects Forst's proposal and echoes the conservative position.

As von Hirsch points out, we do not know with certainty exactly who is going to commit crimes in the future. Tremendous methodological and statistical problems arise in such forecasting. See Richard A. Berk's "Subjectivity in Criminal Prediction," *Criminal Justice Ethics* (Winter/Spring 1988). For a review of recent Canadian trends in this area that reveals a grave concern that Canada might emulate the United States, see Tadeusz Grygier's "A Canadian Approach or an American Bandwagon?" *Canadian Journal of Criminology* (April 1988).

Recent discussions on selective incapacitation that are of a high caliber include those of the British criminologists Leon Radzinowicz and R. Hood's "Incapacitating the Habitual Criminal," *Michigan Law Review*, vol. 78: 1305–1389; Mark H. Moore et al., *Dangerous Offenders: Endangered Justice* (Harvard University Press, 1984); and K. R. Feinberg's "Selective Incapacitation and the Effort to Improve the Fairness of Existing Sentencing Practices," *New York University Review of Law and Social Change* (1983–84).

Criminologists continue to be awed by a series of Rand studies beginning just over a decade ago on career criminals. See Joan Petersilia et al., *Criminal Careers of Habitual Felons* (Rand Corporation, 1977), and J. M. Chaiken and M. R. Chaiken's *Varieties of Criminal Behavior* (Rand Corporation, 1982). These studies, based on questionnaires administered to incarcerated felons, revealed that the vast majority of crimes were committed by a very small number of inmates. However, there are serious methodological flaws with each of these studies, and from both a policy and ethical perspective, most scholars view selective incapacitation as unworkable and/or unjust: for example, see R. Haapanen's *Selective Incapacity and the Serious Offender* (Springer-Verlag, 1990). The issue, though, will continue into the twenty-first century as the public demands that something more be done to control crime and as studies continue to show that relatively few offenders are responsible for the bulk of certain types of crimes.

ISSUE 12

Should Capital Punishment Be Abolished?

YES: Jack Greenberg, from "Against the American System of Capital Punishment," *Harvard Law Review* (1986)

NO: Ernest van den Haag, from "The Ultimate Punishment: A Defense," *Harvard Law Review* (1986)

ISSUE SUMMARY

YES: Columbia Law School professor Jack Greenberg maintains that capital punishment is unfairly administered and ineffective, both as a deterrent and as a punishment.

NO: Fordham University professor Ernest van den Haag challenges those who claim that capital punishment is barbaric and unfair and insists that capital punishment does deter criminals and is just retribution for terrible crimes.

In 1968, only 38 percent of all Americans supported the death penalty for certain crimes. In 1972, when the Supreme Court handed down its decision in *Furman v. Georgia* stating that capital punishment violated the Eighth Amendment, which prohibits cruel and unusual punishment, many Americans were convinced that capital punishment was permanently abolished. After all, even though at the time there were 500 inmates on death row, there had been a steady decline in the number of executions in the United States: In the 1930s, there were on average 152 executions per year; in 1962, there were 47 executions; and in 1966, there was one. Polls in the late 1960s showed that most Americans opposed the death penalty, and virtually every other Western industrial nation had long since eliminated the death sentence or severely modified its use.

A poll in 1988 showed that close to 80 percent of all Americans supported capital punishment, and there are currently over 1,800 inmates on death row awaiting execution. The 1988 presidential election was won by George Bush, who favors the death penalty. His opponent, Michael Dukakis, is against capital punishment.

What happened? Naturally, we will probably never know the full answer to this question. But there are some clues. To begin with, in *Furman v.*

Georgia, the Supreme Court did not really ban capital punishment because it was cruel and unusual in itself. It simply argued that it was unconstitutional for juries to be given the right to decide arbitrarily and discriminatorily on capital punishment. Thus, if states can show that capital punishment is not arbitrary or discriminatory and that the sentencing process is performed in two separate stages—first guilt or innocence is established and *then* the determination of the sentence occurs—then some offenses are legally punishable by death. This was the Supreme Court's ruling in 1976 in *Gregg v. Georgia,* which "restored" the death penalty.

In addition to court decisions clearing the way for the resumption of capital punishment, the mood of the nation has changed since the late 1960s. Americans have become more conservative. Fear of crime has greatly increased, although the number of crimes, as discussed in Issue 6, may not have changed. Moreover, many of the measures taken under the Omnibus Safe Streets Act to reduce crime, speed up judicial processes, and rehabilitate criminals are now viewed by both professionals and laypeople alike as failures. The national mood is now solidly behind "getting tough" on criminals, especially drug dealers and murderers. Support and utilization of capital punishment make sense within the logic of the present cultural and political situation.

Not only are the public and politicians shifting their attitudes toward capital punishment, so are many criminologists. There is a movement to reassess studies done before the 1960s that claimed that states in which capital punishment prevailed had just as high homicide rates as those in which it was not a penalty and that executions did not deter others from committing crimes. Isaac Ehrlich, for instance, in an extensive statistical analysis of executions between the years 1933 and 1967 (over 3,000 were put to death during that period, the vast majority of them in the 1930s and 1940s), reached very different conclusions. He contends that not only did the executions reduce the murder rate, but one additional execution per year between 1933 and 1967 would have caused 7 or 8 fewer murders per year!

Many scholars have bitterly attacked Ehrlich's empirical findings. Most attempt to fault his methods, but others assert that even if he is empirically correct, the trade-off is not worth it. The state should not have the right to extract such a primitive "justice" as murder from a human being, even a convicted killer. Other scholars reemphasize the well-known fact that there have been a disproportionate number of blacks executed (between 1930 and 1967, 2,066 blacks were executed to 1,751 whites, even though blacks were only 10% of the total population then).

Should capital punishment be abolished? If not, what crimes ought it be reserved for? Murder? Rape? Espionage? Drug dealing? Kidnapping? How should it be carried out? If you support it, would you support showing executions on television if studies indicated that that might be a better deterrent?

YES

Jack Greenberg

AGAINST THE AMERICAN SYSTEM
OF CAPITAL PUNISHMENT

Over and over, proponents of the death penalty insist that it is right and useful. In reply, abolitionists argue that it is morally flawed and cite studies to demonstrate its failure to deter. Were the subject not so grim and compelling, the exchanges would, by now, be tiresome.

Yet all too frequently, the debate has been off the mark. Death penalty proponents have assumed a system of capital punishment that simply does not exist: a system in which the penalty is inflicted on the most reprehensible criminals and meted out frequently enough both to deter and to perform the moral and utilitarian functions ascribed to retribution. Explicitly or implicitly, they assume a system in which certainly the worst criminals, Charles Manson or a putative killer of one's parent or child, for example, are executed in an evenhanded manner. But this idealized system is *not* the American system of capital punishment. Because of the goals that our criminal justice system must satisfy—deterring crime, punishing the guilty, acquitting the innocent, avoiding needless cruelty, treating citizens equally, and prohibiting oppression by the state—America simply does not have the kind of capital punishment system contemplated by death penalty partisans.

Indeed, the reality of American capital punishment is quite to the contrary. Since at least 1967, the death penalty has been inflicted only rarely, erratically, and often upon the least odious killers, while many of the most heinous criminals have escaped execution. Moreover, it has been employed almost exclusively in a few formerly slave-holding states, and there it has been used almost exclusively against killers of whites, not blacks, and never against white killers of blacks. This is the American system of capital punishment. It is this system, not some idealized one, that must be defended in any national debate on the death penalty. I submit that this system is deeply incompatible

From Jack Greenberg, "Against the American System of Capital Punishment," *Harvard Law Review* (1986). Copyright © 1986 by the Harvard Law Review Association. Reprinted by permission.

with the proclaimed objectives of death penalty proponents.

I. THE AMERICAN SYSTEM OF CAPITAL PUNISHMENT

Here is how America's system of capital punishment really works today. Since 1967, the year in which the courts first began to grapple in earnest with death penalty issues, the death penalty has been frequently imposed but rarely enforced. Between 1967 and 1980, death sentences or convictions were reversed for 1899 of the 2402 people on death row, a reversal rate of nearly eighty percent. These reversals reflected, among other factors, a 1968 Supreme Court decision dealing with how juries should be chosen in capital cases, a 1972 decision declaring capital sentences unconstitutional partly because they were imposed arbitrarily and "freakishly," and a 1976 decision holding mandatory death sentences unconstitutional. Many death sentences were also invalidated on a wide variety of commonplace state law grounds, such as hearsay rule violations or improper prosecutorial argument.

This judicial tendency to invalidate death penalties proved resistant to change. After 1972, in response to Supreme Court decisions, many states adopted new death penalty laws, and judges developed a clearer idea of the requirements that the Court had begun to enunciate a few years earlier. By 1979, the efforts of state legislatures finally paid off when John Spenkelink became the first person involuntarily executed since 1967. Nevertheless, from 1972 to 1980, the death penalty invalidation rate declined to "only" sixty percent. In contrast, ordinary noncapital convictions

and sentences were almost invariably upheld.

Today, the death row population has grown to more than 1600 convicts. About 300 prisoners per year join this group, while about 100 per year leave death row, mainly by reason of judicial invalidations but also by execution and by death from other causes. Following Spenkelink's execution, some states began to put some of these convicted murderers to death. Five persons were executed involuntarily in 1983, twenty-one in 1984, and fourteen in 1985. . . . Yet even if this number doubled, or increased fivefold, executions would not be numerous either in proportion to the nation's homicides (approximately 19,000 per year) or to its death row population (over 1600).

One reason for the small number of executions is that the courts continue to upset capital convictions at an extraordinarily high rate, albeit not so high as earlier. Between January 1, 1982 and October 1, 1985, state supreme courts invalidated thirty-five percent of all capital judgments. State post-appellate process undid a few more. The federal district and appeals courts overturned another ten percent, and last Term the Supreme Court reversed three of the four capital sentences it reviewed. Altogether, about forty-five percent of capital judgments which were reviewed during this period were set aside by one court or another. One index of the vitality of litigation to reverse executions is that while legal attacks on capital punishment began as a coordinated effort by civil rights lawyers, they now come from a variety of segments of the bar. . . .

Why are there so few executions? Convictions and sentences are reversed, cases move slowly, and states devote relatively meager resources to pursuing *ac-*

tual executions. Even Florida, which above all other states has shown that it can execute almost any death row inmate it wants to, has killed only 13 of 221 inmates since 1979, 12 since 1982. (It now has 233 convicts on death row.) Outside the former slave-holding states, more than half the states are now abolitionist either de jure (fourteen states) or de facto (five states have no one on death row). Moreover, past experience suggests that the execution level will not go very high. Before the 1967–76 moratorium, the number of executions exceeded fifty only once after 1957—fifty-six in 1960. At that time there were fewer abolitionist states and more capital crimes. This experience suggests that executions will not deplete the death row population.

The limited number of actual executions seems to me to reflect the very deep ambivalence that Americans feel about capital punishment. We are the only nation of the Western democratic world that has not abolished capital punishment. By contrast, countries with whose dominant value systems we ordinarily disagree, like the Soviet Union, China, Iran, and South Africa, execute prisoners in great numbers.

II. THE FAILURES OF CAPITAL PUNISHMENT

We have a system of capital punishment that results in infrequent, random, and erratic executions, one that is structured to inflict death neither on those who have committed the worst offense nor on defendants of the worst character. This is the "system"—if that is the right descriptive term—of capital punishment that must be defended by death penalty proponents. *This* system may not be justified by positing a particularly egregious killer like Charles Manson. Our commitment to the rule of law means that we need an acceptable *general* system of capital justice if we are to have one at all. However, the real American system of capital punishment clearly fails when measured against the most common justifications for the infliction of punishment, deterrence, and retribution.

If capital punishment can be a deterrent greater than life imprisonment at all, the American system is at best a feeble one. Studies by Thorsten Sellin showed no demonstrable deterrent effect of capital punishment even during its heyday. Today's death penalty, which is far less frequently used, geographically localized, and biased according to the race of the victim, cannot possibly upset that conclusion. The forty-three persons who were involuntarily executed from 1982 to 1985 were among a death row population of more than 1600 condemned to execution out of about 20,000 who committed nonnegligent homicides per year. While forty-three percent of the victims were black, the death penalty is so administered that it overwhelmingly condemns and executes those who have killed whites.

Very little reason exists to believe that the present capital punishment system deters the conduct of others any more effectively than life imprisonment. Potential killers who rationally weigh the odds of being killed themselves must conclude that the danger is nonexistent in most parts of the country and that in the South the danger is slight, particularly if the proposed victim is black. Moreover, the paradigm of this kind of murderer, the contract killer, is almost by definition a person who takes his chances like the soldier of fortune he is.

But most killers do not engage in anything like a cost-benefit analysis. They are impulsive, and they kill impulsively. If capital punishment is to deter them, it can do so only indirectly: by impressing on potential killers a standard of right and wrong, a moral authority, an influence on their superegos that, notwithstanding mental disorder, would inhibit homicide. This conception of general deterrence seems deeply flawed because it rests upon a quite implausible conception of how this killer population internalizes social norms. Although not mentally disturbed enough to sustain insanity as a defense, they are often highly disturbed, of low intelligence, and addicted to drugs or alcohol. In any event, the message, if any, that the real American system of capital punishment sends to the psyches of would-be killers is quite limited: you may in a rare case be executed if you murder in the deepest South and kill a white person. . . .

To my mind, the moral force of any retribution argument is radically undercut by the hard facts of the actual American system of capital punishment. This system violates fundamental norms because it is haphazard, and because it is regionally and racially biased. To these moral flaws, I would add another: the minuscule number of executions nowadays cannot achieve the grand moral aims that are presupposed by a serious societal commitment to retribution.

Some retribution proponents argue that it is the pronouncement of several hundred death sentences followed by lengthy life imprisonment, not the actual imposition of a few executions, that satisfies the public's demand for retribution. Of course, the public has not said that it wants the death penalty as it exists— widely applicable but infrequently used.

Nor, to the best of my knowledge, is there any solid empirical basis for such a claim. Like other statutes, death penalty laws are of general applicability, to be employed according to their terms. Nothing in their language or legislative history authorizes the erratic, occasional, racially biased use of these laws. But my objections to this argument go much deeper. I find morally objectionable a system of many pronounced death sentences but few actual executions, a system in which race and region are the only significant variables in determining who actually dies. My objection is not grounded in a theory that posits any special moral rights for the death row population. . . . I cannot reconcile an erratic, racially and regionally biased system of executions with my understanding of the core values of our legal order.

Death penalty proponents may respond to this argument by saying that if there is not enough capital punishment, there should be more. If only killers of whites are being executed, then killers of blacks should be killed too; and if many sentences are being reversed, standards of review should be relaxed. In the meantime, they might urge, the death penalty should go on. But this argument is unavailing, because it seeks to change the terms of the debate in a fundamental way. It seeks to substitute an imaginary system for the real American system of capital punishment. If there were a different kind of system of death penalty administration in this country, or even a reasonable possibility that one might emerge, we could debate its implications. But any current debate over the death penalty cannot ignore the deep moral deficiencies of the present system.

NO
Ernest van den Haag

THE ULTIMATE PUNISHMENT: A DEFENSE

In an average year about 20,000 homicides occur in the United States. Fewer than 300 convicted murders are sentenced to death. But because no more than thirty murderers have been executed in any recent year, most convicts sentenced to death are likely to die of old age.[1] Nonetheless, the death penalty looms large in discussions: it raises important moral questions independent of the number of executions.

The death penalty is our harshest punishment. It is irrevocable: it ends the existence of those punished, instead of temporarily imprisoning them. Further, although not intended to cause physical pain, execution is the only corporal punishment still applied to adults. These singular characteristics contribute to the perennial, impassioned controversy about capital punishment.

I. DISTRIBUTION

Consideration of the justice, morality, or usefulness, of capital punishment is often conflated with objections to its alleged discriminatory or capricious distribution among the guilty. Wrongly so. If capital punishment is immoral *in se*, no distribution among the guilty could make it moral. If capital punishment is moral, no distribution would make it immoral. Improper distribution cannot affect the quality of what is distributed, be it punishments or rewards. Discriminatory or capricious distribution thus could not justify abolition of the death penalty. Further, maldistribution inheres no more in capital punishment than in any other punishment.

Maldistribution between the guilty and the innocent is, by definition, unjust. But the injustice does not lie in the nature of the punishment. Because of the finality of the death penalty, the most grievous maldistribution occurs when it is imposed upon the innocent. However, the frequent allegations of discrimination and capriciousness refer to maldistribution among the guilty and not to the punishment of the innocent.

Maldistribution of any punishment among those who deserve it is irrelevant to its justice or morality. Even if poor or black convicts guilty of capital

From Ernest van den Haag, "The Ultimate Punishment: A Defense," *Harvard Law Review,* vol. 99 (May 1986). Copyright © 1986 by the Harvard Law Review Association. Reprinted by permission.

offenses suffer capital punishment, and other convicts equally guilty of the same crimes do not, a more equal distribution, however desirable, would merely be more equal. It would not be more just to the convicts under sentence of death.

Punishments are imposed on persons, not on racial or economic groups. Guilt is personal. The only relevant question is: does the person to be executed deserve the punishment? Whether or not others who deserved the same punishment, whatever their economic or racial group, have avoided execution is irrelevant. If they have, the guilt of the executed convicts would not be diminished, nor would their punishment be less deserved. To put the issue starkly, if the death penalty were imposed on guilty blacks, but not on guilty whites, or, if it were imposed by a lottery among the guilty, this irrationally discriminatory or capricious distribution would neither make the penalty unjust, nor cause anyone to be unjustly punished, despite the undue impunity bestowed on others.

Equality, in short, seems morally less important than justice. And justice is independent of distributional inequalities. The ideal of equal justice demands that justice be equally distributed, not that it be replaced by equality. Justice requires that as many of the guilty as possible be punished, regardless of whether others have avoided punishment. To let these others escape the deserved punishment does not do justice to them, or to society. But it is not unjust to those who could not escape.

These moral considerations are not meant to deny that irrational discrimination, or capriciousness, would be inconsistent with constitutional requirements. But I am satisfied that the Supreme Court has in fact provided for adherence to the constitutional requirement of equality as much as possible. Some inequality is indeed unavoidable as a practical matter in any system.[2] But, *ultra posse neo obligatur.* (Nobody is bound beyond ability.)

Recent data reveal little direct racial discrimination in the sentencing of those arrested and convicted of murder. The abrogation of the death penalty for rape has eliminated a major source of racial discrimination. Concededly, some discrimination based on the race of murder victims may exist; yet, this discrimination affects criminal victimizers in an unexpected way. Murderers of whites are thought more likely to be executed than murderers of blacks. Black victims, then, are less fully vindicated than white ones. However, because most black murderers kill blacks, black murderers are spared the death penalty more often than are white murderers. They fare better than most white murderers. The motivation behind unequal distribution of the death penalty may well have been to discriminate against blacks, but the result has favored them. Maldistribution is thus a straw man for empirical as well as analytical reasons.

II. MISCARRIAGES OF JUSTICE

In a recent survey Professors Hugo Adam Bedau and Michael Radelet found that 7000 persons were executed in the United States between 1900 and 1985 and that 25 were innocent of capital crimes. Among the innocents they list Sacco and Vanzetti as well as Ethel and Julius Rosenberg. Although their data may be questionable, I do not doubt that, over a long enough period, miscarriages of justice will occur even in capital cases.

Despite precautions, nearly all human activities, such as trucking, lighting, or construction, cost the lives of some innocent bystanders. We do not give up these activities, because the advantages, moral or material, outweigh the unintended losses. Analogously, for those who think the death penalty just, miscarriages of justice are offset by the moral benefits and the usefulness of doing justice. For those who think the death penalty unjust even when it does not miscarry, miscarriages can hardly be decisive.

III. DETERRENCE

Despite much recent work, there has been no conclusive statistical demonstration that the death penalty is a better deterrent than are alternative punishments. However, deterrence is less than decisive for either side. Most abolitionists acknowledge that they would continue to favor abolition even if the death penalty were shown to deter more murders than alternatives could deter. Abolitionists appear to value the life of a convicted murderer or, at least, his nonexecution, more highly than they value the lives of the innocent victims who might be spared by deterring prospective murderers.

Deterrence is not altogether decisive for me either. I would favor retention of the death penalty as retribution even if it were shown that the threat of execution could not deter prospective murderers not already deterred by the threat of imprisonment.[3] Still, I believe the death penalty, because of its finality, is more feared than imprisonment, and deters some prospective murderers not deterred by the threat of imprisonment. Sparing the lives of even a few prospective victims by deterring their murderers

is more important than preserving the lives of convicted murderers because of the possibility, or even the probability, that executing them would not deter others. Whereas the lives of the victims who might be saved are valuable, that of the murderer has only negative value, because of his crime. Surely the criminal law is meant to protect the lives of potential victims in preference to those of actual murderers.

Murder rates are determined by many factors; neither the severity nor the probability of the threatened sanction is always decisive. However, for the long run, I share the view of Sir James Fitzjames Stephen: "Some men, probably, abstain from murder because they fear that if they committed murder they would be hanged. Hundreds of thousands abstain from it because they regard it with horror. One great reason why they regard it with horror is that murderers are hanged." Penal sanctions are useful in the long run for the formation of the internal restraints so necessary to control crime. The severity and finality of the death penalty is appropriate to the seriousness and the finality of murder.

IV. INCIDENTAL ISSUES: COST, RELATIVE SUFFERING, BRUTALIZATION

Many nondecisive issues are associated with capital punishment. Some believe that the monetary cost of appealing a capital sentence is excessive. Yet most comparisons of the cost of life imprisonment with the cost of execution, apart from their dubious relevance, are flawed at least by the implied assumption that life prisoners will generate no judicial costs during their imprisonment. At any rate, the actual monetary costs are trumped by the importance of doing justice.

Others insist that a person sentenced to death suffers more than his victim suffered, and that this (excess) suffering is undue according to the *lex talionis* (rule of retaliation). We cannot know whether the murderer on death row suffers more than his victim suffered; however, unlike the murderer, the victim deserved none of the suffering inflicted. Further, the limitations of the *lex talionis* were meant to restrain private vengeance, not the social retribution that has taken its place. Punishment—regardless of the motivation—is not intended to revenge, offset, or compensate for the victim's suffering, or to be measured by it. Punishment is to vindicate the law and the social order undermined by the crime. This is why a kidnapper's penal confinement is not limited to the period for which he imprisoned his victim; nor is a burglar's confinement meant merely to offset the suffering or the harm he caused his victim; nor is it meant only to offset the advantage he gained.[4]

Another argument heard at least since Beccaria is that, by killing a murderer, we encourage, endorse, or legitimize unlawful killing. Yet, although all punishments are meant to be unpleasant, it is seldom argued that they legitimize the unlawful imposition of identical unpleasantness. Imprisonment is not thought to legitimize kidnapping; neither are fines thought to legitimize robbery. The difference between murder and execution, or between kidnapping and imprisonment, is that the first is unlawful and undeserved, the second a lawful and deserved punishment for an unlawful act. The physical similarities of the punishment to the crime are irrelevant. The relevant difference is not physical, but social.[5]

V. JUSTICE, EXCESS, DEGRADATION

We threaten punishments in order to deter crime. We impose them not only to make the threats credible but also as retribution (justice) for the crimes that were not deterred. Threats and punishments are necessary to deter and deterrence is a sufficient practical justification for them. Retribution is an independent moral justification. Although penalties can be unwise, repulsive, or inappropriate, and those punished can be pitiable, in a sense the infliction of legal punishment on a guilty person cannot be unjust. By committing the crime, the criminal volunteered to assume the risk of receiving a legal punishment that he could have avoided by not committing the crime. The punishment he suffers is the punishment he voluntarily risked suffering and, therefore, it is no more unjust to him than any other event for which one knowingly volunteers to assume the risk. Thus, the death penalty cannot be unjust to the guilty criminal.

There remain, however, two moral objections. The penalty may be regarded as always excessive as retribution and always morally degrading. To regard the death penalty as always excessive, one must believe that no crime—no matter how heinous—could possibly justify capital punishment. Such a belief can be neither corroborated nor refuted; it is an article of faith.

Alternatively, or concurrently, one may believe that everybody, the murderer no less than the victim, has an imprescriptible (natural?) right to life. The law therefore should not deprive anyone of life. I share Jeremy Bentham's view that any such "natural and imprescriptible rights" are "nonsense upon stilts."

Justice Brennan has insisted that the death penalty is "uncivilized," "inhuman," inconsistent with "human dignity" and with "the sanctity of life," that it "treats members of the human race as nonhumans, as objects to be toyed with and discarded," that it is "uniquely degrading to human dignity" and "by its very nature, [involves] a denial of the executed person's humanity." Justice Brennan does not say why he thinks execution "uncivilized." Hitherto most civilizations have had the death penalty, although it has been discarded in Western Europe, where it is currently unfashionable probably because of its abuse by totalitarian regimes.

By "degrading," Justice Brennan seems to mean that execution degrades the executed convicts. Yet philosophers, such as Immanuel Kant and G. F. W. Hegel, have insisted that, when deserved, execution, far from degrading the executed convict, affirms his humanity by affirming his rationality and his responsibility for his actions. They thought that execution, when deserved, is required for the sake of the convict's dignity. (Does not life imprisonment violate human dignity more than execution, by keeping alive a prisoner deprived of all autonomy?)

Common sense indicates that it cannot be death—or common fate—that is inhuman. Therefore, Justice Brennan must mean that death degrades when it comes not as a natural or accidental event, but as a deliberate social imposition. The murderer learns through his punishment that his fellow men have found him unworthy of living; that because he has murdered, he is being expelled from the community of the living. This degradation is self-inflicted. By murdering, the murderer has so dehumanized himself that he cannot remain among the living. The social recognition of his self-degradation is the punitive essence of execution. To believe, as Justice Brennan appears to, that the degradation is inflicted by the execution reverses the direction of causality.

Execution of those who have committed heinous murders may deter only one murder per year. If it does, it seems quite warranted. It is also the only fitting retribution for murder I can think of.

NOTES

1. Death row as a semipermanent residence is cruel, because convicts are denied the normal amenities of prison life. Thus, unless death row residents are integrated into the prison population, the continuing accumulation of convicts on death row should lead us to accelerate either the rate of executions or the rate of commutations. I find little objection to integration.

2. The ideal of equality, unlike the ideal of retributive justice (which can be approximated separately in each instance), is clearly unattainable unless all guilty persons are apprehended, and thereafter tried, convicted and sentenced by the same court, at the same time. Unequal justice is the best we can do; it is still better than the injustice, equal or unequal, which occurs if, for the sake of equality, we deliberately allow some who could be punished to escape.

3. If executions were shown to increase the murder rate in the long run, I would favor abolition. Sparing the innocent victims who would be spared, *ex hypothesi*, by the nonexecution of murderers would be more important to me than the execution, however just, of murderers. But although there is a lively discussion of the subject, no serious evidence exists to support the hypothesis that executions produce a higher murder rate. Cf. Phillips, *The Deterrent Effect of Capital Punishment: New Evidence on an Old Controversy*, 86 AM. J. Soc. 139 (1980) (arguing that murder rates drop immediately after executions of criminals).

4. Thus restitution (a civil liability) cannot satisfy the punitive purpose of penal sanctions, whether the purpose be retributive or deterrent.

5. Some abolitionists challenge: if the death penalty is just and serves as a deterrent, why not televise executions? The answer is simple. The death even of a murderer, however well-de-

served, should not serve as public entertainment. It so served in earlier centuries. But in this respect our sensibility has changed for the better, I believe. Further, television unavoidably would trivialize executions, wedged in, as they would be, between game shows, situation comedies and the like. Finally, because televised executions would focus on the physical aspects of the punishment, rather than the nature of the crime and the suffering of the victim, a televised execution would present the murderer as the victim of the state. Far from communicating the moral significance of the execution, television would shift the focus to the pitiable fear of the murderer. We no longer place in cages those sentenced to imprisonment to expose them to public view. Why should we so expose those sentenced to execution?

POSTSCRIPT

Should Capital Punishment Be Abolished?

One of the elements that is the most striking about the issue of capital punishment is that most of the public, the politicians, and even many criminological scholars seem not to be fazed by empirical evidence. Each side ritualistically marshalls empirical evidence to support their respective position. Opponents of capital punishment often draw from Thorsten Sellin's classic study *The Penalty of Death* (Sage Publications) to "prove" that the number of capital offenses is no lower in states that have the death penalty as compared to states that have abolished executions.

Supporters of capital punishment draw from numerous studies including I. Ehrlich's "The Deterrent Effect of Capital Punishment," *American Economic Review*, vol. 65:397–417 (1975), and his "Capital Punishment and Deterrence: Some Further Thoughts and Additional Evidence," *Journal of Political Economy*, vol. 85:741–788 (1977). They also draw from Walter Berns's, *For Capital Punishment: Crime and the Morality of the Death Penalty* (Basic Books, 1979).

Generally, as Greenberg tries to show, the empirical research indicates that the death penalty cannot conclusively be proven to deter others from homicides and other serious crimes. Entire scientific commissions have been charged with the responsibility of determining the deterrent effects of the death penalty (for example, The National Academy of Sciences in 1975). The gist of their conclusions was that the value of the death penalty as a deterrent "is not a settled matter."

As is typical with most aspects of human behavior, including crime and crime control, the issue is filled with much irony, paradox, and contradiction. First, clashing views over capital punishment rely largely on emotion. The public's attitudes, politicians' attitudes, and, as mentioned, even scholarly attitudes are frequently shaped more by sentiment and preconceived notions than rational discourse. As F. Zimring and G. Hawkins indicate in their outstanding work (which is also an attack on capital punishment) *Capital Punishment and the American Agenda* (Cambridge University Press, 1986), very few scholars have ever changed their opinions about capital punishment.

Zimring and Hawkins are correct that in the short run "very few come to oppose or support capital punishment as a result of analysis of the statistical evidence. . . . It is quite clear . . . that neither proponents nor opponents of the death penalty . . . are engaged in a disinterested pursuit of the truth."

For a discussion of the controversy of executing juveniles, see Issue 19 as well as "Execution at an Early Age: Should Young Killers Face the Death Penalty?" *Newsweek* (January 13, 1986) and "Should Teenagers Be Executed?" by C. Whitaker, *Ebony* (March 1988).

As we rapidly approach the twenty-first century, capital punishment should be a dead issue. Yet it is still with us and may possibly continue into the next century. For dissenting views see "The Death Penalty Dinosaur . . ." by Richard C. Dieter, *Commonweal* (January 15, 1988); "A Court Divided: The Death Penalty," by Paul Reidinger, *American Bar Association Journal* (January 1, 1987); "Public Support for the Death Penalty: Retribution as Just Deserts or Retribution as Revenge?" by J. O. Finckenauer, *Justice Quarterly*, vol. 5, no. 1 (1988); *Challenging Capital Punishment: Legal and Social Scientific Approaches,* edited by K. Haas and J. Inciardi (Sage, 1988); and "The Symbolic Death of Willie Darden," *U.S. News and World Report* (March 28, 1988). Also see Hugo A. Bedau's *Death Is Different* (Northeast University Press, 1987); *When the State Kills,* Amnesty International, U.S.A. (1989); and *Facing the Death Penalty,* edited by M. L. Radelet (Temple University Press, 1989).

ISSUE 13

Does Arrest Reduce Domestic Violence?

YES: Joan Meier, from "Battered Justice," *The Washington Monthly* (May 1987)

NO: Franklyn W. Dunford, David Huizinga, and Delbert S. Elliott, from "The Role of Arrest in Domestic Assault: The Omaha Police Experiment," *Criminology* (May 1990)

ISSUE SUMMARY

YES: Attorney Joan Meier, after surveying several studies and reports on domestic violence, concludes that these victims must be supported by the police and courts and claims that, even if research did not show assault deterrence resulting from arrests, spouse attackers should still be dealt with punitively because their crime is so odious.

NO: University of Colorado criminologists F. W. Dunford, D. Huizinga, and D. Elliott, registering far more caution after their study of alleged domestic assault cases, cite among their surprising findings that the incidences of future assaults did not increase or decrease as a consequence of arrest; the authors also suggest alternative strategies besides arrest.

A child hunched over in fear cries, "Mommy, Mommy, please don't hit Mommy." Two other children, hardly teens, stand frightened as their eyes move cautiously from the two police officers, unaccustomed strangers in their home, to their mother, who only moments ago was sprawled semi-conscious on the floor after being beaten by their father. A neighbor, who had been summoned by their cries, helps the woman to her feet and tries to comfort her, while the husband sits defiantly on their sofa and explains to the police how she "had been asking for it."

Such scenarios are repeated literally millions of times throughout America each year. Some estimates of abuse within families run as high as one-fourth to one-half of the population, based on such reported assaults.

Several interesting factors emerge from our new sensitivity toward domestic violence. First, far more people are likely nowadays to report domestic assaults than ever before. Some of this, of course, may be a result of the expansion of public telephone service into impoverished areas of the nation's cities; neighbors can now help easily—indirectly and anonymously—by "dropping a quarter" to help some child or woman in such distress. Much of the increasing sensitivity to abuse is also a consequence of political, professional, and social pressure to inform on abusers. In fact, in many states, professionals who do not report child and/or spouse abuse are subject to tort and criminal sanctions. So, whether domestic assault has increased, has remained the same, or has even decreased is insignificant next to the fact that people will now report it—and *that* is a change. Currently, the highest number of calls to the police stem from family violence.

Getting back to statistics, we find most studies indicating that at least 8 million family members are assaulted each year. Violence is highest among lower-class city dwellers with four or more children and a father who is unemployed. However, domestic assault knows no class boundaries, and spouse/child abuse—in the form of kicking, pinching, scratching, shoving and the like—is not uncommon.

For feuding spouses, the received wisdom among police has been first to separate them temporarily, to calm the husband down, and then to allow them to be together again. It was assumed after even repeated complaints of assault that the couple eventually would have to "work it out" on their own, so why intrude at all? Domestic assaults also were viewed as being the most dangerous for the police officers themselves, although studies now question that assumption.

In a landmark study published in 1984 that served to revolutionize police practices nationally (although it was based primarily on findings from Minneapolis), Lawrence Sherman and R. A. Berk established an empirical link between the arrest of domestic assaulters and the reduction of subsequent domestic violence. Their study was rigorous, and, although they were remarkably modest in their conclusions and policy recommendations based on their work, the thrust of their findings struck an ideological chord throughout the country. Unlike most social science research, including that within criminology and criminal justice, Sherman and Berk's work has been partially replicated by subsequent studies, and none, apparently, have been as rigorous as that of Dunford, Huizinga, and Elliott.

But how do we end the violence of domestic assault? Even if arrest does not reduce it (as Dunford, Huizinga, and Elliott suggest), should we still arrest people because any such abuse is both wrong and illegal? Meier, who in addition to being an attorney is on the Board of Directors of the Washington, D.C., Coalition Against Domestic Violence, certainly feels this way. Many other Americans agree.

Some raise other questions. Are not those who are usually arrested for domestic assault poor and relatively powerless? After the arrest, is the family not subject to additional reproach, inconvenience, possibly lost time at work or even a lost job, the burden of unpaid bills? Also, if as Dunford, Huizinga, and Elliott suggest, officers separating assaulters from their victims and/or mediating between the two works just as well as arrest, why not go that route? Others would respond that the depth of the problem has not been addressed: the extensiveness, the brutality, the horror of domestic assault.

YES

Joan Meier

BATTERED JUSTICE

Last August in Somerville, Massachusetts, Pamela Nigro-Dunn was coming home from work and got off the bus at the stop where her mother met her each day. A man drove up and insisted Nigro-Dunn get into his car. When she and her mother resisted, he threw mace into her mother's face. Then he shot Pamela, who was five months pregnant, in the abdomen and dragged her into the car. Her body was found in a garbage dump nine hours later. She had been shot, strangled, and stabbed. The murderer was arrested three months later in Florida. He was her husband.

Roughly 1,350 women were killed by their spouses, ex-spouses, or boyfriends in 1985. They were the victims of the most extreme form of wife battering but represent only a faction of those who have suffered from what appears to be an epidemic of violence within marriages. National surveys have suggested that as many as one out of four married couples endure at least one act of serious violence during their marriage.

This domestic violence is one-sided: 85-95 percent of assault victims and two-thirds of domestic murder victims are women. And it usually is not an isolated event but part of a pattern of escalating violence. Where there has been murder, there has usually been a history of beating. Consequently, many killings were predictable and could have been stopped. In most cases, the victims had brought their abusers' earlier assaults to the attention of the police, prosecutors, or courts. Pamela Nigro-Dunn had been to court four times trying to stop her husband's attacks before she was murdered. She received a restraining order, but the judge refused to give her police protection. Similarly, the murder of Leedonyell Williams in Washington, D.C. . . . was committed the day after charges against her attacker were dropped. One Minneapolis study found that in 85 percent of spousal murder cases there had been prior contact with the police; in 50 percent they had been called at least five times in the preceding two years.

Many people are aware that wife-beating is a problem. But few are aware of the shocking way that violence is ignored by the criminal justice system. When called for help, police rarely make arrests. When they do, prosecutors

From Joan Meier, "Battered Justice," *The Washington Monthly*, vol. 19, no. 4 (May 1987). Copyright © 1987 by The Washington Monthly Company, 1611 Connecticut Avenue, N.W., Washington, D.C. 20009; (202) 462-0128. Reprinted by permission of *The Washington Monthly*.

rarely bring charges. And when cases are brought to court, judges too often have the attitude of Paul Heffernan, the Massachusetts judge who was sitting on the bench when Pamela Nigro-Dunn requested help.

In the first affidavit Pamela filed, just six weeks after her wedding, she stated, "I'm a prisoner in my apartment. He locks me in and takes the phone cord out. He choked me and threatened to kill me if I try to leave. He made me work only where he works. . . . My life is in danger so long as he is around."

Pamela asked Heffernan to order Paul Dunn out of the apartment, but the judge refused and then asked her, "Did he demonstrate this type of behavior before you married him?" presumably reasoning that, if the husband had hit her before they were married, she was not entitled to police protection if she was beaten—however badly—after she was married. Pamela moved out.

Five days later, she returned to court to obtain a police escort so she could return to the apartment for her clothes. "I don't think it's the role of this Court to decide down to each piece of underwear who owns what," Heffernan said. "This is pretty trivial. . . . This court has a lot more serious matters to contend with. We're doing a terrible disservice to the taxpayers here." Heffernan then turned to her husband and said, "You want to gnaw on her and she on you fine, but let's not do it at the taxpayers' expense."

Pamela moved in with her parents, but after pressure from Paul to return and promises that he'd reform, she reconciled with him for several weeks. The abuse resumed. She didn't go back to court to seek further protection. Why would she? She moved back to her parents', and her mother began accompanying her to and from the bus stop because they had seen Paul circling in his car. Shortly thereafter he murdered her.

It is appalling that so many women suffer as Pamela did at the hands of their spouses. But it is perhaps even more appalling that so many are further abused by the criminal justice system. Although in recent years several cities have moved toward reform, domestic violence remains at best a low priority. There are many reasons for the reluctance of police, prosecutors, and judges to handle these cases, but at the root is the belief that wife-beating is simply not criminal behavior.

POLICE WHO WON'T ARREST

The passivity of police in dealing with domestic assaults was made clear in a landmark case in New York City in 1976. Twelve battered wives sued the city police department and family court for failing to arrest and prosecute men who attacked their wives—simply because the victim and assailant were married. The out-of-court settlement required the police department to change its policies and was hailed as a turning point in the country's police and court treatment of domestic violence cases.

But in the four years I have represented battered women in Chicago and Washington, D.C., it has become clear that little has changed since the New York case. Catherine Klein, who has worked with about five hundred women over the past five years, cannot recall a single arrest that happened without her intervention. . . . [F]or example, the D.C. police were called by nurses at a hospital where Dawn Ronan,* who was five months pregnant, had gone for treat-

*Some of the victims' names have been changed.

ment after being kicked in the back by Jimmy Smith, her boyfriend and the father of her child. The police refused to arrest Jimmy because they hadn't seen the assault. "It's a domestic problem. We really don't get involved," they explained to the nurse.

Fearing what might happen if she continued to live with Jimmy, Dawn moved in with his sister. About two weeks after the baby was born he found her there and attacked her in her bed, splitting her cheek open with a belt buckle, and cutting her eye with the heavy ring he wore. When his sister tried to stop him, he threw her against a dresser. The police, called in from the street by the sister, again refused to arrest because they had not "seen" the assault, even though there was a witness. Instead, they simply advised Dawn to go to the hospital for her bleeding cheek and eye.

Similarly, in December 1985, D.C. police were called to the home of Barbara Nelson after her husband, who no longer lived there, broke into the house, brandishing a razor and yelling, "I'm going to kill you . . . in the basement." There was no other man in the house. When Nelson asked the police to arrest him, they refused. When later asked why, one officer responded that Barbara had seemed more excited and hysterical than her husband.

This reluctance to arrest is corroborated by studies conducted in the late seventies in Colorado and California that showed only 5 to 6 percent of domestic violence complaints to the police resulted in arrest.

Why don't police arrest these abusers? Some states have historically prohibited arrests on misdemeanor—though not felony—charges unless the police have witnessed the crime. Many states, however, have changed the law so police can make misdemeanor arrests in domestic violence cases without having seen the assault if there is sufficient evidence of probable cause. In D.C., police concede they have always been authorized to make arrests for misdemeanors they didn't witness. They simply don't—sometimes not even when they can see blood streaming down a woman's face.

The legal excuses often give way to the real reasons for not arresting. "They always said they couldn't do anything because he was my husband," recalls Jean Cook, whose husband had, on various occasions, thrown a brick through her window, broken a beer bottle over her head, threatened to kill her, and lurked with a gun around the shelter where she was staying. Barbara Nelson was advised by a supportive police officer to tell the dispatcher there was "a man with a knife" when she called for help, rather than say "my husband has a knife." . . . [A]nother D.C. woman was on the floor being kicked by her boyfriend when the police arrived. The police told the man that if the couple had lived together at least six months, making them common law husband and wife, they couldn't do anything. The police then asked how long the two had lived together. The man said six months; she denies they had ever lived together. The police left. Yet another recent D.C. victim, who had been held hostage all of one night and hit repeatedly in the head with a hammer, was told by the police, "he'd have to kill you or damn near kill you" for them to take any action.

The hands-off approach that still operates in most police departments gained theoretical justification in the early seventies when social work alternatives to punishment were popular for a number of offenses, including drug use and prostitution. In 1970, Morton Bard, a clinical psychologist, set up a demonstration project to teach police special counseling skills for intervening in family disputes. Even though the project did not show a reduction in violence, it was hailed as a success. Other well-intended psychologists followed suit. By 1977, a national survey of the larger police departments found that more than 70 percent had implemented some kind of family crisis intervention training program.

At best, such policies help the victim. Police should usually be applauded for their efforts to be more human, but it is curious, given their occupational bias toward punishing offenders, that they eagerly embrace a soft approach towards domestic violence. Unfortunately, experts in domestic violence now agree that mediation as a substitute for arrest is the wrong answer when there is violence.

D.C. police officers typically say they are reluctant to arrest wife-beaters because these "fights"—a term reflecting a belief that spousal violence is minor and mutual—"are much more dangerous for police." They also reason that, as one said, "when people are in a relationship, I assume she could leave and avoid the man if she wanted to."

Both reasons contain a kernel of truth. That police fear domestic violence cases is understandable, although it contrasts strikingly with their notion that such cases are trivial and not very dangerous for the women. When police respond to a domestic call, tempers are usually still hot, and often get hotter at the sight of a cop. One 1983 study by the D.C. Metropolitan Police Department stated that "nationally, more police officers were injured while responding to disturbance calls than in any other type of call for service." But recent FBI Uniform Crime Reports show that police fears are overstated and that a domestic call is one of the least likely of all calls to lead to assaults on officers or to their deaths. Similarly, Don Pfouts, a detective with the Baltimore City Police Department who has been reviewing his department's records, confirms that domestic calls are "not that dangerous."

NOWHERE TO HIDE

Underlying police reluctance to arrest is the feeling that domestic violence is not a real crime. The perception, shared by many people, is that women in some way consent to the violence by being in a relationship with the man. To put it crudely: "If she doesn't take it seriously enough to stay away, why should society take it seriously enough to arrest the man?"

But the assumption that women have control over the situation is mistaken. It can be almost impossible for a woman to relocate, especially when she has children to care for or when she has no independent income. More important, many women don't leave their spouses for fear that the violence will get worse. Angela Browne, a social psychologist at the University of New Hampshire, says, "Some women who have left an abusive partner have been followed and harrassed for months and even years; some have been killed." Jean Cook left her husband only to begin seven months of moving from shelter to shelter in an attempt to hide from him. He always found her. From restaurant to shelter, from shelter to work, to and from church, wherever she went, he tracked and harrassed her. Twice, when she sought court protection he assaulted her the next day. Cook was not truly free of her husband's terrorizing until he was finally put in jail and she left the state.

In her many attempts to get away from her abuser, Dawn Ronan went to her parents', a shelter with a supposedly secret address, and the house of a shelter counselor. Jimmy Smith tracked her down each time. On the last occasion, he forced her into the car, held a knife to her neck, then thrust her head out the car window and choked her.

The legal system also makes it impossible for women to avoid their batterers when it enforces the man's "rights." Even if Dawn could somehow escape Jimmy, she would still have to be in contact with him by order of the court since he has been awarded visitation rights with their baby. Many judges appear to share the opinion of Massachusetts Judge Tempone, who said, in refusing a woman's plea to deny her batterer visitation rights, "Even Dillinger could have made a good father. . . . How about Manson?"

While misperceptions about women's ability to end the violence may make the reluctance of police to arrest more understandable, their behavior in many instances indicates something far worse: an identification with the male attacker and a lack of sympathy for the woman. In the landmark New York case, a policeman who had been called to a scene where a man had stabbed his wife with a knife, said to the husband, "Maybe if I beat my wife, she'd act right too."

Police sympathies can be more subtly expressed. Jimmy Smith broke into the shelter where Dawn Ronan was staying and attacked several of those who lived there. After three calls, a policeman came but stood outside at least ten minutes before coming in. When he got inside, a shelter worker was holding Jimmy down, but the officer, smiling, addressed Jimmy: "What's up Jimmy, what are you doing in here?" He then asked Jimmy, but not the women, if he was hurt. Then the officer escorted him out of the house and proceeded to smoke a cigarette with him, both of them talking and laughing. The officer stood silent when Jimmy said to Dawn, "I'm going to kill you, if that's the last thing I do." Only when Dawn got angry did the officer finally take action: He insisted that she go inside. He than escorted Jimmy to the hospital, though he had no noticeable injuries.

There was no subtlety, however, in the response to Tracy Thurmon, who later won a suit against the Torrington, Connecticut, police department. She had successfully prosecuted her husband in 1982 for repeatedly beating her and threatening her and their child's life. Despite a probation order barring him from further harassment, he assaulted her twice and repeatedly threatened and harassed her. The police consistently refused to respond to her calls. In June 1983, Thurman called the police again when her husband came to her house. By the time they arrived, he had already stabbed her in front of the house. While the police watched, her husband dropped the bloody knife, kicked her in the head, went into the house, came back out, dropped her child on her, kicked her in the head again, and walked around the crowd that had gathered to watch. Not until he approached Thurman a third time, as she lay on a stretcher, did the police arrest him. Thurman said the police frequented the restaurant where her husband worked and that he had boasted to them that he intended to kill her. . . .

VIOLENCE IS VIOLENCE

Slowly, things are changing. . . . [P]olice departments, including D.C.'s, are beginning to adopt policies that favor arrests or require that domestic violence cases be treated no differently from other assault cases. When Denver recently adopted a pro-arrest policy, arrests jumped 60 percent one year and 46 percent the next.

Recently, the Attorney General's Task Force on Domestic Violence, the Bureau of Justice Statistics, and the National Institute of Justice produced reports urging that domestic violence be treated as a serious crime. Justice Department funding, although far lower than in the past, now supports eight demonstration projects to develop new policies and procedures for police and prosecutors.

A firm criminal justice response works. After Duluth, Minnesota, instituted a mandatory arrest program, 70 of a group of 86 women reported at the end of two years that the combined assistance of police, courts, and shelters was helpful in ending their abusers' violence. According to Dr. Anne Ganley, a psychologist and counselor for batterers, "Perpetrators tend to minimize and deny the violence and place the blame on others." Therefore, she says, it is crucial that batterers be held responsible for their violence. As one former abuser said in the National Institute of Justice report: "It was such an extreme experience having actually been arrested and dealt with rather harshly . . . that I sought help." Advocates frequently comment that even the slightest acknowledgment from an official that women do not deserve to be beaten can give victims an enormous boost of strength and energy to take action to end the abuse. Even if the couple stays together, outside disapproval can make both aware that the man does not have "the right to beat" the woman. Barbara Nelson's husband, who was finally arrested and jailed after ten years of violence now says, "There's nothing I want to do enough to go back there. . . . You don't have to be afraid of me; it's not worth it to go back."

If the message is clear, the actual punishment is less important. A study of the Minneapolis Police Department by the Police Foundation concluded that when the officer "advised" the suspect and did not lock him up, violence recurred within the next six months in 37 percent of the cases; when the suspect was arrested, even if he wasn't prosecuted later, violence recurred in only 19 percent of the cases. In Jean Cook's case, a mere warning letter from her attorney to her abuser brought a sudden halt to seven months of almost daily harassment.

Even if the evidence weren't as clear as it is that criminal justice intervention reduces domestic violence, it would still be called for. Society punishes behavior it finds morally opprobrious. The refusal of the police and courts to insist that domestic violence is a crime allows people to go on believing it's not so bad. It's time to teach a different set of lessons.

NO

Franklyn W. Dunford, David Huizinga, and Delbert S. Elliott

THE ROLE OF ARREST IN DOMESTIC ASSAULT: THE OMAHA POLICE EXPERIMENT

In what has come to be known as a landmark study, the Minneapolis Domestic Violence Experiment (Sherman and Berk, 1984a, 1984b) assessed the effects of different police responses on the future violence of individuals apprehended for domestic assault. The authors . . . reported that

> arrest was the most effective of three standard methods police use to reduce domestic violence. The other police methods—attempting to counsel both parties or sending assailants away—were found to be considerably less effective in deterring future violence in the cases examined.

Sherman and Berk specified arrest and initial incarceration, "alone," as deterring continued domestic assault and recommended that the police adopt arrest as the favored response to domestic assault *on the basis* of its deterrent power. These findings and recommendations came at a time when advocacy for increased sensitivity to women's rights was strong and pressure was mounting to change the social service approach to domestic violence that had dominated law enforcement and court policy over the preceding two decades. . . . Sherman and Berk's recommendations were uniquely appealing for the times and were received by many women's advocates and law enforcement administrators as justification for change (Cohn and Sherman, 1987, Sherman and Cohn, 1989).

The overwhelming reaction of the research community to the Minneapolis experiment, with its recommendation for presumptory arrests in cases of misdemeanor domestic assault, was a call for additional studies to corroborate its conclusions. . . . The Omaha Domestic Violence Police Experiment, funded by the National Institute of Justice, was conceived and designed to determine if the findings reported for the Minneapolis experiment could be replicated elsewhere.

From Franklyn W. Dunford, David Huizinga, and Delbert S. Elliott, "The Role of Arrest in Domestic Assault: The Omaha Police Experiment," *Criminology*, vol. 28, no. 2 (1990). Reprinted by permission. Some notes omitted.

THE OMAHA RESEARCH DESIGN

Omaha is a city of approximately 400,000 inhabitants, 10% of whom are black and 2% of Hispanic origin (U.S. Department of Commerce, 1983). The city is split into three sectors (south, west, north) for police purposes. In concert with Chief Robert Wadman of the Omaha Police Division and after surveying 911 dispatch records, it was determined that approximately 60% of all disturbance calls were reported during the hours of "C" shift (4 p.m. to midnight). On this basis, the decision was made to limit the replication experiment in Omaha to eligible domestic assaults coming to the attention of the police throughout the city (all three sectors) during the hours of "C" shift. In this way, no segment of the city (e.g., socioeconomic status [SES] or ethnic group) would be excluded from participation in the experiment by the research design, and the majority of domestic violence calls would be included in the study.

Following the design of the Minneapolis experiment, police calls for domestic violence found to be eligible for the study were randomly assigned to "arrest," "separation," or "mediation" for all instances in which both victims and suspects were present when the police arrived. A case was eligible for the experiment if (1) probable cause for an arrest for misdemeanor assault existed, (2) the case involved a clearly identifiable victim and suspect, (3) both parties to the assault were of age (18 or older), (4) both parties had lived together sometime during the year preceding the assault, and (5) neither party to the offense had an arrest warrant on file. Cases for which the police had no legal authority to make an arrest (i.e., no probable cause to believe that an assault had occurred) were excluded from the experiment, as were more serious cases (i.e., felony cases). . . .

DESCRIPTION OF THE EXPERIMENT

In February 1986 all of the command and patrol officers assigned to "C" (and "D") shift were trained during a succession of three-day training sessions. Training focused on the rationale, content, and mechanics of the experiment. At each shift change thereafter, officers new to "C" shift were similarly trained. A total of 194 officers were ultimately assigned to the participating shifts and received training on the methods and procedures of the experiment. Of that number, 31 (16%) did not refer any cases to the study, and 61 (31%) accounted for approximately 75% of the referrals.

One of the greatest challenges faced when implementing random assignment in field settings is monitoring and identifying all violations of randomized outcomes. Although researchers may not be able to prevent violations of randomly designated treatments (e.g., arresting when treatment is randomized to mediating), they should be able to ensure that such violations do not go undetected when they occur. . . . Some of the discrepancies between Treatment as Assigned and Treatment as Immediately Delivered appear to have involved differences in perceptions of what happened rather than any real differences, while others were clear misdeliveries of treatment.[1] . . .

As a check on the misapplication of treatment, the disparities between Treatments as Assigned and Treatments as Delivered were examined. As presented in Table 1, 95% of the cases assigned to an arrest received an arrest, 92% of those assigned to be separated were separated, and 89% of the mediation cases were mediated; overall, 92% of the treatments were delivered as assigned. . . .

Table 1

Assigned and Delivered Treatments

Assigned Disposition	Mediate	As Delivered Separate	Arrest
Mediate			
N	102	8	2
%	89	7	2
Separate			
N	5	98	3
%	5	92	3
Arrest			
N	3	2	104
%	3	2	95

DISCUSSION

Conclusions based on the results of the research conducted in Omaha must be consider together with the outcomes of the five other research efforts currently funded by the National Institute of Justice to replicate the Minneapolis experiment. Since the results from all of these studies are not yet available, what follows must be considered tentative. It must also be remembered that the results of the Omaha experiment cannot be generalized beyond Omaha. . . .

Given the strength of the experimental design used in Omaha and the absence of any evidence that the design was manipulated in any significant way, the inability to replicate findings associated with the Minneapolis experiment calls into question any generalization of the Minneapolis findings to other sites. First, arrest in Omaha, by itself, did not appear to deter subsequent domestic conflict

any more than did separating or mediating those in conflict. Arrest, and the immediate period of custody associated with arrest, was not the deterrent to continued domestic conflict that was expected. If the Omaha findings should be replicated in the other five sites conducting experiments on this issue, policy based on the presumptory arrest recommendation coming out of the Minneapolis experiment may have to be reconsidered. Second, although arrest, by itself, did not act as a deterrent to continued domestic conflict for the misdemeanor domestic assault cases coming to the attention of the Omaha police, neither did it increase continued domestic conflict between parties to an arrest for assault. This is, victim-reported measures of repeated conflict, which are measures of behavior (as opposed to arrest and complaint data, which are measures of official police reaction to known violations of the law), clearly did not indicate that victims whose partners were arrested were at greater risk of subsequent conflict than were those whose partners were handled informally (mediated or separated) by the police. Arrest did not appear to place victims in greater danger of increased conflict than did separation or mediation. It would appear that what the police did in Omaha after responding to cases of misdemeanor domestic assault (arrest, separate, mediate), neither helped nor hurt victims in terms of subsequent conflict.

The failure to replicate the Minneapolis findings will undoubtedly cast some doubt on the deterrent power of a mandatory or even a presumptory arrest policy for cases of misdemeanor domestic assault. At this point, researchers and policymakers are in the awkward position of having conflicting results from two experiments and no clear, unambiguous direction from the research on this issue. Nevertheless, the data from the Omaha police experiment clearly suggest that the adoption of an arrest policy for cases of misdemeanor domestic assault may not, by itself, have any impact on the likelihood of repeated violent acts. From those who are directly involved in responding to domestic assaults, it might be profitable to begin thinking about new or additional strategies for dealing with this problem.

NOTES

1. Victims were not always sure of what happened as a result of police interventions. Some of their confusion was to be expected. The police, for example, would mediate a dispute, after which the suspect would leave, but at the time of the interview the victim would report a separation as the intervention. Or, after the police left, one of the parties to a separation treatment would return and the event would be recalled as a mediation. This kind of confusion is even more understandable given that (by responding officer estimates) over 30% of the victims had been drinking at the time of the police intervention, which may have affected what victims remembered as happening during those time periods. Further, many victims were clearly traumatized by the presenting assault, which also may have affected their recall.

REFERENCES

Sherman, Lawrence W. and Richard A. Berk 1984a The Minneapolis Domestic Violence Experiment. Police Foundation Reports. Washington, D.C.: Police Foundation. 1984b The specified deterrent effects of arrest for domestic assault. American Sociological Review 49(2):261–272.

Cohn, Ellen G. and Lawrence W. Sherman 1987 Police policy on domestic violence. Paper presented at the annual meeting of the Academy of Criminal Justice Sciences, St. Louis. Sherman, Lawrence W. and Ellen G. Cohn 1989 The impact of research on legal policy: The Minneapolis domestic violence experiment. Law and Society Review 23(1):117–144.

POSTSCRIPT

Does Arrest Reduce Domestic Violence?

One of the aspects of human behavior, including criminal behavior, that makes research both so fascinating and so exasperating is its multifaceted and multicausal nature. There simply are no straightforward relationships between some specific cause and some specific effect in social relations. For instance, families living in poverty will frequently have a high crime rate, yet many living in the meanest conditions, surrounded by vice and poverty, have children that rarely get into trouble. In many parts of the world, communities living in poverty far more terrible than we know often exhibit a crime rate far below ours. Moreover, there are many doctors, lawyers, college professors, or the like, who have children who are criminals—or who abuse *their* wives or children. No social situation *inevitably* leads to a specific outcome. In social relations, we have only at best *probabilities* that some conditions will produce certain outcomes.

Domestic violence, as has been shown in these articles, is a multifacted issue. It includes violence of parents against their children, of husband against wife, of wife against husband, and of adult child against an elderly parent. The causes are usually obscure and complex. In short, as in many areas of human behavior, *why* anyone assaults another is problematic, as are the "cures" for such assaults. There likely is no single panacea. The initial research in the early 1980s by Sherman and Berk was based on a limited sample. Although it was full of cautions, many quickly embraced their findings because they fit in nicely with current ideological leanings. Attorney Joan Meier's position exemplifies this.

Unfortunately, the domestic violence phenomenon having multiple causes compels multiple solutions—with no single treatment modality being considered universally effective. Yet if arrest does indeed reduce domestic assault recidivists or if the threat of it can prevent someone from initiating such terrible behavior to begin with, then arrests should be encouraged. Moreover, even if it is not a powerful deterrent in many cases, arrest has an important symbolic function: It signals that society will no longer tolerate this form of brutality. Certainly, Meier feels that this is an excellent argument for arrest. However, Dunford, Huizinga, and Elliott suggest that arrests might be dysfunctional, not only because their research finds no proof of its deterring such assaults, but also because it might be taking the focus off the search for more meaningful treatment programs.

"Deterrent Effects of Arrest for Domestic Assault," by L. W. Sherman and R. A. Berk, *American Sociological Review* (April 1984) remains the seminal article on this issue. Also consider reading "Handling Battering Men: Police Action in Wife Abuse Cases," by E. W. Gondolf and J. R. McFerron in

Criminal Justice and Behavior (December 1989) and "Use of Police Services by Battered Women," by E. M. Abel and E. K. Suh in *Social Work: Journal of the National Association of Social Workers* (November–December 1987). See also K. R. Williams and R. Hawkins's "The Meaning of Arrest for Wife Assault," *Criminology,* vol. 27 (1989), and L. Sherman and E. G. Cohn's "The Impact of Research on Legal Policy," *Law and Society Review,* vol. 23 (1989). For one of the earliest books bringing together many excellent discussions, see M. Straus, R. Gelles, and S. Steinmatz's *Behind Closed Doors* (Anderson, 1980). For studies of attempted solutions, see "Managing Domestic Violence in Two Urban Police Districts," by R. Caputo in *Social Casework* (October 1988), and "Batterers' Reports of Recidivism after Counselling," by A. DeMaris and J. K. Jackson in *Social Case Work* (October 1987). For a comparison of battering wives and husbands, see "Generalization and Containment: Different Effects of Past Aggression for Wives and Husbands," by J. Malone et al. in *Journal of Marriage and the Family* (August 1989).

For an overview of some of the most current research, see Volume 11 of *Crime and Justice: An Annual Review,* a special issue on family violence edited by Lloyd Ohlin and M. Tonry (University of Chicago Press, 1989), and *Family Violence: Research and Public Policy Issues,* edited by D. J. Besharov (The American Enterprise Institute Press, 1990). For an especially acrimonious debate over both the conceptualization of domestic violence and the extent of female-initiated violence, see R. L. McNeely and G. Robinson-Simpson's "The Truth About Domestic Violence: A Falsely Framed Issue," in *Social Work* (November–December 1987), and their follow-up, "The Truth About Domestic Violence Revisited," in *Social Work* (March–April 1988). Included in that issue are several articles bitterly attacking McNeely and Robinson-Simpson. For a discussion of black family violence, see *Violence in the Black Family,* edited by R. L. Hampton (Lexington Books, 1987). For a focus on this issue involving police and social work practitioners, see *Working with Violent Families: A Guide for Clinical and Legal Practitioners,* by F. G. and S. B. Bolton (Sage, 1987).

Drug Enforcement Agency

PART 4

Future Trends

Forecasting in the social sciences, including criminology and criminal justice, can be lots of fun. It can also be an important device for extrapolating from present trends and projecting future solutions. Most of the issues here pertain, at least according to one side of the argument, to possible significant reductions in crime. If we send prisoners to boot camps, will it cost less than conventional prison programs and reduce recidivism? If we could control guns, we could possibly reduce violence, others maintain. If we decriminalized drugs, would that significantly reduce the amount of crime plaguing America? And is it possible that the victims' movement is causing more problems for both criminals and victims, with neither group really benefiting?

Do Boot Camps Work?
_____

Will Gun Control Reduce Crime?
_____

Are Drug Arrests of Pregnant Women
   Discriminatory?
_____

Will Drug Legalization Help the
   Criminal Justice System?
_____

Should Juveniles Be Executed?
_____

Is the Victims' Rights Movement
   Succeeding?

ISSUE 14

Do Boot Camps Work?

YES: Doris L. MacKenzie, Larry A. Gould, Lisa M. Riechers, and James W. Shaw, from "Shock Incarceration: Rehabilitation or Retribution?" *Journal of Offender Counseling, Services & Rehabilitation* (1989)

NO: Merry Morash and Lila Rucker, from "A Critical Look at the Idea of Boot Camp as a Correctional Reform," *Crime and Delinquency* (April 1990)

ISSUE SUMMARY

YES: National Institute of Justice scientist Doris MacKenzie and Louisiana State University coauthors L. Gould, L. Riechers, and J. Shaw examine several "shock-incarceration," or military boot camp–style, prisons, including Louisiana's IMPACT, and find them relatively inexpensive, frequently helpful, and usually humane.
NO: Michigan State University criminal justice researcher Merry Morash and University of South Dakota political scientist Lila Rucker reject both the concept and the use of such boot camps for rehabilitation, insisting that they are inhumane and are more likely to reinforce violence and other negative reactions by inmates.

Words from an old song that "something's gotta give, something's gotta give" aptly describe the present situation of America's prisons and jails. In 1990, the Bureau of Justice Statistics showed that municipal jails house over 350,000 inmates, double the number from 1980. In 1990, federal and state prisons held over 700,000 residents, a ten-percent increase from the year before and a 113 percent increase from a mere ten years ago. At midyear (of 1990), there were approximately 43,541 women and 711,884 men in state or federal prisons. In many states, prison expansion and maintenance budgets presently rival their education expenditures, with no leveling-off in sight. And with police policies, political rhetoric, and public sentiment seeming to consolidate a new "get tough" agenda, we can expect more and more Americans to be arrested and incarcerated. The present cost of constructing a single jail cell can reach as high as $100,000. The cost of housing a single prisoner ranges from approximately $12,000 to $25,000 per year. Meanwhile, studies consistently show that for the majority of inmates, prisons are revolving doors. In some states, as many as 70 percent of all inmates recidivate within three months. Moreover, 41 states plus Puerto Rico, the

Virgin Islands, and the District of Columbia are under court orders to correct immediately unconstitutional conditions within their prisons and/or to relieve overcrowding. The heat is on to find alternatives.

Shock-incarceration, or military boot camp–style, prisons—in which younger inmates are housed for relatively short periods of time (frequently under six months) are somewhat novel in the United States as alternatives to traditional incarceration. Apparently originating in Oklahoma and Georgia in 1983, they now exist in over a dozen states and will probably increase significantly in the actual number of both programs and inmates.

The first thing about boot camps that has caught both politicians' attention and the public's eye is that relative to standard prisons, they are inexpensive. In New York, for example, inmates assigned to shock incarceration who successfully complete the program serve only one-third of their original sentences. In Florida and Georgia, boot-camp participants may end up serving only three months' worth of their original sentences of up to six years. The three-month cost for a prisoner in the Georgia shock-incarceration program is approximately $3,3000—far less than the yearly cost for inmates in standard prisons. New York saves for every 100 graduates from one of its four boot camps an estimated $1.5 million.

Scientifically, a real problem for criminologists is systematically measuring boot-camp "successes" and "failures" based on the important criterion of recidivism. In some states, as many as 40 percent of eligible inmates do *not* apply for boot camp and less than 25 percent of those that do are accepted. Between 20 to 25 percent of those accepted eventually drop out or are kicked out of the program and transferred back to prison. Moreover some judges are sentencing young first-offenders to boot camp who otherwise would have been placed on probation. All of these factors confound the comparison of boot-camp results with those of prisons. Especially difficult to treat empirically is the fact that boot-camp "rejects" are often not counted as "failures," but are simply ignored statistically. The fact that up to 25 percent of all boot-camp recruits are transferred out suggests a significant failure rate that seems ignored in official claims of equal-or-better success for these camps.

Which would you prefer: prison or military boot camp? Why? What of the claims by some critics that boot camps, even "good ones," are a problem because they deflect our concern over America's having by far the highest incarceration rate, with inmates serving longer sentences than in all other industrial societies? If they made you a warden for a week, what kind of correctional system would you want to create? Why?

YES

**Doris Layton MacKenzie,
Larry A. Gould, Lisa M. Riechers,
and James W. Shaw**

SHOCK INCARCERATION: REHABILITATION OR RETRIBUTION?

Shock incarceration is a relatively new type of alternative to standard prison incarceration. The specific components of shock incarceration programs vary. The similarity among all programs is the short period of imprisonment in a military "boot camp" type program involving participation in military drills, rigorous exercise and maintenance of living quarters. Programs differ, however, in whether activities such as work, community service, education or counseling are also incorporated in the schedule of activities. In addition, some jurisdictions stress the need for intensive supervision upon release if the behavioral changes brought about by the shock incarceration are to be continued on the outside.

The major incentive for developing shock incarceration programs appears to be the need for cost-effective methods of reducing overcrowding in prisons (Parent, 1988). Many people also feel that the enhanced discipline addresses a common problem of offenders and will, therefore, have rehabilitative benefits. After a national survey of shock incarceration programs, Parent . . . stated that these programs have strong face validity to the public and to criminal justice personnel. In his opinion this may account for their ready acceptance. Proponents of these programs argue that the short-term, demanding and rigorous boot camp component of the programs will be rehabilitative and deter future criminal behavior.

In the past there have been programs, called shock probation, which required offenders to spend a short period of time in prison. . . . The major difference between the earlier shock probation programs and shock incarceration is the required participation in the drills and physical training that are components of the recent programs.

The earliest shock incarceration programs began in 1983 in Georgia and Oklahoma. . . . Since then another five states have started shock incarceration programs, five are developing programs and nine are seriously considering initiating such programs. Thus it is probable that in the next few years over 40 percent of the state correctional jurisdictions will have some type of shock incarceration program.

Of the seven state jurisdictions which presently have programs, most are designed for the young, non-violent, first offender who has a short sentence. In most jurisdictions offenders must volunteer, and additionally, they must not have any physical or mental impairment which would prohibit full participation in the program. There are large differences in the programs in terms of who controls placement and release decisions (judge, department of corrections or parole board). Jurisdictions also vary in whether, upon release, the offender receives intensive parole supervision.

To our knowledge there have been few formal evaluations of the shock incarceration programs. There are some early results from Georgia's Special Alternative Incarceration Program (SAIP) and from Oklahoma's Regimented Inmate Discipline Program (RID). During 1984, 260 offenders entered Georgia's SAIP and 92 percent of them successfully completed the program. . . . Of those who completed the program, 21.3 percent returned to prison within one year of program completion. This return rate was lower than the rate for those released from diversion centers (23.4 percent), higher than the rate for those on intensive probation supervision (18.8 percent) and much higher than those on regular probation supervision (7.5 percent).

One thing that must be kept in mind in comparing Georgia's program with other shock incarceration programs is the fact that in Georgia the "fundamen-tal program concept is that a brief period of incarceration under harsh physical conditions, strenuous manual labor and exercise within a secured environment will 'shock' the younger and less seriously criminally oriented offender out of a future life of crime". . . . Thus the emphasis may be directed more towards a punishment model than are other shock incarceration programs that involve counseling, problem-solving or other treatments. SAIP was designed based in part on the earlier shock incarceration models.

In contrast to Georgia's shock incarceration program, treatment and individualized rehabilitation plans are an important ingredient of Oklahoma's RID program. In fact the program is part of the Nonviolent Intermediate Offender (NIO) program which is designed to be a method of planning rehabilitation programs for youthful offenders convicted of nonviolent crimes.

A study of 403 males, who completed the RID program between March 1984 and March 1985, revealed that 63 (15.7 percent) had been reincarcerated before March 1986 (Oklahoma Department of Corrections, 1986). The authors report this reincarceration rate is lower than the rate (45 to 77 percent) for the general population. However, it is difficult to make a meaningful comparison because the RID offenders are a carefully selected group who are most likely very different from the general population offender.

COMPONENTS OF SUCCESSFUL REHABILITATION PROGRAMS

In recent reviews of the literature on correctional rehabilitation it has been argued, contrary to a commonly expressed opinion, that there *is* empirical evidence of successful rehabilitation in some programs (Gendreau and Ross, 1987). . . . However, rather than broad generalizations about types of programs (e.g., shock incarceration, intensive supervision, education) these reviewers suggest that it is necessary to consider the principles and strategies which have been associated with successful programs. That is, a program which incorporates anticriminal modeling or problem solving, two principles that appear to be associated with successful correctional programs, should be more successful than one which does not incorporate these elements.

Early shock probation programs were attempts at getting tough and were designed to inculcate fear in offenders so they would be deterred from future criminal behavior (Vito, 1984; Vito and Allen, 1981). Such negative reinforcement does not appear to have strong support as a successful method of rehabilitation. . . . Although such programs may help by reducing overcrowding in the short run, there is little evidence of a reduction in recidivism. Thus the impact on overcrowding may be relatively short lived.

There is little evidence that the "getting tough" element of shock incarceration will, by itself, lead to behavioral change. This would just be another type of punishment; and there is little research support for the effectiveness of punishment alone. . . . However, voluntary participation in a "tough" program may be a test of commitment to change and other components (e.g., self-confidence) that may be indicative of success. Some of the other elements which have been identified as components of successful correctional rehabilitation programs are: formal rules, anticriminal modeling and reinforcement, problem solving, use of community resources, quality of interpersonal relationships, relapse prevention and self-efficacy, and therapeutic integrity (Gendreau and Ross, 1987). . . . Within the military framework of shock incarceration any or all of these elements could be present, although it is extremely difficult to tell to what degree or intensity they exist.

The goal of this paper is to describe the development and implementation of shock incarceration in one jurisdiction, Louisiana. In particular the elements of the program will be examined in terms of the principles which have been found to exist in successful rehabilitation programs according to recent reviews of the literature. This is part of a comprehensive evaluation of shock incarceration in Louisiana. The data reported are from correctional records and interviews with correctional personnel.

LOUISIANA'S IMPACT PROGRAM

Shock incarceration programs differ so widely at this point in time that any evaluation of them must begin with a description of the specific components of the program. Louisiana's Intensive Motivational Program of Alternative Correctional Treatment (IMPACT) is a two-phase shock incarceration program begun in 1987 by the Louisiana Department of Public Safety and Corrections (LDPSC). In the first phase of IMPACT offenders are incarcerated for 90 to 180 days in a rigorous boot camp type atmosphere (LDPSC, 1987). Following this period of incarceration offenders are placed under intensive parole supervision for the second phase of the program.

At the system level, the IMPACT program was designed to be an alternative for youthful first offenders, to help alleviate overcrowding, to promote a positive image of corrections, and to improve public relations. In regard to the individual, LDPSC (1987) states that IMPACT was designed to teach the offender responsibility, respect for self and others, and self confidence. Others stated goals of the program are to reduce recidivism, improve skills in everyday living and to generally improve the lives of the participants.

Selecting Offenders for IMPACT

To be legally eligible for the program offenders must be parole eligible, this must be their first felony conviction, they must have a sentence of seven years or less and they must volunteer. Furthermore, they must be recommended by (1) the Division of Probation and Parole, (2) the sentencing court and (3) a classification committee at the LDPSC diagnostic center. To be admitted to IMPACT the offender must receive a positive recommendation from all three evaluators (e.g., probation and parole agent, judge, and classification committee).

The law also states that offenders who are selected for the program must be those who are "particularly likely to respond affirmatively to participation" (LDPSC, 1987). As a consequence of this requirement a list of characteristics or disqualifiers have been developed to be used by the three groups who are required to make recommendations about the program. During the first year of operation this list of disqualifiers was gradually lengthened. At the end of 1987 the following characteristics were considered viable reasons for excluding an offender from the program: pending charges; sex offense; felony DWI; mental or physical health problem; over age 40; pattern of assaultive behavior; assaultive

escape; overt homosexuality; no acceptable residence identified for the intensive supervision phase of the program.

An important rationale for the three-group recommendation process was to insure that offenders who were sent to IMPACT would be drawn from the population of offenders who would normally be sent to prison not from those who would normally be given probation. Therefore, if for some reason the offender is disqualified at the diagnostic center, he or she is sent to the general prison population to serve time until the date of parole eligibility.

By the fall of 1987 (approximately October) 327 offenders had arrived at the LDPSC diagnostic center with recommendations for IMPACT from the judge and from the Division of Probation and Parole. The classification committee at the diagnostic center recommended IMPACT for 230 (or 70.3 percent) of these offenders. The remaining 97 offenders (29.7 percent) were excluded from (never entered) the program and almost all went into the general population. Thirty two (33 percent) of the 97 offenders were excluded because they did not volunteer, 23 (23.7 percent) because of a medical or psychological condition, and 21 (21.6 percent) because of an assaultive history. The reasons the remaining 21 (21.6 percent) were excluded varied widely (sexual conduct, pending charges, not first offense, etc.).

Graduation or Dismissal from IMPACT

Once an offender enters the program there are rigorous requirements which must be satisfactorily completed to move through stages of the boot camp. Along with military training, the incarceration phase of IMPACT involves treatment programs such as ventilation therapy, re-educative therapy, substance abuse education, and pre-release education.

Offenders may be returned to general population after they enter the IMPACT program if they fail to receive satisfactory evaluations within the 180 days, if they commit some serious rule infraction (assault, escape, etc.), if a medical or psychological condition is identified, or if a pending change is uncovered. Furthermore, at any time inmates may decide that they no longer wish to participate. In all of the above cases the offender would be returned to general population to await the regular parole hearing.

The first class of IMPACT inmates entered the program on February 8, 1987. By the end of December 1987, there were approximately 15 classes of entrants with an average of 18.3 offenders in each, for a total of 274 IMPACT entrants. Of these entrants, 117 offenders had completed the incarceration phase of the program and were paroled. Parole had been revoked for technical violations for nine (7.7 percent) of the parolees. Fifty four offenders were still in the program at the end of the year. The remaining 103 offenders (37.6 percent) left the program before completing the incarceration phase. Those who were admitted to IMPACT and then left before completing the incarceration phase left for the following reasons: medical (n = 9), voluntary (n = 63), disciplinary (n = 17), other (n = 14).

Overall the average offender who entered IMPACT was a male 23.3 years old with a sentence of 3.7 years. Only 12 women entered. More blacks (58.4 percent) than whites (41.6 percent) entered. A little less than one half of the entrants entered as probation violators and the others entered with a new crime. Most of those who entered were convicted of burglary or theft (63.1 percent) or drugs (22.1 percent).

Once an offender has completed between 90 and 180 days in IMPACT with satisfactory performance evaluations, institutional staff prepare a final report describing adjustment and progress. The parole board is responsible for release decisions. Once paroled the offender graduates from IMPACT and is released to the intensive parole phase of the program. This is a three-stage program involving less restrictions as offenders earn their way out of each stage. . . .

Selection and Dismissal Issues

A large number of the inmates recommended for IMPACT do not enter the program and still others do not complete the program. Personnel in the Division of Probation and Parole report some frustration with the large number of inmates who are dropped at the diagnostic center before entering IMPACT. According to probation and parole staff some judges are frustrated because the offenders they recommend for IMPACT are rejected at the diagnostic center. Everyone seems to understand a medical or psychological condition may be a legitimate reason for denying an offender access to the program. Less agreed upon are the denials due to a past history of violence. However, the specific reasons for denial of an individual may not always be known by those outside the diagnostic center. Judges and probation and parole staff may believe an inmate has been denied entry to IMPACT when actually the offender failed to volunteer or asked to be dropped from the program.

Probation and parole staff believe that their experience in supervising offenders on the street, makes them good judges of who will perform well on parole. Therefore, in their opinion, they should have a major role in deciding who should enter IMPACT. On the other hand, personnel at the diagnostic center believe that they must make decisions very carefully and conservatively, first because any serious offense by an IMPACT offender may destroy the program. And, second, offenders must see the reward of early release at the end of the incarceration phase of the program. It is assumed that early release must be assured for the offenders who take part in the program. If the offenders who enter IMPACT are not the type who will be released by the Parole Board then inmates will no longer feel assured that they will be released if they successfully complete the program. For this reason, the diagnostic staff try to anticipate the decisions of the parole board and omit offenders who are traditionally denied parole at the first hearing. . . .

In summary, there is some debate about the offenders who are most apt to benefit from IMPACT, how to identify these offenders and who can best identify them. The offenders who are selected appear to [be] relatively low-risk offenders. The high number of voluntary dropouts suggests a relatively rigorous program.

Staff and Inmate Interaction

The attitude of the staff toward inmates was examined. In particular we were interested in whether the drill instructors (DIs) saw their task as one of instilling obedience and respect for authority, and maintaining control, or whether they attempted to influence the offenders in other ways. The question was whether staff viewed themselves also as models, counselors, and as agents of behavior change through positive reinforcement and support.

In general, the philosophy of the program seems to be that the drill instructors, who work most closely with the inmates, are supposed to be authority figures who are also models and provide a supportive environment conducive to growth and change. For example, offenders are rewarded for good behavior by moving to more advanced squads or to higher positions within squads. They also earn privileges such as time to watch TV, visits and use of the canteen.

The DIs work closely with the squads. They march, exercise or run with the participants. The program is arranged so that early during training the control and authority of the DIs is emphasized. During this period military bearing, courtesy, drills and ceremony, and physical training are the major focus.

"Even though its framework is military, institutional IMPACT is more than a boot camp for criminal offenders" (LDPSC, 1987, p6). This becomes particularly salient after the offender moves out of the beginners squad. The DIs hold courses for the more advanced squads in which concepts and information related to work and work behaviors are discussed. To emphasize the supportive role of the staff, the parole agents pick up the offenders when they leave the institutional phase and take them home.

In summary, those who are assigned the task of setting the rules do not appear to see their job as only authority and control. They also take steps to be supportive and helpful in other areas.

Authority and Abuse

The emphasis from the administration is on both the supportive and authoritative position of the drill instructors. As is obvious, in programs such as this the line between abuse and authority (and control) is hard to define. It was reported that some correctional officers had difficulty changing from their traditional role of control to a role incorporating both the control and supportive guidance which they are expected to assume in this program. The administration is well aware of the need to carefully watch for signs of abuse. Overzealous control-oriented DIs have been removed from the program.

Facility Location

The program is located within a large mixed (medium/maximum) security facility surrounded by the general population. At first glance this appears to be a disadvantage. However several important advantages have been identified. One advantage in having the program located within a large facility is that the program has close scrutiny from various personnel within (various administrators) and outside of the Department (visitors, news media). This is helpful in guarding against abuse.

A second important advantage in the location is the fact that staff can be easily rotated into and out of the program. One reason this is needed is if a correctional officer has difficulty in making the change to the DI job and appears to be having trouble in the roles expected (counselor, model or teacher) or if a DI's performance appears to be crossing the line from control/authority to abuse. In such cases staff can quickly be reassigned to another area of the prison. A second advantage in being able to rotate staff into and out of the program is burnout. Because the program is located in a large facility, staff who burnout or who might be abusive can be easily rotated.

Burnout

There does appear to be a high burnout rate for DIs (one estimate was that DIs have, on the average, spent only 6 months in the program). Burnout might also be expected for the parole agents. They work in pairs and have a 50 per pair caseload. According to the administration, many of the "best" agents have volunteered to work with IMPACT offenders. A new title has been given to those taking this assignment. Newly hired agents in these positions receive higher pay. However, the type and amount of work is heavy—for example, agents are required to write narratives for every contact made with the offender and they are required to make at least four face-to-face contacts per week in the first phase of intensive incarceration.

Rehabilitative Components

This examination of the IMPACT program did not suggest that either negative reinforcement (punishment) nor just a busier program were the major goals or organizing principles of the program. IMPACT does appear to include many of the elements that have been associated with successful rehabilitation in the opinion of several authors who have reviewed the correctional rehabilitation literature. . . . Based on these reviews, we examined possible rehabilitative elements: rules and authority; anticriminal modeling and reinforcement; problem solving; use of community resources; interpersonal relationships; and an overall therapeutic integrity.

The most outstanding aspect of IMPACT, of course, is the approach to formal rules and authority (e.g., enforced contingencies), one characteristic that has been found to be associated with rehabilitation. This is a highly visible component of the IMPACT program. The high number of those dropping out or being forced to drop the program attests to the enforcement and, also, the rigor of the rules. For those who are able to complete the program it would appear that their belief in their own ability to control events (or a sense of responsibility) would be increased because the program is difficult and they were able to complete it.

Other factors that have been associated with successful rehabilitation programs are anticriminal modeling and reinforcement. Again there is evidence that these are components of IMPACT. The DIs do participate in the drills and physical exercise that are required of the offenders. Time and activities are carefully controlled in the program, for example, the first squad is only permitted to watch the evening news on TV (which could be considered a prosocial activity) during the early weeks of the program. Group support and working together is encouraged during military drill and also in group counseling sessions. Furthermore the DIs encourage "positive thinking."

Many of the aspects of successful behavior modification programs are incorporated in the design of IMPACT. Most of the target behaviors (drill, attention to detail, hygiene, attitude, communication and physical training) are clearly defined and prosocial. . . . The offender's peer group is involved in a positive way and it is the offender's choice as to whether to become involved in the program.

Problem-solving is another component that has been associated with rehabilitation. This component is less obvious in the IMPACT schedule. It may be somewhat addressed during the prerelease and group counseling sessions. During the intensive supervision phase offenders are required to work (or show evidence of an intensive job search), complete community service, go to school, and keep to an early evening curfew among other requirements. Many of these would require problem solving skills. For example how to schedule ones time to arrive at work at the required hour, how to get a job, etc. are problems that must be solved, and the parole agent is there to assist the offender. Thus, problem solving is done in an applied setting.

The two phase structure of the program does make maximum use of community resources with some obvious advantages. For one, the intensive supervision on the street enables the parole agent to advise the offender about the availability and use of resources in the community. The parolee who has an alcohol problem can join AA and work with other nonoffenders (possibly better models). The offender learns to compete for resources with the help of the parole agent. Since resources in the community can be made available to everyone, the IMPACT program is more "acceptable" than other prison programs which are frequently criticized on the basis of why "excellent, costly" programs should be made available to offenders rather than to nonoffenders on the outside. This attitude almost always limits what is available to offenders in prison. Thus, maximizing the parolees use of community programs means that better programs may be available to them outside the prison than would be possible within prison. . . .

The quality of interpersonal relationships is another factor which has been associated with successful rehabilitation. This also seems to be an aspect of the IMPACT program. Offenders are encouraged to cooperate and work as a team with members of their squads. The DIs report that they often receive letters from graduates of the program thanking them for their help and support. The parole agents report that they now feel as if they are really doing something in assisting the IMPACT graduates on parole. However the depth and consistency of this is difficult to objectively evaluate. At the least the philosophy of the program leans towards encouraging quality interpersonal relationships.

Therapeutic integrity or "to what extent do treatment personnel actually adhere to the principles and employ the techniques of the therapy they purport to provide?" . . . might be considered the underlying requirement of any successful program. There is some evidence that the program has therapeutic integrity. For example, the high burnout rate of staff suggests that they are committed to the program and work hard. The program is so all encompassing that it does not appear to be diluted in the prison environment. Neither does it appear to be treatment in name only, there is definitely something going on or so many offenders would not leave the program and choose to spend a longer period of time in general population in prison. . . .

In summary, this paper has reviewed Louisiana's shock incarceration program and examined the components of the program in regard to rehabilitative potential. One of the major goals of the program is to foster prosocial changes in participants. The findings suggest that the term "shock incarceration" alone does not give enough information about the elements of a program to determine whether it includes components which might be expected to result in prosocial changes in the inmates. The examination of Louisiana's programs suggests that many elements associated with successful rehabilitation are incorporated in IMPACT. Particularly important may be the intensity of the program, its volunteer nature and the two-phase (incarceration and intensive parole supervision) structure. The danger is that the punishment and retribution aspects of shock incarceration are emphasized and the possible rehabilitative components go unrecognized. Such an occurrence might lead to a rejection of such programs before their potential has been explored.[1]

NOTES

1. The comparisons with programs in other jurisdictions is taken from [D.] Parent's 1988 address to the American Correctional Association ["Shock Incarceration Programs"] based on his National Institute of Justice, U.S. Department of Justice funded research project.

REFERENCES

Gendreau, P. and R.R. Ross. 1987. Revivification of Rehabilitation: Evidence From the 1980s. *Justice Quarterly*, 4:349–407.

Louisiana Department of Public Safety and Corrections. 1987. IMPACT: *Purposes, Policies and Procedures*. Baton Rouge, LA.

Vito, G.F. 1984. Developments in Shock Probation: A Review of Research Findings and Policy Implications. *Federal Probation*. 48:22–27.

Vito, G.F. and H.E. Allen. 1981. Shock Probation in Ohio: A Comparison of Outcomes. *International Journal of Offender Therapy and Comparative Criminology*, 25:70–76.

NO   Merry Morash and Lila Rucker

A CRITICAL LOOK AT THE IDEA OF BOOT CAMP AS A CORRECTIONAL REFORM

INTRODUCTION: THE BOOT CAMP IDEA

In several states, correctional boot camps have been used as an alternative to prison in order to deal with the problem of prison overcrowding and public demands for severe treatment. . . . Correctional boot camps are styled after the military model for basic training, and, similar to basic training, the participants are primarily young males. However, the "recruits" are offenders, though usually nonviolent and first-time ones. . . . Boot camps vary in their purpose, but even when they are instituted primarily to reduce overcrowding, the implicit assumption is that their programs are of equal or greater deterrent or rehabilitative value than a longer prison sentence.

By the end of 1988, boot camps were operating in one county (Orleans Parish, Louisiana) and in eight states (Georgia, Oklahoma, Mississippi, Louisiana, South Carolina, New York, Florida, and Michigan), they were planned in three states (North Carolina, Kansas, and New Hampshire), and they were being considered in at least nine other states. . . . The model was also being considered for a large number of youthful Detroit offenders. And in the summer of 1989, the boot camp model was put forth by the House Crime Subcommittee chairman as a potential national strategy for treating drug abusers. . . .

The purpose of this article is to provide . . . a critical analysis of the history and assumptions underlying the use of a military model in a correctional setting.

The popular image of military boot camp stresses strict and even cruel discipline, hard work, and authoritarian decision making and control by a drill sergeant. It should be noted that this image does not necessarily conform to either current practices in the U.S. military or to all adaptations of boot camp in correctional settings. However, in a survey of existing correctional boot camp programs, Parent (1988) found commonality in the use of

From Merry Morash and Lila Rucker, "A Critical Look at the Idea of Boot Camp as a Correctional Reform," *Crime and Delinquency*, vol. 36 (April 1990), pp. 204-221. Copyright © 1990 by Sage Publications, Inc. Reprinted by permission of Sage Publications, Inc.

strict discipline, physical training, drill and ceremony, military bearing and courtesy, physical labor, and summary punishment for minor misconduct. Some programs have combined selected elements of the military boot camp model with more traditional forms of rehabilitation. In Oklahoma, for example, the paramilitary structure, including the use of regimentation, has been only one aspect of an otherwise "helping, supportive environment" that is considered by the administration to be a prerequisite if "change is to last or have any carry over". . . . In Michigan, the major emphasis has been on developing the "work ethic" by utilizing various motivational tactics (e.g., chants), strong discipline, and rehabilitation. . . . All participants work from 8:00 a.m. to 3:30 p.m. daily; evenings involve educational and therapeutic programs. When more traditional methods of rehabilitation are included, a consideration of the boot camp idea is more complex, requiring an analysis of both the costs and benefits of mixing the imagery or the reality of a boot camp approach with other measures.

Regardless of the actual degree to which a militaristic, basic training model has been emphasized, the press has taken this emphasis as primary and usually has portrayed it in a positive light. Numerous stories have been printed under titles such as "Boot Camp—In Prison: An Experiment Worth Watching" (Raspberry, 1987, p. H21). "New York Tests a Boot Camp for Inmates" (Martin, 1988), " 'Squeeze You Like A Grape': In Georgia, A Prison Boot Camp Sets Kids Straight" (Life, 1988), and "Some Young US Offenders Go To 'Boot Camp'—Others Are Put in Adult Jails" (Sitomer, 1987, p. 1). The text similarly has reflected a positive evaluation of the approach. For ex-

ample, Raspberry (1987) wrote of the Louisiana boot camp that "[t]he idea [is] to turn a score of lawbreakers into disciplined, authority-respecting men." He quoted the warden: "[W]e're giving an inmate a chance to get out of prison in 90 days instead of seven years. But you're making him work for it. . . . We keep them busy from the time they wake up until they fall asleep with chores that include such sillinesses as cleaning latrines with a toothbrush." The warden concluded that the approach "teaches them self-discipline and self-control, something many of these men have never had" (Raspberry, 1987). Similarly, Martin (1988, p. 15) wrote about the New York program:

> Days are 16 hours long, and two-mile runs and calisthenics on cold asphalt are daily staples. Work is chopping down trees or worse. The discipline recalls Parris Island. . . . those who err may be given what is genteelly termed 'a learning experience,' something like carrying large logs around with them everywhere they go or, perhaps, wearing baby bottles around their necks.

Life's (1988, p. 82) coverage of the Georgia program included the following statement by one of the sergeants: "[Here] being scared is the point. You have to hit a mule between the eyes with a two-by-four to get his attention . . . and that's exactly what we're doing with this Program."

The journalistic accounts of boot camps in corrections have celebrated a popular image of a relatively dehumanizing experience that is marked by hard, often meaningless, physical labor. The inmate has been portrayed as deficient, requiring something akin to being beaten over the head in order to become "a man."

The imagery of the people that we send to boot camp as deserving of dehumanizing treatment is in itself troubling, but even more so in light of the fact that the inmates are disproportionately minorities and underclass members. The boot camp idea also raises the disturbing question: Why would a method that has been developed to prepare people to go into war, and as a tool to manage legal violence, be considered as having such potential in deterring or rehabilitating offenders? . . . In . . . summary of the values stressed in military basic training, Merryfinch (1981, p. 9) identified "a commitment to organized violence as the most effective way to resolve conflicts, a glorification of 'hard' emotions (aggression, hatred, brutality) and a strict channeling of 'soft' emotions (compassion, love, suffering). . . . " Clearly, many of the objectives of military basic training are not shared by the policymakers who promote correctional boot camps. What is even more striking is that none of them make sense as a means to promote either rehabilitation or deterrence, and the emphasis on unquestioned obedience to authority and aggression is inconsistent with prosocial behavior.

WHAT HAS BEEN TRIED AND WHAT WORKS IN CORRECTIONS?

The correctional boot camp model has been touted as a new idea. However, militarism, the use of hard labor, and efforts to frighten offenders—most recently surfacing in the "Scared Straight" programs—have a long history in prison settings. . . .

By 1896, the industrial reformatory at Elmira had " . . . well coordinated discipline which centered around the grading and marking system, an honest application of the indeterminate sentence, trade and academic schools, military organization and calisthenic exercises" (McKelvey, 1977). . . . Similar to many of the contemporary boot camps, at Elmira the philosophy was to combine both rehabilitation approaches and work with military discipline and physical activity to, among other things, improve self-esteem. However, the legacy of Brockway's Elmira Reformatory was not a move toward rehabilitation (Johnson, 1987, p. 41). Instead, the militaristic atmosphere set the stage for abusive punishment, and the contradiction between military discipline and rehabilitation was apparent. . . .

Some might counter the argument that the militaristic approach opens the door for abusive punishment by pointing out that in contemporary correctional settings, physical punishment and harm are eliminated. However, as Johnson (1987) . . . noted, nonphysical abuse can be viewed as a "civilized" substitute. Also, in some cases physical abuse is a matter of definition, as is seen in the accounts of dropouts from one contemporary boot camp. They reported being treated like "scum," working 18-hour days, being refused permission to use the bathroom, being provoked to aggression by drill instructors, being forced to push a bar of soap along the floor with their noses, and being forced to participate in an exercise called "air raids" in which trainees run and dive face down, landing on their chests with arms stretched out to their sides. . . . At least in some settings, the military model has provided a legitimization of severe punishment. It has opened the door for psychological and even physical abuse that would be rejected as cruel and unusual punishment in other correctional settings.

Turning now to work in correctional settings, its persistent use has been supported by its congruence with alternative objectives, including punishment, incapacitation, rehabilitation, and control inside the institution. . . . In contemporary discussions of correctional boot camp programs, work has been justified as both punitive and rehabilitative, as both exemplifying the harsh result of breaking the law and teaching the "work ethic." However, the economic constraints imposed by limited budgeting for rehabilitation efforts and the shrinking number of jobs for unskilled workers have shaped the form of work. Thus, hard physical labor, which has no transfer to the contemporary job market, has been the choice in correctional boot camps.

Further criticism of the form of work used in the boot camp settings rests on empirical research. The literature on work programs in general has not supported the conclusion that they produce a decrease in recidivism. . . . Especially pertinent to the present analysis, in a recent article Maguire, Flanagan and Thornberry (1988) showed that labor in a correctional institution was unrelated to recidivism after prisoner differences were taken into account. . . . Clearly, the evaluation literature contradicts the idea that hard, often meaningless, labor in the boot camp setting has some positive effect. . . .

The "Scared Straight" programs, a contemporary version of correctional efforts intended to deter offenders through fright, also are not supported by empirical research. In a San Quentin program of this type, older adolescent participants were arrested less often but for more serious crimes than a comparison group. . . . An evaluation of a similar New Jersey program showed that participants were more seriously delinquent than a control group. . . . In general, then, the program elements of militarism, hard labor, and fear engendered by severe conditions do not hold much promise, and they appear to set the stage for abuse of authority.

MILITARY BOOT CAMPS

The idea of boot camp as applied in correctional settings is often a simplification and exaggeration of an outdated system of military training that has been examined and rejected as unsatisfactory by many experts and scholars and by the military establishment itself. The difficulties that the military has discovered with the traditional boot camp model, and the resulting implications for reforms, could be instructive to people in search of positive correctional measures.

A number of difficulties with what will be referred to as the "traditional" military boot camp approach that is now mimicked in correctional settings were uncovered by a task force appointed in the 1970s. . . . The first difficulty with the traditional boot camp approach involved inconsistent philosophies, policies, and procedures. Ten years after the task force report was published, a followup study provided further insight into the problem of inconsistency and the related patterns of unreasonable leadership and contrived stressful situations. The study documented the "severe effects" of lack of predictability in such areas as standards for cleanliness and how cadence was called (Marlowe et al., 1988, p. 10). According to the study, "predictability and reasonableness contribute to trainee self esteem, sense of being valued by the unit and commitment to the organization." Further, "when authority is arbitrarily imposed, or when leaders lead strictly by virtue of their power or authority, the result is often anger and disrespect" (Marlowe et al., 1988, pp. 11–12). Also, "dysfunctional stress [which results when work is irrelevant or contrived], heightens tensions, shortens tempers, and increases the probability of abuse while generally degrading the effectiveness of training" (Raupp, 1978, p. 99). . . .

The second difficulty that the task force identified with traditional boot camp training was a widespread "we-versus-they" attitude and the related view that trainees were deserving of degrading treatment. . . . The we-versus-they attitude was manifested by different behavioral and/or dress standards for trainees and for other personnel. Specifically, trainees were given "skin-head" haircuts and were prohibited from swearing and shouting, and physical training was used as punishment.

Aside from the investigative reports sponsored by the military, empirical studies of the effects of military boot camps, the effects of physical training (which is a major component of many correctional boot camp programs), and learning in general have provided relevant findings. Empirical evidence regarding the psychological impact of traditional military basic training on young recruits between the ages of 18 and 22 has demonstrated that "there was no increase in scores on ego-strength, or any other evidence of beneficial psychological effects accruing from basic training". . . . Administration of the MMPI to recruits revealed that "the change in the shape of the [MMPI] profiles suggests that aggressive, impulsive, and energetic features became slightly more prominent". . . . The authors concluded that the changes on the subscales imply that

more callous attitudes, a tendency to ignore the needs of others, and feelings of self-importance increase slightly during basic training. The recruits appear less prone to examine their own responsibility for conflicts, and more ready to react aggressively. (Ekman et al., 1962, p. 104)

The importance of this finding is heightened by the conclusion of Gendreau, Grant, and Leipciger . . . that components of self-esteem that were good predictors of recidivism include the very same characteristics, namely, "self-centered, exploitive of others, easily led, and anxious to please." Sonkin and Walker (1985; see also Walker, 1983) . . . also speculated that basic training in the military can result in the transfer of violent solutions to family settings. . . . Although correctional boot camps do not provide training in the use of weapons or physical assault, they promote an aggressive model of leadership and a conflict-dominated style of interaction that could exacerbate tendencies toward aggression.

In another empirical study of military basic training, Wamsley . . . contrasted the effects of Air Force Aviation Cadet Pre-Flight Training School with Air Force Officer's Training School. The Cadet School employed harsh techniques—including such activities as head shaving, marching miles in stiff shoes, and impromptu exercises as physical punishment—to inculcate basic values and eliminate that "unfit." After one week, 33% of recruits left. Wamsley . . . wrote that "Those with low capacities for anxiety, insufficient self-esteem to withstand and discredit abuse, inability to control or suppress anger, or those with latent neuroses or psychoses literally 'cracked' under the stress, and attempted suicides and psychiatric referrals were not uncommon." The purpose of constant exhortations to "get eager, mister" or "get proud, Raunch" was to promote an aggressive fighter spirit, and the "common misery and despair created a bond" among the trainees.

Increased aggression and a bond among inmates are not desired outcomes of correctional boot camps, so again the efficacy of using the military boot camp model is in question. Moreover, it is unlikely that the offenders in correctional boot camps are more mentally healthy than Air Force recruits. What is the effect of using such techniques when there is no escape valve through dropping out of the program? And, if only the best-adjusted stay, what is accomplished by the program? The contrast of the Cadet School with the Officer's Training School, which did not use humiliation and severe physical conditions and punishment, provides convincing evidence of the ineffectiveness of such an approach to training people. . . .

Also contradicting the negatively oriented training strategy that is characteristic of the old-style military boot camp model, virtually no empirically supported criminology theories have suggested that aggressive and unpredictable reactions by authority figures encourage prosocial behavior. The opposite has been promulgated by most learning theorists. . . . Finally, there has been considerable theory and research showing that antisocial behavior is increased when authority figures provide aggressive models for behavior. . . . Research in the sociology of sport has provided further evidence that physical training under the direction of an authoritarian trainer increases aggression. . . .

There is no systematic evidence of the degree to which the problems in traditional-style military boot camps are manifested in correctional settings, but there is evidence that they do occur. The introductory descriptions of the correctional boot camp model clearly reveal a tendency for some of the "drill sergeants" to use negative leadership. Telephone interviews with representatives of nine correctional boot camps show a tendency to focus on "tearing down the individuals and then building them back up." Reflective of his philosophy are negative strategies alluded to earlier, such as the utilization of debasing "welcoming speeches," the "chair position," and "learning experiences" that require men to wear baby bottles around their necks or to carry tree limbs with them all day.

Correctional boot camps also provide settings conducive to high levels of unpredictability and contrived stress. In one program (Bellew, 1988), . . . dropouts, current trainees, and parolees who had completed the program all reported that "differences between DI [drill instructor] styles made it tough to avoid trouble. Trainees' beds may be made to satisfy DI 'A,' but at shift change, if DI 'B' doesn't approve of that particular style, trainees are punished." As further illustration, another inmate reported that on the first day of participation in the boot camp, he was told that he had quit and could not participate. When the inmate sat down for the rest of the day, he was reportedly "kicked out for sitting down," and his having left the program was listed as voluntary. The inmate reported that he had tried to participate but that the drill instructor kept telling him that he had quit. The interviewer reported that at the time of the interview, the offender was "still confused as to what actually had happened that day." . . .

It is true that, as proponents of correctional boot camps claim, many military recruits feel that their survival of basic training is evidence of maturity and a major achievement in their lives. . . . However, the sense of achievement is linked to the notion that the experience is the first step in preparing them for the unique role of a soldier. Moreoever, military boot camp is intended as just a prelude to acquaint the recruits with their new environment, in which they will take more control of their lives. . . . It is not obvious that the boot camp experience alone, including elements of capricious and dehumanizing treatment, would be seen in such a positive light by inmate participants. . . .

It could be argued that the purpose of correctional boot camp is not to bind soldiers to their leaders or to develop group solidarity. Thus, the failure of the outmoded military boot camp model to achieve these results may not be a serious concern. Even is we accept this argument, the research on military basic training raises serious questions about the potential for undesirable outcomes, including increased aggression.

STEREOTYPES OF MASCULINITY AND CORRECTIONAL MEASURES

The very idea of using physically and verbally aggressive tactics in an effort to "train" people to act in a prosocial manner is fraught with contradiction. The idea rests on the assumption that forceful control is to be valued. . . .

There is little doubt that the military is a male-dominated institution . . . and that there is a military ideology that rejects both women and stereotypically female characteristics. . . . As Enloe . . . wrote, there is a common assumption that "the military . . . is a *male* preserve, run by men and for men according to

masculine ideas and relying solely on *man* power." In some military settings, terms such as "little girl," "woman," and "wife" have been routinely used to negatively label a trainee who is viewed as having failed in some way. . . . Traditional marching chants have included degrading comments about women, and sexist terms for women and their body parts have been common in military settings. . . . Stiehm . . . concluded from her research that even after the mandated inclusion of women in the U.S. Military Academy, considerable derogatory name calling and ridicule of women were common. The implication is that to fail is to be female, or, conversely, to succeed is to be aggressive, dominant, and therefore unquestionably "male." . . .

Aside from overt rejection of women and femaleness, the boot camp model, with its emphasis on unquestioned authority and aggressive interactions and its deemphasis on group cooperation and empathy, promotes a limited image of the "true man." . . .

This result has been echoed in the use of a military model that similarly extols the virtues that are often associated with both masculinity and aggression in our society. . . .

The irony in emphasizing an aggressive model of masculinity in a correctional setting is that these very characteristics may explain criminality. Theorists working in the area of crime causation have focused on both the identification with male stereotypical traits and roles, which are consistent with illegal behavior . . . and the frustration that males feel when they cannot achieve these stereotypes because of low social status. . . .

An additional irony is found in the inclusion of women in correctional boot camps. . . . There is serious doubt about the efficacy of placing women in a militaristic environment that emphasizes masculinity and aggressiveness and that in some cases rejects essentially prosocial images and related patterns of interaction associated with the stereotype of femininity.

ALTERNATIVE MODELS IN CORRECTIONS

Correctional policymakers and program staff are not alone in their application of the traditional boot camp model as an approach for training people outside of military settings. Looking again at news reports, we see that the boot camp type of training has been accepted in a variety of organizations as a means to increase the productivity, skill levels, efficiency, and effectiveness of participants. Such enterprises are as diverse as the Electronic Data Systems Corporation, . . . the Nick Bollettieri Tennis Academy, . . . and Japan's Managers' Training School. . . . In keeping with the boot camp model, participants are made to endure humiliation so that a bond can develop with the teacher. . . . There appear to be social forces supporting acceptance of the general idea that the boot camp model is appropriate as a method for promoting training and human development. In spite of societal pressures to use such a model, our assessment has a number of negative implications for the application of boot camps in correctional settings. . . .

Our review and analysis suggest that even when the elements of the military boot camp model are mixed with traditional rehabilitative approaches, there can be negative outcomes. Thus, the boot camp model is unlikely to provide a panacea for the needs of rehabilitation or for the pressures arising from the problems of both prison overcrowding and public demands for severe punishment. Whether the point is to provide rehabilitation, to deter, or to divert people from prison, alternatives other than boot camp should be given careful consideration.

REFERENCES

Ekman, Paul, Wallace V. Friesen, and Daniel R. Lutzker. 1962. "Psychological Reactions to Infantry Basic Training." *Journal of Consulting Psychology* 26:103–104.

Johnson, Robert. 1987. *Hard Time*. Monterey, CA: Brooks/Cole.

Maguire, Kathleen E., Timothy J. Flanagan, and Terence P. Thornberry. 1988. "Prison Labor and Recidivism." *Journal of Quantitative Criminology* 4:3–18.

Marlowe, David H., James A. Martin, Robert J. Schneider, Larry Ingraham, Mark A. Vaitkus, and Paul Bartone. 1988. *A Look at Army Training Centers: The Human Dimensions of Leadership and Training*. Washington, DC: Department of Military Psychiatry, Walter Reed Army Institute of Research.

Martin, Douglas. 1988. "New York Tests a Boot Camp for Inmates." *New York Times* March 4:15.

McKelvey, Blake. 1977. *American Prisons: A History of Good Intentions*. Montclair, NJ: Patterson Smith.

Merryfinch, Lesley. 1981. "Militarization/Civilization." Pp. 9–13 in *Loaded Questions: Women in the Military*, edited by W. Chapkis, Washington, DC: Transnational Institute.

Parent, Dale. 1988. "Shock Incarceration Programs." Paper Presented at the American Correctional Association Winter Conference, Phoenix.

Raspberry, William. 1987. "Boot Camp—In Prison: An Experiment Worth Watching." *Washington Post* March 21: Section H, 21.

Raupp, Edward R. 1978. *Toward Positive Leadership for Initial Entry Training. A Report by the Task Force on Initial Entry Training Leadership*. Fort Monroe, VA: United States Army Training and Doctrine Command.

Sitomer, Curtis J. 1987. "Some Young U.S. Offenders Go to 'Boot Camp'—Others are Put in Adult Jails," *Christian Science Monitor* October 27:1.

Sonkin, Daniel Jay, Del Martin, and Leonard E. Aurbach Walker. 1955. *The Male Batterer: A Treatment Approach*. New York: Springer.

POSTSCRIPT

Do Boot Camps Work?

Clearly, this is an issue that calls for more research. About the only thing that is known for certain right now is that boot camps (somewhat like half-way houses) are considerably less expensive than maximum security prisons. However, whether they are nearly as humane as half-way houses or rehabilitate more inmates than prisons do is inconclusive.

Boot camps (like private prisons, a current correctional fad that has been tried many times in the correctional past) involve numerically only a small portion of the incarcerated population. Although private concerns have expanded somewhat into the business of juvenile training schools by utilizing the boot camp concept, almost all adult shock-incarceration programs are run by state administrators. By contrast, private industry now manages over 40 adult facilities housing some 14,000 inmates. Boot camps apparently have a population closer to 10,000. Yet even combining the two estimated populations still totals less than 2 percent of the entire incarcerated U.S. population. However, based on current trends and public sentiment, the present programs could rapidly escalate until they could conceivably constitute a statistically significant percentage of this population, and this in itself necessitates our careful consideration of the shock-incarceration concept.

The majority of published reports on boot camps thus afar are popular media accounts and/or in-house state publications. Both, unfortunately, are sometimes little more than glowing reports advocating a new "fad" rather than a sustained analytical reflection on the concept. See, for instance, "Boot Camp in Prison: An Experiment Worth Watching," by W. Raspberry, *Washington Post* (March 21 1987); D. Martin's "New York Tests a Boot Camp for Inmates," *New York Times* (June 8, 1989); *Life* magazine's "Squeeze You Like a Grape: In Georgia a Prison Boot Camp Sets Kids Straight" (July 1988); J. Dillon's "Hardship, Help for Drug Dealers" *Christian Science Monitor* (November 10, 1989); and T. W. Waldron's "Boot Camp Prison Offers Second Chance to Young Felons," *Corrections Today* (July 1990).

For an attack on prison effectiveness that generated tremendous debate, see R. Martinson et al., *Effectiveness of Correctional Treatment* (Praeger, 1975); for a current response to these authors' position as well as a discussion of private prisons, see *The American Prison: Issues in Research and Policy,* edited by L. Goodstein and D. L. MacKenzie (Plenum Publishing Co., 1989). A recent discussion of private prisons and a summary of the work of Charles Logan is "Private Prisons—Profitable and Growing," by R. Welch in *Corrections Compendium* (April 1990). A good discussion of U.S. proclivities for correctional panaceas is J. Finckenauer's *Scared Straight and the Panacea Phenomenon* (Prentice-Hall, 1982).

ISSUE 15

Will Gun Control Reduce Crime?

YES: Josh Sugarmann, from "The NRA Is Right: But We Still Need to Ban Handguns," *Washington Monthly* (June 1987)

NO: James D. Wright, from "Second Thoughts About Gun Control," *Public Interest* (Spring 1988)

ISSUE SUMMARY

YES: Josh Sugarmann, formerly with the National Coalition to Ban Handguns, identifies several problems with legalized handguns, including what he describes as unacceptably high rates of suicides with guns, family homicides, and accidents.

NO: Massachusetts Institute of Technology sociologist James D. Wright argues that banning small handguns would not reduce crime and sets forth what he classifies as the many legitimate uses of "Saturday night specials."

According to some estimates in the 1980s, one in every four families in the United States owns a gun. And because of the growing fear of crime, many citizens express increased unwillingness to give up their guns. Guns are seen as necessary to protect home and family. An excellent example of this is the complicated situation that the nationally syndicated columnist Carl Rowan confronted. A well-known supporter of strict firearm controls, he was allegedly threatened by an intruder in his own backyard. Rowan quickly produced a pistol and shot the intruder. While conservatives (who consistently support the right to bear arms and oppose most kinds of gun control) jeered Rowan for his hypocrisy, other Americans were sympathetic. Rowan was later acquitted of criminal charges in the incident. He, like approximately 50 million other Americans, continues to possess a handgun.

This reflects another paradox in our society. On the one hand, many, if not most, Americans support handgun control. On the other hand, they feel that law-abiding citizens should have the right to possess a gun, at least inside their own homes, and to use it to protect themselves and their families. The argument is that weapons are needed for simple protection.

According to the FBI, out of the eight serious crimes that are Part I crimes of Index Offenses included in the Uniform Crime Reports, robbery, aggravated assault, murder, nonnegligent homicide, and forcible rape are violent crimes. Simple assault is the most common crime of violence, followed by aggravated assault, which is the use of or threat of a weapon to inflict bodily harm. Other than robbery, most violent crimes are not committed with a gun. Knives, fists, and blunt instruments are more likely to be the weapons of choice. Homicide is the least frequent form of assault in the United States.

However, for most years between 1960 and 1985, violent crimes increased as reported to the police. In the late 1970s and in the 1982–1984 period, there was a slight decrease, but between 1984 and 1985, there was an approximate 4 percent increase. There are about 500,000 violent crimes per year and just under 20,000 murders. The South has approximately 38 percent of the nation's assaults and 43 percent of its murders. Users of guns account for anywhere between 30 percent to 50 percent of these crimes.

The debate over gun control, specifically control of if not complete elimination of Saturday night specials, continues. These are inexpensive handguns that are used in many assaults, robberies, and murders. Josh Sugarmann of the National Coalition to Ban Handguns acknowledges that the issue is complex but still feels banning handguns is recommendable. In a rare example of a reversal of position within the social sciences, MIT sociologist James D. Wright decides that neither empirically nor morally can Americans demand of other Americans that they give up their handguns.

Do *you* own a handgun? Would you willingly give it up if a law were passed? If a burglar has been working your neighborhood, would you still forgo purchasing one? Would you be willing to be a close friend of someone who has handguns? Why or why not? Are folks with guns safer than those without them?

YES

Josh Sugarmann

THE NRA IS RIGHT:
BUT WE STILL NEED TO BAN HANDGUNS

One tenet of the National Rifle Association's faith has always been that handgun controls do little to stop criminals from obtaining handguns. For once, the NRA is right and America's leading handgun control organization is wrong. Criminals don't buy handguns in gun stores. That's why they're criminals. But it isn't criminals who are killing most of the 20,000 to 22,000 people who die from handguns each year. We are.

This is an ugly truth for a country that thinks of handgun violence as a "crime" issue and believes that it's somehow possible to separate "good" handguns (those in our hands for self-defense) from "bad" handguns (those in the hands of criminals).

Contrary to popular perception, the most prevalent form of handgun death in America isn't murder but suicide. Of the handgun deaths that occur each year, approximately 12,000 are suicides. An additional 1,000 fatalities are accidents. And of the 9,000 handgun deaths classified as murders, most are not caused by predatory strangers. Handgun violence is usually the result of people being angry, drunk, careless, or depressed—who just happen to have a handgun around. In all, fewer than 10 percent of handgun deaths are felony-related.

Though handgun availability is not a crime issue, it does represent a major public health threat. Handguns are the number one weapon for both murder and suicide and are second only to auto accidents as the leading cause of death due to injury. Of course there are other ways of committing suicide or crimes of passion. But no means is more lethal, effective, or handy. That's why the NRA is ultimately wrong. As several public health organizations have noted, the best way to curb a public health problem is through prevention—in this case, the banning of all handguns from civilian hands.

THE ENEMY IS US

For most who attempt suicide, the will to die lasts only briefly. Only one out of every ten people attempting suicide is going to kill himself no matter what. The success or failure of an attempt depends primarily on the lethality of the means. Pills, razor blades, and gas aren't guaranteed killers, and they take time. Handguns, however, lend themselves well to spontaneity. Consider that although women try to kill themselves four times as often as men, men succeed three to four times as often. For one reason: women use pills or less lethal means; men use handguns. This balance is shifting, however, as more women own or have access to handguns. Between 1970 and 1978 the suicide rate for young women rose 50 percent, primarily due to increased use of handguns.

Of course, there is no way to lock society's cupboard and prevent every distraught soul from injuring him or herself. Still, there are ways we can promote public safety without becoming a nation of nannies. England, for instance, curbed suicide by replacing its most common means of committing suicide—coal stove gas—with less toxic natural gas. Fifteen years after the switch, studies found that suicide rates had dropped and remained low, even though the number of suicide *attempts* had increased. "High suicide rates seem to occur where highly lethal suicidal methods are not only available, but also where they are culturally acceptable," writes Dr. Robert Markush of the University of Alabama, who has studied the use of handguns in suicide.

Most murders aren't crime-related, but are the result of arguments between friends and among families. In 1985, 59 percent of all murders were committed by people known to the victim. Only 15 percent were committed by strangers, and only 18 percent were the result of felonious activity. As the FBI admits every year in its *Uniform Crime Reports*, "murder is a societal problem over which law enforcement has little or no control." The FBI doesn't publish separate statistics on who's killing whom with handguns, but it is assumed that what is true of all murders is true of handgun murders.

CONTROLLING THE VECTOR

Recognizing that eliminating a disease requires prevention, not treatment, health professionals have been in the forefront of those calling for a national ban on handguns. In 1981, the Surgeon General's Select Panel for the Promotion of Child Health traced the "epidemic of deaths and injuries among children and youth" to handguns, and called for "nothing short of a total ban." It is estimated that on average, one child dies from handgun wounds each day. Between 1961 and 1981, according to the American Association of Suicidology, the suicide rate for 15- to 24-year-olds increased 150 percent. The report linked the rise in murders and suicides among the young to the increased use of firearms—primarily handguns. In a 1985 report, the Surgeon General's Workshop on Violence and Public Health recommended "a complete and universal ban on the sale, manufacture, importation, and possession of handguns (except for authorized police and military personnel)." . . .

Comparing the relationship between handguns and violence to mosquitos and malaria, Stephen P. Teret, co-director of the Johns Hopkins Injury Prevention Center, says, "As public health professionals, if we are faced with a disease that is carried by some type of vehicle/vector like a mosquito, our initial response would be to control the vector. There's no reason why if the vehicle/vector is a handgun, we should not be interested in controlling the handgun."

The NRA refers to handgun suicides, accidental killings, and murders by acquaintances as "the price of freedom." It believes that handguns right enough wrongs, stop enough crimes, and kill enough criminals to justify these deaths. But even the NRA has admitted that there is no "adequate measure that more lives are saved by arms in good hands than are lost by arms in evil hands." Again, the NRA is right.

A 1985 NCBH study found that a handgun is 118 times more likely to be used in a suicide, murder, or fatal accident than to kill a criminal. Between 1981 and 1983, nearly 69,000 Americans lost their lives to handguns. During that same period there were only 583 justifiable homicides reported to the FBI, in which someone used a handgun to kill a stranger—a burglar, rapist, or other criminal. In 1982, 19 states reported to the FBI that not once did a private citizen use a handgun to kill a criminal. Five states reported that more than 130 citizens were murdered with handguns for each time a handgun was justifiably used to kill a criminal. In no state did the number of self-defense homicides approach the murder toll. Last year, a study published in the *New England Journal of Medicine* analyzing gun use in the home over a six-year period in the Seattle, Washington area, found that for every time a firearm was used to kill an intruder in self-defense, 198 lives ended in murders, suicides, or accidents. Handguns were used in more than 70 percent of those deaths.

Although handguns are rarely used to kill criminals, an obvious question remains: How often are they used merely to wound or scare away intruders? No reliable statistics are available, but most police officials agree that in a criminal confrontation on the street, the handgun-toting civilian is far more likely to be killed or lose his handgun to a criminal than successfully use the weapon in self-defense. "Beyond any doubt, thousands more lives are lost every year because of the proliferation of handguns than are saved," says Joseph McNamara, chief of police of San Jose, who has also been police chief in Kansas City, a beat cop in Harlem, and is the author of a book on defense against violent crime. Moreover, most burglaries occur when homes are vacant, so the handgun in the drawer is no deterrent. (It would also probably be the first item stolen.)

Faced with facts like these, anti-control advocates often turn to the argument of last resort: the Second Amendment. But the historic 1981 Morton Grove, Illinois, ban on handgun sale and possession exploded that rationale. In 1983, the U.S. Supreme Court let stand a lower court ruling that stated, "Because the possession of handguns is not part of the right to keep and bear arms, [the Morton Grove ordinance] does not violate the Second Amendment."

CRIMINAL EQUIVOCATION

Unfortunately, powerful as the NRA is, it has received additional help from the leading handgun control group. Handgun Control Inc. (HCI) has helped the handgun lobby by setting up the perfect strawman for the NRA to shoot down.

"Keep handguns out of the wrong hands," HCI says. "By making it more difficult for criminals, drug addicts, etc., to get handguns, and by ensuring that law-abiding citizens know how to maintain their handguns, we can reduce handgun violence," it promises. Like those in the NRA, HCI chairman Nelson T. "Pete" Shields "firmly believe(s) in the right of law-abiding citizens to possess handguns . . . for legitimate purposes."

In its attempt to paint handgun violence solely as a crime issue, HCI goes so far as to sometimes ignore the weapon's non-crime death tally. In its most recent poster comparing the handgun murder toll in the U.S. with that of nations with strict handgun laws, HCI states: "In 1983, handguns killed 35 people in Japan, 8 in Great Britain, 27 in Switzerland, 6 in Canada, 7 in Sweden, 10 in Australia, and 9,014 in the United States." Handguns *killed* a lot more than that in the United States. About 13,000 suicides and accidents more.

HCI endorses a ban only on short-barrelled handguns (the preferred weapon of criminals). It advocates mandatory safety training, a waiting period during which a background check can be run on a purchaser, and a license to carry a handgun, with mandatory sentencing for violators. It also endorses mandatory sentencing for the use of a handgun in a crime. According to HCI communications director Barbara Lautman, together these measures would "attack pretty much the heart of the problem."

HCI appears to have arrived at its crime focus by taking polls. In his 1981 book, *Guns Don't Die—People Do*, Shields points out that the majority of Americans don't favor a ban on handguns. "What they do want, however, is a set of strict laws to control the easy access to handguns by the criminal and the violence prone—*as long as those controls don't jeopardize the perceived right of law-abiding citizens to buy and own handguns for self defense* [italics his]." Shields admits "this is not based on any naive hope that criminals will obey such laws. Rather, it is based on the willingness of the rest of us to be responsible and accountable citizens, and the knowledge that to the degree we are, we make it more difficult for the criminal to get a handgun." This wasn't always HCI's stand. Founded in 1974 as the National Council to Control Handguns, HCI originally called a ban on private handgun possession the "most effective" solution to reducing violent crime rapidly and was at one time a member of NCBH. Michael Beard, president of NCBH, maintains that HCI's focus on crime "started with a public relations concern. Some people in the movement felt Americans were worried about crime, and that was one way to approach the problem. That's the problem when you use public opinion polls to tell you what your position's going to be. And I think a lot of the handgun control movement has looked at whatever's hot at the time and tried to latch onto that, rather than sticking to the basic message that there is a relationship between the availability of handguns and the handgun violence in our society. . . . Ultimately, nothing short of taking the product off the market is really going to have an effect on the problem."

HCI's cops and robbers emphasis has been endlessly frustrating to many in the anti-handgun movement. HCI would offer handgun control as a solution to crime, and the NRA would effectively rebut their arguments with the commonsensical observation that criminals are not likely to obey such laws. I can't help but think that HCI's refusal to abandon the crime argument has harmed the longterm progress of the movement.

SATURATED DRESSER DRAWERS

In a nation with 40 million handguns—where anyone who wants one can get one—it's time to face a chilling fact. We're way past the point where registration, licensing, safety training, waiting periods, or mandatory sentencing are going to have much effect. Each of these measures may save some lives or help catch a few criminals, but none—by itself or taken together—will stop the vast majority of handgun suicides or murders. A "controlled" handgun kills just as effectively as an "uncontrolled" one.

Most control recommendations merely perpetuate the myth that with proper care a handgun can be as safe a tool as any other. Nothing could be further from the truth. A handgun is not a blender.

Those advocating a step-by-step process insist that a ban would be too radical and therefore unacceptable to Congress and the public. A hardcore 40 percent of the American public has always endorsed banning handguns. Many will also undoubtedly argue that any control measure—no matter how ill-conceived or ineffective—would be a good first step. But after more than a decade, the other foot hasn't followed.

In other areas of firearms control there has been increasing recognition that bans are the most effective solution. The only two federal measures passed since the Gun Control Act of 1968 have been bans. In each case, the reasoning was simple: the harm done by these objects outweighed any possible benefit they brought to society. In 1986, Congress banned certain types of armor-piercing "cop-killer" bullets. There was also a silver lining to last year's NRA-McClure-Volkmer handgun "decontrol" bill, which weakened the already lax Gun Control Act of 1968, making it legal, for instance, for people to transport unloaded, "not readily accessible" handguns interstate. A last-minute amendment added by pro-control forces banned the future production and sale of machine guns for civilian use.

Unfortunately, no law has addressed the major public health problem. Few suicides, accidental killings, or acquaintance murders are the result of cop-killer bullets or machine guns.

Outlawing handguns would in no way be a panacea. Even if handgun production stopped tomorrow, millions would remain in the dresser drawers of America's bedrooms—and many of them would probably stay there. Contrary to NRA fantasies, black-booted fascists would not be kicking down doors searching for handguns. Moreover, the absolute last segment of society to be affected by any measure would be criminals. The black market that has fed off the legal sale of handguns would continue for a long while. But by ending new handgun production, the availability of illegal handguns can only decrease.

Of course, someone who truly wants to kill himself can find another way. A handgun ban would not affect millions of rifles and shotguns. But experience shows that no weapon provides the combination of lethality and convenience that a handgun does. Handguns represent only 30 percent of all the guns out there but are responsible for 90 percent of firearms misuse. Most people who commit suicide with a firearm use a handgun. At minimum, a handgun ban would prevent the escalation of killings in segments of society that have not yet been saturated by handgun manufacturers. Further increases in suicides among women, for example, might be curtailed.

But the final solution lies in changing the way handguns and handgun violence are viewed by society. Public health campaigns have changed the way Americans look at cigarette smoking and drunk driving and can do the same for handguns.

For the past 12 years, many in the handgun control movement have confined their debate to what the public supposedly wants and expects to hear—not to reality. The handgun must be seen for what it is, not what we'd like it to be.

NO

James D. Wright

SECOND THOUGHTS
ABOUT GUN CONTROL

Gun control, it has been said, is the acid test of liberalism. All good liberals favor stricter gun controls. After all, doesn't the United States have the most heavily armed population on earth? Are we not the world's most violent people? Surely these facts must be causally connected. The apparently desperate need to "do something" about the vast quantity of firearms and firearms abuse is, to the good liberal, obvious.

At one time, it seemed evident to me, we needed to mount a campaign to resolve the crisis of handgun proliferation. Guns are employed in an enormous number of crimes in this country. In other countries with stricter gun laws, gun crime is rare. Many of the firearms involved in crime are cheap handguns, so-called Saturday Night Specials, for which no legitimate use or need exists. Many families buy these guns because they feel the need to protect themselves; eventually, they end up shooting one another. If there were fewer guns around, there would also be less crime and less violence. Most of the public also believes this, and has supported stricter gun control for as long as pollsters have been asking the question. Yet Congress has refused to act in a meaningful way, owing mainly to the all-powerful "gun lobby" headed by the National Rifle Association. Were the power of this lobby somehow effectively countered by the power of public opinion, stricter gun laws would follow quickly, and we would begin to achieve a safer and more civilized society.

When I first began research on the topic of private firearms, in the mid-1970s, I shared this conventional and widely held view of the issue. Indeed, much of it struck me as self-evidently true. My initial interest in the topic resulted from a life-long fascination with the bizarre: I certainly did not own a gun (I still don't), and neither, as far as I knew, did many of my friends. Still, readily available survey evidence showed that half the families in the United States did own one, and I wondered what unspeakable

From James D. Wright, "Second Thoughts About Gun Control," *Public Interest*, no. 91 (Spring 1988), pp. 23-39. Copyright © 1988 by National Affairs, Inc. Reprinted by permission of the author.

oddities or even pathologies an analysis of this half of the American population would reveal.

My first scholarly paper on the topic, "The Ownership of the Means of Destruction," appeared in 1975. This demographic comparison between gun-owning and non-gun-owning households revealed no shocking information. Gun owners, it turned out, were largely small-town and rural Protestants of higher-than-average income. Fear of crime, interestingly enough, did not seem to be related to gun ownership. The general tone of my piece remained unmistakably "anti-gun," but the findings did not provide much new information to strengthen the "anti-gun" lobby's arguments. At about the same time, I prepared a more polemical version of the paper, which was eventually published in the *Nation*. The General Counsel of the National Rifle Association described the piece as "emotionally supercharged drum-beating masquerading as scholarly analysis." Clearly, I was on the right track; I had managed to offend the right people.

The *Nation* article was abridged and reprinted in the Sunday Chicago *Tribune*, a newspaper read by about two million people, many of whom saw fit to write me after the piece appeared. Almost all the letters I received were provocative; some were very favorable, but most were vitriolic attacks from gun nuts. I was accused of being "incredibly biased," "strange and contradictory," of telling "many outright 100% lies," of being "sophistic" and "intellectually dishonest," of being "unable to grasp truth," and of taking "thousands of words to say *nothing* constructive." I answered every letter I received. In a few cases, a long and profitable correspondence developed. The

first wave of correspondence over the *Tribune* piece affirmed my assumption that many gun owners were crazy. Subsequent waves, however, convinced me that many were indeed thoughtful, intelligent, often remarkably well-read people who were passionately concerned about their "right to keep and bear arms," but were willing, nonetheless, to listen to reason.

Two years later, in 1977, my colleague Peter Rossi and I received a grant from the National Institute of Justice to undertake a comprehensive, critical overview of the research literature on guns, crime, and violence in America. The results of this overview were published in 1981 in a three-volume government report and in 1983 as a commercial monograph, entitled *Under the Gun*. Subsequent to this work, we received another grant to gather original data on gun acquisition, ownership, and use from about 2,000 men doing felony time in ten state prisons all over the United States. We assembled this information in a government report and later in a monograph, *Armed and Considered Dangerous*. The felon survey marked the temporary end of my firearms research program, one that ran roughly from 1974 through 1986, when *Armed and Considered Dangerous* was finally published.

As I have already suggested, at the outset of the research program I had a strong feeling that the pro-gun-control forces had never marshalled their evidence in the most compelling way, that they were being seriously undercut by the more artful polemics of the National Rifle Association and related pro-gun groups. That the best available evidence, critically considered, would eventually prove favorable to the pro-control viewpoint was not in serious doubt—at least not to me, not in the beginning.

In the course of my research, however, I have come to question nearly every element of the conventional wisdom about guns, crime, and violence. Indeed, I am now of the opinion that a compelling case for "stricter gun control" *cannot be made*, at least not on empirical grounds. I have nothing but respect for the various pro-gun-control advocates with whom I have come into contact over the past years. They are, for the most part, sensitive, humane, and intelligent people, and their ultimate aim, to reduce death and violence in our society, is one that every civilized person must share. I have, however, come to be convinced that they are barking up the wrong tree.

WHAT IS "GUN CONTROL"?

Before I describe the intellectual odyssey that led to my change in thinking, it is critical to stress that "gun control" is an exceedingly nebulous concept. To say that one favors gun control, or opposes it, is to speak in ambiguities. In the present-day American political context, "stricter gun control" can mean anything from federal registration of firearms, to mandatory sentences for gun use in crime, to outright bans on the manufacture, sale, or possession of certain types of firearms. One can control the manufacturers of firearms, the wholesalers, the retailers, or the purchasers; one can control the firearms themselves, the ammunition they require, or the uses to which they are put. And one can likewise control their purchase, their carrying, or their mere possession. "Gun control" thus covers a wide range of specific interventions, and it would be useful indeed if the people who say they favor or op-

pose gun control were explicit about what, exactly, they are for and against.

In doing the research for *Under the Gun*, I learned that there are approximately 20,000 gun laws of various sorts already on the books in the United States. A few of these are federal laws (such as the Gun Control Act of 1968), but most are state and local regulations. It is a misstatement to say, as pro-gun-control advocates sometimes do, that the United States has "no meaningful gun control legislation." The problem is not that laws do not exist but that the regulations in force vary enormously from one place to the next, or, in some cases, that the regulations carried on the books are not or cannot be enforced.

Much of the gun legislation now in force, whether enacted by federal, state, or local statutes, falls into the category of reasonable social precaution, being neither more nor less stringent than measures taken to safeguard against abuses of other potentially life-threatening objects, such as automobiles. It seems reasonable, for example, that people should be required to obtain a permit to carry a concealed weapon, as they are virtually everywhere in the United States. It is likewise reasonable that people not be allowed to own automatic weapons without special permission, and that felons, drug addicts, and other sociopaths be prevented from legally acquiring guns. Both these restrictions are in force everywhere in the United States, because they are elements of federal law. About three-fourths of the American population lives in jurisdictions where the registration of firearms purchases is required. It is thus apparent that many states and localities also find this to be a useful precaution against something. And many jurisdictions also require "waiting periods" or "cooling off" periods between application and actual possession of a new firearms purchase. These too seem reasonable, since there are very few legitimate purposes to which a firearm might be put that would be thwarted if the user had to wait a few days, or even a few weeks, to get the gun.

Thus, when I state that "a compelling case for 'stricter gun control' cannot be made," I do not refer to the sorts of obvious and reasonable precautions discussed above, or to related precautionary measures. I refer, rather, to measures substantially more strict than "reasonable precaution," and more specifically, to measures that would deny or seriously restrict the right of the general population to own a firearm, or that would ban the sale or possession of certain kinds of firearms, such as handguns or even the small, cheap handguns known colloquially as "Saturday Night Specials."

EFFECTS OF GUN LAWS

One wonders, with some 20,000 firearms regulations now on the books, why the clamor continues for even more laws. The answer is obvious: none of the laws so far enacted has significantly reduced the rate of criminal violence. *Under the Gun* reviewed several dozen research studies that had attempted to measure the effects of gun laws in reducing crime; none of them showed any conclusive long-term benefits.

As it happens, both sides of the gun-control debate grant this point; they disagree, though as to why there is no apparent connection between gun-control laws and crime rates. The NRA maintains that gun laws don't work because they can't work. Widely ignored

(especially by criminals) and unenforceable, gun-control laws go about the problem in the wrong way. For this reason, the NRA has long supported mandatory and severe sentences for the use of firearms in felonies, contending that we should punish firearms abusers once it is proven that an abuse has occurred, and leave legitimate users alone until they have actually done something illegal with their weapon.

The pro-control forces argue that gun laws don't work because there are too many of them, because they are indifferently enforced, and because the laws vary widely from one jurisdiction to the next. What we need, they would argue, are federal firearms regulations that are strictly enforced all across the nation. They would say that we have never given gun control a fair test, because we lack an aggressive *national* firearms policy. . . .

GUNS, CRIMES, AND NUMBERS

What is the annual firearms toll in this country? Our review of the data sources revealed that some components of the toll, especially the annual fatality count, are well known, whereas other components are not. In recent years, the total number of homicides occurring in the United States has been right around 20,000. Of these, approximately 60 percent are committed with firearms. There are somewhat fewer than 30,000 suicides committed in an average recent year, of which about half involve a firearm. Deaths from firearms accidents have represented about 2 percent of the total accidental deaths in the nation for as long as data have been collected, and add about 2,000 deaths per year to the toll.

Taken together, then, there are about 30,000 deaths from firearms in an average year; this amounts to some 1–2 percent of all deaths from any cause.

Both camps in the gun control war like to spew out exaggerated rhetoric. In the case of gun deaths, the anti-control forces shout that the total deaths due to firearms in a year are less than the deaths due to automobile accidents (about 50,000)—"but nobody wants to ban cars!" To counter, the pro-control people express the gun toll as a number of deaths per unit of time. The resulting figure is dramatic: on average, someone in the United States dies from a firearm every seventeen or eighteen minutes.

Death is not the whole story, of course. One must also include non-fatal but injurious firearms accidents, crimes other than homicide or suicide committed with guns, unsuccessful suicide attempts involving firearms, and so on. None of these things is known with much precision, and the lack of firm data is an invitation to exuberant formulations on both sides. Still, reasonable compromise values for the various components suggest a total incident count of fewer than a million per year—that is, incidents in which a firearm of some sort was involved in some way in some kind of violent or criminal incident (intentional or accidental, fatal or not). Pro-gun people have dismissed this estimate as much too high, and anti-gun people have dismissed it as much too low, so I figure it can't be too far off.

When we shift to the guns side of the "guns and crime" equation, the numbers jump by a few orders of magnitude, although here, too, some caution is needed. In the course of the twentieth century, so far as can be told, some 250 million total firearms (excluding military weapons) have been manufactured in or imported into the United States. Published guesses about the number of guns in private hands in this country run upwards to a billion—an absurd and inconceivably large estimate. Most of the published estimates are produced by advocates and thus are not to be trusted, most of all since both sides have vested interests in publishing the largest possible numbers: the pro-gun people, to show the vast number of people whose rights would be infringed by stricter gun controls; the anti-gun people, to show the obvious urgency of the situation.

It is not known for certain how many of the 250 million guns of the twentieth century remain in private hands; 150 million is a sensible guess. Survey evidence dating from at least 1959 routinely shows that about 50 percent of all American households possess at least one firearm, with the average number owned (among those owning at least one) being just over three. Whatever the exact number, it is obvious that there are lots and lots of guns out there—many tens of millions at the very least. . . .

The numbers do speak clearly to at least one point: if we are going to try to "control" guns as a means of controlling crime, then we are going to have to deal with the guns already in private hands; controls over new purchases alone will not suffice. Taking the highest plausible value for the number of gun incidents—1 million per year—and the lowest plausible value for the number of guns presently owned—say, 100 million—we see rather quickly that the guns now owned exceed the annual incident count by a factor of at least a hundred; in other words, the existing stock is adequate to supply all conceivable nefarious purposes for at least the next century.

These figures can be considered in another way. Suppose we did embark on a program of firearms confiscation, with the ultimate aim of achieving a "no guns" condition. We would have to confiscate at least a hundred guns to get just one gun that, in any typical year, would be involved in any kind of gun incident; several hundred to get just one that would otherwise be involved in a chargeable gun crime; and several thousand to get just one that would otherwise be used to bring about someone's death. Whatever else one might want to say about such a policy, it is not very efficient.

DEMAND CREATES ITS OWN SUPPLY

One of the favorite aphorisms of the pro-gun forces is that "if guns are outlawed, only outlaws will have guns." Sophisticated liberals laugh at this point, but they shouldn't. No matter what laws we enact, they will be obeyed only by the law-abiding—this follows by definition. If we were to outlaw, say, the ownership of handguns, millions of law-abiding handgun owners would no doubt turn theirs in. But why should we expect the average armed robber or street thug to do likewise? Why should we expect felons to comply with a gun law when they readily violate laws against robbery, assault, and murder?

For the average criminal, a firearm is an income-producing tool with a consequent value that is several times its initial cost. According to data published by Phillip Cook of Duke University, the average "take" in a robbery committed with a firearm is more than $150 (in 1976 dollars) and is three times the take for a robbery committed with any other weapon; the major reason for the difference is that criminals with guns rob more lucrative targets. Right now, one can acquire a handgun in any major American city in a matter of a few hours for roughly $100. Even if the street price of handguns tripled, a robber armed with a handgun could (on the average) recoup his entire capital outlay in the first two or three transactions.

As long as there are *any* handguns around (and even "ban handgun" advocates make an exception for police or military handguns), they will obviously be available to anyone *at some price*. Given Cook's data, the average street thug would come out well ahead even if he spent several hundred—perhaps even a few thousand—on a suitable weapon. At those prices, demand will always create its own supply: just as there will always be cocaine available to anyone willing to pay $200 a gram for it, so too will handguns always be available to anyone willing to pay a thousand dollars to obtain one.

The more militant "ban handgun" advocates urge what is easily recognized as the handgun equivalent of Prohibition. Why would we expect the outcome of "handgun prohibition" to differ from its 1920s predecessor? A black market in guns, run by organized crime, would almost certainly spring up to service the demand. It is, after all, no more difficult to manufacture a serviceable firearm in one's basement than to brew up a batch of home-made gin. Afghani tribesmen, using wood fires and metal-working equipment much inferior to what can be ordered from a Sears catalogue, hand-manufacture rifles that fire the Russian AK-47 cartridge. Do we ascribe less ability to the Mafia or the average do-it-yourselfer? . . .

CRIMES OF PASSION

Sophisticated advocates on both sides by now grant most of the preceding points. No one still expects "stricter gun control" to solve the problem of hard-core criminal violence, or even make a dent in it. Much of the argument has thus shifted toward violence perpetrated not for economic gain, or for any other good reason, but rather in the "heat of the moment"—the so-called "crimes of passion" that turn injurious or lethal not so much because anyone intended them to, but because, in a moment of rage, a firearm was at hand. Certainly, we could expect incidents of this sort to decline if we could somehow reduce the availability of firearms for the purpose. Or could we?

Crimes of passion certainly occur, but how often? Are "heat of the moment" homicides common or rare? The fact is, nobody knows. . . .

The "crime of passion" most often discussed is that of family members killing one another. One pertinent study, conducted in Kansas City, looked into every family homicide that occurred in a single year. In 85 percent of the cases examined, the police had previously (within the prior five years) been called to the family residence to break up a domestic quarrel; in half the cases, the police had been there five or more times. It would therefore be misleading to see these homicides as isolated and unfortunate outbursts occurring among normally placid and loving individuals. They are, rather, the culminating episodes of an extended history of violence and abuse among the parties.

Analysis of the family homicide data reveals an interesting pattern. When women kill men, they often use a gun. When men kill women, they usually do it in some more degrading or brutalizing way—such as strangulation or knifing. The reason for the difference seems obvious: although the world is full of potentially lethal objects, almost all of them are better suited to male than to female use. The gun is the single exception: all else held constant, it is equally deadly in anyone's hands. Firearms equalize the means of physical terror between men and women. In denying the wife of an abusive man the right to have a firearm, we may only be guaranteeing her husband the right to beat her at his pleasure. One argument against "stricter gun control" is thus that a woman should have as much right to kill her husband as a man has to kill his wife.

Some will gasp at this statement; no one, after all, has a "right" to kill anyone. But this, of course, is false: every jurisdiction in the United States recognizes justifiable homicides in at least some extenuating circumstances, and increasingly a persistent and long-standing pattern of physical abuse is acknowledged to be one of them. True, in the best of all possible worlds, we would simply do away with whatever gives rise to murderous rage. This is not, regrettably, the world in which we live. . . .

THE SATURDAY NIGHT SPECIAL

The notorious Saturday Night Special has received a great deal of attention. The term is used loosely: it can refer to a gun of low price, inferior quality, small caliber, short barrel length, or some combination of these. The attention is typically justified on two grounds: first, these guns have no legitimate sport or recreational use, and secondly, they are the firearms preferred by criminals.

Thus, the argument goes, we could just ban them altogether; in doing so, we would directly reduce the number of guns available to criminals without restricting anyone's legitimate ownership rights.

The idea that the Saturday Night Special is the criminal's gun of choice turns out to be wrong. Our felon survey showed, overwhelmingly, that serious criminals both prefer to carry and actually do carry relatively large, big-bore, well-made handguns. Indeed, not more than about one in seven of these criminals' handguns would qualify as small and cheap. Most of the felons wanted to be and actually were at least as well armed as their most likely adversaries, the police. There may well be good reason to ban Saturday Night Specials, but the criminal interest in such weapons is not one of them. Most serious felons look on the Saturday Night Special with considerable contempt.

It is too early to tell how these data will be interpreted among "Ban Saturday Night Special" advocates. The most recent wrinkle I have encountered is that they should be banned not because they are preferred or used by criminals, but because, being cheap, they tend to be owned by unknowledgeable, inexperienced, or irresponsible people. One may assume that cheap handguns, like cheap commodities of all sorts, tend to be owned by poor people. The further implication—that poor gun owners are less knowledgeable, experienced, or responsible than more affluent owners—has, however, never been researched; it is also the sort of "elitist" argument that ordinarily arouses liberal indignation.

What about the other side of the argument—that these guns have no legitimate use? It is amazing how easily people who know little about guns render such judgments. When I commenced my own research, it occurred to me that I ought to find out what gun owners themselves had to say on some of these matters. So I picked up the latest issues of about a half-dozen gun magazines. It is remarkable how informative this simple exercise turned out to be.

One magazine that surfaced is called *Handgunning*, which is specifically for devotees of handgun sports. Every issue of the magazine is full of articles on the sporting and recreational uses of handguns of all kinds. I learned, for example, that people actually hunt game with handguns, which never would have occurred to me. In reading a few articles, the reason quickly became obvious: it is more sporting than hunting with shoulder weapons, and it requires much more skill, which makes a successful handgun hunt a much more satisfying accomplishment.

In my journey through this alien turf, I came upon what are called "trail guns" or "pack guns." These are handguns carried outdoors, in the woods or the wilds, for no particular reason except to have a gun available "just in case" one encounters unfriendly fauna, or gets lost and needs small game for food, or is injured and needs to signal for help. The more I read about trail guns, the more it seemed that people who spend a lot of time alone in the wilds, in isolated and out-of-the-way places, are probably being pretty sensible in carrying these weapons.

One discussion went on in some detail about the characteristics to look for in a trail gun. It ought to be small and light, of course, for the same reason that serious backpackers carry nylon rather than canvas tents. "Small and light" implies small caliber. . . . And suddenly it dawned on me: the small, low-caliber, short-barreled, imported, not-too-expensive guns the article was describing were what are otherwise known as Saturday Night Specials. And thus I came to learn that we cannot say that Saturday Night Specials have "no legitimate sport or recreational use."

It would be sophistic to claim that most Saturday Night Specials are purchased for use as trail guns; my point is only that some are. Most small, cheap handguns are probably purchased by persons of modest means to protect themselves against crime. It is arguable whether protection against crime is a "legitimate" or "illegitimate" use; the issues involved are too complex to treat fairly in this article. It is worth stressing, however, that poor, black, central-city residents are by far the most likely potential victims of crime; if self-protection justifies owning a gun, then a ban on small, cheap handguns would effectively deny the means of self-protection to those most evidently in need of it.

There is another argument against banning small, cheap handguns: a ban on Saturday Night Specials would leave heavy-duty handguns available as substitute weapons. It is convenient to suppose that in the absence of small, cheap handguns, most people would just give up and not use guns for whatever they had in mind. But certainly some of them, and perhaps many of them, would move up to bigger and better handguns instead. We would do well to remember that the most commonly owned handgun in America today is a .38 caliber double-action revolver, the so-called Police Special that functions as the service revolver for about 90 percent of American police. If we somehow got rid of all the junk handguns, how many thugs, assailants, and assassins would choose to use this gun, or other guns like it, instead? And what consequences might we then anticipate?

The handgun used by John Hinckley in his attack on President Reagan was a .22 caliber revolver, a Saturday Night Special. Some have supported banning the Saturday Night Special so as to thwart psychopaths in search of weapons. But would a psychopath intent on assassinating a President simply give up in the absence of a cheap handgun? Or would he, in that event, naturally pick up some other gun instead? Suppose he did pick up the most commonly owned handgun available in the United States, the .38 Special. Suppose further that he got off the same six rounds and inflicted the same wounds that he inflicted with the .22. A .38 slug entering Jim Brady's head where the .22 entered would, at the range in question, probably have killed him instantly. The Washington policeman would not have had a severed artery but would have been missing the larger part of his neck. The round deflected from its path to President Reagan's heart might have reached its target. One can readily imagine at least three deaths, including the President's, had Hinkley fired a more powerful weapon.

POSTSCRIPT

Will Gun Control Reduce Crime?

In the fall of 1988, citizens in Maryland voted by a wide margin for handgun controls in that state. This vote was in spite of the fantastically heavy lobbying by the National Rifle Association and other pro-gun groups. In the same fall election, the people of Nebraska turned out to amend their state constitution so that individuals could continue to have the right to possess firearms. Probably less than two-thirds of all Americans would support a total ban on guns. Yet there seems little doubt that concern with crime, especially street crimes committed with firearms, continues to be a top priority for Americans—at least 80 percent support automatic criminal sanctions for any crime committed with a gun.

For a discussion of the effectiveness of gun control laws, see J. Wright and P. Rossi's, *Armed and Considered Dangerous: A Survey of Felons and Their Firearms* (Aldine De Gruther, 1986); D. McDowall, B. Wiserema, and C. Loftin's "Did Mandatory Firearm Ownership in Kennesaw Really Prevent Burglaries?" *Sociology and Social Research* (October 1989); and F. Zimring's "The Problem of Assault Firearms," *Crime and Delinquency* (May 1989).

On gun control and public sentiment, see "The Arms Race in Your Own Back Yard," *U.S. News and World Report* (April 4, 1988); "Furor Over Fire Arms," by R. Dolphin, *Macleans* (January 9, 1989); "The NRA Comes Under the Gun," *Newsweek* (March 21, 1989); "The Other Arms Race," by G. J. Church, *Time* (February 6, 1989); and "Under Fire: The NRA," by R. Lacayo, *Time* (January 29, 1990).

To clarify the historical roots of American's attachment to firearms as well as the ongoing empirical research, see W. R. Tonso's, *Guns and Society: The Social and Existential Roots of the American Attachment to Firearms* (University Press of America, 1982). For an elaboration of gun control policy, see P. Shields's *Guns Don't Die, People Do* (Arbor House, 1981); Tony Lesce's "Is Gun Control the Answer?" *Law Enforcement News* (January 12, 1988); and "Gun Control and Rates of Firearms Violence in Canada and the U.S.," by R. J. Mundt, *Canadian Journal of Criminology* (January 1990).

A different conceptualization of the debate is M. Bijefeld's "How Others Restrict Firearms" versus G. M. Gottlieb's "Better Crime Control Will Save More Lives," in *USA Today* (June 21, 1990). For research findings that sadden, see Lois Fingerhut and J. Kleinman's *Firearm Mortality Among Children and Youth* (U.S. National Center for Health Statistics, 1989).

ISSUE 16

Are Drug Arrests of Pregnant Women Discriminatory?

YES: Wendy K. Mariner, Leonard H. Glantz, and George J. Annas, from "Pregnancy, Drugs and the Perils of Prosecution," *Criminal Justice Ethics* (Winter/Spring 1990)

NO: Paul A. Logli, from "Drugs in the Womb: The Newest Battlefield in the War on Drugs," *Criminal Justice Ethics* (April 1990)

ISSUE SUMMARY

YES: Boston University professors W. K. Mariner, L. H. Glantz, and G. J. Annas flatly reject prosecuting drug-abusing pregnant women. They cite the difficulty of ascertaining a causal relationship between drug abuse and specific harm to neonates and argue that such prosecution only adds to the existing discrimination these women face and that they need massive hospital and social service assistance, not legal harassment.

NO: Winnebago County, Illinois, state's attorney Paul A. Logli argues that, since our society already has laws to protect the unborn, these laws should be used to punish women who abuse a fetus—including drug-taking pregnant women—and he calls for new laws to control their substance abuse and for more services to assist them.

Forty years ago, doctors assumed that a fetus was almost hermetically sealed within the mother's womb, which made it basically impervious to outside influences. Now it is known that substances in the mother's body get quickly passed to the fetus. These include the effects of smoking, drinking, and substance abuse. One well-known result, documented for several years, is fetal alcohol syndrome; the newborn is sickly, frequently premature, and often mentally retarded.

Recently in many urban area hospitals but especially in New York City and Baltimore, medical staff have been inundated with "crack babies." These are neonates born of crack-using mothers. Their physical and mental retardation is now well known. AIDS is becoming another tragic factor for babies born of mothers exposed to the disease through IV drug abuse. An apparently growing number of these babies are being abandoned by their mothers. Annual costs for hospital and medical care are sometimes more than $100,000 per infant, and the social costs for the rest of society are also staggering.

Crack babies and their mothers have become a social dilemma. Most of the babies are "illegitimate," the majority are black, and they are all by definition addicted to drugs. Moral crusaders warn that those who survive to adulthood run a high risk of being both criminal victims and offenders, a prime reason for instituting "get tough" social programs: These mothers should be arrested not only for substance abuse but for baby neglect as well, some maintain.

Others worry that the "attack" on crack-using mothers is yet another abuse of impoverished teenage females and is also a blatant attempt to restore male hegemony. They link the recent efforts at the federal and state levels to reverse *Rowe v. Wade* (the 1973 decision permitting abortions) with efforts to prosecute pregnant mothers. Both actions are seen as efforts to control women and what they may do with their bodies.

However, police, judges, district attorneys and others who feel that society has a responsibility to protect defenseless babies dismiss these concerns. They argue that a law against abortion and a law against a pregnant woman's endangering the fetus are completely separate issues and insist that there are no conspiracies against either women or ethnic and racial minorities.

While laws attempting to control women as well as laws against substance abuse are hardly new, linking the two as a societal and legal attempt to prevent harm to fetuses is novel. Presently, the practical policy consequences of such legal actions are highly problematic. Would such legal crackdowns, regardless of their fairness, be part of a solution or add to the problem of fetal endangerment from drug abuse?

Does the state have the right to punish pregnant women for their lifestyle? Can society do nothing about the thousands of babies born into such agony because of alleged negligence? Does the concept of "punishment" of a pregnant woman who makes such unhealthy choices have a place in a civilized world?

YES

Wendy K. Mariner,
Leonard H. Glantz,
and George J. Annas

PREGNANCY, DRUGS, AND THE PERILS OF PROSECUTION

In the war on drugs an offensive has been launched against pregnant women who use drugs. Over the past four years, prosecuting attorneys have been indicting women who use drugs while pregnant. In South Carolina alone, eighteen women who allegedly took drugs during pregnancy were indicted last summer for criminal neglect of a child or distribution of drugs to a minor. In the only successful prosecution so far, Jennifer Johnson was convicted in Florida for delivering illegal drugs to a minor via the umbilical cord in the moment after her child was born and before the cord was clamped. No one seriously maintains that the transitory "delivery" was the conduct on trial. Rather, the crime was the mother's use of illegal drugs during pregnancy. But the indictment contorted the statute's prohibition against drug "delivery" to characterize as criminal the kind of conduct that could not have been considered within its scope by the enacting legislation.

No new law had been passed making it a special criminal offense to use drugs during pregnancy. Rather, the prosecutions have been based on obviously strained interpretations of existing law, such as child endangerment or delivery of drugs to a minor. Since both drug use and criminal laws prohibiting sale, distribution, or possession of drugs have been with us for decades, why should prosecuting attorneys be searching the statute books today for creative ways to prosecute pregnant women who use drugs? The answer may lie in a peculiar confluence of changing attitudes toward pregnancy and drug use. Public attitudes are pro-natalist in the broad sense of supporting efforts to overcome infertility and to have children. Advances in medical technology have produced new methods for detecting and sometimes correcting fetal abnormalities, which enables us to think of fetuses as "patients" separately from their mothers. Public health studies have found that pregnant women can have a positive impact on the outcome

From Wendy K. Mariner, Leonard H. Glantz, and George J. Annas, "Pregnancy, Drugs, and the Perils of Prosecution," *Criminal Justice Ethics*, vol. 9, no. 1 (Winter/Spring 1990), pp. 30-39. Copyright © 1990 by W. K. Mariner, L. H. Glantz, and G. J. Annas. Reprinted by permission. Some notes omitted.

of their pregnancies through prenatal care, improved nutrition, and the avoidance of teratogenic or toxic substances like alcohol and drugs. This had led to a close scrutiny of the behavior of pregnant women. Finally, the war on illegal drugs announced by the Reagan Administration has spurred intense publicity about the dangers of drug use and has tended to legitimize virtually any action to suppress drugs. Indeed, the civil liberties of individuals are often seen as a hindrance to winning the "war." Media reports of increases in the number of infants born with traces of drugs in their systems have linked the horrors of drugs with our concern for healthy babies.

The influence of changing knowledge and values has led us to see the mother as responsible for many ills that befall her newborn. If she did not receive prenatal care, ate poorly, drank too much, or took drugs, she is assumed to be the cause of any injury to the baby—she is a bad mother. It is easy to feel outrage at the behavior that seems avoidable and that risks injury to a newborn. So it is understandable that many have argued for controlling women to protect a fetus. Few would argue that a pregnant woman has no moral responsibility to her developing fetus. However, violation of this moral responsibility not to harm is being tranformed into a punishable crime.

Prosecuting women for prenatal drug use offers immediate and visible action against an identifiable "wrongdoer." It is always a news story. Unable to make significant inroads against drug traffickers, prosecutors can appear to take a strong stand against illegal drugs and for protecting children. The alternatives— intercepting the drug supply, finding effective treatment for drug dependency, and providing drug treatment programs—are tedious, expensive, and rarely newsworthy.

No one really disagrees that drug use, among other things, risks jeopardizing fetal health, and that, ideally, such drug use should be eliminated. The question is who should be responsible for, and who will be effective in, taking steps to protect fetal health—the public health community or the criminal justice system?

This article examines the assumptions that underlie current prosecutions of pregnant women who use drugs. It argues that the professed goals of such prosecutions cannot be achieved through the criminal law. The offense that pregnant women are thought to commit cannot be defined in terms of any intelligble duty enforceable by the criminal law. Prosecuting pregnant women for drug use is unlikely to alter the spread of drugs or the health prospects of children. Instead, it is likely to threaten the rights of women as autonomous individuals and, ultimately, the future of their children.

THE GOAL OF PROSECUTION

Most prosecutors argue that their actions are not intended to punish women. For example, one prosecutor was reported to say, "We are not really interested in convicting women and sending them to jail. We're just interested in getting them to stop using drugs before they do something horrible to their babies."[1] If the goal is to stop drug use, there is no need to resort to rationalizations about protecting the fetus in order to prosecute. In virtually all states, the manufacture, delivery, or possession of controlled substances (illicit drugs) is already a criminal offense. This applies to everyone, not just pregnant women. Women are not immune from prosecution for these crimes merely because they are pregnant. Few pregnant women, however, are involved in drug trafficking. At most they might be guilty of illegal drug possession. Yet because they are not ordinarily discovered until their children are born and drug metabolites are found in the newborn's system, there is not likely to be proof sufficient to permit a conviction for the offense of possession. Thus, as a practical matter, pregnant women are not likely to be successfully prosecuted for drug possession.

Drug use, by itself, is not ordinarily a criminal offense, largely because of the difficulty of proof and because offenders can ordinarily be charged with possession. Moreover, if drug use results in harm to another person, such as an assault, the undesirable behavior is ordinarily proscribed by another criminal statute, such as that making assault a criminal offense. In such cases, however, the prosecution is limited to the crime of assault, independent of drug use. Thus, drug use that results in harm to a fetus cannot be prosecuted unless either drug use alone or harm to the fetus by itself is an independent crime. If neither is punishable as a crime, their co-existence should not constitute a crime. If drug use alone is not a criminal offense, then what is being punished is the status of being pregnant. This makes pregnancy a necessary element of a remarkable new criminal offense: pregnancy by a drug-dependent person, or drug use by a pregnant woman. . . .

Pregnancy is symbolic of the continuation of the human race. For individuals, it is, ideally, a time of joy, of preparing for an expanded family. It involves nurturing and growth. To convert it into a symbol of woman as threat is likely to profoundly affect the way society views women in general and to transform pregnant women from nurturers into suspects.

The justifications for wanting to stop pregnant women from taking drugs have to do with preventing harm to the fetus and insuring the birth of a health[y] baby. This raises several questions. What is the harm to be prevented? What acts or omissions cause the harm? What kind of duty can a pregnant woman have to prevent the harm? Can the duty be enforced and the harm prevented by prosecuting pregnant women under the criminal law?

DUTY

Criminal prosecutions of women's conduct during pregnancy assume that women have a special duty to the fetus. But precisely what is this duty? And what qualifies as a violation of the duty? General discussions of the subject appear to assume that women have a legal duty not to *harm* the fetus. . . .

One of the truisms of criminal law is that it exists to prevent harm. What is the harm to be prevented in the case of pregnant women who use drugs? The most extreme case of harm would be the death of the fetus. Criminal law governing killing a fetus is already in place. In most states, homicide can be committed against the fetus, but only if it dies after live birth. . . . There are good reasons why the criminal law has treated feticide differently from homicide. The harm ordinarily sought to be prevented is that directed against the pregnant woman herself. Ascribing legal personhood to fetuses for purposes of applying homicide laws would unnecessarily subject most stillbirths to criminal investigation. It could also create two independent rights-holders within the body of one pregnant woman—the woman and the fetus—with controversial implications for both criminal and civil law that society has not yet agreed on and is not likely soon to accept. . . .

[T]here is the problem of determining the cause of any harm. The physical and mental status of a child is affected by a multitude of [f]actors, some genetic, some gestational, some perinatal, some environmental in the postnatal period, many unknown. Many of these lie outside a woman's control, such as her genetic contribution to the child or her exposure to rubella or toxic air pollutants. How is the state or anyone else to know whether and when a crime has been committed? Must every birth with an Apgar score of less than 10 be investigated? There is no general duty to produce a perfect or even a healthy or "normal" child. Thus, this cannot be the duty that pregnant women are said to violate. Moreover, any general duty to perform or refrain from specific acts that harm the fetus in some clearly identifiable way would be derivative of a more general duty not to harm the fetus.

Interestingly, few prosecutions of drug-using women have demonstrated that a drug actually caused harm to a newborn. The offense that is prosecuted is not the materialization of harm at birth. It is the conduct that exposes the child to risk. This conduct takes place during pregnancy, not after birth. This suggests that it is not enough to avoid harm. The duty implied is really a duty to prevent any *risk* of harm. Since the fetus is integrally connected to the pregnant woman, preventing risks of harm to the fetus requires caring for the woman's body or at least preventing harm to her. Thus, the woman's duty to the fetus is necessarily a duty to protect her own body, for she cannot take proper care of the fetus unless she cares properly for her own body. This duty to prevent risk to the fetus amounts to imposing on a pregnant woman a state-defined standard of care for her own body, or conduct toward herself. It is noteworthy that while the state justifies its prosecutions on the basis of its interest in protecting the fetus, it does not undertake any duty to ensure the necessary care for the woman's body. Instead, it imposes that duty on the pregnant woman. . . .

CAUSATION

The evidence that drug use harms the fetus is suggestive but problematic as a basis for criminal offense. The harmful effects of heroin and alcohol when taken frequently in very large quantities are well known. Yet a surprising number of children of substance abusers escape damage. For example, the Public Health Services has estimated that 86 percent of women drink at least once during pregnancy, with 20 to 35 percent drinking regularly. Most of their children are born quite healthy. Alcohol appears to be teratogenic only if used on a few specific days of gestation. Different substances have different effects on the fetus at different times during pregnancy. For example, significant damage to organs generally occurs early in pregnancy; birth weight problems happen later; there is still uncertainty about when brain damage can occur. Given the difficulties in estimating gestation in general, how are we to know whether a particular substance caused a particular harm in one infant?

The evidence with respect to cocaine use is still being accumulated. Women who use cocaine have newborns with low birth weight (5.5. pounds or less), reduced head circumference, some congenital malformations, and an increased risk of premature birth and of *abruptio placentae* resulting in stillbirth. However, cocaine's precise contribution to these and other risks remains uncertain and under study. The effect of occasional as opposed to regular heavy use is unclear. Studies indicate that the health of women who used cocaine during pregnancy is often impaired by other factors, such as poor nutrition and the use of alcohol, cigarettes, marijuana, and other drugs. Some researchers studied only poor minority women, who typically have poorer prenatal health than the general population. Poverty, poor nutrition, lack of prenatal care, and even stress adversely affect fetal development. One of the most important determinants of low birth weight (itself a major risk factor for infant mortality) is inadequate prenatal care. Thus, drug use may not be the primary determinant of poor birth outcomes. Stopping drug use during pregnancy will not guarantee a healthy baby. Continued drug use does not always cause damage. Moreover, the long-term effects of drug use are still under study. The degree to which children who are born prematurely, or with low birth weight or small head size, are actually prejudiced in their development remains to be seen. Caretaking and their environment contribute significantly to their developmental functioning.

Women who use drugs typically are beset with problems in addition to substance abuse—from lack of housing and income to family difficulties—that contribute to poor birth outcomes. Yet, when a bad outcome occurs, it is easier to blame it on a drug the women took during pregnancy than to recognize the constellation of possible causes. As a practical matter, it seems almost impossible to satisfy the standard of proof of causation in a criminal prosecution, given the complexity of fetal development and the multiplicity of factors that affect it. While drug use is certainly a risk factor, focusing on drugs draws attention away from the much more global problem of inadequate prenatal care.

SOURCES OF HARM

If harm is what is to be prevented, then the source of the harm should not matter. Anything that causes serious harm should be the subject of prosecution. Women who fail to get adequate prenatal care or proper nourishment should be prosecuted. This approach was used in California when Pamela Rae Stewart's baby died six weeks after birth. She was prosecuted not just for taking amphetamines but also for disregarding her physician's advice to refrain from sex with her husband and to get to the hospital at the first sign of bleeding. The court dismissed the criminal action on the grounds that the child support statute under which it was brought was not intended to apply to refusals to follow physician's orders. Amending the statute to prohibit pregnant women from having sex with their husbands might protect some fetuses from harm but would be seen by most people as an outrageous violation of liberty.

A recent study compared the neurological development of children born prematurely whose heart rates were monitored electronically before and during delivery with children (also born prematurely) whose heart rates were checked periodically by auscultation of "listening" through the pregnant woman's abdomen. Children who were monitored with state-of-the-art electronic fetal monitors had cerebral palsy 2.9 times as often as children monitored by ordinary auscultation. After adjustment for other risk factors, the risk of cerebral palsy was 3.8 higher for the electronically monitored children than the other group. Does this mean that the use of electronic fetal monitors is or should be a criminal offense? Such a law would merely require women and physicians to avoid using something that creates a risk of fetal harm.

Variations in medical practice should make us wary of relying on current medical standards as ideal pregnancy care. Over the decades, women have been alternately praised and chastised for gaining more than ten pounds during pregnancy. Attitudes toward giving birth outside the hospital have varied from acceptance as normal to rejection as dangerous or crazy. A former president of a state chapter of the American College of Obstetrics and Gynecology reportedly said that people who have home births are "kooks, the lunatic fringe, people who have emotional problems they're acting out." Physicians in Alaska even requested the attorney general to charge a physician with murder after a baby died following a home birth he attended. Such incidents are reminders of the fallibility of medical opinion and how quick some are to equate unfashionable conduct with crime.

There is little doubt that drug use during pregnancy presents a risk of harm to the fetus. But it is hardly the only risk. How are we to distinguish the harm from drug use from harm arising from poor nourishment during infancy and childhood, from poor parenting practices such as emotional detachment, excessive discipline, or lack of supervision? What kind of duty will prevent such similar harms? Should we require a license to have children, as some have suggested, obtainable upon proof of adequate parenting capabilities? How will we define these? Can they be predicted before one has a child?

The duty pregnant women who use drugs are assumed to have cannot, in fact, be explained in terms of the harm to the fetus or child or even risk of harm. Harm can be caused by more than just drug use. Thus, the duty cannot be justified by the desire to prevent the harm itself. It must be justified, if at all, by the need to proscribe specific drug use that causes harm that does not result from other sources. The only distinction between cases of possible harm to a child from drug use and cases of harm arising from alcohol, tobacco, malnutrition, lack of prenatal care, and physical trauma is the assumed source of the harm—the drugs. The duty that is really imposed here is the duty not to use drugs, a duty that may already exist regardless of pregnancy. If the real concern is to avoid fetal harm, there is no principled way to distinguish between harm caused by drugs and harm caused by these other avoidable factors, and, therefore, no principled way to limit prosecutions to drug using pregnant women.

But, it might be argued, the harm from drug use can be singled out because drug use is already illegal in some states or could be made unlawful. Certainly drug use could be prosecuted as an offense. But its illegality does not distinguish it from other risks of harm to a fetus. Anyone—male or female—could be prosecuted for illegal drug use. Prosecuting *only* pregnant women for drug use requires a justification beyond illegality based on harm to the fetus that other risk factors do not create.

DUTY TO WHOM?

The idea of a duty raises the additional question of to whom the duty is owed. If the law is criminal, then the duty is owed to the state. This transforms any normal desire to avoid harm to the fetus into an obligation to the government. . . .

Children who are abused can be removed from parental custody because they are physically separate persons. "Fetal abuse," however, cannot be stopped without physically intervening on the mother, or at the least, seriously restricting her liberty. As long as the two are physiologically united, such an intervention subordinates the woman to the fetus. The concept of fetal abuse can be justified only by granting to the fetus rights of an independent live-born person and denying such rights to the woman. Pregnant women would be treated as chattel, as inert "fetal containers." Even temporary denial of the rights of personhood to women is incompatible with the fundamental principles of individual autonomy and equal respect for persons that form the core of our law. If there is a duty to the fetus, it cannot be bootstrapped into a fetal abuse hypothesis.

INTENT

Attaching criminal liability to drug use raises the issue of criminal intent—whether, in taking drugs, the woman could be said to have intended the harm in question. Criminal intent is sometimes attributed to reckless conduct, in which the risk of harm is consciously disregarded, even though the actor has no reason or desire to cause harm. What is often thought to provide an explanation or reason for the action—the motive—is generally considered to be irrelevant. Were motive relevant, the absence of any purpose to harm would render many reckless actions nonculpable.

Motive and intention are not always easily distinguished in fact. . . . A pregnant woman who intentionally walked on an icy sidewalk might be said to have acted criminally if a fall causes injury or death to the fetus. Indeed, if the goal is to prevent any *risk* of fetal harm, then the crime is committed once the woman sets foot on the ice, even if no injury results. Similarly, a pregnant woman who has sex with her husband could be guilty of endangering her fetus. In fact, when such an event results in injury, it is considered a tragedy and not a crime. This suggests that it is not the behavior alone that determines liability. Rather, it is society's perception of the behavior as desirable or undesirable that controls. From the fetus's perspective, walking on ice and taking drugs may have the same unwanted consequences. The only explanation for making the latter a crime is that we think drug use is bad.

The focus on pregnant women who use illegal drugs is best explained by societal disapproval of mothers who need or want to get high, an attitude that "betrays a profound suspicion of pregnant women." It is as though we believe that women are taking a drug for the purpose of harming the fetus. Yet it is doubtful that any woman has taken any drug for the express purpose of harming her fetus. However the initial use of a drug might be characterized, its continued use by addicts is rarely, if ever, truly voluntary. Drug addiction tends to obliterate rational, autonomous decision making about drug use. Drugs become a necessity for dependent users, even when they would much prefer to escape their addiction. In virtually all instances, a user specifically does *not* want to harm her fetus. Yet she cannot resist the drive to use the drug. Thus, it is not plausible to attribute to drug-using women a motive of causing harm to the fetus. The only intent the women form is to take the drug. But this is the traditional definition of intent merely to do the act, which is not sufficient to define *this* crime.

CRIMINALIZING DRUG USE IS COUNTERPRODUCTIVE

Even if one could plausibly argue that pregnant women have a duty to have healthy children, and that they intend by drug use to injure a child, and even if the causal link between drug use and harm to the fetus could be proved beyond a reasonable doubt, use of the criminal law to protect fetuses from their drug-using mothers should still be opposed because it will be counterproductive.

One of the goals of prosecuting women who use drugs seems to be to create an incentive for pregnant women to stop using drugs, as by entering a drug treatment program. But treatment is rarely available to pregnant women. Dr. Chavkin's survey showed that about 54 percent of New York City's drug treatment programs excluded pregnant women. Moreover, 67 percent refused to admit pregnant women whose source of payment was Medicaid. Eighty-seven percent excluded pregnant Medicaid patients who used crack. In Massachusetts, there are only thirty state-funded residential beds for pregnant women in drug treatment programs. Ten of these are in a new program that opened only last year; fif-

teen are in the women's correctional facility.

In part, the scarcity of treatment for pregnant women reflects a history of ignoring drug treatment for women. Even now, little is known about how to eliminate drug dependence among women. The absence of child care has made it impossible for many women to enter or remain in treatment. Also, few programs deal with the problems of domestic violence or husbands or partners who introduce women to drugs, so that women return to circumstances that foster drug use. . . .

The general absence of drug treatment programs for pregnant women means that there is little likelihood that women who want to get off drugs will be able to. In these circumstances, there is little justification for making the pregnant woman's drug use a crime. The woman would be punished for society's more general failure to provide treatment. Some prosecutors have claimed that they prosecuted women in order to get them into treatment, and indeed, have recommended sentencing them to a treatment program instead of prison. This type of sentence assumes an obligation on the part of drug users to join a treatment program, an obligation they cannot meet because of the woefully inadequate treatment facilities available. The irony of requiring a criminal conviction in order to gain access to treatment is apparent. Prosecutions cannot be justified as long as there are insufficient treatment programs to meet the needs of pregnant women.

Finally, criminalizing drug use during pregnancy is likely to be counterproductive in protecting the fetus. There is reason to believe that women will avoid prenatal delivery care if detection of their drug use could lead to their arrest or loss of child custody. Several states currently require that health care providers report to the state women or their newborns who are drug dependent or exhibit drug withdrawal symptoms. The state may act to take custody of the newborn and may notify the district attorney to initiate criminal charges.

Newborns are rarely protected by such a system. If women avoid prenatal care for fear of losing their babies or going to jail, the child's birth weight and development are likely to be prejudiced. Removing the child from the mother after birth compounds the injury. There are already too few foster homes available without adding more children to the system. Many of these children languish as boarder babies in hospitals waiting for placement. The emotional deprivation that is necessarily typical of institutional care may harm these children more than living at home with their mothers. The paucity of resources devoted to caring for children belies the assertion that the purpose of separating mother and child is to protect the child. William Bennett, the Bush Administration's "drug czar," has recommended removing children from every woman who uses drugs. But prenatal drug use, by itself, does not predict postnatal abuse or neglect. If the mother demonstrates conduct sufficient to constitute child abuse or neglect after birth, existing law is more than adequate to take the child into custody for its own protection.

It seems clear that punishment is the only goal that is served by defining drug use by pregnant women as a crime. No one can seriously maintain that prosecution serves the traditional goal of deterrence. Existing prohibitions and increased penalties have not stopped the distribution or use of drugs. In the absence of adequate treatment programs, "rehabilitation" cannot be provided. Rehabilitation is generally conceived as appropriate for recalcitrant offenders who have refused to comply with the law. Creating a new crime for the sole purpose of getting pregnant women into treatment stands the goal of rehabilitation on its head. . . .

If neither deterrence nor rehabilitation is served by prosecuting pregnant women, only punishment remains. Pregnant women who use drugs need help, not punishment. But all that prosecution can accomplish is conviction and punishment.

CONCLUSION

Prosecution of drug-using pregnant women are based on an illusion, and a dangerous one at that. They foster the illusion that society is protecting its future generations. In reality, such prosecutions substitute punishment for protection. By treatment women as threats to their own progeny, society rejects the only source of fetal sustenance. It separates mother and child at the time the child most needs a mother, and relegates the child to the woefully inadequate system of institutional or foster care.

Criminal prosecutions assume that women have a special duty to the fetus that men do not have. But when they are examined closely, that duty cannot be found. Any duty not to harm the fetus would cover a wide range of concededly lawful behavior. The more expansive duty to avoid any risk to the fetus would prohibit an even larger sphere of ordinary conduct. A pregnant women might be assured of satisfying such a duty only by having an abortion.

Singling out pregnant women highlights the fact that they are being punished not for any act harming the fetus but because they are pregnant and use drugs. Making pregnancy one of the elements of a crime is disturbing. It affects the way we think about pregnancy, making all pregnant women suspect. Moreover, punishment cannot remotely be believed to deter either drug use or pregnancy. . . .

Finally, criminalizing certain conduct by pregnant women is likely to be counterproductive, deterring women not from drug use but from prenatal care and other services that have a realistic probability of improving the health of their children.

The effects of drug use are tragic for women, children, and society. Injecting the criminal law can only deepen the tragedy. The answer lies not in punishing women but in helping them to emerge from their own misery. It is an expensive and lengthy process requiring better education about pregnancy care, expansion of prenatal care facilities, research into addiction treatment, and the creation of treatment facilities. It won't get headlines, but it can work. Drug use during pregnancy is a *real* problem. It is a public health problem that can only be compounded by treating it as a crime.

NOTES

1. Lewin, *Drug Use in Pregnancy: New Issues for the Courts,* N.Y. Times, Feb. 5, 1990, at A14.

NO

Paul A. Logli

DRUGS IN THE WOMB: THE NEWEST BATTLEFIELD IN THE WAR ON DRUGS

INTRODUCTION

The reported incidence of drug-related births has risen dramatically over the last several years. The legal system and, in particular, local prosecutors have attempted to properly respond to the suffering, death, and economic costs which result from a pregnant woman's use of drugs. The ensuing debate has raised serious constitutional and practical issues which are far from resolution.

Prosecutors have achieved mixed results in using current criminal and juvenile statutes as a basis for legal action intended to prosecute mothers and protect children. As a result, state and federal legislators have begun the difficult task of drafting appopriate laws to deal with the problem, while at the same time acknowledging the concerns of medical authorities, child protection groups, and advocates for individual rights.

THE PROBLEM

The plight of "cocaine babies," children addicted at birth to narcotic substances or otherwise affected by maternal drug use during pregnancy, has prompted prosecutors in some jurisdications to bring criminal charges against drug-abusing mothers. Not only have these prosecutions generated heated debates both inside and outside of the nation's courtrooms, but they have also expanded the war on drugs to a controversial new battlefield—the mother's womb.

A 1988 survey of hospitals conducted by Dr. Ira Chasnoff, Associate Professor of Northwestern University Medical School and President of the National Association for Perinatal Addiction Research and Education (NAPARE) indicated that as many as 375,000 infants may be affected by maternal cocaine use during pregnancy each year. Chasnoff's survey in-

From Paul A. Logli, "Drugs in the Womb: The Newest Battlefield in the War on Drugs," *Criminal Justice Ethics*, vol. 9, no. 1 (Winter/Spring 1990), pp. 23-39. Copyright © 1990 by *Criminal Justice Ethics*. Reprinted by permission of *Criminal Justice Ethics* and the author. Notes omitted.

cluded 36 hospitals across the country and showed incidence rates ranging from 1 percent to 27 percent. It also indicated that the problem was not restricted to urban populations or particular racial or socio-economic groups. More recently a study at Hutzel Hospital in Detroit's inner city found that 42.7 percent of its newborn babies were exposed to drugs while in their mothers' wombs.

The effects of maternal use of cocaine and other drugs during pregnancy on the mother and her newborn child have by now been well-documented and will not be repeated here. The effects are severe and can cause numerous threats to the short-term health of the child. In a few cases it can even result in death.

Medical authorities have just begun to evaluate the long-term effects of cocaine exposure on children as they grow older. Early findings show that many of these infants show serious difficulties in relating and reacting to adults and environments, as well as in organizing creative play, and they appear similar to mildly autistic or personality-disordered children.

The human costs related to the pain, suffering, and deaths resulting from maternal cocaine use during pregnancy are simply incalculable. In economic terms, the typical intensive-care costs for treating babies exposed to drugs range from $7,500 to $31,000. In some cases medical bills go as high as $150,000.

The costs grow enormously as more and more hospitals encounter the problem of "boarder babies"—those children literally abandoned at the hospital by an addicted mother, and left to be cared for by the nursing staff. Future costs to society for simply educating a generation of drug-affected children can only be the object of speculation. It is clear, however, that besides pain, suffering, and death the economic costs to society of drug use by pregnant women is presently enormous and is certainly growing larger.

THE PROSECUTOR'S RESPONSE

It is against this backdrop and fueled by the evergrowing emphasis on an aggressively waged war on drugs that prosecutors have begun a number of actions against women who have given birth to drug-affected children. A review of at least two cases will illustrate the potential success or failure of attempts to use existing statutes.

People v. Melanie Green On February 4, 1989, at a Rockford, Illinois hospital, two-day old Bianca Green lost her brief struggle for life. At the time of Bianca's birth both she and her mother, twenty-four-year-old Melanie Green, tested positive for the presence of cocaine in their systems.

Pathologists in Rockford and Madison, Wisconsin, indicated that the death of the baby was the result of a prenatal injury related to cocaine used by the mother during the pregnancy. They asserted that maternal cocaine use had caused the placenta to prematurely rupture, which deprived the fetus of oxygen before and during delivery. As a result of oxygen deprivation, the child's brain began to swell and she eventually died.

After an investigation by the Rockford Police Department and the State of Illinois Department of Children and Family Services, prosecutors allowed a criminal complaint to be filed on May 9, 1989, charging Melanie Green with the offenses of Involuntary Manslaughter and Delivery of a Controlled Substance.

On May 25, 1989, testimony was presented to the Winnebago County Grand Jury by prosecutors seeking a formal indictment. The Grand Jury, however, declined to indict Green on either charge. Since Grand Jury proceedings in the State of Illinois are secret, as are the jurors' deliberations and votes, the reason for the decision of the Grand Jury in this case is determined more by conjecture than any direct knowledge. Prosecutors involved in the presentation observed that the jurors exhibited a certain amount of sympathy for the young woman who had been brought before the Grand Jury at the jurors' request. It is also likely that the jurors were uncomfortable with the use of statutes that were not intended to be used in these circumstances.

It would also be difficult to disregard the fact that, after the criminal complaints were announced on May 9th and prior to the Grand Jury deliberations of May 25th, a national debate had ensued revolving around the charges brought in Rockford, Illinois, and their implications for the ever-increasing problem of women who use drugs during pregnancy.

People v. Jennifer Clarise Johnson On July 13, 1989, a Seminole County, Florida judge found Jennifer Johnson guilty of delivery of a controlled substance to a child. The judge found that delivery, for purposes of the statute, occurred through the umbilical cord after the birth of the child and before the cord was severed. Jeff Deen, the Assistant State's Attorney who prosecuted the case, has since pointed out that Johnson, age 23, had previously given birth to three other cocaine-affected babies, and in this case was arrested at a crack house. "We needed to make sure this woman does not give birth to another cocaine baby."

Johnson was sentenced to fifteen years of probation including strict supervision, drug treatment, random drug testing, educational and vocational training, and an intensive prenatal care program if she ever became pregnant again.

SUPPORT FOR THE PROSECUTION OF MATERNAL DRUG ABUSE

Both cases reported above relied on a single important fact as a basis for the prosecution of the drug-abusing mother: that the child was born alive and exhibited the consequences of prenatal injury.

In the Melanie Green case, Illinois prosecutors relied on the "born alive" rule set out earlier in *People v. Bolar.* In *Bolar* the defendant was convicted of the offense of reckless homicide. The case involved an accident between a car driven by the defendant, who was found to be drunk, and another automobile containing a pregnant woman. As a result, the woman delivered her baby by emergency caesarean section within hours of the collision. Although the newborn child exhibited only a few heart beats and lived for approximately two minutes, the court found that the child was born alive and was therefore a person for purposes of the criminal statutes of the State of Illinois.

The Florida prosecution relied on a live birth in an entirely different fashion. The prosecutor argued in that case that the delivery of the controlled substance occurred after the live birth via the umbilical cord and prior to the cutting of the cord. Thus, it was argued, that the delivery of the controlled substance occurred not to a fetus but to a person who enjoyed the protection of the criminal code of the State of Florida.

Further support for the State's role in protecting the health of newborns even against prenatal injury is found in the statutes which provide protection for the fetus. These statutes proscribe actions by a person, usually other than the mother, which either intentionally or recklessly harm or kill a fetus. In other words, even in the absence of a live birth, most states afford protection to the unborn fetus against the harmful actions of another person. Arguably, the same protection should be afforded the infant against intentional harmful actions by a drug-abusing mother.

The state also receives support for a position in favor of the protection of the health of a newborn from a number of non-criminal cases. A line of civil cases in several states would appear to stand for the principle that a child has a right to begin life with a sound mind and body, and a person who interferes with that right may be subject to civil liability. In two cases decided within months of each other, the Supreme Court of Michigan upheld two actions for recovery of damages that were caused by the infliction of prenatal injury. In *Womack v. Buckhorn* the court upheld an action on behalf of an eight-year-old surviving child for prenatal brain injuries apparently suffered during the fourth month of the pregnancy in an automobile accident. The court adopted with approval the reasoning of a New Jersey Supreme Court decision and "recognized that a child has a legal right to begin life with a sound mind and body." Similarly, in *O'Neill v. Morse* the court found that a cause of action was allowed for prenatal injuries that caused the death of an eight-month-old viable fetus.

Illinois courts have allowed civil recovery on behalf of an infant for a negligently administered blood transfusion given to the mother prior to conception which resulted in damage to the child at birth. However, the same Illinois court would not extend a similar cause of ac-

tion for prebirth injuries as between a child and its own mother. The court, however, went on to say that a right to such a cause of action could be statutorily enacted by the Legislature.

Additional support for the state's role in protecting the health of newborns is found in the principles annunciated in recent decisions of the United States Supreme Court. The often cited case of *Roe v. Wade* set out that although a woman's right of privacy is broad enough to cover the abortion decision, the right is not absolute and is subject to limitations, "and that at some point the state's interest as to protection of health, medical standards and prenatal life, becomes dominant."

More recently, in the case of *Webster v. Reproductive Health Services*, the court expanded the state's interest in protecting potential human life by setting aside viability as a rigid line that had previously allowed state regulation only after viability had been shown but prohibited it before viability. The court goes on to say that the "fundamental right" to abortion as described in *Roe* is now accorded the lesser status of a "liberty interest." Such language surely supports a prosecutor's argument that the state's compelling interest in potential human life would allow the criminalization of acts which if committed by a pregnant woman can damage not just a viable fetus by eventually a born-alive infant. It follows that, once a pregnant woman has abandoned her right to abort and has decided to carry the fetus to term, society can well impose a duty on the mother to insure that the fetus is born as healthy as possible.

A further argument in support of the state's interest in prosecuting women who engage in conduct which is damaging to the health of a newborn child is especially compelling in regard to maternal drug use during pregnancy. Simply put, there is no fundamental right or even a liberty interest in the use of psycho-active drugs. A perceived right of privacy has never formed an absolute barrier against state prosecutions of those who use or possess narcotics. Certainly no exception can be made simply because the person using drugs happens to be pregnant.

Critics of the prosecutor's role argue that any statute that would punish mothers who create a substantial risk of harm to their fetus will run afoul of constitutional requirements, including prohibitions on vagueness, guarantees of liberty and privacy, and rights of due process and equal protection. . . .

In spite of such criticism, the state's role in protecting those citizens who are least able to protect themselves, namely the newborn, mandates an aggressive posture. Much of the criticism of prosecutorial efforts is based on speculation as to the consequences of prosecution and ignores the basic tenet of criminal law that prosecutions deter the prosecuted and others from committing additional crimes. To assume that it will only drive persons further underground is to somehow argue that certain prosecutions of crime will only force perpetrators to make even more aggressive efforts to escape apprehension, thus making arrest and prosecution unadvisable. Neither could this be accepted as an argument justifying even the weakening of criminal sanctions. . . .

The concern that pregnant addicts will avoid obtaining health care for themselves or their infants because of the fear of prosecution cannot justify the absence of state action to protect the newborn. If the state were to accept such reasoning, then existing child abuse laws would have to be reconsidered since they might deter parents from obtaining medical care for physically or sexually abused children. That argument has not been accepted as a valid reason for abolishing child abuse laws or for not prosecuting child abusers. . . .

The far better policy is for the state to acknowledge its responsibility not only to provide a deterrant to criminal and destructive behavior by pregnant addicts but also to provide adequate opportunities for those who might seek help to discontinue their addiction. Prosecution has a role in its ability to deter future criminal behavior and to protect the best interests of the child. The medical and social welfare establishment must assume an even greater responsibility to encourage legislators to provide adequate funding and facilities so that no pregnant woman who is addicted to drugs will be denied the opportunity to seek appropriate prenatal care and treatment for her addiction.

ONE STATE'S RESPONSE

The Legislature of the State of Illinois at the urging of local prosecutors moved quickly to amend its juvenile court act in order to provide protection to those children born drug-affected. Previously, Illinois law provided that a court could assume jurisdiction over addicted minors or a minor who is generally declared neglected or abused.

Effective January 1, 1990, the juvenile court act was amended to expand the definition of a neglected or abused minor. . . .

those who are neglected include . . . any newborn infant whose blood or urine contains any amount of a controlled substance . . .

The purpose of the new statute is to make it easier for the court to assert jurisdiction over a newborn infant born drug-affected. The state is not required to show either the addiction of the child or harmful effects on the child in order to remove the child from a drug abusing mother. Used in this context, prosecutors can work with the mother in a rather coercive atmosphere to encourage her to enter into drug rehabilitation and, upon the successful completion of the program, be reunited with her child.

Additional legislation before the Illinois Legislature is House Bill 2835 sponsored by Representatives John Hallock (R-Rockford) and Edolo "Zeke" Giorgi (D-Rockford). This bill represents the first attempt to specifically address the prosecution of drug abusing pregnant women. . . .

The statute provides for a class 4 felony disposition upon conviction. A class 4 felony is a probationable felony which can also result in a term of imprisonment from one to three years.

Subsequent paragraphs set out certain defenses available to the accused.

It shall not be a violation of this section if a woman knowingly or intentionally uses a narcotic or dangerous drug in the first twelve weeks of pregnancy and: 1. She has no knowledge that she is pregnant; or 2. Subsequently, within the first twelve weeks of pregnancy, undergoes medical treatment for substance abuse or treatment or rehabilitation in a program or facility approved by the Illinois Department of Alcoholism and Substance Abuse, and thereafter discontinues any further use of drugs or narcotics as previously set forth.

. . . A woman, under this statute, could not be prosecuted for self-reporting her addiction in the early stages of the pregnancy. Nor could she be prosecuted under this statute if, even during the subsequent stages of the pregnancy, she discontinued her drug use to the extent that no drugs were present in her system or the baby's system at the time of birth. The statute, as drafted, is clearly intended to allow prosecutors to invoke the criminal statutes in the most serious of cases.

CONCLUSION

Local prosecutors have a legitimate role in responding to the increasing problem of drug abusing pregnant women and their drug-affected children. Eliminating the pain, suffering and death resulting from drug exposure in newborns must be a prosecutor's priority. However, the use of existing statutes to address the problem may meet with limited success since they are burdened with numerous constitutional problems dealing with original intent, notice, vagueness, and due process.

The juvenile courts may offer perhaps the best initial response in working to protect the interests of a surviving child. However, in order to address more serious cases, legislative efforts may be required to provide new statutes that will specifically address the problem and hopefully deter future criminal conduct which deprives children of their important right to a healthy and normal birth.

The long-term solution does not rest with the prosecutor alone. Society, including the medical and social welfare establishment, must be more responsive in providing readily accessible prenatal care and treatment alternatives for pregnant addicts. In the short term however, prosecutors must be prepared to play a vital role in protecting children and deterring women from engaging in conduct which will harm the newborn child. If prosecutors fail to respond, then they are simply closing the doors of the criminal justice system to those persons, the newborn, who are least able to open the doors for themselves.

POSTSCRIPT

Are Drug Arrests of Pregnant Women Discriminatory?

The immediate costs of medical care for crack babies are staggering. However, ignoring citizens' civil liberties, singling out a visible group for differential negative treatment, and thereby further increasing the miseries of America's underclass, no matter how critical the situation, is to many simply unacceptable. This response, defenders of crack mothers maintain, is simply too draconian. They shout: Do not arrest them! Moreover, Mariner, Glantz, Annas, and a growing legion of scholars argue that legal "controls" simply do not work. The pregnant women who are crack users will either take their chances and possibly go to jail or avoid medical and social welfare care for themselves or their child because they fear that they may be arrested. Thus, the legal response would only make matters worse, defenders claim. For an extension of these arguments, see *Criminal Justice Ethics* (Winter/Spring 1990), in which there is a symposium on "Criminal Liability for Fetal Endangerment."

For an article that reviews some of the issues specifically pertaining to women and the law, see Robin West's "Jurisprudence and Gender," *University of Chicago Law Review* (Winter 1988); for two articles that partially agree with Logli's argument for legal sanctions against pregnant drug users, see "The Problem of the Drug-Exposed Newborn: A Return to Principled Intervention," by Bonnie I. Robin-Vergeer in *Stanford Law Review* (February 1990); and "Crack and Kids" by D. J. Besharov in *Society* (July/August 1990). For a broader discussion of disease and reproductive rights, see R. Bayer's AIDS and the Future of Reproductive Freedom" in *Milbank Quarterly*, vol. 68 (1990).

ISSUE 17

Will Drug Legalization Help the Criminal Justice System?

YES: Arnold S. Trebach, from *"Law Enforcement News* Interview with Trebach," *Law Enforcement News* (April 30, 1988)

NO: John Kaplan, from "Taking Drugs Seriously," *Public Interest* (Summer 1988)

ISSUE SUMMARY

YES: American University School of Justice professor Arnold S. Trebach pulls no punches by insisting that the war against illegal drugs is lost and says that the only sensible path remaining is immediately to make many drugs legal.
NO: John Kaplan, from Stanford Law School, counters that legalization is not the answer and instead the lesser evil is to step up our fight against hard-core drug use and sales in order to reduce crime.

Throughout the twentieth century, America's problems have often been traced to dubious origins that have served primarily as scapegoats. The shifting nature of the American family, the changing behavioral patterns of the young, the broadening of opportunities for blacks, women, and other minority groups, increasing political disenchantment—which were all partially the result of increasing modernization, an unpopular war, and other specific structural precipitants—were variously blamed on the movie industry, comic books, bolshevism, gambling, booze, the Mafia, and now and then, the devil himself. Currently, the continued concern with the changing nature of the American family, the increasing fear of crime, and the widening generation gap are linked with drug use. If only we could get the dealers off the streets or at least get the kids to say "No" to drugs, then we could restore our family system. If only we could arrest everyone taking drugs, then we could eliminate crime, since it is drugs that cause most people to commit crimes. If only the students in our junior high schools, high schools, and our college students were not taking drugs, then they would not only do better on their academic achievement scores but once again love and obey Mom and Dad!

It is precisely this kind of thinking that has generated the recent, surprisingly venomous attacks on those scholars and political leaders who simply have called for a dialogue to consider the decriminalization of drugs, along with other creative alternatives to the existing drug policies. For instance, Baltimore mayor Kurt Schmoke was vilified by fellow politicians, news commentators, and members of a variety of religious groups for his proposed forum simply to *discuss* alternatives to present policies, including decriminalization.

Exactly what laws have been passed in the twentieth century to stem drug manufacturing, distribution, and consumption? Although there were a few local regulations in the late 1800s that prohibited the sale of over-the-counter drugs containing narcotics, it was not until 1906 that Congress passed the Pure Food and Drug Act. It was concerned primarily with the availability of patent medicines and with prohibiting the sale of dangerous drugs.

The Harris Act passed in 1914 and the Volstead Act (prohibiting alcohol) passed in 1919 were even broader than the Pure Food and Drug Act. Many use this as a benchmark for the first anti-drug campaign in the United States. In 1937, the Marijuana Tax Act was passed, and during the 1950s, stiffer penalties were legislated for possession and sale of drugs. However, it was not until 1970 with the passage of the Controlled Substance Act (Title II of the Comprehensive Drug Abuse and Control Act) that efforts were made to standardize the many existing local and state drug laws.

In June 1986, 1.7 billion additional dollars were added to the budget by Congress to fight drugs. Currently over 9 billion dollars per year are spent on drug control. Toward the end of 1988, Congress authorized the death penalty for murders related to drug deals. It also called for considerably stiffer penalties for the manufacture, distribution, and use of illegal drugs. Between March and June of 1988, during the height of "zero tolerance," or active government interdiction, over 1,500 boats, bikes, and cars were seized. At the San Diego–Mexican border alone, over 20 drivers per week were arrested for illegal possession.

In spite of these efforts, 25 million Americans occasionally or regularly use drugs, according to some estimates. And the U.S. Justice Department estimates that 70 percent of all criminals arrested for serious offenses are regular drug users. Yet the link between crimes and drug use is problematic—there is no firm proof that all serious offenders, or even the majority, committed their crimes *because* of drugs.

Should we lock up drug dealers and users? Would that keep your friends from using pot, pills and/or trying to obtain other illicit highs? Exactly how often has the regulation of personal conduct "worked" in America? After users are arrested, should they be imprisoned to punish them or to administer treatment? Is the use of hard-core drugs really a "victimless" crime? Can we as a society afford to "say Yes" to drug use? These and other highly emotional issues are addressed here.

YES
Arnold S. Trebach

LOSING THE WAR ON DRUGS

Law Enforcement News interview by Peter Dodenhoff

LAW ENFORCEMENT NEWS: In a nutshell, why is America losing the war on drugs, as the title of your newest book suggests?

TREBACH: Well, for a whole variety of reasons, not least of which is that the whole concept of a "war" on drugs is inappropriate. There's no way you can have a war on a chemical. What you really have is a war on a significant segment of the American people. Roughly one in four Americans used an illegal drug within the past 12 months, so what you're saying is that we're going to go to war against 25 percent of the American people. That's a civil war. If it's only a war in rhetoric, then it's just great political fun. But it's becoming a war, especially when Mrs. Reagan talks of occasional users of illegal drugs as accomplices to murder, and when other people take this as an invitation to lynch law. So we are in a position where this is becoming a real war, more or less a sectarian or civil war, and we should tremble to think where such attitudes could lead us.

That's the first part of the problem. Another reason why we're losing the war is because we do not distinguish between the legal drugs and the illegal drugs with any degree of rationality. We act as if there is a distinction, when in fact there isn't. To say we're going to war against the illegal drugs, which really are not a great health threat on the whole to the American people, and virtually ignore the legal drugs is irrational.

Another reason why it's failing is that we have never shown any great ability at Prohibition. We failed at it in the 20's, we are now failing at it in the 80's, and there's no evidence whatsoever that we can succeed at it in the future, even if we turn the society into a police state.

LEN: If cost were no object, is the war winnable?

TREBACH: I know of no way to do it. Suppose a new Democratic administration gets in, and they say, "Let's get this curious fellow Trebach, he claims to know a little bit about these drugs, and let's make him the drug war czar and give him $10 billion." I would have to say to the President, "I'm more

From *"Law Enforcement News* Interview with Trebach," *Law Enforcement News* (April 30, 1988). Reprinted by permission of *Law Enforcement News*, John Jay College of Criminal Justice, New York.

stunned than flattered that you asked me, but I would not know how to use those $10 billion or $20 billion to successfully win a war as that war is currently defined." There's nothing in our history, nothing in the history of any other major country to suggest that that can be done.

LEN: So you're suggesting, then, that winning this war, if in fact it's feasible, would entail costs that go far beyond monetary expenditures?

TREBACH: Yeah. What most objective observers have seen is that to even push the war rationally and logically further down the current path will go very far in the direction of creating a police state. We are doing that already and it's not working. We're moving in that direction. And mind you, these thoughts are not mine alone. President Nixon's commission on marijuana and drug abuse, headed by Governor [William] Schafer, said that it is possible to really increase the level of police power and military power applied to the drug war, but this could well mean the invasion of many of the most cherished rights of Americans.

LEN: That commission recommended that current marijuana laws be replaced by a decriminalized approach. Why were those recommendations written off?

TREBACH: Well, first remember that every major commission that has studied marijuana has come to remarkably similar conclusions. Every one of them went out there probably expecting to find how marijuana was tearing up the people. Each of them concluded that while marijuana was not harmless—and I agree, it's not harmless—it simply did not present a great threat, on the whole, to the people of the country where it was being used.

President Nixon went out there, I'm sure, with the hope that the commission would come back and damn this evil weed. They didn't. They said, "We looked at the evidence, and though marijuana can be a difficult problem for many people, on the whole it's not a very damaging presence in our society, and we should be somewhat more lenient with it." As in the past, it's the last thing that the people who set up the commission wanted to hear. Nixon didn't want to hear this stuff. He didn't want rationality. It was politically unacceptable, and that's been our problem with most of the drugs. We set up political standards for science, for objective research, and when the science and objective research don't comport, we go with politics rather than with science.

ALCOHOL IS BAD, PROHIBITION WORSE

LEN: Some argue that in the context of the war on drugs, the object lessons of Prohibition appear to have been lost in the shuffle . . .

TREBACH: There are many people—including some of the leading experts in the country—who chastise me and shake their fingers at me, saying "How can you compare this with Prohibition? It's just not the same." Well, alcohol was a drug that was widely accepted, and we attempted to take it away from the people. And also, it wasn't that harmful on the whole. Moreover, they say that Prohibition had a good impact. It controlled the overall use of alcohol. They say that when we removed Prohibition, alcohol use nearly doubled. So there are a host of reasons, I think, why we don't see exact similarities, and why, indeed, many people liked Prohibition. I see the situation quite the opposite. Number one, I think what we're doing now is very close to what we did in the 20's, except that now it's more savage. In the 20's we did not go after users; we went after sellers and racketeers. Now we're saying that going after the user is the answer to the problem. Secondly, the analogy in terms of the police corruption, the crime of the traffickers, the erosion of civil liberties, all of these are precise. If we were to legalize some of these drugs, it's possible that use might go up. So I think the analogies with Prohibition are very good. . . .

LEN: As you mentioned, there are those who suggest that the moment drugs were legalized, should they be, use will go up, perhaps significantly. Others, however, have surmised that use might actually decrease, simply because the curiosity of trying something that's illegal will have been removed, and young people might find the idea of drug experimentation to be rather ho-hum . . .

TREBACH: The evidence would suggest the possibility of both responses. As I pointed out in "The Great Drug War," clearly the experience of Holland and Alaska with respect to marijuana, which are really the only two examples we have of a very lenient approach toward any of the illicit drugs, suggests that nothing terrible would happen if we remove some of the criminal sanctions. In Alaska, as I documented, there's been no dramatic change in drug use. . . . The youth of Holland can buy all the drugs they want, and there you have indications of a drop from the old days. Any survey of Dutch use that I've studied shows that one-half of one percent use marijuana daily. That's in a country where the kids can get all the pot they want, right off the menus of coffee houses. In this country, as I found when I wrote the book, it's about four to five percent. In other words, it's about 10 times as much in this country. . . . [t]he Dutch rely more on cultural, familial and social controls, and they are generally a very conservative people. . . . the major controls are where they should be: in the family, in the church, in the culture. Also, I think the Dutch youths are bored with marijuana; there's nothing deviant about it. . . .

DRUG PEACE, NOT SURRENDER

LEN: You refer to the alternative to a war on drugs as "drug peace." If the war on drugs is not winnable, is the alternative, as some have said, mere surrender?

TREBACH: Not al all. We are now engaged in working out peace with the Russians. We worked our peace with the Red Chinese. I hope none of those involved surrender. My hope is that peace means we can now work out our conflicts, which will certainly be there, within the framework of the peaceful methods of a democracy. That means you seek out compromises and the middle ground between the extremes. I called it "drug peace" because I think people use "drug war" like it's one word—like "damn Yankees" used to be. So if you need a word, call it "drug peace," and let's say we're going to approach this in a peaceful way and seek compassionate compromises. Well, what could that involve? A whole series of things, as it turns out. For example, one of the first things we'd do is to recognize who the true victims of the war are, and help them. And I think most people would agree that some of the most pitiful victims of the war are sick people, people denied heroin for pain relief in cancer cases, people denied marijuana for relief of the agonies of chemotherapy in cancer cases, people with glaucoma who are denied the help that marijuana can provide in preventing the onset of glaucoma-related blindness, people with multiple sclerosis, where marijuana might well help the tremors and the shaking and the lack of control that comes from that disease. There's no reason in the world why sick people should be denied drugs because we think dope fiends will eventually get their hands on the drugs.

LEN: Or that the sick people will themselves become drug addicts as a result of using these substances?

TREBACH: That's right. That should be irrelevant. In addition, I would like us to start thinking of narcotic addicts as sick people with a bad habit, who might make nice neighbors if they were treated right. One compromise might be to offer them a wide array of affordable, legal treatments that could range from the standard drug-free treatment to oral methadone and on to other oral drugs, all of which are now illegal for maintenance, and then on to injectable drugs. We must consider the possibility of providing injectable drugs and clean needles, . . . we'd better start accepting that, because the major engine for the transmission of AIDS is not the homosexual couple, but the heterosexual injecting addict. . . .

LEN: Wouldn't legalization carry with it the implicit suggestion that the government is getting into the business of drug dealing? Or could the matter be opened up to private entrepreneurship under a regulatory scheme such as we now have with alcoholic beverages?

TREBACH: We ought to look at our experiment with alcohol and learn from that. When we allowed the states to legalize alcohol, we did not carry with that national campaign enough warnings about alcohol. I think where research ought to be going in this field is along the lines of what new control schemes make sense beyond prohibition. Because if anybody thinks that one day we're going to simply get rid of all the laws and everything will be fine, they're as mistaken as the drug warriors. What we need is to think out new, more effective laws and policies. So my hope would be that we would provide for a wide array of experiments in the states on how to control drugs. A good part of that ought to provide for private control, but I wouldn't object in those states where they have state package stores for liquor to sell some of the drugs there. Sell the drugs in the store, make sure it's sold only to adults, make sure it has health warnings on it, because all of these drugs are dangerous. There should be tax stamps on the drugs, we should make sure they're pure, that they meet all the FDA requirements for safety and efficacy. I can see that kind of scheme in some states. In other states, I can see it sold in private stores as well, so long as there were health warnings on the packages, so long as purity was assured, so long as it was clear that there were age limits and tax stamps, so you can earn a lot of money that's now going to criminals. . . .

COULD THE MILITARY SUCCEED?

LEN: Among the new approaches that have been advocated are those that suggest that the drug war has been a failure because we haven't really taken a war-

like posture, and thus the military should be involved in the suppression effort.

TREBACH: Well, let's talk practicalities and forget the Constitution for a moment. Forget it totally, which we'd have to do to use the military here. Remember that both of our recent Secretaries of Defense, Cap Weinberger and Frank Carlucci, have opposed this, and no one's going to call them left-leaning hippie liberals, or "soft on drugs." Both of them have said that they don't want to use the military forces in this effort. It violates basic American traditions and it will decrease our military effectiveness. Forget that for the moment, and forget the Constitution. Let's just say the next President says, "I don't give a damn, I want to use the military." What's the military going to do? How does it even interdict drugs at the border? The esteemed Mayor of New York, Ed Koch, has suggested strip-searching all visitors from Asia or Mexico. Let's assume you put aside your compunctions and you put aside the Constitution and our history, and we do what he suggests. How many drugs are we going to get? And at what point do people say, "Well, we're strip-searching everybody coming in from Asia and from Mexico, and the drugs are flooding down from the Canadian border. What do we do now?" Well, we close the Canadian border. How many divisions would it take to close the Canadian border? Well, you might say we could close the Canadian border, but then drugs might start coming in through Florida again. So let's close down Florida. You begin to recognize that we simply can't do it. It isn't like you're trying to prevent an invasion by several divisions of Russian troops. You are trying to prevent people from smuggling very small packages of goods, some of which, because of our drug war, are now worth $10,000 for a little bit of cocaine about the size of a couple cigarette packs. There's no way in the history of the world where the military has ever been able to prevent that kind of traffic from occurring. So in the end, forgetting the Constitution and forgetting our tradition, I see nothing to suggest that the military could even do it.

LEN: One other approach that has been suggested involves redirecting the war on drugs to the demand side of the equation, given the absence of genuine, meaningful successes in the war on drug traffickers. Would such an effort hold any greater promise?

TREBACH: Again, put aside the Constitution and all our petty, technical concerns about such things as decency and privacy. I see no evidence that it would work. The nature of drug-taking is like the nature of sexual relationships. It's done quietly, it's often done in the dark, it's often done between consenting adults in the privacy of their own bedrooms or living rooms. There's nothing to indicate that you could control this even in a totalitarian state. . . . You can put a few big-time criminals away, but any notion that you can fill the jails with misdemeanants for possession is preposterous, because at a given point you simply have run out of room, and exhausted the prison option. And we pretty much have done that now.

LEN: Wouldn't urinalysis drug screening hold some promise for scaring people away from drug use?

TREBACH: Well, that would be the major way in which you'd go about getting at the users. If you listen to the statements of Attorney General Meese, the use of urinalysis is clearly the use of criminal law power in an illegal way to scare people out of drug use. It's very clear what they're trying to do. And to an extent it will work; it will scare some people away. But remember what you're going to come up with, for the most part, because of the nature in which the drugs are secreted from the body. Ninety-five percent of the time you'll come up with occasional marijuana users. This will have very little effect on cocaine and heroin users, because generally the stuff is secreted from the body very rapidly. . . . So in the end, I don't see this having much of an impact, or as a victory. We're going to scare people away from occasional marijuana use and perhaps encourage the use of other drugs. . . .

SAYING "NO" TO DRUGS

LEN: Has the latest war on drugs given rise to any positive aspects, in your estimation? One that comes readily to mind as a possibility might be the increase in drug-abuse education efforts, or the "Just Say No" campaign . . .

TREBACH: I think there are some good things there. More and more youngsters are saying, "Hey, there may be something wrong with these drugs, and I shouldn't just take 'em because my friends like to." More and more are accepting the idea that they can say "no." I like "Just Say No" as one approach to dealing with the problem. But the difficulty is that it's not enough. You need other approaches. In the end, we must recognize that the greatest controls are familial, cultural, personal, ethical. What we've got to say is that we must build up honest education and treatment as the

major ways in which we control drug abuse. . . .

LEN: So in your estimation there is such a thing as responsible drug use?

TREBACH: Absolutely. I say that not because I approve of the drug use, and not because I urge people to do it, or because I want people to do it. But that's what the facts say, and as a scholar I must report what I find. . . .

POLICE AS DRUG-WAR VICTIMS

LEN: In "The Great Drug War," you describe law enforcement personnel as being among the victims of the drug war. In what ways?

TREBACH: I view my friends in law enforcement with great admiration, and I worry about them. It's the same way I feel about sending Marines into Beirut, or keeping the armed forces in Vietnam for such a long time. They were attempting to carry out a very difficult mission, a fuzzy mission—certainly the Marines in Beirut didn't know what the hell they were doing—and the tragedies that resulted are somewhat like the tragedies that are happening now to our police. But for our police in the drug war, it's more complicated, because they are subjected to immense temptations of corruption, they are subjected to immense temptations to violate the law in order to enforce it, and I really think you can say that not only policemen, but the entire police institution in America is being corroded by the continued work in the drug field.

LEN: In the course of your professional contacts, do you run across many police officials, or even street cops, who are

sympathetic to your views on the drug issue?

TREBACH: More and more police people are coming forward. It's hard for them, because basically—and God bless 'em for feeling this way—most of the police I know say, "It's the law, and I'm going to enforce it." I want them to do that, but more and more are also saying, "We've got to think of different ways of dealing with this, because this is not working." Many police thinkers have said that. The great August Vollmer said that police have no role in the vice field. It just corrodes their institution. My colleague Jim Fyfe, who spent 16 years as a New York City policeman, has come out and said that. Wes Pomeroy, the former chief of police in Berkeley, and a man who, by the way, fought with the Marines in the Pacific, spoke at our first drug policy forum, at which he said that police are victims of the drug war. I find a number of street cops coming to me and saying that we've got to do something different.

One other thing that's struck me, and that is it may look like personal failing when you see these corrupt police, but I'm willing to bet that if you took all the rabbis, priests and nuns in New York City, say, and you had 'em change uniforms with the cops, within a very short time they'd be acting the same way. We say to the cops, in effect, go out and work in this drug and crime sewer, and when they do things bad, we say to them, "You smell like you've been working in a sewer." We created the sewer for them, and unless we change it, we're still going to find corrupt cops, cops who violate the law in order to enforce it, cops becoming increasingly ineffective in other areas of law enforcement because we've got them mired in the dangerous and corrupt drug field. . . .

A POINT OF NO RETURN?

LEN: If the answer to the drug war is to call it off, to put it in simple terms, is there a point in time past which it is no longer possible to call things off, simply because criminal drug traffickers are so powerful that no degree of decriminalization will make a difference?

TREBACH: I don't think so. I think we're all united in wanting to see drug traffickers caught. I don't think any sensible person opposes that. I support the police, and many people support the police in their going after organized crime syndicates that traffic in drugs, or any kind of predatory drug trafficker. But my support has nothing to do with my belief in that action as a way to control drug use. To these organized criminal syndicates, drugs are irrelevant. They'd sell peanut butter if there were that much profit in it. So by changing the rules on drugs, I have every belief that these groups will be into something else. There are plenty of lucrative things for people in organized crime to get involved in.

But the big point here is to emphasize that we can compromise on this. We can come up with sensible, humane methods of dealing with this problem that are not at the extremes on either side of the argument. That's what we should be reaching for. We should be seeking out those new positions in the middle ground. That's the big message.

NO

John Kaplan

TAKING DRUGS SERIOUSLY

It would be difficult to deny that the efforts and resources expended in our attempt to prevent the production of heroin and cocaine in other countries, and to keep out of the United States those drugs that are produced, have passed the point of diminishing returns. The outcry over drugs in the newspapers and on the political hustings, and a look at what is occurring in many public-housing projects and in the large lower-class black and Hispanic neighborhoods of our central cities, should be enough to convince sober observers that our present drug policies have simply not been successful enough. . . .

The problem, then, for those who realize that our present efforts have bogged down, is what to do. In this respect, drug policy must proceed by elimination. None of the policy options is attractive. All involve great costs— either in expenditures on law enforcement or in damage to public health. Since no option is without severe disadvantages, we can aim only to choose the policy that is least bad.

At one level, the simplest solution would be simply to get out of the way, legalize heroin and cocaine, and allow their sale as we do alcohol's. Until recently this was rarely advocated in print, though for years one would hear such recommendations in private conversation with intellectuals. Now, however, the legalization movement is becoming respectable, and even popular. . . .

Probably the central problem with the solution of legalization is that it ignores basic pharmacology. There is such a thing as a dangerous drug, and both heroin and cocaine undoubtedly fall into this category. . . .

A PRESCRIPTION SYSTEM?

Of course, criminalization and legalization are not the only possibilities. We are probably correct in using a prescription system for valium, for example, which is quite a dangerous drug—but also a useful one. When heroin addicts in England consisted overwhelmingly of middle-aged, middle-class men and

From John Kaplan, "Taking Drugs Seriously," *Public Interest*, no. 92 (Summer 1988), pp. 32-50. Copyright © 1988 by National Affairs, Inc. Reprinted by permission of the author.

women who had become addicted during the course of medical treatment, a prescription system was successfully used to dispense the drug. (Sale without a prescription was a rather serious crime.) However, when an increasingly higher percentage of those addicted came to be more like American addicts—lower-class, criminal, and thrill-seeking—the "British system" was abandoned. England stopped using the prescription system for more than a tiny and diminishing number of addicts, adopting instead a legal-control method much like that used in the United States. . . .

Various commentators have considered the social costs of marijuana's criminalization and the projected public-health costs of legalization. And though they have been shouted down by parent groups and those who seek their votes, these commentators, by and large, have leaned toward legalization. . . .

Nor need we devote any attention to LSD, mescaline, PCP, or any number of other illegal drugs here; for the illegal status of these drugs has not created a significant social problem.

Needless to say, this is not the case with heroin and cocaine. The costs of restricting supply of these drugs are substantial. Since space does not permit discussions of both heroin and cocaine, I will discuss only the anticipated costs of legalizing cocaine. . . .

THE CASE OF COCAINE

At a minimum, it is clear that anyone advocating the legalization of cocaine would have to make a serious estimate of how many more people would use the drug after it was legalized; how many of these users would become dependent on the drug; and how much harm this would cause them and society. Instead, there has been no serious discussion of all this. Moreover, no one has seriously considered the impact of a "new" drug upon a culture that has yet to develop patterns of self-control with respect to its use; by contrast, we should recall that over many generations our culture has developed a variety of informal controls over alcohol use, which allow most people to lessen the harm that alcohol does both to them in particular and society in general. Societies not accustomed to alcohol, however, such as England prior to the "gin epidemic" of the late seventeenth and early eighteenth centuries, and many Native American and Eskimo cultures, have experienced a public-health catastrophe of huge proportions as a result of the introduction of distilled spirits.

Nor have the advocates of the legalization of cocaine considered how we would be able to prevent teenagers from gaining access to the now legal drug. Many people assume that legalization of a drug would affect only adults, since, as with alcohol, we would make it illegal to sell the drug to minors. The problem, however, is that legal access for adults makes a drug *de facto* available to the young. This has been the experience with alcohol and tobacco. Cocaine is far less bulky and more concealable than alcohol, and its use does not leave the telltale aroma of smoke; thus it would be even more difficult to keep away from minors.

Yet another problem is the possibility of changes in public consciousness and values. Such changes can make use of a drug less dangerous, but they can also greatly augment its dangers. There are many examples of changes in public consciousness, entirely apart from governmental action, that have influenced drug use. The use of tobacco, alcohol, and marijuana seems to have dropped in the last several years, just as jogging and low-fat diets have increased, all as a consequence of the nation's greater fixation on health. Unfortunately, we cannot guarantee that such cultural trends will continue, or even that they will not be reversed, as has often happened in the past.

Youth culture, moreover, seems to be subject to dramatic fluctuations. The rapid changes in styles of dress, hair, music, and entertainment among the young have bewildered their elders for generations; and the appearance of a charismatic proselytizer for cocaine (as Timothy Leary was for LSD and marijuana) could change youth attitudes toward cocaine. Such a cultural change, even if only temporary, could present us with a permanent problem of large numbers of young people who became drug-dependent during the period of the drug's "window of acceptability."

Consider the case of heroin. Though most people have not noticed, the epidemic of heroin use stopped about ten years ago. Each year, the average age of heroin addicts goes up by about a year. Nevertheless, the last heroin epidemic has left us with an endemic problem of about 500,000 addicts who impose large social costs upon us.

THE DANGERS OF COCAINE

This is not to say that problems like these cannot be solved, or that more careful thought and research might not satisfy us. As far as we now know, however, there is no particular cause for comfort. The pharmacological nature of cocaine,

in fact, is especially worrisome. We need not list all the serious negative effects cocaine may have on its users, since an impressive list of such effects can be drawn up for any of the psychoactive drugs. The problem is to determine just how prevalent these effects would be if the drug were legalized. . . .

The most important fact about cocaine is that it is an extremely attractive drug. In the 1950s a double-blind experiment on the "enjoyability" of a number of injected drugs was undertaken with twenty normal volunteers. Although fewer than half of the subjects found heroin or morphine euphoric, fully 90 percent liked an amphetamine (which is a pharmocological relative of cocaine), giving it by far the highest "pleasure score."

Probably related to its "pleasure score" is the fact that cocaine is the most "reinforcing" drug known to us. . . .

This problem is exacerbated by several other properties of cocaine. Along with amphetamines, it is one of the few drugs that can improve one's mental and physical performance of a task. In fact, this improvement is limited to performance under conditions of fatigue, and the improvement is only temporary. Nonetheless, there will be many occasions during work, athletics, or studies when an individual will be willing to mortgage his future for a little more energy and mental clarity. . . .

The damage wrought by heavy cocaine use in terms of psychiatric symptoms and general debilitation is now widely known. What is less appreciated are the more subtle changes that regular cocaine use can cause. Unlike alcohol and heroin, cocaine use can easily be integrated with every day activities. Its use can be quite inconspicuous, and, like cigarette smoking, can accompany a host of everyday activities. Cocaine use makes one feel good, then highly competent, then nearly omnipotent. It is easy to see why the use of such a drug would be damaging in a complex, mechanized, and interdependent society such as ours.

Nor should we take much comfort from the fact that most of those who use cocaine today have not become dependent upon the drug. As long as the drug is expensive and relatively difficult to procure, most of its users will be able to avoid dependence. When the drug is easily available, however, we can expect the temptations toward use to increase considerably. . . .

When one considers that there are about fifty "hits" of cocaine in a gram, one is startled by the realization that at $20 per gram* the cost of a hit will be only forty cents—a figure well within the budget of almost all grade-school children. Nor is the specter of very young children destroyed by the use of cocaine in any way unrealistic; there are ten-year-old cocaine addicts on the streets of Bogota today.

It is true that if the number of those dependent upon cocaine merely doubled, we would arguably be well ahead of the game, considering the large costs imposed by treating those users as criminals. But what if there were a fifty-fold increase in the number of those dependent on cocaine? We simply cannot guarantee that such a situation would not come to pass; since we cannot do so, it is the height of irresponsibility to advocate risking the future of the nation.

If all this is not enough to convince reasonably prudent people that legalizing cocaine is too risky a course, we can

*[Estimated cost if legalized. Current cost is $80–$100 per gram.—ED.]

also consider the consequences of taking the risk and being wrong. After all, if we had legalized cocaine five years ago, we would not have known how easy it is to make cocaine into "crack," universally considered to be a much more habit-forming and dangerous form of the drug. If we legalize cocaine now, how long should we wait before deciding whether we made a mistake? And if we decided that we had, how would we go about recriminalizing the drug? By then, substantial inventories of legal cocaine would have been built up in private hands, and large numbers of new users would have been introduced to the drug. And once a drug has been made legally available, it is very difficult to prohibit it. This consideration helps to explain why Prohibition failed, and also explains why almost no one advocates the criminalization of tobacco. . . .

In an ideal world, the best way to reduce the damage done by illegal drugs would be to convince everyone not to use them. In this world, however, we will probably have to reconcile ourselves to using some coercion. On the other hand, once we give up on finding an inexpensive solution, we may take the problem seriously and apply more careful thought and more resources to the job.

SUPPLY-SIDE ENFORCEMENT

So long as we are unable to suppress the sale of drugs, we will be remitting large parts of our cities to the terrorization of innocent people, drug-related killings, and the brutalization that comes from constant exposure to the use of drugs. Perhaps equally demoralizing is the sight of the large number of teenage drug lords who own Jaguars or Ferraris before they are old enough to have driver's licenses. Nonetheless, we can accomplish much more than we have in the past.

Apart from our efforts in other countries and at the borders, the major thrust of enforcement within the United States has been the attempt to break up large-scale drug rings, arrest small-scale dealers when they sell drugs outside the areas in which drug use is endemic, and punish users when they commit other crimes. In recent years local police have stepped up their efforts to restrain street-level selling, and private employers have exerted greater efforts to apprehend their workers' "connection," and to weed out illegal drug users from their work force. The result has been a slow but steady loss of ground for law-enforcement agencies.

One cannot say that careful thought and greatly augmented law-enforcement resources will solve our drug problem. There are large numbers of sellers arranged hierarchically within the United States as part of loose but fairly sizable organizations, taking the drug from its importation into the United States through smaller wholesalers down to the small-scale sellers who provide the drug to users. Unfortunately, we cannot expect to achieve much of a reduction in the number of drug suppliers, even if we jail a sizable percentage of them. The high profits at every level of the drug trade guarantee a huge reservoir of individuals prepared to take the places of those who have been imprisoned. At each level in the distribution scheme there are more than enough competitors; and even at the lowest ranks, those who do minor jobs for the sellers (such as acting as lookouts for the police) seem ready to enter the business.

On the other hand, pressure upon the retailing of heroin and cocaine is not necessarily an unattractive option. In fact, it is probably the major governmental means of restraining drug use in the United States today. The number of locations in which an ordinary middle-class individual can buy heroin and cocaine is not very large. In most of the country, cocaine is not widely available to most people. Heroin is less so. A major task of law-enforcement resources is to increase that area of drug unavailability. At the very least, the police should act immediately to suppress the open-air drug markets that spring up whenever the police are distracted by other duties. In most of our urban areas, greater efforts could drive much of the dealing indoors, where a large percentage of potential customers are afraid to go.

At least for the foreseeable future, it is hard to imagine the police being able to do more than gradually drive the dealing back into the public-housing projects and other relatively small areas in which the police are unable to maintain a presence. Nonetheless, increases in law-enforcement efforts at the retail level may lower the availability of heroin and cocaine to large numbers of people without creating a need to involve ourselves in the most hard-core drug-trafficking areas, in which the police would have to maintain a virtual army of occupation.

Apart from the difficulty of policing the hard-core drug areas, the most important constraint upon our ability to suppress the sale of drugs is the cost of incarceration space. Our prisons and jails are full, and despite a massive and continuing effort to provide the infrastructure to imprison more and more lawbreakers, the demand threatens to permanently outrun the supply. Drug sales, moreover, are especially difficult and expensive to restrain through imprisonment. The deterrence we expect from the legal threat is in large part neutralized by the high profits at all levels of the drug trade. And incapacitation, the other major restraint provided by imprisonment, is weakened by the fact that the skills necessary to participate in the drug trade are not at all scarce.

Although we must allocate a large percentage of prison space to the incarceration of drug dealers if we are to make headway, there are other methods that can help. At the higher levels of the drug trade, the forfeiture of assets have proven quite successful. We cannot show that the threat has caused any drug dealers to get out of the business, but at the margin it should have that effect; depriving sellers of working capital makes their reentry into the industry more difficult. At the very least, it assuages our sense of justice, as well as providing additional resources with which to further enforcement. It is likely that we can go a great deal lower in the drug-trade hierarchy before forfeiture is no longer worthwhile. It will require a little more ingenuity by the police and cooperation from the agencies of the criminal-justice system before we can strike at the pocketbook of the small-scale seller, but it can be done—and to good effect.

DEMAND-SIDE ENFORCEMENT

While pressure on the small-scale sale of drugs represents an attempt to influence drug supply, it also has an impact on drug demand—perhaps a greater one. The buyer who does not reside in an area of heavy drug sales must not only come up with the money to pay for the drugs; he may also have to search longer to make a purchase and worry more about the danger of being robbed or assaulted. He may also be more conspicuous to the police. To some extent, we can take advantage of this problem faced by drug buyers by using a relatively inexpensive means of lessening the number of those who are willing to obtain their supplies from the areas of heavy drug dealing. On a few occasions police have seized the automobiles of those who drove them to purchase drugs. This is not only inexpensive, but also far less brutal than imprisoning otherwise law-abiding drug users—and it may have more of an impact. This should be a regular feature of all drug enforcement.

Probably the most important aspect of the attack on drugs is the attempt to lower the amount of predatory crime that drug use engenders. We know, for example, that those who use illegal drugs commit a substantial proportion of our urban burglaries, robberies, and thefts. A number of studies have demonstrated that the criminality rate of those using heroin daily—that is, those who were addicted—was about seven times as great as the criminality rate of the same people when they were using the drug only sporadically or temporarily not using it at all.

Newer studies have shown an even higher correlation between criminality and drug use, and have implicated cocaine as well. Urinalysis of those arrested from crimes in 1986 has revealed that a staggering percentage of those apprehended had recently used cocaine or heroin. In the District of Columbia, 74 percent of non-drug-felony arrestees tested positive for at least one illegal drug other than marijuana. (No one has alleged that marijuana use helps to cause predatory crime, in part because the drug is cheap, in part because it has a tranquilizing effect.) In New York City the figure was 72 percent; in Chicago, 60 percent; and in Los Angeles, 58 percent. It turns out that in large cities about 70 percent of those arrested for robbery, weapons offenses, and larceny tested positive for heroin, cocaine, or (in the few cities where use is common) PCP.

The data on urinalysis suggest an obvious course of action. We must institutionalize routine urinalysis for those arrested for any of the typical crimes arising out of drug use. Then we must act on this information by making maintenance of a urine clean of cocaine, heroin, and PCP a requirement for all those who are released on bail or, after conviction, are placed on probation or released on parole.

A positive urine sample must reliably and immediately mean a return to jail. It is far more important that the enforcement of these rules be consistent than that the jail terms be long. We do not have the jail space that would be needed to provide long terms for this type of offense. And if we try, our efforts will backfire: we will deprive the system of the consistency necessary to get the message through to drug users. But a properly implemented system of imprisonment can make possible a more lasting cure for drug dependency.

This kind of regimen is not without disadvantages. There will inevitably be a dispute over whether we can demand "clean" urine before releasing someone on bail. On the one hand, our jurisprudence tells us that bail is to be used only to guarantee the presence of the accused at judicial proceedings, and there is no firm evidence that drug users are less likely than others to show up in court.

On the other hand, more recent precedent seems to allow consideration of the danger to the community if an arrestee is released on bail, and those who use illegal drugs are, on average, much more likely to commit crimes after they have been freed.

Such a system of mandatory urinalysis will also require more money. Parts of the criminal-justice system will simply not give up—temporarily—the funds they already have and need, even though doing so may help to save money in the long run. The jails are already full, and in many cases under court order not to exceed their present population. Even at two days per failed urinalysis, the increased demand upon those institutions will be substantial. And the maintenance of such a system will require the police to go looking for those who miss urinalysis appointments, a burden that may initially be only partially compensated for by the lower criminality of those now compelled to be drug-free.

Furthermore, the inexpensive urine test, which costs only about $5, but is less than completely accurate, will have to be supplemented by a system in which an arrestee who was confident that he had not used an illegal drug could simply file an affidavit to that effect and be tested by a more expensive but foolproof method (costing about $70). Although there will have to be some sanction for a false affidavit, expensive prosecutions for perjury will not be necessary to deter such conduct (though it is hard to imagine a simpler case to prosecute). The judge, in revoking bail or probation, can simply revoke it for longer.

Then there are the privacy concerns. It should be noted that urinalysis for those who have been arrested involves far fewer restraints on the citizen's right to privacy than the usual attempt to require urinalysis of government employees or members of other large groups, who, as individuals, give us no reason to suspect their drug use. (Nor is it nearly so expensive.) Our statistics on the drug use of those arrested for street crimes already single them out. And apart from the use of urinalysis in the bail decision, there are no real constitutional doubts. If there is a good reason, those arrested for drunken driving, for example, may constitutionally be subjected to blood, urine, or breath analysis, and those released on bail or, after conviction, on probation or parole, forfeit even more of their privacy. They are subject not only to intrusive searches but also to various restrictions on their autonomy. Very few of the restrictions on the privacy and autonomy of defendants in the criminal-justice system make as much practical sense as requiring urinalysis in order to monitor their drug use.

THE PROGNOSIS

What, then, could we expect from the institutionalization of such a regimen? Many of those using drugs will find themselves constantly in and out of jail. Some would simply decide that enough is enough and clean themselves up. We do know that this can occur when the consequences are immediate and certain enough. Nonetheless, in most cases we will have to rely upon drug treatment to prevent the urinalysis system from becoming a huge, inhumane, and expensive revolving-door operation. . . .

The approach I am recommending may have another important effect. For years, the drug-producing nations have argued that the United States must share the blame for the drug problem: if they cannot control the production of illegal drugs, neither can we control our consumption. We may now be able to have some success. Those users who are both criminals and drug consumers appear to be not merely a random selection of drug users; they tend, rather, to be the heaviest users. . . .

[T]hose users we will be focusing on will be those who do the most to support the illegal market. On average, each seller is supported by three heavy users. If we can bring their use under control—in addition to decreasing the number of predatory crimes—we may finally be able to deal a major blow to the illegal retail-distribution networks. We may also create a sizable cohort of former drug users who can help discourage drug use. If the zeal of the convert in this area is as strong as it seems to be in others—think of exsmokers, for example—we may reap unanticipated and sizable dividends from our efforts. For decades we have attempted to get at the sellers as a way of preventing use; now we may have the means to get at the users as a means of restraining sales.

I do not mean to suggest that we will be able to solve the problem easily. For the foreseeable future we will have a serious drug problem, but we can lessen it considerably if we have the will. Where will the money to accomplish this come from? The additional resources we need for law enforcement and drug treatment will come from the federal government, or they will not come at all. Whether the resources will come is simply a question of whether we have finally begun to take our drug problem seriously. It will be interesting to find out.

POSTSCRIPT

Will Drug Legalization Help the Criminal Justice System?

The decriminalization (frequently referred to as the medicalization) of drugs, and the impact on society and the criminal justice system of such a policy, is very much in the forefront of the public's mind. Within criminology, it is a current preoccupation as well. Trebach and Kaplan provided us with a stimulating overview. Although both acknowledge the dangers of hard-core drugs, neither is satisfied with current policy. The reader also gets the impression that neither feels that law enforcement agents chasing down marijuana users is particularly rational either.

James A. Inciardi in *The War on Drugs* (Mayfield, 1986) suggests that efforts to control drugs might not be worth the price. Large segments of some countries' economies are dependent on the drug trade, not to mention the fact that many local, state, and federal agencies in the United States depend directly and/or indirectly on funds allocated for fighting drugs. The multi-billion-dollar expenditures for law enforcement do not even include the extra billions for trying, counseling, and imprisoning drug abusers. Simply put: The supply side of drug trafficking has too much going for it for too many influential people to permit decriminalization, according to this view.

In his inimitable way, the astute psychiatrist Thomas Szasz, who is possibly America's greatest unrecognized sociologist, delineates many additional contradictions in the system. See his *Ceremonial Chemistry: The Ritual Persecution of Drugs, Addicts, and Pushers*, revised edition (Learning Publications, 1985).

A very different approach is found in recent National Institute of Justice Reports employing Drug Use Forecasting (DUF). In one survey, 65 percent of all males and 59 percent of all females arrested tested positive for one or more drugs. See, for example, the *1988 Drug Use Forecasting Annual Report* and the *Federal Drug Data for National Policy* (1990). Also see *Drug Abuse Treatment: A National Study of Effectiveness* by R. L. Hubbard et al. (University of North Carolina Press, 1989). Two contrasting perspectives are Jane E. Bahls's "Life Lessons: Just Say Know: Education Is Working in the Battle on Drugs," *Student Lawyer* (May 1990) and Gerry Fitzgerald's "Dispatches from the Drug War: Tough Sentences Sound Great But Don't Work," *Common Cause Magazine* (January/February 1990).

For consideration of problems inherent in controlling drug supplies, see Peter Reuter's "Can the Borders Be Sealed?" *The Public Interest* (Summer 1988). In that same journal issue is an argument agreeing in parts with Trebach: see E. A. Nadelmann's "The Case for Legalization."

ISSUE 18

Should Juveniles Be Executed?

YES: Antonin Scalia, from Dissenting Opinion, *Thompson v. Oklahoma*, U.S. Supreme Court

NO: Victor L. Streib, from *Death Penalty for Juveniles* (Indiana University Press, 1987)

ISSUE SUMMARY

YES: Supreme Court justice Antonin Scalia, joined by Chief Justice Rehnquist and Justice White, assails the plurality and concurring opinion in *Thompson v. Oklahoma,* which vacated the death penalty against Wayne Thompson, who at 15 brutally murdered his brother-in-law, and he argues that states have the right to impose the death penalty on those under 18.

NO: Cleveland State University professor Victor L. Streib insists that executing citizens under 18 violates contemporary standards of decency and that capital punishment for juveniles makes no measurable contributions to justice because they simply do not have the reasoning abilities of adults and executing them serves neither retribution nor deterrence.

In August 1990, two boys 13 years of age were charged with sexual assault and murder of two younger children (one 8, the other 7). The victims were strangled with their own shoelaces in St. Charles, Missouri. That same month, a 16-year-old found guilty along with two youthful confederates of raping and beating a 30-year-old female jogger in Central Park, New York, mocked the court with a rap monologue before being sentenced to 5 to 10 years. Manhattan Supreme Court justice Thomas B. Galligan assailed the vicious self-confessed assaulters for turning the park "into a torture chamber." Four boys—aged 14, 15, 16, and 17—were arrested in Fresno, California, following a random shooting spree that killed one person and wounded nine others. The police confiscated three shotguns, one rifle, one handgun, and crack cocaine. These are a small sample of incidents involving youngsters under 18 that were reported in the last half of 1990.

Since the mid-1600s, there have been 281 known executions of juveniles in the United States. The majority of executed youths in the 1800s and 1900s were black. Some youths executed in the United States have been as young as 10 years old, but most were 16 or 17. Sixteen of them were females, all nonwhite. Currently, there are approximately 40 people on death row who were under 18 when they committed a capital offense. Of the over 8,000 executions that are known to have taken place in the United States, approximately 2.5 percent have been of juveniles.

Most polls show that more Americans now support capital punishment than at any other time in our recent history. However, the intensity of that support is problematic (see Issue 13), and far fewer support the death penalty for juveniles. Yet the rate of violent crimes among juveniles seems to be rising dramatically. Clearly, the concern of the public with controlling violent crime, especially that which is drug-related, is growing.

Most experts contend that capital punishment as a pragmatic deterrent or ethical response to crime is shaky, at best. With juveniles, Streib and others say, it serves no purpose at all other than to separate the United States from most other industrial nations (the vast majority of which oppose capital punishment for anyone, but especially those under 18). People under 18 simply have not developed reasoning capacity in many cases. They often do not know right from wrong and sometimes feel that they are omnipotent. They do not understand or fear death. They are very likely to act on impulse with no perception of future consequences. Thus, execution is not a deterrent or a sensible punishment. And, furthermore, Streib and others contend that executing juveniles is a violation of the Eighth Amendment, which prohibits cruel and unusual punishment.

It is interesting to note several things in Judge Scalia's dissenting opinion. First, he feels that there is no proof that public sentiment is necessarily against executing juveniles, although he acknowledges that executions have become, and probably should remain, relatively rare. However, he definitely feels that state courts should have the right in especially heinous cases to sentence even 15-year-olds to death. He dismisses claims that juveniles are immature, impressionable, and vulnerable with the assertion that so are many adults on death row. Scalia acknowledged that world opinion opposes juvenile executions but dismisses it, along with a large number of U.S. professionals who oppose capital punishment, as irrelevant.

While clearly embracing the ideal of *parens patria* (the state being a parent for errant juveniles), Streib offers no solution to capital offenses by juveniles. Do you think Judge Scalia's ideas provide a basis for crime control? Should we execute a 17-year-old convicted criminal? What about a 16-year-old? A 15-year-old? Why or why not?

YES

Antonin Scalia

THOMPSON v. OKLAHOMA

CERTIORARI TO THE COURT OF CRIMINAL APPEALS OF OKLAHOMA

No. 86–6169. Argued November 9, 1987—Decided June 29, 1988

Petitioner, when he was 15 years old, actively participated in a brutal murder. Because petitioner was a "child" as a matter of Oklahoma law, the District Attorney filed a statutory petition seeking to have him tried as an adult, which the trial court granted. He was then convicted and sentenced to death, and the Court of Criminal Appeals of Oklahoma affirmed.

Held: The judgment is vacated and the case is remanded. . . .

JUSTICE STEVENS, joined by JUSTICE BRENNAN, JUSTICE MARSHALL, and JUSTICE BLACKMUN, concluded that the "cruel and unusual punishment" prohibition of the Eighth Amendment, made applicable to the States by the Fourteenth Amendment, prohibits the execution of a person who was under 16 years of age at the time of his or her offense. . . .

JUSTICE SCALIA, with whom CHIEF JUSTICE REHNQUIST and JUSTICE WHITE join, dissenting.

If the issue before us today were whether an automatic death penalty for conviction of certain crimes could be extended to individuals younger than 16 when they commit the crimes, thereby preventing individualized consideration of their maturity and moral responsibility, I would accept the plurality's* conclusion that such a practice is opposed by a national consensus, sufficiently uniform and of sufficiently long standing, to render it cruel and unusual punishment within the meaning of the Eighth Amendment. We have already decided as much, and more, in *Lockett* v. *Ohio*, . . .**

---

*[Plurality is the winning decision. Concurring is justice(s) who agree with the decision, but provide their own rationale. In this case, Justice O'Connor provides a concurring opinion which Justice Scalia also rejects.—ED.]

**[From a Supreme Court decision.—ED.]

From *Thompson v. Oklahoma*, 487 U.S. 815 (1988). Some case citations omitted.

(1978). I might even agree with the plurality's conclusion if the question were whether a person under 16 when he commits a crime can be deprived of the benefit of a rebuttable presumption that he is not mature and responsible enough to be punished as an adult. The question posed here, however, is radically different from both of these. It is whether there is a national consensus that no criminal so much as one day under 16, after individuated consideration of his circumstances, including the overcoming of a presumption that he should not be tried as an adult, can possibly be deemed mature and responsible enough to be punished with death for any crime. Because there seems to me no plausible basis for answering this last question in the affirmative, I respectfully dissent.

I

I begin by restating the facts since I think that a fuller account of William Wayne Thompson's participation in the murder, and of his certification to stand trial as an adult, is helpful in understanding the case. The evidence at trial left no doubt that on the night of January 22–23, 1983, Thompson brutally and with premeditation murdered his former brother-in-law, Charles Keene, the motive evidently being, at least in part, Keene's physical abuse of Thompson's sister. As Thompson left his mother's house that evening, in the company of three older friends, he explained to his girl friend that "we're going to kill Charles." . . .

Several hours after they had left Thompson's mother's house, Thompson and his three companions returned. Thompson's girl friend helped him take off his boots, and heard him say: "[W]e killed him. I shot him in the head and cut

his throat and threw him in the river." Subsequently, the former wife of one of Thompson's accomplices heard Thompson tell his mother that "he killed him. Charles was dead and Vicki didn't have to worry about him anymore." During the days following the murder Thompson made other admissions. One witness testified that she asked Thompson the source of some hair adhering to a pair of boots he was carrying. He replied that was where he had kicked Charles Keene in the head. Thompson also told her that he had cut Charles' throat and chest and had shot him in the head. Another witness testified that when she told Thompson that a friend had seen Keene dancing in a local bar, Thompson remarked that that would be hard to do with a bullet in his head. Ultimately, one of Thompson's codefendants admitted that after Keene had been shot twice in the head Thompson had cut Keene "so the fish could eat his body." Thompson and a codefendant had then thrown the body into the Washita River, with a chain and blocks attached so that it would not be found. On February 18, 1983, the body was recovered. The Chief Medical Examiner of Oklahoma concluded that the victim had been beaten, shot twice, and that his throat, chest, and abdomen had been cut.

On February 18, 1983, the State of Oklahoma filed an information and arrest warrant for Thompson, and on February 22 the State began proceedings to allow Thompson to be tried as an adult. Under Oklahoma law, anyone who commits a crime when he is under the age of 18 is defined to be a child, unless he is 16 or 17 and has committed murder or certain other specified crimes, in which case he is automatically certified to stand trial as an adult. . . . In addition, under the statute the State invoked in the present case, juveniles may be certified to stand trial as adults if: (1) the State can establish the "prosecutive merit" of the case, and (2) the court certifies, after considering six factors, that there are no reasonable prospects for rehabilitation of the child within the juvenile system. . . .

At a hearing on March 29, 1983, the District Court found probable cause to believe that the defendant had committed first-degree murder and thus concluded that the case had prosecutive merit. A second hearing was therefore held on April 21, 1983, to determine whether Thompson was amenable to the juvenile system, or whether he should be certified to stand trial as an adult. A clinical psychologist who had examined Thompson testified at the second hearing that in her opinion Thompson understood the difference between right and wrong but had an antisocial personality that could not be modified by the juvenile justice system. The psychologist testified that Thompson believed that because of his age he was beyond any severe penalty of the law, and accordingly did not believe there would be any severe repercussions from his behavior. Numerous other witnesses testified about Thompson's prior abusive behavior. Mary Robinson, an employee of the Oklahoma juvenile justice system, testified about her contacts with Thompson during several of his previous arrests, which included arrests for assault and battery in August 1980; assault and battery in October 1981; attempted burglary in May 1982; assault and battery with a knife in July 1982; and assault with a deadly weapon in February 1983. She testified that Thompson had been provided with all the counseling the State's Department of Human Services had

available, and that none of the counseling or placements seemed to improve his behavior. She recommended that he be certified to stand trial as an adult. . . .

Thompson was tried in the District Court of Grady County between December 4 and December 9, 1983. During the guilt phase of the trial, the prosecutor introduced three color photographs showing the condition of the victim's body when it was removed from the river. The jury found Thompson guilty of first-degree murder. At the sentencing phase of the trial, the jury agreed with the prosecution on the existence of one aggravating circumstance, that the murder was "especially heinous, atrocious, or cruel." As required by our decision in *Eddings* v. *Oklahoma*, . . . (1982), the defense was permitted to argue to the jury the youthfulness of the defendant as a mitigating factor. The jury recommended that the death penalty be imposed, and the trial judge, accordingly, sentenced Thompson to death. Thompson appealed, and his conviction and capital sentence were affirmed. Standing by its earlier decision in *Eddings* v. *State*, . . . the Oklahoma Court of Criminal Appeals held that "once a minor is certified to stand trial as an adult, he may also, without violating the Constitution, be punished as an adult." . . . (1986). It also held that admission of two of the three photographs was error in the guilt phase of the proceeding, because their prejudicial effect outweighed their probative value; but found that error harmless in light of the overwhelming evidence of Thompson's guilt. It held that their prejudicial effect did not outweigh their probative value in the sentencing phase, and that they were therefore properly admitted, since they demonstrated the brutality of the crime. Thompson petitioned for certiorari with respect to both sentencing issues, and we granted review . . . (1987).

II

A

As the foregoing history of this case demonstrates, William Wayne Thompson is not a juvenile caught up in a legislative scheme that unthinkingly lumped him together with adults for purposes of determining that death was an appropriate penalty for him and for his crime. To the contrary, Oklahoma first gave careful consideration to whether, in light of his young age, he should be subjected to the normal criminal system at all. That question having been answered affirmatively, a jury then considered whether, despite his young age, his maturity and moral responsibility were sufficiently developed to justify the sentence of death. In upsetting this particularized judgment on the basis of a constitutional absolute, the plurality pronounces it to be a fundamental principle of our society that no one who is as little as one day short of his 16th birthday can have sufficient maturity and moral responsibility to be subjected to capital punishment for any crime. As a sociological and moral conclusion that is implausible; and it is doubly implausible as an interpretation of the United States Constitution.

The text of the Eighth Amendment, made applicable to the States by the Fourteenth, prohibits the imposition of "cruel and unusual punishments." The plurality does not attempt to maintain that this was originally understood to prohibit capital punishment for crimes committed by persons under the age of 16; the evidence is unusually clear and unequivocal that it was not. The age at which juveniles could be subjected to capital punishment was explicitly addressed in Blackstone's Commentaries on the Laws of England, published in 1769 and widely accepted at the time the Eighth Amendment was adopted as an accurate description of the common law. According to Blackstone, not only was 15 above the age at which capital punishment could theoretically be imposed; it was even above the age (14) up to which there was a rebuttable presumption of incapacity to commit a capital (or any other) felony. . . . Streib, Death Penalty for Children: The American Experience with Capital Punishment for Crimes Committed While under Age Eighteen, 36 Okla. L. Rev. 613, 614–615 (1983) (hereinafter Streib, Death Penalty for Children). The historical practice in this country conformed with the common-law understanding that 15-year-olds were not categorically immune from commission of capital crimes. One scholar has documented 22 executions, between 1642 and 1899, for crimes committed under the age of 16. See Streib, Death Penalty for Children 619.*

Necessarily, therefore, the plurality seeks to rest its holding on the conclusion that Thompson's punishment as an adult is contrary to the "evolving standards of decency that mark the progress of a maturing society." . . . Of course the risk of assessing evolving standards is that it is all too easy to believe that evolution has culminated in one's own

*[This is the same Streib who represents the "No" position in this issue. While Streib does provide documentation of juvenile executions, he clearly interprets those deaths and supporting policies radically differently than Justice Scalia.—Ed.]

views. To avoid this danger we have, when making such an assessment in prior cases, looked for objective signs of how today's society views a particular punishment. . . . The most reliable objective signs consist of the legislation that the society has enacted. It will rarely if ever be the case that the Members of this Court will have a better sense of the evolution in views of the American people than do their elected representatives.

It is thus significant that, only four years ago, in the Comprehensive Crime Control Act of 1984, . . . Congress expressly addressed the effect of youth upon the imposition of criminal punishment, and changed the law in precisely the opposite direction from that which the plurality's perceived evolution in social attitudes would suggest: It lowered from 16 to 15 the age at which a juvenile's case can, "in the interest of justice," be transferred from juvenile court to Federal District Court, enabling him to be tried and punished as an adult. . . . This legislation was passed in light of Justice Department testimony that many juvenile delinquents were "cynical, street-wise, repeat offenders, indistinguishable, except for their age, from their adult criminal counterparts." Hearings . . . before the Subcommittee on Criminal Law of the Senate Committee on the Judiciary . . . (1983), and that in 1979 alone juveniles under the age of 15, *i.e.*, almost a year *younger* than Thompson, had committed a total of 206 homicides nationwide, more than 1,000 forcible rapes, 10,000 robberies, and 10,000 aggravated assaults. . . . Since there are federal death penalty statutes which have not been determined to be unconstitutional, adoption of this new legislation could at least theoretically result in the imposition of the death penalty upon a 15-year-old.

There is, to be sure, no reason to believe that the Members of Congress had the death penalty specifically in mind; but that does not alter the reality of what federal law now on its face permits. Moreover, if it is appropriate to go behind the face of the statutes to the subjective intentions of those who enacted them, it would be strange to find the consensus regarding criminal liability of juveniles to be moving in the direction the plurality perceives for capital punishment, while moving in precisely the opposite direction for all other penalties.

Turning to legislation at the state level, one observes the same trend of *lowering* rather than raising the age of juvenile criminal liability. As for the state status quo with respect to the death penalty in particular: The plurality chooses to "confine [its] attention" to the fact that all 18 of the States that establish a minimum age for capital punishment have chosen at least 16. . . . But it is beyond me why an accurate analysis would not include within the computation the larger number of States (19) that have determined that no minimum age for capital punishment is appropriate, leaving that to be governed by their general rules for the age at which juveniles can be criminally responsible. A survey of state laws shows, in other words, that a majority of the States for which the issue exists (the rest do not have capital punishment) are of the view that death is not different insofar as the age of juvenile criminal responsibility is concerned. And the latter age, while presumed to be 16 in all the States, . . . can, in virtually all the States, be less than 16 when individuated consideration of the particular case warrants it. Thus, what Oklahoma has done here is precisely what the majority of capital-punishment States would do.

When the Federal Government, and almost 40% of the States, including a majority of the States that include capital punishment as a permissible sanction, allow for the imposition of the death penalty on any juvenile who has been tried as an adult, which category can include juveniles under 16 at the time of the offense, it is obviously impossible for the plurality to rely upon any evolved societal consensus discernible in legislation—or at least discernible in the legislation of *this* society, which is assuredly all that is relevant.* Thus, the plurality falls back upon what it promises will be an examination of "the behavior of juries." . . . It turns out not to be that, perhaps because of the inconvenient fact that no fewer than 5 murderers who committed their crimes under the age of 16 were sentenced to death, in five different States, between the years 1984 and 1986. . . . Instead, the plurality examines the statistics on capital executions, which are of course substantially lower than those for capital sentences because of various factors, most notably the exercise of executive clemency. . . . Those statistics show, unsurprisingly, that capital punishment for persons who committed crimes under the age of 16 is rare. We are not discussing whether the Constitution requires such procedures as will continue to cause it to be rare, but whether the Constitution prohibits it entirely. The plurality takes it to be persuasive evidence that social attitudes have changed to embrace such a prohibition—changed so clearly and permanently as to be irrevocably enshrined in the Constitution—that in this century all of the 18 to 20

executions of persons below 16 when they committed crimes occurred before 1948.

Even assuming that the execution rather than the sentencing statistics are the pertinent data, and further assuming that a 4-decade trend is adequate to justify calling a constitutional halt to what may well be a pendulum swing in social attitudes, the statistics are frail support for the existence of the *relevant* trend. There are many reasons that adequately account for the drop in executions other than the premise of general agreement that no 15-year-old murderer should ever be executed. Foremost among them, of course, was a reduction in public support for capital punishment in general. . . . A society less ready to impose the death penalty . . . will of course pronounce death for a crime committed by a person under 16 very rarely. There is absolutely no basis, however, for attributing that phenomenon to a modern consensus that such an execution should never occur. . . .

In sum, the statistics of executions demonstrate nothing except the fact that our society has always agreed that executions of 15-year-old criminals should be rare, and in more modern times has agreed that they (like all other executions) should be even rarer still. There is no rational basis for discerning in that a societal judgment that no one so much as a day under 16 can *ever* be mature and morally responsible enough to deserve that penalty; and there is no justification except our own predeliction for converting a statistical rarity of occurrence into an absolute constitutional ban. One must surely fear that, now that the Court has taken the first step of requiring individualized consideration in capital cases, today's decision begins a second stage of

*[In a lengthy footnote, Justice Scalia rejects the relevancy of capital punishment policies in other nations.—ED.]

converting into constitutional rules the general results of that individuation. One could readily run the same statistical argument with respect to other classes of defendants. Between 1930 and 1955, for example, 30 women were executed in the United States. Only 3 were executed between then and 1986—and none in the 22-year period between 1962 and 1984. Proportionately, the drop is as impressive as that which the plurality points to in 15-year-old executions. . . . Surely the conclusion is not that it is unconstitutional to impose capital punishment upon a woman.

If one believes that the data the plurality relies upon are effective to establish, with the requisite degree of certainty, a constitutional consensus in this society that no person can ever be executed for a crime committed under the age of 16, it is difficult to see why the same judgment should not extend to crimes committed under the age of 17, or of 18. The frequency of such executions shows an almost equivalent drop in recent years. . . . It seems plain to me, in other words, that there is no clear line here, which suggests that the plurality is inappropriately acting in a legislative rather than a judicial capacity. . . .

B

Having avoided any attempt to justify its holding on the basis of the original understanding of what was "cruel and unusual punishment," and having utterly failed in justifying its holding on the basis of "evolving standards of decency" evidenced by "the work product of state legislatures and sentencing juries," . . . the plurality proceeds, . . . to set forth its views regarding the desirability of ever imposing capital punishment for a murder committed by a 15-year-old. That discussion begins with the recitation of propositions upon which there is "broad agreement" within our society, namely, that "punishment should be directly related to the personal culpability of the criminal defendant," and that "adolescents as a class are less mature and responsible than adults." . . . It soon proceeds, however, to the conclusion that "[g]iven the lesser culpability of the juvenile offender, the teenager's capacity for growth, and society's fiduciary obligations to its children," none of the rationales for the death penalty can apply to the execution of a 15-year-old criminal, so that it is "nothing more than the purposeless and needless imposition of pain and suffering. . . . On this, as we have seen, there is assuredly not general agreement. Nonetheless, the plurality would make it one of the fundamental laws governing our society solely because it has an " 'abiding conviction' " that it is so. . . .

I reject that proposition in the sense intended here. It is assuredly "for us ultimately to judge" what the Eighth Amendment permits, but that means it is for us to judge whether certain punishments are forbidden because, despite what the current society thinks, they were forbidden under the original understanding of "cruel and unusual." . . . On its face, the phrase "cruel *and unusual* punishments" limits the evolving standards appropriate for our consideration to those entertained by the society rather than those dictated by our personal consciences. . . .

. . . [T]here is another point of view, suggested in the following passage written by our esteemed former colleague Justice Powell, whose views the plurality several times invokes for support, . . .

"Minors who become embroiled with the law range from the very young up to those on the brink of majority. Some of the older minors become fully 'streetwise,' hardened criminals, deserving no greater consideration than that properly accorded all persons suspected of crime." *Fare* v. *Michael C.,* . . . (1979) (dissenting opinion).

The view that it is possible for a 15-year-old to come within this category uncontestably prevailed when the Eighth and Fourteenth Amendments were adopted, and, judging from the actions of the society's democratically elected representatives, still persuades a substantial segment of the people whose "evolving standards of decency" we have been appointed to discern rather than decree. . . .

III

If I understand JUSTICE O'CONNOR's separate concurrence correctly, . . . it proceeds . . . to state that since (a) we have treated the death penalty "differently from all other punishments" . . . imposing special procedural and substantive protections not required in other contexts, and (b) although we cannot actually *find* any national consensus forbidding execution for crimes committed under 16, there may *perhaps* be such a consensus, therefore (c) the Oklahoma statutes plainly authorizing the present execution by treating 15-year-old felons (after individuated findings) as adults, and authorizing execution of adults, are not adequate, and what is needed is a statute explicitly stating that "15-year-olds can be guilty of capital crimes."

. . . I am unaware of any national consensus, and the concurrence does not suggest the existence of any, that the death penalty for felons under 16 can only be imposed by a single statute that explicitly addresses that subject. Thus, part (c) of the concurrence's argument, its conclusion, could be replaced with almost anything. There is no more basis for imposing the particular procedural protection it announces than there is for imposing a requirement that the death penalty for felons under 16 be adopted by a two-thirds vote of each house of the state legislature, or by referendum, or by bills printed in 10-point type. . . .

. . . What the concurrence proposes is obviously designed to nullify rather than effectuate the will of the people of Oklahoma, even though the concurrence cannot find that will to be unconstitutional.

. . . It is difficult to pass a law saying explicitly "15-year-olds can be executed," just as it would be difficult to pass a law saying explicitly "blind people can be executed," or "white-haired grandmothers can be executed," or "mothers of two-year-olds can be executed." But I know of no authority whatever for our specifying the precise form that state legislation must take, as opposed to its constitutionally required content. We have in the past studiously avoided that sort of interference in the States' legislative processes, the heart of their sovereignty. Placing restraints upon the manner in which the States make their laws, in order to give 15-year-old criminals special protection against capital punishment, may well be a good idea, as perhaps is the abolition of capital punishment entirely. It is not, however, an idea it is ours to impose. . . .

. . . If 15-year-olds must be explicitly named in capital statutes, why not those of extremely low intelligence, or those over 75, or any number of other appealing groups as to which the existence of a national consensus regarding capital punishment may be in doubt for the same reason the concurrence finds it in doubt here, viz., because they are not specifically named in the capital statutes? Moreover, the motto that "death is different" would no longer mean that the firm view of our society demands that it be treated differently in certain identifiable respects, but rather that this Court can attach to it whatever limitations seem appropriate. I reject that approach, and would prefer to it even the misdescription of what constitutes a national consensus favored by the plurality . . .

IV

Since I find Thompson's age inadequate grounds for reversal of his sentence, I must reach the question whether the Constitution was violated by permitting the jury to consider in the sentencing stage the color photographs of Charles Keene's body. Thompson contends that this rendered his sentencing proceeding so unfair as to deny him due process of law.

The photographs in question, showing gunshot wounds in the head and chest, and knife slashes in the throat, chest and abdomen, were certainly probative of the aggravating circumstances that the crime was "especially heinous, atrocious, or cruel." The only issue, therefore, is whether they were unduly inflammatory. We have never before held that the excessively inflammatory character of concededly relevant evidence can form the basis for a constitutional attack, and I would decline to do so in this case. If there is a point at which inflammatoriness so plainly exceeds evidentiary worth as to violate the federal Constitution, it has not been reached here. The balancing of relevance and prejudice is generally a state evidentiary issue, which we do not sit to review. . . .

For the foregoing reasons, I respectfully dissent from the judgment of the Court.

NO

Victor L. Streib

JUVENILES IN LAW AND SOCIETY

Fundamental to our American legal system is the premise that "children have a very special place in life which law should reflect." Children are significantly different from adults and simply cannot be shuttled mindlessly into adult legal processes. Law has reflected the unique nature of childhood in many ways, both for children who are offenders and for children who are victims. . . . The Supreme Court has made clear its view that the death penalty is uniquely harsh and that such a severe and irrevocable penalty for crime must be subjected to the most stringent safeguards. One category of such stringent safeguards has been the appropriateness of the death penalty given the individual characteristics of the defendant. Among the individual characteristics singled out for particular constitutional scrutiny in death penalty cases has been the youthful age of the defendant.

The Supreme Court has been quite willing to "assume juvenile offenders constitutionally may be treated differently from adults." Manifestations of this different treatment are limitations on youths' right to vote, make a contract, purchase liquor, sue or be sued, dispose of property by will, serve as jurors, enlist in the armed services, drive vehicles, marry, or accept employment. As Justice Frankfurter aptly noted, "Children have a very special place in life which law should reflect." That juveniles are less mature and responsible than adults is a premise often recognized by the Supreme Court. Given the great instability of the behavior of adolescents, it has stated, they "cannot be judged by the more exacting standards of maturity." . . .

Contemporary Standards of Decency

Criminal punishments that run contrary to popular sentiment can and ought to be banned. The death penalty for juveniles is such a punishment because it is in conflict with contemporary theory and practice. An example of the reaction that may be precipitated is the public outcry that resulted from death sentences for a sixteen- and a seventeen-year-old imposed in the late 1960s.

Leaders in the legal, criminological, and social policy fields almost universally oppose the death penalty for juveniles. The prestigious American Law

From Victor L. Streib, *Death Penalty for Juveniles* (Indiana University Press, 1987). Reprinted by permission. Notes omitted.

Institute excluded the death penalty for crimes committed while under age eighteen from its influential Model Penal Code, concluding that "civilized societies will not tolerate the spectacle of execution of children." This position was also adopted by the National Commission on Reform of Criminal Law.

In August 1983 the American Bar Association adopted as its formal policy a resolution stating that the association "opposes, in principle, the imposition of capital punishment upon any person for any offense committed while under the age of eighteen. . . ." That was the first time in the history of the organization that it took a formal position on any aspect of capital punishment. . . .

MEASURABLE CONTRIBUTION TO GOALS OF PUNISHMENT

Regardless of any controversy surrounding the death penalty in general, this criminal sanction has been characterized by the Supreme Court in its major death penalty opinions as achieving, to varying degrees, the goals of retribution, general deterrence, and specific deterrence or incapacitation while obviously rejecting the goals of reformation, rehabilitation, and treatment of the offender. The death penalty cannot be justified, however, unless it makes a measurable contribution to the goals of retribution and deterrence, since it is otherwise too harsh compared with long-term imprisonment. A careful analysis of the death penalty for juveniles reveals that it makes no such measurable contribution to these goals for these offenders. It is not reasonably capable of advancing a legitimate state interest and thus cannot be justified under the United States Constitution. . . .

Retribution

. . . Even if the execution of an adult for revenge or retribution is constitutionally permissible, this justification for the death penalty loses its appeal when the object of righteous vengeance is a child. Juveniles do not "deserve" harsh punishments in the same way that mature, responsible adults might. Society does not feel the same satisfying, cleansing reaction when a child is executed. Nonresponsible actors, whether children, retarded adults, or insane persons, by their very nature deserve and usually receive pity and treatment rather than the revenge of an outraged society anxious to "kill them back." Experts in sentencing youthful offenders have concluded as much:

[A]dolescents, particularly in the early and middle teen years, are more vulnerable, more impulsive, and less self-disciplined than adults. Crimes committed by youths may be just as harmful to victims as those committed by older persons, but they deserve less punishment because adolescents may have less capacity to control their conduct and to think in long-range terms than adults. Moreover, youth crime as such is not exclusively the offender's fault; offenses by the young also represent a failure of family, school, and the social system, which share responsibility for development of America's youth. [Twentieth Century Fund Task Force on Sentencing Policy Toward Young Offenders (1978).]

Execution of persons whose crimes were committed while under age eighteen is not necessary to serve the ends of retribution. More than sufficient retribution is achieved by sentencing such persons to long prison terms.

General Deterrence

General deterrence from the death penalty has been the subject of heated debate among criminology scholars. Various members of the Supreme Court have disagreed about the general deterrent effects of the death penalty. . . .

The Supreme Court has observed that young persons are inexperienced and unable to avoid detrimental choices in general. They are going through "the period of great instability which the crisis of adolescence produces." Juveniles "generally are less mature and responsible than adults." The *Eddings* majority noted favorably the generally accepted conclusions about the impulsiveness and irresponsibility of juveniles.

Most social scientists would agree that juveniles live primarily for today with little thought of the future consequences of their actions. Adolescents are in a developmental stage of defiance of danger and death and are attracted to flirtations with death from a feeling of omnipotence. Such well-known adolescent behavior was noted long ago for juveniles sentenced to death: "On one occasion a boy showed delight at being placed in the condemned cell, apparently because it gave him status in the eyes of his fellow prisoners."

Child development research reveals that the ability to engage in mature moral judgments develops significantly during middle and late adolescence, reaching a plateau only after an individual leaves school or reaches early adulthood. Most adolescents have insufficient social experience for making sound value judgments and understanding the long-range consequences of their decisions. Supreme Court opinions have recognized this universally understood principle: "[D]uring the formative years of childhood and adolescence, minors often lack the experience, perspective, and judgment to recognize and avoid choices that could be detrimental to them." All of this generally accepted information about typical adolescent behavior leads to the conclusion that juveniles do not commonly engage in any "cold calculus that precedes the decision to act." Thus the Supreme Court's premises behind its assumed general deterrence of the death penalty simply do not apply to any reasonable manner to juveniles.

Even if a few juveniles might engage in a cold, premeditated calculus before committing the act, they would know that even though the death penalty might be authorized for juveniles the probability of their ever being executed for their acts is almost nil. Without some reasonable degree of certainty, any possible general deterrent effect disappears.

Specific Deterrence and Incapacitation

Proponents of the death penalty, whether for juveniles or for all offenders, point out that at least execution of an offender specifically deters and incapacitates that individual offender. An executed prisoner will never commit another murder. This justification for the death penalty for juveniles is not of course incorrect; it simply sanctions too much punishment for too little additional result. . . .

. . . If the goal is prevention of future murders by these juveniles, long-term imprisonment is of comparable specific deterrent impact and negates any need for the death penalty for juveniles.

Reformation, Rehabilitation, and Treatment

The inescapable conclusion is that the death penalty for juveniles makes no measurable contribution to the constitutionally accepted goals of the death penalty. This ultimate punishment does, however, totally reject the one sentencing alternative normally thought most appropriate for young offenders—rehabilitation. Execution irreversibly abandons all hope of reforming a teenager and thus is squarely in opposition to the fundamental premises of juvenile justice and comparable sociolegal systems. A Kentucky court stated that "incorrigibility is inconsistent with youth; . . . it is impossible to make a judgment that a fourteen-year-old youth, no matter how bad, will remain incorrigible for the rest of his life."

Capital punishment of our children inherently rejects humanity's future, which begins with the habilation and rehabilitation of today's youth. Such costly rejection should not be made if it makes no measurable contribution to the goals of criminal justice in general or to the death penalty in particular.

CONCLUSIONS

Does the eighth amendment prohibit the death penalty for crimes committed while under age eighteen? The Supreme Court has avoided giving a direct answer to this question but has provided a general analytical framework from which answers may be derived. The foregoing analysis suggests that the most persuasive answer, given this general analytical framework, is yes—the death penalty for juveniles is cruel and unusual under the eighth amendment. This answer follows from a step-by-step consideration of the supporting arguments for the death penalty as they apply to adolescents. In this application, the force of these supporting arguments either disappears or in some

cases suggests that the threat of the death penalty may become an attraction to death-defying adolescents.

Presently the thirty-six death penalty jurisdictions are doing whatever they wish. All must give the age of the offender great weight in mitigation of the death penalty, and most expressly prohibit application of their death penalties to their juveniles, at least at some age minimum. While some state courts have tried to resolve the constitutional question themselves, most simply have left the issue to the state legislatures, which are increasingly considering amending their statutes to join the trend against the death penalty for juveniles.

A uniform, nationwide policy is needed, and such a policy flows most reasonably from the eighth amendment.* It is beyond argument that American law would not permit the death penalty for a very young child—the three-year-old toddler, say, who shoots Mommy to death with Daddy's handgun. It is also settled that American law may permit the death penalty for adults—the thirty-year-old, say, who shoots his mother to death with his father's handgun. The only issue, then, is at what age the line will be drawn between these two polar positions. At present no universally accepted line exists, except the line at age seven for criminal responsibility of any kind.

The line should be drawn at age eighteen, since that is by far the most common age for similar restrictions and limitations. This line should emanate from the eighth amendment and should be imposed by the Supreme Court.

---

*[The Eighth Amendment prohibits cruel and unusual punishment.—ED.]

POSTSCRIPT

Should Juveniles Be Executed?

Conservative justice Antonin Scalia's dissenting opinion in *Thompson v. Oklahoma* reflects a pragmatic position. He is mindful that capital punishment is rarely applied but feels that if states have the option to execute those juveniles who have committed very vicious, premeditated crimes with no mitigating excusing factors, then execution, however infrequent that option may be, will both punish them and deter others. Streib sees no practical value in juvenile executions and would still oppose them even if they did "work." Streib, like many others, views executions for juveniles as morally reprehensible. For these critics, the very concept of juvenile executions is as horrible as medieval torture chambers.

Many excellent studies critiquing the constitutionality of juvenile executions have been published in the last 10 years. These include W. Williams's "Juvenile Offenders and the Electric Chair: Cruel and Unusual Punishment or Firm Discipline for the Hopeless Delinquent?" *University of Florida Law Review* (Spring 1983); Helen B. Greenwald's "Eighth Amendment—Minors and the Death Penalty: Decision and Avoidance," in *Journal of Criminal Law and Criminology*, vol. 73 (1983); B. C. Feld's "The Juvenile Court Meets the Principle of the Offense: Legislative Changes in Juvenile Waiver Statutes," *Journal of Criminal Law & Criminology*, vol. 78 (1987); and S. M. Simmons's "*Thompson v. Oklahoma*: Debating the Constitutionality of Juvenile Executions," *Pepperdine Law Review*, vol. 16 (1989). For research on public support of juvenile executions, see "The Death Penalty for Juveniles: An Assessment of Public Support," by S. E. Skovran et al., *Crime and Delinquency* (October 1989). For a somewhat neutral viewpoint in the midst of recent discussions sympathetic to capital punishment for juveniles, see R. A. Fine's *Escape of the Guilty* (Dodd, Mead & Co., 1988) and "Behavioral Science and the Juvenile Death Penalty," by G. B. Leong and S. Eth in *Bulletin of the American Academy of Psychiatry and the Law*, vol. 17 (1983). W. Davison II et al. provide an interesting set of alternatives for delinquents in their *Alternative Treatment for Troubled Youth* (Plenum Press, 1990). See also the suggested readings in the Postscript for Issue 13.

ISSUE 19

Is the Victims' Rights Movement Succeeding?

YES: Frank Carrington and George Nicholson, from "Victims' Rights: An Idea Whose Time Has Come—Five Years Later: The Maturing of an Idea," *Pepperdine Law Review* (1989)

NO: Robert Elias, from *The Politics of Victimization: Victims, Victimology, and Human Rights* (Oxford University Press, 1986)

ISSUE SUMMARY

YES: Frank Carrington, attorney and executive director for Victims Assistance Legal Organization, and Sacramento municipal court judge George Nicholson are convinced that the victims' movement "has arrived," and, after reviewing its progress within various court systems and committees, they conclude that the movement has been a success in spite of some remaining hurdles.

NO: Political scientist Robert Elias contends that the victims' movement has hurt both victims and defendants in several unexpected ways, and he sees it as only helping certain people within the criminal justice system that may not have any real interest in either victims or their rights.

While exact statistics on both crime and victimization rates are debatable (see Issues 5 and 6), there is little doubt that almost every American family contains one or more members who have been or will be victims of a serious crime. The vast majority of crimes either do not get reported or do not result in arrests or convictions. At times, the courts have appeared to be openly unsympathetic toward many victims. Recently, the Bureau of Justice Statistics reported that 7 out of 8 Americans will be victims of personal theft three or more times within their lifetimes. Most Americans over the course of their lives will be victims of at least one assault. And we have not even considered statistics on domestic violence.

Until fairly recently, victims per se were peripheral to the entire criminal justice process. It was the status of either the victim or the offender (or both) that infused the crime with added meaning. The victim's economic or racial status might have aroused a response, or a lack thereof, but the concept of a victim with rights and privileges, politically articulated, was generally nonexistent in the United States. The modern victims' movement is both amorphous and diffuse as well as relatively novel. Its consequences can be easily observed and measured by several indicators dating back approximately 20 years.

These indicators include an outpouring of articles, pamphlets, books, and films on victims and their rights, as well as the emergence of scientific journals dealing with victims (for example, *Victimology*). Also, there are now dozens of victims' organizations at the local, state, and national levels, such as the Stephanie Roper Committee, the Parents of Murdered Children and Other Survivors of Homicide Victims Foundation, and the National Organization for Victim Assistance. The hundreds of local shelters and centers for victims of rape, child abuse, or wife abuse are other indicators.

The victims' movement is frequently linked with the women's movement. Such a linkage is quite logical since women have always been more likely to be victims of strikingly brutal and inhumane crimes, such as battering and rape. Moreover, female victims typically had far fewer rights than others, and their victimization was likely to be minimized or even mocked. For instance, until the past few years, no husband was ever charged with, let alone found guilty of, raping his wife. It was quite possible that a rape victim would find her personal life held up for public display by a defense attorney trying to discredit her testimony. It was not unusual for a woman to have to disclose exactly how many men she had had voluntary sexual relations with, and, if it numbered "excessively" (which usually meant more than one or two), then the defense attorney would routinely insinuate that the victim either made a practice of "giving it away" or indeed was really a prostitute. In the public's mind and in many courts of law, this tacit understanding was taken for granted. The horrified victim would find herself regretting ever having reported the terrible crime, let alone being so foolish as to testify in open court.

Not surprisingly, then, many of the initial supporters of victims' rights were concerned about women as victims. They were interested in obtaining justice for victims through minimizing court-related stresses and maximizing punishment for assailants. The callous treatment of many victims by the police, by prosecuting and defense attorneys, and by the courts all compounded victims' dissatisfaction with the existing criminal justice system.

Taking all these facts into account, what right-thinking person could fault the victims' rights movement? Why do some experts maintain that the movement has failed and that we need a new conceptualization of what we mean by a "victim"? In the jargon of the social sciences, have there been unanticipated negative consequences?

337

YES

Frank Carrington and
George Nicholson

VICTIMS' RIGHTS: AN IDEA WHOSE TIME HAS COME—FIVE YEARS LATER: THE MATURING OF AN IDEA

> [T]oday, due to energetic leadership by policy makers at the federal, state, and local levels, and a great deal of hard work at the same levels by private parties devoted to victims' rights, an effective inexorable and cooperative national endeavor is underway to guarantee crime victims their rightful places everywhere in America's legal system.[1]

This article will track the major advances in the victims' movement since the publication of the 1984 *Pepperdine Law Review Symposium*. Notwithstanding a few major setbacks, primarily at the hands of the United States Supreme Court, the victims' movement has matured in the last five years, with a number of positive signs indicating that, indeed, victims' rights' have truly arrived.

LEGISLATION

Federal Legislation

The Victims of Crime Act of 1984 established a fund making grants available to states for victim compensation, victim assistance programs, and child abuse prevention and treatment. Funds for these grants arise from fines in federal criminal cases, penalty assessments, forfeitures of federal bail bonds, as well as a federal "Son of Sam" law, whereby funds from literary or other exploitation of the criminal's activities must be escrowed for the benefit of the victim. . . .

The Act also provides funding for federal crime victim assistance programs, including crisis intervention, forensic services, and salaries of victim service providers. Finally, the Act mandates that at least forty-five percent of the Crime Victims Fund shall be distributed to states for the purpose of aiding state crime victim programs.

From Frank Carrington and George Nicholson, "Follow-Up Issue on Victims' Rights," *Pepperdine Law Review*, vol. 17, no. 1 (1989). Copyright © 1989 by the Pepperdine University School of Law. Reprinted by permission. Some notes omitted.

State Legislation

Any effort to catalog the various laws which have been enacted by state legislatures during the last five years would far exceed the scope of this . . . article. Suffice it to say that the legislatures of every state continued to respond enthusiastically to the victims' movement. Major initiatives were seen in areas such as victim impact statements, victims' rights to allocution at sentencing (and in some cases even at the plea bargaining stage), rape shield laws, extension of statutes of limitations in child sexual abuse cases, and other areas as well.

Compendia of this kind of legislative action, state by state, can be obtained from two principal sources: the National Victim Center (formerly the Sunny von Bulow National Victim Advocacy Center) [2] and the National Organization for Victim Assistance (NOVA).[3] The work of NOVA, described in the 1984 article, will be updated below, and the work of the National Victim Center, new on the scene since the 1984 article, also will be discussed.

One example of how the state courts are taking the victims' rights issue and its related legislation seriously is provided by the Illinois case of *Myers v. Daley*. Mr. Myers, a Chicagoan, had been the victim of a violent crime, which he reported to the State's Attorney's office. Subsequently, he exercised his right under the Illinois Bill of Rights for Victims and Witnesses of Violent Crime Act and wrote to the State's Attorney's office requesting the status of his case, but he received no reply. He then sued the State's Attorney to obtain the information, which ultimately was forwarded to him. Upon an agreed dismissal of the case, the court awarded Mr. Myers $92.32 in court costs. The State's Attor-

ney appealed. The Illinois Court of Appeals affirmed the award, holding that the State's Attorney had a legal duty to furnish the information, and that it would frustrate the purposes of the Act if court costs were not allowed to one who was invoking his legal rights under the Act.

EXECUTIVE BRANCH INITIATIVES

. . .Ronald Reagan was the first United States President to put the full weight and influence of that office behind the victims' movement. . . . Such support on the national level gave enormous impetus to similar state proclamations by various governors. The presidential imprimatur embodied in this initiative elevated concern for victims to a level never before attained.

The Victims' Week proclamations came under the heading of "moral support," albeit from the highest national level. An initiative on a far more substantive level soon followed in the form of the President's Task Force on Victims of Crime, the first such presidential-level commission in the nation's history. . . . [T]he task force reported to President Reagan with sixty-eight specific recommendations geared to preventing victimization and to alleviating the plight of those unfortunate enough to become victims or survivors of crime. As of 1989, seventy-five percent of the recommendations had been acted upon, usually in a highly bipartisan spirit of cooperation between the Administration and Congress.

Pursuant to the 1984 Victims Act, the Administration established the Office on Victims, which administers funds appropriated for crime victims by Congress and assists victims' organizations through the expertise of the Office's staff. The impact of the coordinated efforts of the executive and legislative branches has been felt on a nationwide basis. . . .

For victims and their advocates, there is every reason to believe that President Bush will continue to encourage government initiatives on behalf of crime victims. For example, one of his first acts in office was the proclamation of National Victims' Rights Week, 1989.

THE SUPREME COURT

. . . While it is difficult to neatly categorize the Justices into voting blocs, certainly a rough sketch of voting trends may be useful in ascertaining how the Court *generally* views crime victims' rights.

The current Justices may be fairly characterized as "conservatives," "swing votes," or "liberals" regarding criminal justice issues.

The "conservatives" are those Justices who will likely vote to affirm convictions or otherwise rule in favor of the prosecution, law enforcement, and the safety of society. They include Chief Justice Rehnquist and Justices White, O'Connor, Scalia, and Kennedy. The "swing votes," Justices Blackmun and Stevens, lean heavily toward the rights of accused or convicted criminals, while the "liberals," Justices Brennan* and Marshall, vote almost invariably for the rights of accused or convicted criminals. . . .

For an issue as important and volatile as the rights of crime victims, there are surprisingly few Supreme Court cases. The lack of legal precedent primarily is

*[Justice William J. Brennan, Jr., retired from the Supreme Court July 20, 1990. He had been appointed by President Eisenhower in 1956.—ED.]

due to the fact that, until recently, the American legal system, including the United States Supreme Court, did not really recognize that crime victims *had* any legal rights.

CASES IN WHICH CRIME VICTIMS DID NOT PREVAIL

The first major victims' rights case to reach the Supreme Court during the past decade was *Martinez v. California*,[4] in which the Court held that a California statute provided blanket immunity to correctional officials for the murder of a fourteen-year-old girl by a prisoner who had been released under grossly negligent circumstances. The Court found that the statute violated neither the Federal Civil Rights Act,[5] nor the Due Process Clause of the United States Constitution. Justice Stevens, writing for a unanimous court, stated that the child's murder, six months after the release of her murderer, was too remote in time to sustain a cause of action, and that, in any event, the murder was the "action" of the murderer himself rather than "state action" for purposes of the Federal Civil Rights Act.

In *United States v. Shearer*,[6] an action was brought under the Federal Tort Claims Act by the parents of a soldier who had been murdered by another soldier. The latter had been convicted of murder and then released under allegedly negligent circumstances. The Court held that the parents failed to state a cause of action because Section 2680(h) of the Federal Tort Claims Act retained the immunity of the United States for "any claim arising out of assault or battery." The Court also held that the action was barred by the *Feres* doctrine, named for the landmark case, *Feres v. United*

States [(1950)]. *Feres* is cited for the proposition that a soldier cannot recover under the Federal Tort Claims Act for injuries arising "out of or . . . in the course of activity incident to service." . . .

By 1987, a number of states had passed legislation mandating that "victim impact statements" could be reviewed by the courts when considering the sentences to be imposed upon criminals. In *Booth v. Maryland*, the Court, in a five-to-four decision, held that statutorily approved victim impact statements could not be used during the penalty phase of capital cases because they might "inflame" the jurors' minds against the defendant. Justice Powell wrote the opinion, in which Justices Brennan, Marshall, Blackmun, and Stevens concurred. . . .

Also, in 1989, a majority of the Court took "Suffer, Little Children" as its text in *DeShaney v. Winnebago County Dep't of Social Services*. Chief Justice Rehnquist, who wrote the majority opinion, in which Justices White, Stevens, O'Connor, Scalia, and Kennedy joined, framed the issue before the Court:

> Petitioner is a boy who was beaten and permanently injured by his father, with whom he lived. The respondents are social workers and other local officials who received complaints that petitioner was being abused by his father and had reason to believe that this was the case, but nonetheless did not act to remove petitioner from his father's custody. Petitioner sued respondents claiming that their failure to act deprived him of his liberty in violation of the Due Process Clause of the Fourteenth Amendment to the United States Constitution. We hold that it did not.

In more detail, the facts show that the Winnebago County authorities were aware of the danger posed to the victim, Joshua DeShaney, by his father, who had custody of the child. Joshua was hospitalized twice with suspicious injuries which indicated child abuse, but each time he was returned to his father. Finally, Joshua's father beat him so severely that permanent brain damage ensued. . . .

After *DeShaney* and *Martinez*, it is clear that while the conservative majority of the Court are willing to protect society from the criminals themselves, they are not willing to extend that protection to those endangered by the negligence of bureaucrats, thus leaving unprotected the likes of four-year-old Joshua DeShaney or fourteen-year-old Mary Ellen Martinez.

The cases described above are devastating to the burgeoning campaign of enhancing the legal rights of crime victims in the legislatures and the courts. The news, however, is not *all* bad as the Court also has rendered some decisions sympathetic to the victims' point of view. . . .

The Court's October 1987 term furnished two cases reasonably favorable to crime victims. In *Kelly v. Robinson*, the Court held that court-ordered restitution to the state, imposed on a woman who had been convicted of welfare fraud, was not a debt that was dischargeable in bankruptcy. . . . Justice Powell, the author of the opinion, intimated that a similar rationale would prevail in cases involving restitution to private parties from their assailants. . . .

In *Pennsylvania v. Ritchie*, the Court reversed a decision of the Supreme Court of Pennsylvania holding that the defendant in a rape-sodomy-incest case had a discovery right to *all* of the records of the Pennsylvania Children and Youth Services (CYS) pertaining to the victim.

Justice Powell, writing for a plurality, cited Pennsylvania's efforts to combat child abuse and provided that the defendant's right to review CYS records was limited to having the trial court, in camera, review such records to determine if they contained any information favorable to the defendant which probably would have changed the outcome of the trial. As a result, the defendant's attorney would not be permitted to rummage through the victim's statements on a generalized fishing expedition. . . .

It is perhaps premature to predict what the Court's ultimate posture on victims' rights issues will be. Victims' attorneys have been winning major victories in state courts in the past ten to fifteen years, and it is possible that, as a sizeable body of victims' law is established in lower courts, even the Supreme Court will take a fairer and more realistic attitude towards victims' rights. Additionally, because the Court reviews so few cases, primarily concerned with cosmic constitutional issues, the above-mentioned body of victim-oriented civil cases will continue to develop despite some setbacks by the Court.

PRIVATE VICTIMS' RIGHTS ACTIVITIES

. . . [I]t is not an understatement to assert that without the tireless and dedicated work of the hundreds of thousands of volunteers in service to crime victims, there would be no victims' movement as we know it today.

. . . The First such organization, founded in 1976 by a small group of victim advocates in Fresno, California, was the National Organization for Victim Assistance, Inc. (NOVA).[7] NOVA's literature highlights some of its major accomplishments: (1) assistance in formulating and passing the Victims of Crime Act, the Victim and Witness Protection Act, the Justice Assistance Act, and bills of rights for victims; (2) providing through its advocates, crisis counseling, information, referral, and assistance; and (3) providing local victim assistance programs with updated information on how to serve the victims with whom they have contact. NOVA's annual National Forums on Victims Rights and various conferences provide vehicles for victims' advocates from all over the country to meet, to share ideas, and to be heard.

The second national victim organization, the National Victim Center (the Center), formerly the Sunny von Bulow National Victim Advocacy Center, was founded in 1985. Its broad-ranging programs include: (1) seminar training across the country of direct-line victim service personnel involved in such areas as rape crisis counselling, child protection activities, assistance with domestic violence cases, and counselling survivors of homicide victims; (2) work for constitutional amendments creating "Victims' Bills of Rights" in the several states; (3) information referral to individual crime victim service agencies (since its establishment, the Center has made some 4000 such referrals); (4) maintaining a data base of some 13,000 pieces of legislation that concern victims' rights, directly or indirectly; and (5) maintaining another data base of the names and addresses of, and key individuals involved with, over 7000 victim assistance agencies nationwide. Current information about victims' issues is made available to these individuals and agencies upon request through the Center's quarterly newsletter, *Networks*.

Of principal interest to attorneys, paralegals, law students, and faculty, as well as to others who are concerned with the legal rights of crime victims, is the Center's Crime Victims Litigation Project (the Project). Initiated late in 1986, the Project has established the only data base in the country that is concerned specifically and exclusively with victims' legal rights. . . .

The Project began with the establishment of its data base. Categories of victims' cases in which redress for injuries were to be sought in the civil courts were selected. Categorization was surprisingly easy because the majority of lawsuits fell into one of two major classifications: (1) suits by victims against the perpetrators of crime or (2) suits by victims against third parties whose simple or gross negligence caused or facilitated the criminal acts which had victimized them. . . .

In 1988, the Project established the Coalition of Victims' Attorneys and Consultants (COVAC) as its membership, educational, research, and referral arm. COVAC Update, which presents the most important victim cases decided during a given quarter, refers members to victims who have not yet retained attorneys and to other attorneys, and provides direct counseling services by telephone or by letter to interested parties. The Project's services are available to all attorneys and others involved in victim cases. There is no charge for COVAC members or attorneys handling *pro bono* cases, and only a nominal charge in other instances.

CONCLUSION

It is apparent from the foregoing that the above-characterized "maturing process"

for the victims' movement is well under way. The ultimate goal, that of elevating the rights of crime victims and their survivors to their proper status in our system of justice, is being approached with a rapidity that few would have predicted with any great degree of confidence only two decades ago.

NOTES

1. Carrington & Nicholson. *The Victims' Movement: An Idea Whose Time Has Come,* 11 PEPPERDINE L. REV. 1 (Symposium 1984).

2. The National Victim Center is located at 307 West 7th Street, Suite 1001, Fort Worth, Texas 76102; (817) 877-3355; E. Gene Patterson, Executive Director.

3. NOVA is located at 717 D. Street, N.W., Suite 1989, Washington, D.C. 20004; (202) 393-NOVA; Dr. Marlene A. Young, Executive Director; John Stein, Esq., Associate Executive Director.

4. 444 U.S. 277 (1980).

5. U.S.C. § 1983 (1982).

6. 473 U.S. 52 (1983).

7. NATIONAL ORGANIZATION FOR VICTIM ASSISTANCE, FROM THE DARKNESS OF CRIME . . . TO THE LIGHT OF HOPE: THE CAMPAIGN FOR VICTIMS' RIGHTS (1989).

NO   Robert Elias

THE POLITICS OF VICTIMIZATION

Victims have progressed significantly in the last quarter century, but they
have not yet shaken their second-class status. When victimized, they lack
confidence in receiving the aid they need, and for good reason—they often
must tolerate inadequate services, cultural insensitivity, political insignificance, and official maltreatment. The many worthy initiatives for victim
rights and services have provided valuable help, yet have been impeded by
numerous obstacles. Most important, we have been very unsuccessful in
preventing victimization in the first place. . . .

To prevent victimization, and to further victim rights, we might well
consider new vehicles for increasing victims' political influence. As an
applied science, victimology might also consider political influences on its
work. Our quest both to better understand victims and to promote their
interests may depend substantially on victimology's embracing some new
directions, preferably a "new" victimology, encompassing both criminal
victimization and human rights violations.

POLITICS, SCIENCE, AND POWER

The rise of victims and victimology has reflected numerous political clashes.
Victims first began losing their equal status and prominent criminal justice
role in conflicts with the emerging power of the state. As governments took
greater interest and received increasing benefits from controlling law enforcement and the definition of deviance, the victim's role receded. . . .

In our conservative, success-oriented society, victims have often suffered
not only as crime victims, but also as cultural victims. This has made their
resurgence more difficult, yet ultimately their rise may depend mostly on
their political functions. Insufficiently supported and promoted, victims will
probably achieve little political power and substantive relief. Yet, even when
relatively influential, their real power may depend just as much on their
political uses as on their political victories. In other words, victims may

perform certain functions that governments now find valuable to promote.

Research suggests that victims may function to bolster state legitimacy, to gain political mileage, and to enhance social control. By championing the victim's cause, government may deflect criticism about ineffective law enforcement, and portray itself as the friend of victims, instead of as possibly their greatest threat. Victims may provide considerable political advantage for officials seeking re-election and political support, such as by sponsoring popular victim compensation programs. And victims may help promote greater social control, not benevolently as an age-old formula for reducing victimization,[1] but rather as a rationale for enhancing state power.

Victims have risen partly through some progressive initiatives taken by the women's and human rights movements, and related efforts, but mostly from the hardline, conservative law-and-order backlash against defendants' rights and rampant crime. Most pro-victim policies have been promoted in the name of reducing defendants' rights and enhancing criminal punishments. In fact, national, conservative support would likely have been even greater had it not been impeded by other, conservative themes of fiscal austerity and state's rights.[2] Since 1980, the hardline efforts for victims have redoubled.

Victimology seems less directly affected by these political developments, yet their influence shows nevertheless. Begun as a broad, humanitarian concern for human rights and all victims, victimology has evolved very narrowly. It quickly abandoned all victims for an almost exclusive emphasis on crime victims. It has almost invariably accepted state definitions of victimization. And it has often championed victim policies invoked to strengthen government power and weaken defendants' rights. . . .

POLITICS AND SOCIAL REALITY

Some believe our limited social reality of victimization reflects a worldview almost perfectly suited to maintaining existing political, social, and economic arrangements. As such, it may serve as an ideology, reflecting certain beliefs, and having certain goals and functions. That ideology's development and inculcation may begin with how we define victimization in the first place. The legislative process, reflecting special interests more than general public interests, may selectively define the criminal law, ignoring many harmful actions and actors while encompassing others, and even criminalizing many acts that have no apparent victims at all. Official definitions may help ingrain stereotypes and perceptions publicly, and help control certain populations much more than others. Our definitions, often reflecting an imbalance of political power, seem to emphasize lower-class wrongdoing while largely ignoring much more harmful upper-class wrongdoing. Overcriminalization, wrought by double standards, extends law and enforcement into the lives of (again, mostly lower-class) people who produce no victims, and yet who get defined as criminal and become subject to greater social controls.

Likewise, measuring crime and conveying victimization publicly may also reflect prevailing political configurations. We may rely on official indicators that only selectively portray the crime problem and that respond to crime waves that have less to do with crime levels and more with organizational and political needs. Besides our misleading measures, our concept of victimization gets further distorted by its media portrayal. The media's concept of victimization seems to faithfully reproduce official definitions and measures; provide superficial, misleading, and sensationalist accounts; convey false stereotypes and scapegoats; and ingrain and intensify an astounding level of social violence. The media may inculcate, in other words, a social reality of victimization almost perfectly suited to promote not only its own private and public goals, but also state objectives. Among other things, this may help intensify a considerable public fear of crime and help justify enhanced state control and power and reduced rights and freedoms. By breeding insecurity, it may promote the public's "escape from freedom."[3]

In this ideological process, the victim may play a considerable role. Especially in recent years, the political use of victims has helped promote government power and justify our hardline response. Victims could as easily represent the state's failure, but by coopting victims and the victim movement, the state may use them to portray its apparent concern and promote its legitimacy instead. As such, victims may help perform an ideological and political function, justifying state actions and deflecting attention from the interests it promotes and the much more extensive harms it commits. Our social reality profoundly affects our responses to public problems.

THE POLITICAL ECONOMY OF HELPLESSNESS

Victims face many problems, such as how to take precautionary measures, how to cope with victimization's financial and psychological effects, and how to avoid further victimization in law enforcement. Victimologists and victim advocates have worked hard to eliminate these problems, yet we have done comparatively little to solve the victim's greatest dilemma: how to escape victimization in the first place. We refer not merely to protective devices or behavior, but rather to the sources of victimization, whose elimination or reduction will be the only really effective protection against crime. . . .

Our futility may reflect a "political economy of helplessness" more than objective barriers to reducing victimization. Some believe that we may fail to examine sources, and take action against them less because we cannot do so, and more because to do so would challenge American mainstream life,[4] particularly our political economy. We must examine the political uses of various crime causation theories and their impact on victims.

Our prevailing crime theories blame regulations, criminals, or victims. We stress either institution blaming or offender blaming or victim blaming. Intentionally or not, each one may amount much more to "system defending." Institution blaming finds crime's sources in regulatory failures, particularly in law enforcement and criminal justice. Politically, it pleads for greater resources, efficiency, and power for law enforcement, and asks victims to be more cooperative and supportive, but not to expect much against the intractable crime problem. Offender blaming finds crime's sources in the inherent traits either of all people or in a select group of evil people. Politically, it suggests that we can only be more vigilant in identifying, punishing, and isolating the dangerous criminal element. Victims must constantly be on their guard and help authorities root out the threat. Victim blaming finds crime's sources in victim traits and behavior, and warns victims to reform their precipitatory habits. Politically, it diverts the blame for crime onto its victims, and implores them to change their behavior to avoid crime. The opposite view, victim defending, usually only shifts the blame back to offenders and institutions.

But these theories may only reveal some of the more important symptoms of crime. While they sometimes indicate important factors upon which we could immediately act, like overcriminalization, the prison system, handgun proliferation, and certain victim behaviors, they usually ignore the primary sources of victimization. They deflect attention away from the American system—that is, away from basic American political, economic, and social structures. They emphasize secondary symptoms of crime, against which we can hope to achieve little. Instead, critics believe the best evidence for victimization's sources lies in structural characteristics of the American system which, in their view, produce the factors on which most crime rests: poverty, inequality, racism, sexism, classism, competition, bureaucracy, alienation, violence, and political inequities. In other words, to challenge criminal victimization fundamentally, we must stop defending a system that produces victimization generally.

Obviously, this view has substantially different implications for both politics and victims than conventional crime theories. Politically, it suggests that reducing victimization will rely on fundamental structural reform. For victims, it suggests not that they should cooperate and support conventional political and administrative forces, but rather challenge them. The structural theory of crime proposes a new "social reality" of victimization up-

on which victims and the public could act. . . .

THE POLITICS OF DISENCHANTMENT

When victimized, we expect authorities to defend us, helping us to effectively reduce our suffering and redress the wrongs committed against us. Instead, we often find ourselves further victimized in the law enforcement process. While we have long recognized this "second" victimization (in fact, it has substantially propelled the victim movement), we rarely consider its political sources.

Victims of enforcement arise from both state and organizational politics. To begin with, law enforcement may not fundamentally seek to reduce victimization. Criminal justice may have more to do with political or social control than with crime control. Thus, law enforcement may primarily perform political functions beyond its ostensible activities. Moreover, it reflects official and selective criminal definitions, frequently pressed discriminantly against some offenders and offenses while ignoring many others, and often corresponding to the society's overall distribution of political and economic power. It begins a process that some view as "weeding out the wealthier" from consideration, thus also ignoring the extensive victimization they produce. Thus, many victims have no claim for relief or remedies since their victimization has not been officially recognized.

When recognized, their experience may reflect their political and economic power and status. While officials encourage victim participation ostensibly to help enforcement, some believe it has much more to do with bolstering the government's legitimacy and support. When they try to participate, most victims find it impossible, often relegated to influencing by their demeanor and characteristics, when they have any effect at all. When they sometimes participate more extensively, they often find themselves mechanically employed through some kind of witness management scheme. In the rare instance when they participate in a full trial, they often find themselves on trial as much as the offender. These may be the typical victim experiences because typical victims have little political status or power, coming largely from middle- and especially lower-class backgrounds.

Besides this general powerlessness, victims regularly clash with criminal justice's internal organizational politics. They symbolize official failures, and represent outsiders whose participation will more than likely interfere in official routines. Contrary to our adversarial ideals, criminal justice personnel usually form cooperative "work-groups," which seek rapid case dispositions, usually through plea bargaining, free from outside participants and surprises. Personal objectives bolster these organizational goals, making it especially difficult for victims to become institutionalized into a process that already routinely considers crime as a victimization of society, not individual victims. In a way, crime victims suffer from what officials consider as their own victimization and exploitation by the criminal justice system. Victims suffer not by competing with defendants, whose rights are regularly honored in the breach, but rather by competing with officials objectives. For victims, and undoubtedly others, the process is the punishment. And for particular victims, like

women, the punishment can be especially brutal.

Victimization by law enforcement hardly occurs inadvertently, but reflects instead a clash of political interests, some bolstered by considerable power, and others having relatively little. Reforming the criminal process to promote victim interests may depend not merely on involving victim rights or sensitizing officials to victim needs, but rather on addressing entrenched official incentives and even American criminal justice's purposes in the first place. Until that time, we might question any increase in victim participation in a process that will almost invariably alienate, and not satisfy, victims.[5]

THE SYMBOLIC POLITICS OF ADVOCACY

Victimization and the criminal process create many problems for victims. In response, we have developed various programs to promote victim needs and rights. Yet much of this victim advocacy, while it has made some important progress, has nevertheless been much less successful than we had hoped. The limits of advocacy, if not some of its motives, may reflect some important political obstacles.

For all their calls for greater victim participation, officials usually do quite well with little victim (save symbolic) involvement at all. Within criminal justice, officials often consider victims as a threat or interference in their activities. And victim programs may be even more threatening, unless tailored to official objectives. Witness management schemes, for example, may promote official goals, but expensive victim assistance programs may drain scarce resources and thus be resisted. Community crime control closely connected to law enforcement and reflecting official views and approaches may be embraced as improving police-community relations, but popular justice initiatives promoting independent, alternative organizations and techniques that question social structures and police functions will be opposed. This suggests that only victim advocacy carefully tailored to parallel official goals will likely be successful, even if such schemes do not serve victim interests very well or perhaps at all.

More broadly, some believe that victim programs may promote particular political ideologies and certain state interests. Ideologically, victim advocacy may hide quite another political agenda: the desire to curb defendant's rights and bolster the state's enforcement power. It may promote other state interests as well. Victim programs such as victim compensation emerged ostensibly to satisfy victims needs before we even determined their scope or victim preferences. The programs arose while (if only briefly) we were increasingly questioning victimization's sources and wondering whether offenders were not also victims. Some believe that this "opening" in our conventional social reality of victimization may have challenged the state's legitimacy and its ability to control the definition of victims. Victim compensation programs may have emerged to recoup the state's control over labeling victims. The schemes, providing little substantive assistance, did nevertheless redefine the victims society would recognize—namely, the narrow array of victims encompassed by their restrictive eligibility requirements.[6]

Programs such as victim compensation may have had other political goals as well. They may have enhanced the state's legitimacy by conveying the government's apparent concern for victims. They may have emerged for symbolic, political purposes designed to promote victim and public support and enhance social control. Most plans, for example, cover only very selective victimizations, despite public perceptions to the contrary. If very few even qualify, then even fewer actually apply (about 1% of all violent crime victims), and only about one-third of them receive any payments, in amounts often less than what they believe they deserve. While programs often receive considerable general publicity, actual application information is usually very difficult to obtain and rarely a regular part of the victim's initiation to the criminal process.[7] . . .

We need not, and should not, deprecate the many sincere and important efforts at victim advocacy by acknowledging the politics of victim programs. Instead, it only suggests that some victim advocacy, most notably many official initiatives, may have purposes that place victim interests secondary, if it promotes them at all. For good reason, most sincere and experienced advocates have prescribed programs independent from government, if not basically challenging government structures and objectives. To really promote victim interests successfully, we may need strategies that transform victims into a potent and independent political force, and which second-guess apparent government benevolence.

NOTES

1. Eduard Ziegenhagen, *Victims, Crime and Social Control* (New York: Praeger, 1977); Eduard Ziegenhagen, "Controlling Crime by Regulating Victim Behavior: Two Alternative Models," in

Hans Joachim Schneider (ed.), *The Victim in International Perspective* (Berlin: Walter de Gruyter, 1982), 335.

2. Andrew Karmen, *Crime Victims* (Belmont, Calif,: Brooks/Cole, 1984), 221.

3. Erich Fromm, *Escape from Freedom* (New York: Avon, 1970).

4. Stuart A. Scheingold, *The Politics of Law and Order: Street Crime and Public Policy* (New York: Longman, 1984).

5. Robert Elias, "A Political Strategy for Victims," unpublished paper, 1984.

6. David Miers, "Victim Compensation as a Labelling Process," *Victimology,* 5(1980), 3.

7. Robert Elias, *Victims of the System: Crime Victims and Compensation in American Politics and Criminal Justice* (New Brunswick, N.J.: Transaction Books, 1983).

POSTSCRIPT

Is the Victims' Rights Movement Succeeding?

This is one clashing issue that almost makes you wonder if the protagonists are talking about the same thing! Carrington and Nicholson are convinced that significant advances have been made in victims' rights. Carrington himself chaired President Reagan's Task Force on Victims of Crime. Elias has serious concerns. He feels that the victims' movement has indirectly contributed to the criminal justice system's victimization of both victims and defendants.

The President's Task Force on Victims of Crime (U.S. GPO, 1982) made 68 different proposals. Many of these were openly critical of the criminal justice system, especially the courts, which were clearly viewed by the Task Force as being unsympathetic toward victims. Among the many recommendations were that no criminal in the future could profit from his or her crime through the sale of book or movie rights. Profits from such endeavors would have to go to a fund for victims or to pay back court costs. Other proposals were considerably more controversial. They ranged from those reflecting out-and-out vengeance to those that would almost cavalierly dispense with constitutional protections for defendants in a court of law.

For excellent discussions of broader sociolegal aspects of the victims' movement, see Tom Gibbons's "Victims Again," *American Bar Association Journal* (September 1, 1988); the special issue of *Crime and Delinquency* on "Criminal Victimization and Crime" (October 1987); and Claudine Schweber and C. Feinman (editors), *Criminal Justice Politics and Women* (Hayworth Press, 1985). The latter work—along with "Women and Victims of Crime" in *The Criminal Justice System and Women*, edited by B. Price and N. Sokoloff (Clark Boardman, 1982)—is especially helpful in dealing with victimization from the view of the women's liberation movement.

Provocative discussions that reflect some of Elias's concerns include "Prologue: On Some Visible and Hidden Dangers of Victim Movements," by E. A. Fattah, in his edited book *From Crime Policy to Victim Policy* (Macmillan, 1986), and Diane M. Daane's "Rape Law Reform: How Far Have We Come?" *Prison Journal* (Fall/Winter 1988).

Empirical studies of victim participation in legal changes and/or courtroom processes include F. J. Weed's "The Victim-Activist Role in the Anti-Drunk Driving Movement," *Sociological Quarterly* (Summer 1990) and E. Erez and P. Tontodonato's "The Effect of Victim Participation in Sentencing on Sentence Outcome," *Criminology* (August 1990). For excellent articles on the victims' movement within the United Kingdom, see *Victims of Crime: A New Deal?* edited by M. Maguire and J. Pointing (Milton Keynes: Open University Press, 1988).

CONTRIBUTORS
TO THIS VOLUME

EDITOR

RICHARD C. MONK is currently a professor of criminology at Valdosta State College. From 1986 to 1989 he taught at Morgan State University, and from 1984 to 1986 he taught at San Diego State University. Professor Monk received his Ph.D. in sociology from the University of Maryland in 1978. He has been the recipient of two NEH fellowships, and he received a Bureau of Justice Statistics grant to participate in a 1985 Summer Seminar in Quantitative Methods in Criminal Justice at the University of Michigan. His publications include "Scientific Research Programs, Theory and Schools Interregnum in Criminology and Criminal Justice," *Journal of Contemporary Criminal Justice* (February 1988). And he is the editor of *Structures of Knowing* (University Press of America, 1986).

STAFF

Marguerite L. Egan Program Manager
Brenda S. Filley Production Manager
Whit Vye Designer
Libra Ann Cusack Typesetting Supervisor
Juliana Arbo Typesetter
James Filley Graphics
Diane Barker Editorial Assistant
David Dean Administrative Assistant

AUTHORS

ADALBERTO AGUIRRE, JR., is a professor at the University of California at Riverside. He is the author of *An Experimental Sociolinguistic Study of Chicano Bilingualism* (R & E, 1978).

GEORGE J. ANNAS is the Edward R. Utley Professor of Law and Medicine at Boston University Schools of Medicine and Public Health. He is the coauthor, with Sherman Elias, of *Reproductive Genetics and the Law* (Year Book Medical, 1987).

DAVID V. BAKER is a professor in the Department of Sociology at Riverside Community College in Riverside, California.

DANIEL BELL has been a professor of sociology at Harvard University since 1969. He is a member of the President's Commission on Technical Automation and Economic Progress and the author of several books on politics, government, and sociology, including *The Deficits: How Big? How Long? How Dangerous?* (New York University Press, 1985), with Lester Thurow.

A. KEITH BOTTOMLEY is a British criminologist who teaches at the University of Hull. He is the author of *Decisions in the Penal Process* (Rothman, 1973).

STEPHEN J. BRODT is a criminologist at Ball State University in Muncie, Indiana.

FRANK CARRINGTON is an attorney and the executive director of Victims Assistance Legal Organization. He also serves as a legal consultant for the National Victim Center. He is a former member of President Reagan's Task Force on Victims of Crime and a former chairperson for the American Bar Association's Victims Committee.

ELLIOTT CURRIE is an attorney and research associate at the Center for the Study of Law and Society at the University of California at Berkeley. He is coauthor, with Jerome H. Skolnick, of *America's Problems: Social Issues and Public Policy,* 2nd ed. (Scott, Foresman, 1988).

DAVID DOWNES is a professor at the London School of Economics and Political Science and the editor of *The British Journal of Criminology.* He is the coauthor, with Paul Rock, of *Understanding Deviance: A Guide to the Sociology of Crime and Rule Breaking* (Oxford University Press, 1982) and the editor of *Crime and the City: Essays in Memory of John Barron Mays* (Macmillan, 1988).

FRANKLYN W. DUNFORD is a research associate at the Institute of Behavioral Science, University of Colorado at Boulder. He is currently studying the correlates of domestic assault among cases known to the police.

EMILE DURKHEIM (1858–1917) was a French sociologist who profoundly influenced the development of the social sciences.

ROBERT ELIAS is currently visiting scholar at the Center for the Study of Law and Society at the University of California at Berkeley. He is the author of *Victims of the System: Crime Victims and Compensation in American Politics and Criminal Justice* (Transaction Books, 1983).

DELBERT S. ELLIOTT is the associate director of the Program on Problem Behavior in the Institute of Behavioral Science at the University of Colorado at Boulder. He is coauthor, with David Huizinga and Suzanne S. Ageton, of *Explaining Delinquency and Drug Use* (Sage, 1985) and coauthor, with David Huizinga and Scott Menard, of *Multiple Problem Youth: Delinquency, Substance Use, and Mental Health Problems* (Springer-Verlag, 1989).

RALPH ADAM FINE is a Court of Appeals judge in Wisconsin. He is a former attorney with the U.S. Department of Justice.

BRIAN FORST is a member of the faculty of the George Washington University's School of Business and Public Management. He was formerly director of research at the Institute for Law and Social Research and the Police Foundation (INSLAW).

HERMAN FRANKE is a criminologist at the University of Amsterdam and an editor of the Dutch journal of criminology *Tijdschrift voor Criminologie*.

LEONARD H. GLANTZ is a professor of health law in the School of Public Health at Boston University. He is coauthor, with George J. Annas and Barbara Katz, of *Informed Consent to Human Experimentation: The Subject's Dilemma* (Ballinger, 1977).

LARRY A. GOULD is a professor in the Criminal Justice Department at Louisiana State University at Baton Rouge, Louisiana.

JACK GREENBERG is a professor of law at Columbia University. He is the author of *Judicial Process and Social Change: Constitutional Litigation, Cases and Materials* (West, 1977).

RICHARD J. HERRNSTEIN is the Edgar Pierce Professor of Psychology at Harvard University, where he has taught since 1958. He is the coauthor, with James Q. Wilson, of *Crime and Human Nature* (Simon & Schuster, 1985).

DAVID HUIZINGA is a research associate in the Institute of Behavioral Science at the University of Colorado at Boulder. He is coauthor, with Delbert S. Elliott and Suzanne S. Ageton, of *Explaining Delinquency and Drug Use* (Sage, 1985) and coauthor, with Delbert S. Elliott and Scott Menard, of *Multiple Problem Youth: Delinquency, Substance Use, and Mental Health Problems* (Springer-Verlag, 1989).

BRUCE JACKSON is a social critic and criminologist who teaches at the University of Illinois. He is the author of *Law and Disorder: Criminal Justice in America* (University of Illinois Press, 1984) and *Fieldwork* (University of Illinois Press, 1987).

C. R. JEFFERY is a professor of criminology at Florida State University. He is the author of *Attacks on the Insanity Defense: Biological Psychiatry and New Perspectives on Criminal Behavior* (C. C. Thomas, 1985).

JOHN KAPLAN is an associate professor of law at Stanford Law School. He is the author of *The Hardest Drug: Heroin and Public Policy* (University of California Press, 1985) and coauthor, with Robert Weisberg, of *Criminal Law: Cases and Materials* (Little, Brown, 1986).

PAUL A. LOGLI is a state's attorney for Winnebago County, Illinois. He received his J.D. from the University of Illinois and has been a member of the Illinois State Bar since 1974.

DORIS LAYTON MacKENZIE is a visiting scientist with the National Institute of Justice. She is coeditor of *Measuring Crime: Large-Scale, Long-Range Efforts* (State University of New York Press, 1989).

WENDY K. MARINER is an associate professor of health law in the School of Public Health at Boston University.

JOAN MEIER is an attorney with the Public Citizen Litigation Group and a member of the board of directors of the Washington, D.C., Coalition Against Domestic Violence.

MERRY MORASH is a professor in the School of Criminal Justice at Michigan State University. She is coauthor, with Robert C. Trojanowicz, of *Juvenile Delinquency: Concepts and Control*, 4th ed. (Prentice-Hall, 1987).

GEORGE NICHOLSON is a municipal court judge in Sacramento, California. He is a former senior assistant attorney general for the State of California and a former executive director for the California District Attorney's Association.

KEN PEASE is a British criminologist who teaches at the University of Manchester. He is coauthor, with Peter B. Ainsworth, of *Police Work* (Methuen, 1987) and coeditor, with Martin Wasik, of *Sentencing Reform: Guidance or Guidelines?* (St. Martin, 1988).

TONY PLATT is a professor in the School of Criminology at the University of California at Berkeley, where he has taught since 1968. He is coeditor, with Paul Takagi, of *Crime and Social Justice* (B & N Imports, 1981).

RICHARD QUINNEY is a sociologist and criminologist at Northern Illinois University in DeKalb, Illinois, where he has taught since 1983. He is the author of several books on crime and sociology, including *Class, State, and Crime,* 2nd ed. (Longman, 1980) and *Social Existence: Metaphysics, Marxism and the Social Sciences* (Sage, 1982).

ALFRED S. REGNERY is the administrator of the Office of Juvenile Justice and Delinquency Prevention, the federal agency charged with reducing crime by juveniles.

JEFFREY H. REIMAN is a professor of criminal justice at American University in Washington, D.C. He is a member of the American Society of Criminology and the American Philosophical Association. His publications include *In Defense of Political Philosophy* (Harper & Row, 1972) and *The Police in Society* (Lexington, 1974).

LISA M. RIECHERS is a recent graduate of the criminal justice program at Louisiana State University in Baton Rouge. She is currently working in the governor's office in Texas.

LILA RUCKER is an assistant professor in the Department of Political Science at the University of South Dakota.

ANTONIN SCALIA has been serving as an associate justice of the U.S. Supreme Court since his appointment by President Reagan in 1986.

JAMES W. SHAW is a recent graduate of the criminal justice program at Louisiana State University in Baton Rouge. He is currently working at the National Institute of Justice.

J. STEVEN SMITH is a criminologist who teaches at Ball State University in Muncie, Indiana.

VICTOR L. STREIB is a professor at Cleveland State University in Ohio. He is the author of *Juvenile Justice in America* (Associates Faculty Press, 1978) and *The Death Penalty for Juveniles* (University of Illinois Press, 1987).

JOSH SUGARMANN is the executive director of New Right Watch, a non-profit educational foundation that issues reports on topics dealing with the New Right in America. He is the former communications director of the National Coalition to Ban Handguns.

PAUL TAKAGI is associate professor of sociology at the University of California, Los Angeles.

ARNOLD S. TREBACH is a professor in the School of Justice at American University in Washington, D.C. He is also the director of the Drug Policy Center and the author of *The Great Drug War: And Radical Proposals That Could Make America Safe Again* (Macmillan, 1987).

ERNEST van den HAAG is the John M. Olin Professor of Jurisprudence and Public Policy at Fordham University and a regular lecturer at

Columbia University, Yale University, and Harvard University. He is a contributing editor for *National Review* magazine, and has contributed more than 200 articles to magazines and sociology journals in the United States, England, France, and Italy. He is coauthor, with John P. Conrad, of *The Death Penalty: A Debate* (Plenum, 1983).

ANDREW von **HIRSCH** is a professor in the School of Criminal Justice at Rutgers University, where he has taught since 1975. He is the author of *Doing Justice: The Choice of Punishments* (Northeast University Press, 1985) and *Past or Future Crimes: Deservedness and Dangerousness in the Sentencing of Criminals* (Rutgers University Press, 1985).

SAMUEL WALKER has been an associate professor in the Department of Criminal Justice at the University of Nebraska at Omaha since 1974. He is the author of *The Police in America: An Introduction* (McGraw-Hill, 1983) and *In Defense of American Liberties* (Oxford University Press, 1990).

WILLIAM WILBANKS is a criminologist who teaches at Florida International University. He is the author of *Murder in Miami: An Analysis of Homicide Patterns and Trends in Dade County Florida, 1917–1983* (University Press of America, 1984) and *The Myth of a Racist Criminal Justice System* (Brooks/Cole, 1987).

JAMES Q. WILSON has been the Collins Professor of Management

and Public Policy at the University of California, Los Angeles, since 1987. He has published several successful books on politics, government, and urban studies, including *Politics of Regulation* (Basic Books, 1982) and *Bureaucracy: What Government Agencies Do and Why They Do It* (Basic Books, 1989).

JAMES D. WRIGHT is a professor of human relations in the Department of Sociology at Tulane University. He is the author of 13 books, including *Address Unknown: The Tragedy of Homelessness in America* (Aldine de Gruyter, 1989).

KEVIN N. WRIGHT is an associate professor of criminal justice at the State University of New York at Binghamton and director of the Center for Education and Social Research. He is the author of *The Great American Crime Myth* (Greenwood, 1985) and the editor of *Crime and Criminal Justice in a Declining Economy* (Oelgeschlager, 1981).

INDEX